THE REAL GUIDE

W9-CEP-569

HUNGARY

REAL GUIDE CREDITS

Series Editor: Mark Ellingham
Editorial: Martin Dunford, John Fisher, Jack Holland, Jonathan Buckley
US Text Editor: Melissa Kim
Production: Susanne Hillen, Kate Berens, Andy Hilliard
Typesetting: Greg Ward and Gail Jammy
Design: Andrew Oliver

THANKS

to Karen for her total support, and to friends in *Magyarország* for their kind hospitality and advice: Anni, Csaba, Csilla, István, Judit, Laci, Margo, Sola, Szabolcs, Tibor, Zoltán, Zsolt and, last but not least, Zsuzsi. Also to Katalin Koronczi of TOURINFORM (who bears no responsibility for anything critical in this book), Judit (for her forbearance) and Mike Stewart (for an illuminating chat about Gypsies). As for other contributors, thanks to Keith Crane, Julian Duplain, Peter Foersom, Susan Greenberg, Martin Kender, Sophia Lambert, Richard Levy, Bill Lomax, Dr L J Ray, Byron Russell, Karin Steininger, Anne Tillyer, Dick Wash, and Maureen who missed the fair at Kecskemét. On the production front, thanks in particular to Andy Hilliard for his conscientious and imaginative battle with accents and style sheet.

The publishers and authors have done their best to ensure the accuracy and currency of all the information in The Real Guide Hungary; however, they can accept no responsibility for any loss, injury, or inconvenience sustained by any traveler as a result of information or advice contained in the guide.

Published in the United States and Canada by Prentice Hall Trade Division
A division of Simon & Schuster, Inc., 15 Columbus Circle, New York, NY 10023.

Typeset in Linotron Univers and Century Old Style.
Printed in the United States by R.R Donnelley & Sons.

Library of Congress Cataloging-in-Publication Data

Richardson, Dan
Hungary: The Real Guide/written and researched by Dan Richardson; contributors: Jill Denton, Charlie Hebbert, Simon Broughton and Dan L. Andin; edited by Dan Richardson with Charlie Hebbert and Mark Ellingham.
288p Includes index.
Revised edition of Hungary, the rough guide. 1989.
ISBN 0-13-766072-3: $12.95
1. Hungary—Description and travel—1981—Guidebooks.
    I. Denton, Jill. II. Richardson, Dan. Hungary, the rough guide.
    III. Rough Guide to Hungary.
DB905.R53 1990
914.3904' 53—dc20.   89-28764
                                                                        CIP

THE REAL GUIDE

HUNGARY

Written and researched by
DAN RICHARDSON

With additional research and writing by
**Jill Denton, Charlie Hebbert,
Simon Broughton, and Dan L. Andin**

Edited by
Dan Richardson
with Charlie Hebbert and Mark Ellingham

■ PRENTICE HALL ■
NEW YORK LONDON TORONTO SYDNEY TOKYO SINGAPORE

CONTENTS

Introduction viii

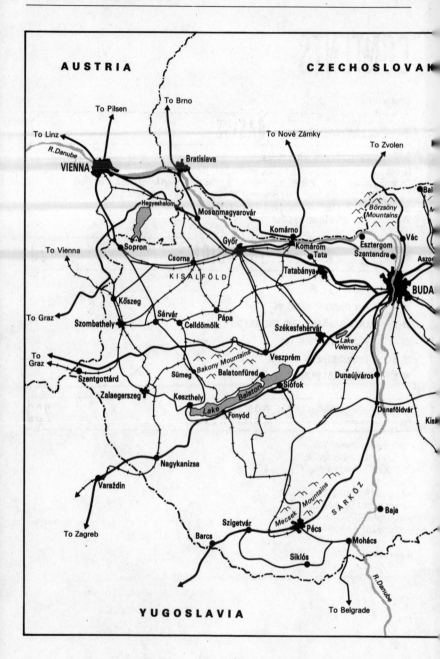

INTRODUCTION

Visitors who refer to **Hungary** as a Balkan country risk getting a lecture on how this small, landlocked nation of 10,658,000 people differs from "all those Slavs." Natives are strongly conscious of Hungary (likened by the poet Endre Ady to a ship sailing westwards against the tide of history) and of themselves as Magyars—of a race that transplanted itself from Central Asia into the heart of Europe, and a nation that identifies with "Western values." There's currently an upsurge of democratic and nationalist aspirations as Hungary prepares for free multi-party elections in 1990, and a Papal tour the following year. Censorship and the Iron Curtain have effectively ceased to exist, earning the West's seal of approval (symbolized by President Bush's visit) and alarming the repressive regimes in neighboring Romania and Czechoslovakia—all of which delights ordinary Hungarians and doesn't seem to bother the Kremlin.

As a result you'll encounter few of the clichés of Eastern European travel: no bread lines or overtly intrusive bureaucracy, or fear of secret police; and hardly a sign of Marx or Lenin, let alone a personality cult of Hungary's political leadership. **Tourism** is neither straitjacketed nor one-way; visitors can travel wherever they please, while plenty of Magyars visit Western Europe despite the expense this entails. Westerners, on the other hand, will find Hungary cheap: the moderately flush can afford a princely lifestyle, and even the impecunious can treat themselves frequently.

Hungary's capital, **Budapest**, inspires a feeling of déjà vu. It's not just the vast Gothic Parliament and other monuments of a bygone imperial era that seem familiar, but the latest fashions on the streets, or a poster advertising something that was all the rage back home a year before. In coffee houses, Turkish baths, and the fad for Habsburg bric-à-brac, there's a strong whiff of *Mitteleuropa*—that ambient culture that welcomed Beethoven in Budapest and Hungarian-born Liszt in Vienna, currently being revived in a new form by rock stars, film directors, environmental activists, and millions of tourists, making Budapest the melting pot of East and West.

After Budapest, **Lake Balaton** and the **Danube Bend** vie for popularity. The Balaton, with its string of brash resorts, styles itself as the "Nation's Playground," enjoying a fortuitous proximity to the Badacsony wine-producing region. The Danube Bend has more to offer in terms of scenery and historic architecture, as do the **Northern Uplands** and **Transdanubia**. Sopron, Győr, and Pécs are rightfully the main attractions in Transdanubia, like the famous wine centers of Tokaj and Eger in the Uplands, but for castle buffs the Zempléni range and the lowlands adjoining Yugoslavia have several treats in store. On the **Great Plain** Szeged hosts a major festival, while its rival city, Debrecen, serves as the jumping-off point for the archaic Erdőhát region and the mirage-haunted Hortobágy *puszta*, where a folkloric gathering at Nagykálló and the equestrian Bridge Fair are staged to coincide with Hungary's National Day, August 20. See the **chapter introductions** for more details about each region.

Finally, Hungary is an excellent point of departure if you're **heading for China or other parts of Eastern Europe**; railroad tickets and *MALÉV* flights from Budapest to these destinations are probably the cheapest in Europe. Travelers bound for Romania, Poland, or the Soviet Union would be well advised to stock up in Hungary's supermarkets first, and all the visas and reservations for the amazingly cheap train ride from Budapest to Beijing can be made in the Hungarian capital.

Where and when to go

Most visitors come in the summer, when nine or ten hours of sunshine are a daily occurrence, interspersed with short, violent storms during August or September. The humidity that causes these is really only uncomfortable in Budapest, where the crowds don't help; elsewhere the **climate** is agreeable. Budapest, with its spring and fall festivals, sights, and culinary delights, is a standing invitation to come out of season. But other parts of Hungary have little to offer during the winter, and the weather doesn't become appealing until late spring. May, warm but showery, is the time to see the Danube Bend, Tihany, or Sopron before everyone else arrives; June is hotter and drier, a pattern reinforced throughout July, August, and September. There's more of a variation in tourism than temperatures across the country: the Great Plain is drier, and the highlands are wetter, during summer, but that's about as far as climatic changes go, whereas some areas get mobbed while others receive few visitors, even during the high season.

AVERAGE DAYTIME TEMPERATURES				
	Budapest		**Debrecen**	
	°F	°C	°F	°C
January	29	-2	27	-3
February	32	0	31	-1
March	42	6	41	5
April	53	12	51	10
May	61	16	60	16
June	68	20	66	19
July	72	22	70	21
August	70	21	68	20
September	63	17	61	16
October	52	11	51	11
November	42	6	41	5
December	34	1	32	0

°F = (°C x 9/5) + 32

PART ONE

THE
BASICS

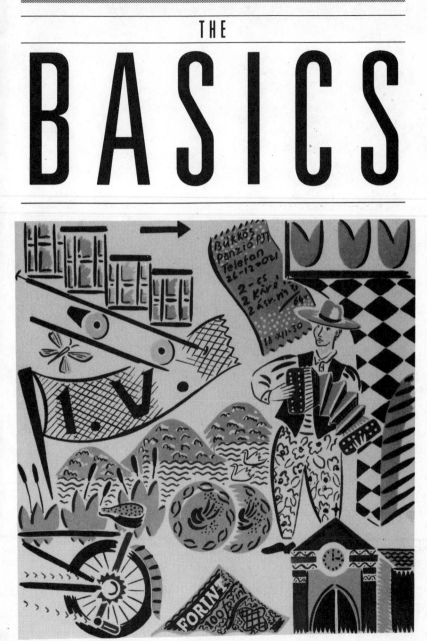

GETTING THERE

FLIGHTS FROM THE US

The simplest way to reach Hungary from the US is to fly **direct to Budapest**, which entails flying out from New York using either *MALÉV*, the national airline of Hungary, or *Pan Am*. Although *MALÉV* flies from other American cities (Boston, Miami, Chicago, San Francisco, Philadelphia, Washington, and Atlanta in the US, and Montreal and Toronto in Canada), this entails a European connection and works out more expensive.

MALÉV (630 5th Avenue, New York, NY; ☎212/757-6480) flies to Budapest twice weekly, with fares ranging from $919 in the low season to around $1000 in the high. *Pan Am* (☎800/221-1111) flies out of New York three times a week, with connections from most US cities. The Apex (non-refundable) fare is $698 in the low season, $798 in the shoulder, and $973 in the high season, all tickets remaining valid for three months.

Of the **other airlines** that fly to Europe, *KLM* (☎800/777-5553), *TWA* (☎800/221-2000) and *Lufthansa* (☎800/645-3880) fly from many American cities, including New York, Los Angeles, San Francisco, Chicago, Dallas, and Boston. *KLM* and *TWA* have similar prices, a non-refundable fare from New York starting at $698 in the low season, rising to $798 in the high season, while *Lufthansa* is slightly cheaper. From cities on the West Coast, fares on scheduled flights generally start at around $950 in the low season and $1150 in the high season.

A variety of **discount and student flights** to Budapest are also available, from agencies such as *STA, CIEE*, and *Nouvelles Frontières* (see box), *Council Travel Service* (205 East 42nd Street, New York, NY 10017; ☎212/661-1450), *Access International* (250 West 57th Street, Suite 511, New York, NY 10107; ☎212/333-7280) and *McTravel* (130 S. Jefferson St., Chicago, Illinois; ☎800/333-3335). *STA* offers fares starting at $580 for a low season midweek flight from New York, and $640 in early summer, though obviously prices vary so it pays to shop around. It's worth remembering too, that while *STA, CIEE* and *Nouvelles Frontières* specialize in the youth/student market, they offer **low-cost fares to all travelers**, irrespective of age or student status. In addition, there are many discount travel clubs, who operate in various ways. Some charge an annual fee and sell unsold airline tickets at discounts of fifteen to sixty percent, with members calling a hot-line for information on what's available. Others, such as *Airhitch*, sell last minute **standbys** to Europe from several US cities for one very low price ($160 from New York, $229 from Los Angeles), though precise dates and destinations are not guaranteed—you'll be offered a variety of flights that approximate your chosen destination and departure date, with only a few days notice. Obviously this form of travel is very uncertain, and calls for a degree of flexibility in your plans. Note also that in peak periods, standbys will be few and far between—*Airhitch*, for example, closes down for the two weeks over Christmas as most flights are too full to have standbys.

For further information about charter flights to Budapest, consult the Travel Guides in the Sunday papers, especially the *New York Times* and the *L.A. Times.*

Agencies offering discount flights include:

Stand Buys Ltd., 311 West Superior Street, Suite 404, Chicago, IL. 60610; ☎800/255-0200.

Worldwide Discount Travel Club, 1674 Meridian Avenue, Miami Beach, FL. 33139; ☎305/534-2082.

Moments Notice, 40 East 49th Street, New York, NY 19072; ☎212/668-2182.

Airhitch, 2901 Broadway, Suite 100, New York, NY 10025; ☎212/864-2000.

CIEE IN THE U.S.

Main Office: 205 E. 42nd St., New York, NY 10017; ☎800/223-7401

CALIFORNIA
2511 Channing Way, Berkeley, CA 94704; ☎415/848-8604

UCSD Student Center, B-023, La Jolla, CA 92093; ☎619/452-0630

5500 Atherton St., Suite 212, Long Beach, CA 90815; ☎213/598-3338

1093 Broxton Ave., Los Angeles, CA 90024; ☎213/208-3551

4429 Cass St., San Diego, CA 92109; ☎619/270-6401

312 Sutter St., San Francisco, CA 94108; ☎415/421-3473

919 Irving St., San Francisco, CA 94122; ☎415/566-6222

14515 Ventura Blvd., Suite 250, Sherman Oaks, CA 91403; ☎818/905-5777

GEORGIA
12 Park Place South, Atlanta, GA 30303; ☎404/577-1678

ILLINOIS
29 E. Delaware Place, Chicago, IL 60611; ☎312/951-0585

MASSACHUSETTS
79 South Pleasant St., 2nd Floor, Amherst, MA 01002; ☎413/256-1261

729 Boylston St., Suite 201, Boston, MA 02116; ☎617/266-1926

1384 Massachusetts Ave., Suite 206, Cambridge, MA 02138; ☎617/497-1497

MINNESOTA
1501 University Ave. SE, Room 300, Minneapolis, MN 55414; ☎612/379-2323

NEW YORK
35 W. 8th St., New York, NY 10011; ☎212/254-2525

Student Center, 356 West 34th St., New York, NY 10001; ☎212/661-1450

OREGON
715SW Morrison, Suite 1020, Portland, OR 97205; ☎503/228-1900

RHODE ISLAND
171 Angell St., Suite 212, Providence, RI 02906; ☎401/331-5810

TEXAS
1904 Guadalupe St., Suite 6, Austin, TX 78705; ☎512/472-4931

The Executive Tower, 3300 W. Mockingbird, Suite 101, Dallas,TX 75235; ☎214/350-6166

WASHINGTON
1314 Northeast 43rd St., Suite 210, Seattle, WA 98105; ☎206/632-2448

STA IN THE U.S.

BOSTON
273 Newbury St., Boston, MA 02116; ☎617/266-6014

HONOLULU
1831 S. King St., Suite 202, Honolulu, HI 96826; ☎808/942-7755

LOS ANGELES
920 Westwood Blvd., Los Angeles, CA 90024; ☎213/824-1574

7204 Melrose Ave., Los Angeles, CA 90046; ☎213/934-8722

2500 Wilshire Blvd., Los Angeles, CA 90057; ☎213/380-2184

NEW YORK
17 E. 45th St., Suite 805, New York, NY 10017; ☎212/986-9470;☎ 800/777-0112

SAN DIEGO
6447 El Cajon Blvd., San Diego, CA 92115; ☎619/286-1322

SAN FRANCISCO
166 Geary St., Suite 702, San Francisco, CA 94108; ☎415/391-8407

NOUVELLES FRONTIÈRES

In the United States
NEW YORK 19 W. 44th St., Suite 1702, New York, NY 10036; ☎212/764-6494

LOS ANGELES 6363 Wilshire Blvd., Suite 200, Los Angeles, CA 90048; ☎213/658-8955

SAN FRANCISCO 209 Post St., Suite 1121, San Francisco, CA 94108; ☎415/781-4480

In Canada
MONTREAL 1130 ouest, bd de Maisonneuve, Montréal, P.Q. H3A 1M8; ☎514/842-1450

QUEBEC 176 Grande Allée Ouest, Québec, P.Q. G1R 2G9; ☎418/525-5255

PACKAGE DEALS

A variety of **package deals** and arranged tours are also available, offering a range of activities and prices. *Magyar Tours* (☎718/816-6828) run 17-day vacations during the high season starting at around $1800, while the *Hungaria Travel Bureau* (1603 2nd Avenue, New York, NY; ☎212/249-9342) organizes four- to seven-day tours for between $300-600 per person, until October 1. *IBUSZ Hungarian Travel Company* (1 Parker Plaza, Suite 1104, Fort Lee, NJ 07024; ☎201/592-8585) offers tour packages focusing on Hungary's many archaeological, cultural, and folkloric points of interest, and organizes a range of activities including horseback riding, hunting, bicycling, and wine tasting. The *Hungarian Hotels Sales Office* (6033 West Century Boulevard, Suite 670, Los Angeles, CA 90045; ☎800/448-4321) offers a similar range, supplemented with educational courses. Other operators include *Forum Travel International* (91 Gregory Lane, Pleasant Hill, CA 94523; ☎415/671-2900), *The Russian Travel Bureau Inc.* (225 East 44th Street, New York, NY 10017; ☎800/847-1800), and *Fugazy International Travel* (770 US Highway 1, North Brunswick, NJ 08902; ☎800/828-4488), who lead escorted tours through Hungary and can also tailor itineraries for individual travelers.

VIA BRITAIN

If you decide to travel to Hungary via Britain, a range of options becomes available, simplest of which again is to fly. Three companies offer reasonably-priced *British Airways* or *MALÉV* round-trip flights from London to Budapest. Departures are from Heathrow, and travelers are required to stay at least one Saturday night. All Apex flights must be booked at least fourteen days in advance, and paid for in full then; confirmed reservations can't be changed.

Hungarian Air Tours (3 Heddon Street, London W1R 7LE; ☎01/437-9405) offers various deals. In the so-called Money Miser category, there are weekend flights limited to set periods (for example Thurs–Sun, Thurs–Tues, Fri–Mon, and so forth) costing £178 during April, May, and October, and £221 between June and September; plus six- to thirty-day round-trip flights costing £202 and £221 for the same periods. Their Midweek Apex flights (Tues and Wed only) go for £182 and £194, while their Apex round-trips, subject to the same restrictions but valid for up to three months, cost £224 irrespective of the season.

Similar deals are available from *Danube Travel* (6 Conduit Street, London W1R 9TG; ☎01/493-0263) under different names, such as

TRAVEL CUTS IN CANADA

Main Office: 187 College St., Toronto, Ontario M5T 1P7; ☎416/979-2406

ALBERTA

1708 12th St. NW, Calgary T2M 3M7; ☎403/282-7687. 10424A 118th Ave., Edmonton T6G 0P7; ☎403/471-8054

BRITISH COLUMBIA

Room 326, T.C., Student Rotunda, Simon Fraser University, Burnaby, British Columbia V5A 1S6; ☎604/291-1204. 1516 Duranleau St., Granville Island, Vancouver V6H 3S4; ☎604/689-2887. Student Union Building, University of British Columbia, Vancouver V6T 1W5; ☎604/228-6890 Student Union Building, University of Victoria, Victoria V8W 2Y2; ☎604/721-8352

MANITOBA

University Center, University of Manitoba, Winnipeg R3T 2N2; ☎204/269-9530

NOVA SCOTIA

Student Union Building, Dalhousie University, Halifax B3H 4J2; ☎902/424-2054. 6139 South St., Halifax B3H 4J2; ☎902/424-7027

ONTARIO

University Center, University of Guelph, Guelph N1G 2W1; ☎519/763-1660. Fourth Level Unicentre, Carleton University, Ottawa, K1S5B6; ☎613/238-5493. 60 Laurier Ave. E, Ottawa K1N 6N4; ☎613/238-8222. Student Street, Room G27, Laurentian University, Sudbury P3E 2C6; ☎705/673-1401. 96 Gerrard St. E, Toronto M5B 1G7; ☎416/977-0441. University Shops Plaza, 170 University Ave. W, Waterloo N2L 3E9; ☎519/886-0400.

QUÉBEC (Known as *Voyages CUTS*)

Université McGill, 3480 rue McTavish, Montréal H3A 1X9; ☎514/398-0647. 1613 rue St. Denis, Montréal H2X 3K3; ☎514/843-8511. Université Concordia, Edifice Hall, Suite 643, S.G.W. Campus, 1455 bd de Maisonneuve Ouest, Montréal H3G 1M8; ☎514/288-1130. 19 rue Ste. Ursule, Québec G1R 4E1; ☎418/692-3971

SASKATCHEWAN

Place Riel Campus Center, University of Saskatchewan, Saskatoon S7N 0W0; ☎306/343-1601

Weekend Supersaver, 7–30 day Supersaver and Super Apex, but the fares are identical to those of *Hungarian Air Tours*, though *Danube Travel* also does a one-way Euro Budget flight (£214). Round-trip flights from *Canterbury Travel* (248 Streatfield Road, Kenton, Harrow, Middlesex HA3 9BY; ☎01/206-0411) cost £217 (June–Sept), £197 (Oct), and £179 (Nov–March), and *Slade Thrifties* (15 Vivian Avenue, London NW4 3UT; ☎01/202-0111) could also be competitive.

By approaching *MALÉV* (10 Vigo Street, London W1; ☎01/439-0577), *Air France*, *Aeroflot*, *KLM*, *Lufthansa*, or *British Airways* directly, you might shave £10–30 off the above prices, but it's easier to let specialized agents do the work. *STA Travel*, with offices in London (74 Old Brompton Road, SW7 3LH; ☎01/581-1022, and 117 Euston Road, NW1 2SX; ☎01/388-2261), Bristol (25 Queens Road, BS8 1QE; ☎0272/294-399), and Cambridge is highly reliable. Another possibility is to use bargain flights to Vienna or Zagreb, available from *Intasun*, *Jetsave*, *Pegasus*, and various "bucket shops" (see ads in the London magazines *City Limits* and *Time Out*). Round-trips can cost as little as £90, but of course exclude the expense of traveling to and from Hungary, plus accommodation.

The cost of direct flights from other European capitals to Budapest isn't always proportionate to their proximity to Hungary, but it's certainly worth checking out *MALÉV* (who fly four times a week from Dublin), *Air France*, *KLM*, *Alitalia*, *Lufthansa*, or *TAROM* in any country.

BY RAIL

As an alternative to a direct flight, traveling to London (or another European city) and then proceeding by rail has the obvious advantage of allowing you to see more of Europe on your trip, and is attractive economically if you're a **student, under 26,** or **over 60**.

Those in the first two categories qualify for the discount tickets offered by **Eurotrain** (52 Grosvenor Gardens, London SW1; ☎01/730-3402), which are valid for two months and allow stopovers along the way. A round-trip ticket currently costs £142 (£80 one way), and entitles you to 25–30 percent off rail fares in Hungary. Alternatively, if you're under 26 and resident in Europe for at least six months, you can buy an **InterRail** pass, currently sold for £145 at major London railroad stations. This entitles the holder

to one month's travel on most European railways (though only at a 50 percent discount inside Hungary). **Eurail** passes are the American equivalent of InterRail, and come in regular and Youthpass varieties, both sold only in North America. The regular over-26 pass is the more expensive, covering first class travel for fifteen days ($298), a month ($470), two months ($650), or three months ($798), while the under-26 Youthpass covers one month ($320) or two months ($420) of travel in Europe, including Hungary. The *Eurotrain* main office is fairly close to London's Victoria Station (Victoria Underground), from where the trains for Budapest—connecting with the Oostende–Vienna express—depart. If you're 60 or over, the Rail Europ Senior Card gives the benefits of a program very similar to InterRail. You can get details from any British Rail Travel Center. If you qualify for none of the above, ordinary round-trip and one-way tickets will cost more than plane or bus fares.

On the continent, there are two trains **from Paris** (Gare de l'Est)—the midday connection for the *Wiener Waltzer*, and the thoroughly prosaic *Orient Express*. Both take roughly 25 hours to reach Keleti Station in Budapest. **Munich** is the Federal Republic's point of departure for Budapest, which can also be reached from Vienna's Westbahnhof (departures around 6:50 & 8:30am; 3:15 & 6pm) or Südbahnhof (7:45am), from where an ordinary one-way ticket costs roughly $25. During summer, trains from **Rome** join the *Maestral Express* which, like the *Adriatica* (connections to Split) stops at Zagreb in **Yugoslavia** en route to Budapest (also accessible by the *Polonia* from Belgrade). The *Balt–Orient* (Berlin–Dresden–Prague–Bratislava–Budapest) is one of several trains from **the DDR and Czechoslovakia**.

BY BUS

For the over 26s in particular, buses are an economical alternative to trains from **London to Budapest**. From mid-June to mid-September, *Attila Travel* (8 Wimpole Street, London W1N 7AB; ☎01/631-5207) runs a weekly service, with round-trip tickets costing £120—but book early to be sure of getting a seat. *National Express* (International terminal ☎0582/404-511; London inquiries ☎01/730 0202) also run a twice-weekly service to Budapest, although again only in the summer months (April–Sept), priced at £136 adult round-trip, £123 for a youth round-trip. Both journeys last two days, so bring plenty of food and drink and/or Deutschmarks.

If the above can't help and you don't mind leaving the return journey to fate, there's always the Zagreb route, capitalizing on the low fares to Zagreb (upwards of £40) offered by various outfits running buses to Yugoslavia and Greece. Unfortunately, none of the firms advertising in the London magazines *LAW*, *City Limits,* or *Time Out* can be recommended. The driver of my bus kept going for 36 hours on speed, circled Salzburg eight times, and only agreed to drop us near the center (rather than on the outskirts) of Zagreb after much argument. Having flaked-out at the comfortable Omladinski hostel near the railroad station (17, Ul. Petriniska), you can catch a train to Budapest (£10) or a bus to Letenye in southern Hungary (£5) the next day. As it's impossible to arrange a bus back, hard-up travelers might consider hitching—see the advice below.

For details of buses from elsewhere in Western Europe, contact *Deutsche Touring Gmbh*, Hauptbahnhof Europabus (2, Arnulfstrasse 3) in **Munich** 2; *Ungarn und Osteuropapareisen* (Altheimer Eck 1) in **Munich** 2; *Romeatour* (Lista di Spagna 134) in **Venice**; *Heribert Matzer Reisebüro* (Draisgasse 18 and Lendlplatz 38) in **Graz**; or one of several companies in **Vienna**. You'll find the *Österreichische Bundesbahnen* at the Wien Mitte bus terminal (Landstrasser Hauptstrasse 1/b), which is the point from which services to Budapest—charging roughly £15 for a one-way ticket—depart.

BY CAR—DRIVING OR HITCHING

The most direct highway to Budapest from the west is the E5, running via Oostende, Brussels, Aachen, Köln, Frankfurt, Nürnberg, Linz, and Vienna between London and the Hungarian capital (a distance of 1732km). You shouldn't bank on driving this in under 36 hours, however, and many motorists could face an insuperable obstacle should West Germany introduce a ban on cars using leaded gasoline in the near future, as it's currently (and quite rightly) considering. See "Driving" below regarding licenses, insurance, and driving inside Hungary.

Hitching along the same route can take up to three days, so you'd be wise to pack rainwear, a tent, a good road map, and some Deutschmarks

and/or food. On all European freeways it's illegal to hitch anywhere but at gas stations and motels, and police are generally tough with violators although their attitude to "law abiding" hitchers can vary—the Austrian Grenzepolizei seem almost benevolent. The ideal ride would be with a *Hungarocamion* truck going home, but it's realistic to settle for anything heading towards Austria. I found London to Dover the most frustrating stage of the journey, and western Germany to Vienna the most rewarding. To economize on the Vienna stopover, stay at the *Student Hostel* (IX, Säulenpasse 18/☎340-335 or 340-336) or the campground on the Linz side of town (Metro U4 to Hütteldorf, then bus #52B). Continuing on to Budapest, start thumbing just before the rd.10 exit ramp off the Simmeringer Hauptstrasse, more or less accessible by tram #71 from the Schwarzenbergplatz in the center of Vienna.

Hitching back from Hungary, you might be able to take advantage of the Hungarian radio program *Ötödik Sebesség* (at 5pm on Mon, Wed & Fri), which advertises rides to foreign countries. Callers are given the driver's telephone number and then you strike a deal—sharing the cost of gas is the usual arrangement. You'll need a Hungarian friend to understand the broadcast and make the calls, though. For independent hitch-hikers, German is the lingua franca of the road: *Wo fahren sie?* means "Where are you going?," and hitching signs should carry the word *Richtung* ("direction"). Sticking to routes through German-speaking countries and Holland, it's possible to make the English Channel in 24 hours; above all, avoid France, where the hitching's awful.

BY HYDROFOIL FROM VIENNA

Although the frequency of **hydrofoils from Vienna** varies seasonally, the journey to Budapest always takes four and a half hours. Departures occur at 8am daily during the low season (March 1–30 and Sept 4–Oct 1), 2:30pm daily from May 1–Sept 3, with an extra daily service at 8am during the high season (July 3–Sept 3)—but check this in Vienna, since schedules might change. Make reservations at least 24 hours in advance at *IBUSZ*, Kärntnerstrasse 26 (☎53-26-86), or the *DDSG* boat station, Praterkai, II. Mexiko Platz 8 (☎26-56-36), where the hydrofoils depart; the one-way fare costs around $48, payable in Austrian schillings.

VISAS AND RED TAPE

All North American citizens are required to obtain a visa prior to arrival in Hungary, as visas are not issued at the border.

To get a visa in the US, first obtain an application form by sending an SAE to the Hungarian Embassy (3910 Shoemaker Street N.W., Washington DC 20008; ☎202/362–6730, or, in Canada, 7 Delaware Avenue, Ottowa, Ontario K2P 0Z2; ☎613/232-1711), the Hungarian Consulate (8 East 75th Street, New York NY 10021; ☎212/879–4126), or *Ibusz Hungarian Travel Company* (1 Parker Plaza, Suite 1004, Fort Lee NJ 07024). Then send the filled-in application with your passport (which must have at least nine months validity remaining) by certified mail to the embassy or consulate, and enclose two passport-sized photos and a money order or certified check (currently $15) for each person, plus an SAE for return. Allow at least three weeks for processing.

A visa is valid for six months and entitles you to 30 days' stay. Keep the pink "exit visa," since this must be accommodation-stamped (see below) and surrendered on leaving Hungary.

The procedure is similar at **embassies abroad**, but by applying in person (in Britain, for example) it may be possible to get a visa in 48 hours. Payment is by postal order or cash in the local currency, except in other Eastern bloc states where only $US are accepted. Addresses are given in the box below.

VISA EXTENSIONS

Providing you get there 48 hours before it expires, your visa can usually be extended for another 30 days by the local police (Rendőrség), at headquarters (főkapitányság) in provincial towns, or the district station (kerületi rendőrség) nearest to your place of residence in Budapest. For further **extensions** it's necessary to furnish proof of solvency and deal with *KEOKH*, whose main office is **in Budapest** at VI, Népköztársaság útja 12 (open Mon–Fri 10am–12:30pm). Here you'll need two photos and a 300Ft stamp, theoretically available from the photomat and the *IBUSZ* desk on the premises, after which you'll have to wait outside the appropriate room for a final rubber-stamp validation. The process should be much the same at *KEOKH*s in Debrecen, Pécs, etc (addresses in the guide). **Lost passports and visas** must be reported to the police (who'll issue a new exit visa; if found, they'll be forwarded to another *KEOKH* office in Budapest (VI, Rudas u.45; Mon 8am–4pm, Tues–Fri 8:30am–noon).

HUNGARIAN EMBASSIES ABROAD

AUSTRALIA: 79 Hopetown Circuit, Yarralumia a.c.t. 2600 Canberra (☎82-32-26); 351/a Edgecliff Rd, Edgecliff NSW 2027 Sydney (☎328-7859).

AUSTRIA: 1, Bank Gasse 4–6, A–1010 Wien (☎62–36-21).

BRITAIN: 35b Eaton Place, London SW1 (☎01/ 235-2664;open Mon–Fri 10am–noon).

CANADA: 7 Delaware Avenue, Ottawa K2P 0Z2 Ontario (☎613-232-1711).

DENMARK: Strandvej 170, 2920 Charlottenlund, Copenhagen (☎451/63-16-88).

W.GERMANY: 5300 Bonn 2 (Plittersdorf) Trumstr. 30 (☎37-67-97).

HOLLAND: La Haye Hoheweg 14, Den Haag (☎500-405).

NORWAY: Sophus Lies gt. 3 Oslo 2 (☎47-2/56- 46-88).

SWEDEN: Laboratoriegaten 2, 11527 Stockholm (☎47-8/61-67-62).

REGISTRATION WITH THE POLICE

Registration isn't as formidable as it sounds, for although foreigners are obliged to notify the police of their place of residence within 48 hours, in practice it's rarely the visitor's concern. The reception desk at hotels and campgrounds, or any tourist office that fixes you up with private accommodation, will automatically stamp your exit visa and notify the police on your behalf. Only when staying with friends, or in lodgings obtained without official involvement, is it necessary to go to the police yourself. First get an Alien's Registration form (*Lakcímbejelentő lap küföldiek részére*) from any Post Office and have it countersigned by your host; then take it to the district or provincial police station for stamping. If you're staying in unofficial lodgings a lot, it's worth buying several registration forms (10Ft each). Any **gaps** in the record render you liable to a fine of 100Ft per day; so if you fail to register for a while it's better to check into a hotel or campground for an up-to-date stamp than go to *IBUSZ* or the police. Once you've "closed" the gap there shouldn't be any problems afterwards.

HEALTH AND INSURANCE

No inoculations are required for travel in Hungary, and standards of public health are good. Tap water is safe everywhere, while potable springs (*forrás*) and streams are designated on maps, and with signs, as *ivóvíz*. The national health service (*Sz.T.K.*) will provide free emergency treatment in any hospital or doctor's office, though insurance is recommended in the event of serious illness—drugs are charged for.

For information about **health care** in Hungary (and other countries) including the names of English-speaking doctors, contact the *International Association for Medical Assistance to Travelers* (417 Center Street, Lewiston, NY 14092; ☎716/754-4883), or *International SOS Assistance Abroad*, who can help with emergency transportation (Box 11568, Philadelphia PA 19116; ☎800/523-8930).

You may also like to take out some form of insurance which covers trip cancellation (especially for Apex tickets which are non-refundable) and lost property. Obviously, if you're intending to drive, an appropriate policy is essential (see "Driving" below).

Hungarian insurance policies (from the *Állami Biztosító* company) only pay out in forints.

PHARMACIES

Sunburn (*napszúrás*) and insect bites (*rovarcsípés*) are the most common **minor complaints**. Supermarkets sell suntan lotion, while pharmacies stock *Vietnámi balzsam* (Vietnamese-made "Tiger Balm"—the best bug repellent going) and bite ointment. Mosquitoes are pesky, but the bug to beware of in forests is *kullancs*, which bites and then burrows into human skin, causing inflammation. The risk seems fairly small—we've never encountered any—but if you get a bite which seems particularly painful, it's worth having it inspected at a **pharmacy**. All towns and some villages have a *gyógyszertár* or *patika*, with staff (who probably understand German) authorized to issue a wide range of drugs, including pain-killers. However, pharmaceutical products are mainly of Eastern bloc origin, so anyone requiring specific medication should bring a supply with them. Opening hours are normally Monday–Friday 9am–6pm, Saturday 9am–noon or 1pm; signs in the window give the location or telephone number of all-night (*éjjel*) pharmacies.

HOSPITALS

Provincial tourist offices can direct you to local medical centers or doctors' offices (*orvosi rendelő*), while your embassy in Budapest will have the addresses of foreign-language speaking **doctors** and **dentists**, who'll probably be in private (*magán*) practice. Private medicine is much cheaper than in the West, as attested to by the thousands of Austrians who come here for treatment. For muscular, skin, or gynaecological complaints, doctors often prescribe a soak at one of Hungary's numerous **medicinal baths** (*gyógyfürdő*) whose curative properties are described in an *IBUSZ* booklet. In **emergencies**,

dial **04** for the *Mentők* ambulance service, or catch a taxi to the nearest *Kórház*. The standard of **hospitals** varies enormously, but low morale and shortages of beds or equipment are obviously caused by poor wages and general underfunding of the health service. Depending on local conditions, Westerners might get the best available treatment, or be cold-shouldered; in the event of the latter, it's worth trying to bribe the staff as a last resort. When properly funded, Hungarian medicine can work wonders: Budapest's Pető Institute (XII, Kútvölgyi út 6) leads the world in the treatment of children with spina bifida, cerebral palsy, or multiple sclerosis.

COSTS, MONEY, AND BANKS

rare; but this isn't too serious considering the low costs in other areas. A three-course meal with wine can be had for $5–8 in most **restaurants**, and even the classiest *étterem* charge less than their Western counterparts. Cheapest of all is public transit, with 5–6Ft flat fares in urban areas, few railroad or bus journeys exceeding $8, and most costing under $1.50. *Eurotrain* and *Inter-Rail* holders get reductions on domestic railroad tickets, while campgrounds and hostels give discounts to holders of IUS cards (see "Other Things" below). Further **savings** can be made by hitching, making or buying your own food, or eating in workers' canteens.

HUNGARIAN FORINTS

Hungarian **forints** (Ft) come in notes of 10, 20, 50, 100, 500, and 1000Ft; with 1, 2, 5, 10, and 20Ft coins; the little *fillér* (100 fillér = 1Ft) coins are practically useless though still in circulation. Forints can't be exchanged outside the socialist bloc; and while they can be bought at a favorable rate around Vienna's Mexiko Platz, importing or exporting banknotes exceeding 100Ft is illegal. There's no restriction on bringing in or taking out convertible currency—although if all your cash is in small denominations, declare this on entry (since a zealous customs person might suspect you of smuggling them on the way out).

Magyars complain of "paying Swedish taxes on an Ethiopian wage" and the 15–30 percent inflation which forces them to hold down two or even three jobs, but most Westerners find that their money goes a long way at the official rate of exchange (currently around 70Ft = $1), making **costs** low. And if something does exceed your budget, there's usually a cheaper substitute available—particularly in the case of restaurants and **accommodation**. The average three-star hotel charges around $24 for a double room, whereas the same in a Hungarian household costs between $8–11. In both cases, solo travelers are likely to be charged the full rate, since singles are

Note: Forint prices quoted here will inevitably be overtaken by inflation, but tourists should find that real costs haven't risen much unless their own currency has slipped against the forint.

CHANGING MONEY

Providing you produce your passport, **changing money** or travelers' checks is a painless operation at any *IBUSZ* or regional tourist office, or the majority of large hotels and campgrounds; *valuta* desks in *OTP* **banks** take longer over transactions, and work shorter hours (Mon–Fri 8:30am–3:30pm) than tourist offices. Exchange rates are the same everywhere. Keep the **receipts**, which are required should you wish to extend your visa, pay for international tickets in forints, or re-exchange forints back into hard currency when you leave Hungary. At road checkpoints, 50 percent of any remaining forints can be re-exchanged up to the value of $50. The advantages of changing money on the illegal **black market** are minimal (15–20 percent above the official rate), and scalpers are skilled at cheating, or might even be plainclothes police. It's safer to change money with Hungarian acquaintances, who'll find it useful if they're saving for a Western vacation or stereo. At Debrecen's Polish Market (to name but one place) there's a black market **in other Eastern bloc currencies**, nicknamed the "Comecon stock exchange," where one can swap forints or hard currency for Romanian lei, Soviet rubles, DDR Ostmarks, or Polish zloty at favorable rates.

TRAVELERS' CHECKS AND CREDIT CARDS

Although a modest amount of low-denomination dollar bills or Deutschmarks can be useful, it's safest to carry the bulk of your money in **travelers' checks**. Eurochecks and TCs issued by American, Australian, British, Dutch, Norwegian, and West German banks are all accepted; but for speedy refunds in case of loss, *American Express* (represented here by *IBUSZ*) is the only reliable brand. *Amex, Bank of America, Diners' Club, Carte Blanche*, and *Eurocard* **credit cards** can be used to rent cars, buy airline tickets, or pay your bills directly in the fancier hotels and restaurants and in shops catering mainly to tourists. But in everyday Hungarian life, and out in the sticks, they're pretty useless. If you're planning a lengthy stay in Budapest or want to receive money from the West, consider opening an account. Foreigners may hold hard currency **bank accounts** at the *OTP Központi Devisa Fiók* in Budapest (V, Münnich F. u.6), which pay out and give interest in the currency of your choice.

COMMUNICATIONS—MAIL, PHONES, AND MEDIA

style, and underline it; even this may not prevent your mail being misfiled, so ask them to check under all your names. To collect, show your passport and ask "*Van posta a részemre?*". A more secure "drop" is the 24-hour *IBUSZ* bureau in Budapest (V, Petőfi tér 3), where letters marked "c/o American Express" are lovingly guarded until collection, and the staff speak English. Letters (*levél*) can be sent to anywhere in the West for 8Ft (5Ft for postcards). It's quicker to buy stamps (*bélyeg*) at tobacconists; post offices are full of people making complicated transactions or sending telegrams (*távirat*), which can also be dictated by dialling 02.

PHONES

In towns and cities, local calls can be made from public **phones** where 2Ft gets you three minutes (six minutes after 6pm), but in villages you usually have to go to the post office. Long-distance calls are more problematic, for although lines between Budapest and provincial centers are okay, communications between smaller towns are poor, or nonexistent. In villages, calls

POST OFFICES

Post offices (*posta*) are usually open 8am–6pm Monday–Friday and until noon on Saturday, although in Budapest you'll find several offices functioning around the clock. Mail from abroad should be addressed "*poste restante, posta*" followed by the name of the town; tell your friends to write your surname first, Hungarian-

must be placed by the post office or the operator; in towns where it's possible to dial direct from booths (☎06, followed by the area code, eg. 1 for Budapest, and then the subscriber's number), the post office might still get better results. Budapest and some large towns also have red phone booths, taking 10Ft and 20Ft coins, for making **international calls**. Dial 00, the country code (1 for U.S. or Canada) followed by the area code and finally the number—and then keep your fingers crossed. Personally, I found it easier to place calls through the international operator (09), the Telephone Bureau in Budapest (130Ft for 3 minutes), or fancy hotels in the provinces (ask about the cost first).

MEDIA

Without a knowledge of Hungarian you can only hope to recognize some features of the **media**: the obvious dullness of *Népszabadság* (People's Freedom), the Party daily; an appetite for soft porn and celebrity trivia, catered for by *Szextra* and *Reform*; and the inroads made by the Springer press and Murdoch's satellite TV station called Sky Channel. There's no way you can appreciate founts of literature and criticism like *Kortárs*, *Élet és Irodalom*, or the new journal of the Democratic Forum, *Hitel*. In fact, reading material boils down to *Daily News*, an English/German language paper featuring tourist information and a cautious selection of world news, found on newsstands alongside the *Morning Star*, *L'Humanite*, and *Rude Pravo*. Capitalist newspapers used to be sold as furtively as pornography (which is widely available nowadays), and deluxe hotels are still the likeliest places to find *The Times*, *Herald Tribune*, or *Newsweek*, otherwise stocked by a few stands in Budapest (curiously, only right-wing papers are available). If these don't appeal, drop into the British Embassy's library or try the radio. A new German-language station, *Radio Danubius*, lets rip with pop, ads, and rap, broadcasting on a daily basis 6:30am to 10pm until October 31 (100.5, 103.3, or 102 MHz VHF); while *Radio Petőfi* broadcasts news in English at 11am (weekdays) and 11:57am (Sat) between June 1 and September 1. Alternatively, tune into the BBC World Service on the following frequencies:

MHz 24.80, 30.77, 48.54, 49.59

Meters 12.095, 9.75, 6.18, 6:05

The lower frequencies (MHz) tend to give better results early in the morning and late at night, the higher ones during the middle of the day.

INFORMATION AND MAPS

A large number of photo-packed brochures, maps, and special-interest leaflets are available free from *IBUSZ*, the Hungarian tourist organization, and distributed by their agents abroad.

These agents include:

BRITAIN: Danube Travel Ltd. 6, Conduit St, London W1 (☎01- 493-0263).

W.GERMANY: *IBUSZ*, 6000 Frankfurt am Main, Baseler Str.46/48 (☎252-018) (other branches in München, Köln and Stuttgart).

SWEDEN: 10326 Stockholm, Beridarebanan 1, PO box 16322 (☎20-40-40).

USA: 630 Fifth Avenue, Rockefeller Center (Suite 520), New York, NY, 10020 (☎212/582-7412).

The most useful are the large road map (which is perfectly adequate for traveling around Hungary), a pamphlet detailing the year's festivals and events, and the booklet *Hotel-Camping*, which lists all official accommodation, gives an indication of prices, and tells you where to make reservations. There are also maps designed specifically for campers and cyclists (the latter showing which roads may be used).

TOURIST AGENCIES IN HUNGARY

In Hungary itself you'll find *IBUSZ* offices in most towns, together with **other tourist agencies**. Many of them are mentioned in this guide, and a full list of addresses can be found in the *Hotel-Camping* booklet; opening hours are generally (but not invariably) Monday–Saturday 8am–6pm (some main offices until 8pm); 8am–1pm on Sunday. *Volántourist*—an arm of the *Volán* bus company—specializes in handling travel reservations and tour groups; *Cooptourist* deals with the top end of the market—mainly car and apartment rentals; while the "Youth Travel" agency *Express* supposedly caters to impoverished under-35s, although their hotels and campgrounds aren't particularly cheap. In theory, all three can reserve accommodation and/or tickets on a nationwide basis; but for guided tours and on-the-spot lodgings and information, it's usually better to inquire at a regional tourist office (*Siótour, Hajdú Tourist*, etc). The situation is slightly different in the capital, where *Tourinform* dispenses information while *IBUSZ* and *Budapest Tourist* handle sightseeing programs and accommodation. Most tourist offices carry a free monthly magazine, *Programme*, which details tourist **events** throughout Hungary.

MAPS

For reasons of scale, our **town maps** lack the details, accents, and tram and bus routes that appear on Hungarian *városi-térkép*. These cost 15–30Ft, and are available from local tourist offices or, failing that, from bookshops (*könyvesbolt*). Bookshops also stock **hiking maps** or *turistatérkép* covering the Mátra, Bükk, Zempléni, and other highland regions (30–60Ft), which should be purchased in advance, since they may not be available on the spot. The best selections can be found at two **map shops** in Budapest (VII, Nyár u.2 and V, Bajcsy-Zsilinszky út 37), which are outlets for the *Cartographia* company, whose maps of other Eastern bloc capitals are better than anything available there—which is useful to know if you're planning to visit them later.

TROUBLE

The Hungarian police (*Rendőrség*) have a milder reputation than their counterparts in other socialist states; and foreign tourists are handled with kid gloves unless they're suspected of black-marketeering, drug-smuggling, or driving under the influence of alcohol.

However, the rule on registration (see "Red Tape and Visas" above) is taken seriously, and since bored cops ask to inspect passports and visas from time to time, you should make sure that everything's in order. In border regions, it's fairly common to be (politely and briefly) questioned by plainclothes—usually flashily dressed—young secret police; but here too, if your stamps are in order, the security police shouldn't create any problems. Most police officers have at least a smattering of German, but rarely any other foreign language. If you need the police, dial **07** in **emergencies**; should you be arrested or need legal advice, ask to contact your embassy or consulate (see "Listings" in *Budapest* for the addresses).

Violent crimes—and theft in general—are rare in Hungary, and most **trouble** can be avoided. Don't sunbathe nude or topless unless everyone else is, photograph "secret" Russian bases (invariably marked by "no photography" signs), or deal blatantly on the black market, and you've eliminated almost all the likely causes.

SEXUAL HARASSMENT

The exception is **sexual harassment**, which is mainly a problem for women traveling alone, and more likely in certain situations than in others. "Provocative" clothing (or punkish hairstyles) may encourage unwelcome male attention if you visit rural or working-class *italbolt* (bars), or hitch-hike alone; while the "black train" (see "Getting There" in *The Great Plain*) should be avoided, as should Budapest's VIII district and downtown Miskolc after dark.

Mostly, harassment is of the annoying rather than the frightening variety, and it's probably not worth responding with "*nem fogdoss!*" (keep your hands to yourself!) or "*menj a fenébe!*" (go to hell!). The important word to remember is *segítség!*—help!—although it's unlikely that you'll need to use it.

GETTING AROUND

Although it doesn't break any speed records, public transit reaches most parts of Hungary, and despite recent price increases, fares remain remarkably cheap.

The only problem is *információ*, for the staff rarely speaks anything but Hungarian, the only language used for notices and announcements. You'll find some pertinent phrases in the *Contexts* section of this guide, while the following should be useful for **deciphering timetables**. *Érkező járatok* (or *érkezés*) means "arrivals," and *induló járatok* (or *indulás*) "departures." Trains or buses to (*hova*) a particular destination leave from a designated platform (for example *vágány 1*) or bus-stand (*kocsiállás*); and the point of arrival for services from (*honnan*) a place may also be indicated. Some services run (*közlekedik, köz.* for short) *munkaszüneti napok kivételével naponta köz.*—daily, except on rest days, meaning Sunday and public holidays; *munkanapokon (hetfőtől-péntekig) köz.*—weekdays, Monday–Friday; *munkaszüneti napokon köz.*—on rest days; or *09:30–tól 12-ig vasárnap köz.*—on Sunday 9:30am–midnight. *Átszállás* means "change"; *at* "via"; and *kivételével* "except."

TRAINS

The centralization of the **MÁV** railroad network means that many cross-country journeys are easier if you travel via Budapest rather than on branch lines where services are slower and less frequent. Timetables are in yellow (for departures) or white (for arrivals), with express and

Note: Regional transportation schedules are summarized under "Travel Details" at the end of each chapter.

gyorsvonat (fast trains) in red. Express **trains**—stopping at major centers only—require seat reservations (see below), as do *gyorsvonat* (which stop more frequently) indicated on the timetable with an "R" in red; but no reservations are necessary for *személyvonat*, which crawl along halting at every hamlet en route. The latter are obviously the cheapest, but all fares are so low that the money saved is insignificant compared with the time lost by not traveling on a faster service. Most trains have buffets and first and second class (*osztály*) sections; international services routed through Budapest have **sleeping cars and couchettes** (*hálókocsi* and *kusett*), for which tickets can be bought at *MÁV* offices, in advance, or sometimes on the train itself. More details are available from the *UTASELLÁTÓ* company in Budapest (☎140-803), which runs *MÁV*'s catering side.

If you're planning to travel a lot by rail, or take trains to other socialist countries, it's worth investing in a **national timetable**, available from the annex at *MÁV*'s international reservations office in Budapest. Domestic services are covered by the chunky *Hivatalos Menetrend* (80Ft); international ones by *Nemzetközi Menetrend* (20Ft), a slimmer paperback. In both cases you'll need to spend a while decoding them.

Tickets (*jegy*) for domestic services can safely be bought at the station (*pályaudvar* or *vasútállomás*) on the day of departure, but it's possible to reserve them up to sixty days in advance. You can break your journey once between the point of departure and the final destination, but must get your ticket punched within an hour of arrival at the interim station. Most Hungarians purchase one-way tickets (*egy útra*), so specify a *retur* or *oda-vissza* if you want a round-trip ticket. If you're found traveling without a ticket you have to buy one at many times the normal price. **Seat reservations** (*helyjegy*), in the form of a separate numbered bit of card, are obligatory for services marked "R" on timetables; they cost a few forints at the ticket office, and reservations can be made two months in advance at any *MÁV* or *Volántourist* office.

It's best to buy tickets for **international trains** (*nemzetközi gyorsvonat*) at least 36 hours in advance, although this won't get you seats on the oversubscribed trains **to China** (see "From

Budapest to China by Rail" in *Contexts*). Their popularity stems from the fact that Hungary is **the cheapest place to buy tickets** to other socialist countries on the Eurasian continent; and for the return journey, too. Holders of IUS cards (which even non-students can obtain; see "Directory" below) are entitled to a 15–30 percent reduction in the fare; and round-trip tickets (to Bulgaria in particular) generally work out substantially less than the cost of a Hungarian one-way ticket, plus a one-way back to Hungary purchased in another socialist state. One can pay for the "Hungarian stage" of the journey in forints, but the "international" phase must be paid for in hard currency. The central *MÁV* ticket office in Budapest (VI, Népköztársaság útja 35), which handles reservations, gets crowded during summer; and staff and waiting tourists won't thank anybody who tries to pay by check or credit card.

Concessions in the form of reduced fares on domestic services are available for groups of ten or more people (25 percent), *InterRail*ers (50 percent), *Eurotrain* card holders (50 percent) and pensioners with rail permits (33 percent). Children under four travel free if they don't occupy a separate seat. *MÁV* itself issues various **season tickets**, valid on domestic lines nationwide (but not on the international trains within Hungary), or around the Balaton only; for one week or ten days. You'll need to travel fairly intensively to make savings with a seven-day national *Runaround* (800Ft/1200Ft first class), and while a week's train travel around the Balaton comes cheap (200Ft), quite a number of the shoreline settlements are easier to reach by bus. Budapest season tickets are detailed under "Getting Around" in *Budapest*.

Hungary runs a **car train** on the Budapest–Dresden line, which travelers to West Germany via the DDR might find useful, although it doesn't carry campers or mini-buses. On domestic services **bicycles** can ride in the guard's van as personal **luggage** for a charge of about 30Ft per 100 kilometers. Most stations have a left-luggage office (*ruhatár*) which charges 3Ft per day for each item deposited—sometimes including "each item" strapped to your backpack! Beware of huge lines for baggage at Budapest's main stations (and some Balaton terminals) during the summer, and keep *all* of the scrappy little receipts, or you'll never get your gear back. A few main stations have automatic luggage lockers, which take two 2Ft coins and your baggage for up to 24 hours. **Lost property** is kept for two months at the station where it was handed in, and thereafter forwarded to the regional *MÁV* headquarters (except for passports, which are sent to *KEOKH* immediately).

BUSES

Regional **Volán** ("Wheel") companies run the bulk of Hungary's **buses**, which are called *busz* (pronounced "booce," *not* "bus," which means "fuck" in Hungarian!). Buses are often the quickest way to travel **between towns**, and while fares are higher than on the railroads they're still very cheap (roughly 1Ft per km). Details of useful routes are given in the guide, and at the end of each chapter, but in any case, schedules are clearly displayed in bus terminals (*autóbuszállomás* or *autóbusz pályaudvar*) in every Hungarian town. Arrive early to confirm the departure bay (*kocsiállás*) and ensure getting a seat. For long-distance services originating from Budapest or major towns, you can buy tickets with a seat reservation up to half an hour before departure; after that you get them from the driver, and risk standing throughout the journey. Services **in rural areas** may be limited to one a day, and tickets are only available on board the bus. As on trains, children under four travel free if they don't occupy a separate seat, and for halffare up to the age of ten, but otherwise there are no concessions.

Public transit **within towns** is generally excellent, with buses and trolleybuses (*trolibusz*), and sometimes trams (*villamos*), running from dawn until around 10:30 or 11pm. Express buses (numbered in red and prefixed by an "E") halt only at main stops, or not at all between terminals, so be careful about boarding them. **Tickets** for all services are sold in strips by tobacconists and street stands, and punched by the passenger on board the vehicle. Municipalities set their own flat rates, causing some variation in prices nationwide. Generally, the local fare for trams and trolleybuses is identical, so the same kind of ticket can be used on both services; buses require different, slightly more costly tickets. Tickets from one town aren't supposed to be used in another. In Budapest, various types of **passes** are available.

In addition, *Volán* runs **international services** to neighboring countries and a few points farther west. The main depot for these is Engels tér in Budapest (see "The Belváros" in

Budapest), but some services also run from provincial towns like Siófok, Szombathely, Győr, Miskolc, Salgótarján, Szeged, Baja, Mohács, and Debrecen, (detailed under those towns in the guide). It's fractionally cheaper to travel from Budapest to Vienna by bus, but other destinations may cost less by train. Unless you present a receipt showing that your forints were obtained legally, tickets on all international coaches must be purchased in hard currency.

DRIVING

Hungary's geographical location means that the country plays an important part in overland communications across Europe, and the E15 (London–Istanbul) highway goes via Budapest. To drive in Hungary you'll require an international **driving license** and **third-party insurance**. Cars registered in EEC countries (except France, Italy, Portugal, Spain, Greece and Turkey) are assumed to be covered by this; drivers from other countries must have an appropriate insurance extension, or purchase one at the border. This last only covers for damage to third parties in Hungary, so it's wiser to fix it up at home beforehand. **Accidents** not involving injury should be reported to the Motor Vehicle Insurance Dept. in Budapest (XI, Hamzsabégi út 60;☎669-755), within 24 hours if possible; if someone is injured the police must be notified (dial 07).

Drinking and driving is totally prohibited, and offenders with in excess of eight milligrams of alcohol are liable to felony charges. The state requires cars to be roadworthy (steering, brakes, and all lights must work); and carry certain **mandatory equipment**—a triangular breakdown sign; spare bulbs for the indicators, head-, rear- and brake-lights; a first aid box; and a supplementary mud-guard made of a non-rigid material, attached to rear fenders. Passengers must wear three-point safety belts in the front seats, where children are forbidden to travel.

Speed limits for vehicles are 60 kph in town, 80 kph on main roads, and 100 kph on highways; offenders can expect a spot-fine of at least 500Ft. Besides driving on the right, the most important **rules** are the prohibitions against repeatedly switching from lane to lane on highways; passing near pedestrian crossings; and sounding the horn in built-up areas unless to avert accidents. At crossroads, vehicles coming from the right have right-of-way, unless otherwise indicated by signs,

and pedestrians have priority over cars turning onto the road. Remember that trams *always* have right of way, and that some traffic islands serve as bus or tram stops. On highways and secondary roads it's illegal to reverse, make U-turns, or stop at islands. **Pedestrian zones** (found in many towns and shaded blue on maps) are indicated by "Restricted Access" signs—*kivéve célforgalom*.

Roads are generally in good condition, and fall into three categories. Highways, called motorways—prefixed by an "M"—link the Balaton with Budapest, and will doubtless soon do the same for Győr and Miskolc; lesser highways (numbered with a single digit from 1–8) mostly radiate from Budapest like spokes in a wheel; linked by secondary roads identified by two or three digits (the first one indicates the highway which the road joins, for example roads 82 and 811 both meet route 8 at some point). Information on nationwide **driving conditions** can be obtained from *ÚTINFORM* (☎227-643); conditions in Budapest are monitored by *FÖVINFORM* (☎171-173). In rural areas, wagons, cyclists, livestock, and pedestrians are potential **traffic hazards**, so you should drive slowly—especially at night.

Gas—*benzin*—isn't rationed in Hungary, and most AFOR gas stations (*benzinkút*) sell 98 octane *extra*; 92 octane *szuper*; and 86 octane *normál*. However, **diesel** is only obtainable with **coupons** (sold at main hotels and *IBUSZ* agencies; unused coupons aren't refunded). Gas stations usually function 6am–10pm, except on highways and in the capital, where many operate around-the-clock. *IBUSZ* issues a variety of useful, free **road maps**, including one showing Budapest's one-way streets and bypasses. By phoning 220-668 or 160-183 you can summon the "Yellow Angels" **breakdown service**, which is free if the repairs take no longer than one hour to complete and your own motoring organization belongs to the *FIA* or *AIT* federations, to which the **Hungarian Automobile Club**—*MAK*—is also affiliated. The *MAK*'s national headquarters is at Rómer Flóris u.4/a in Budapest's II district (weekdays 8am–2:30pm; alternate Sats 8am–12:30pm; ☎666-404); but their depot for **technical assistance** in the capital is at Boldizsár u.2 in the XI district (☎850-722). **Spare parts** for foreign cars are easier to find in Hungary than elsewhere in Eastern Europe, but may still present problems. See under the Budapest "Listings" and ask the *MAK* for help.

Renting a car is easy provided you're 21 or older, with a valid national driving license that's at least one year old. You can order a car through any *AVIS* or *EUROPCAR* bureau in the world, and from hotel reception desks or certain travel agencies within Hungary, using cash or credit cards. In Budapest these agencies are *FŐTAXI* (VII, Kertész u.24; ☎116-116), *Volántourist* (IX, Vaskapu u.16; ☎334-783), *Cooptourist* (V, Kossuth tér 13–15; ☎118-803) and *IBUSZ* (V, Martinelli tér 8; ☎184-158). *IBUSZ*, *Volántourist* and *Cooptourist* offices offer the same service in the provinces. Rental **costs** vary from $12/175 per day/week for a Lada 1300, to $20/126 for a *Toyota* or *VW Golf*, or $45/238 for a van; there's a minimum deposit of $150, plus a charge of $0.12–0.35 per km and $10 compulsory CASCO insurance to add to this—not to mention the cost of gas. The latter is not included in the price of **fly/drive holidays**.

BY AIR AND BOATS

MALÉV doesn't operate any **domestic flights**, since Hungary is such a small country, but many of their **flights abroad** (departing from Ferihegy airport) are a good deal. If you're heading on to other socialist countries, or to Greece or Turkey, they may prove an attractive alternative to trains—especially for holders of IUS cards, who sometimes qualify for substantial discounts. *MALÉV*s central office (Roosevelt tér 2/☎186-614) is the place to make inquiries, while you can also make reservations at desks in the main Budapest hotels, or by telephone (☎184-333).

The *MAHART* company organizes **passenger boats** in Hungary, which operate on Lake Balaton, between Budapest and Esztergom, on the section of the Danube running through the capital, and on the River Tisza which bisects the Great Plain (although this last service only functions during high season, if at all some years). *MAHART* also operates a daily **hydrofoil service between Vienna and Budapest**. It's a four and a half hour journey downriver to Budapest; an hour longer if one travels upriver to Vienna. Tickets to Vienna are sold at the International Boat Station on the Belgrád rakpart (the Pest embankment), where the hydrofoil departs, or at *IBUSZ* (Tanács körút 3/c); in Vienna, tickets are available from *IBUSZ* (I. Kárntnerstrasse 26) or the Austrian company DDSG (II. Mexiko Platz 8). Prices are subject to regular increase, so the quoted one-way fare of 600 Austrian schillings (roughly $48) is only an indication of the likely cost.

BY BIKE OR HITCHING

Motorcycling seems to be the favorite means of travel for young West German campers in Hungary, although I'd have thought that they'd find the **speed limits** irksomely low: 80 kph on highways, 70 on other roads, and 50 kph in built-up areas. Drivers must be over eighteen, wear a helmet, and have a log book or other registration document, plus an **insurance extension**. Otherwise, rules and conditions are the same as for cars.

If you bring your own bicycle, **cycling** can be a good way to see Hungary. Winds are generally light, there's hardly any rain from July until the end of September, and roads are well surfaced and usually free of heavy traffic. However, cyclists are forbidden on main roads (with single digit numbers), and on some secondary roads between "peak hours": 7–9:30am, 4–6pm. You can obtain a **cycling map** of Hungary from the *Hungarian Camping and Caravaning Club* (VII, Üllői út 6) in Budapest, which makes the permissable routes clear. The most scenic areas of Hungary are the northern uplands, the Danube Bend, and parts of Transdanubia and the Bakony, where you'll find a few stiff climbs and lots of rolling hills. Conversely, the easiest cycling terrain—the Great Plain—is visually the most monotonous. In towns, beware of slippery cobbled streets and sunken tram lines during wet weather. **Renting bikes** (for the day or week) is possible at some Balaton resorts; unfortunately the machines are low-slung and heavy, with limited gears. Your best chance of getting **spares and repairs** is in Budapest (see "Listings" in *Budapest*).

Autostop or **hitch-hiking** is widely practiced by young Magyars and East Germans, and only forbidden on highways. A fair number of drivers seem willing to give lifts, although your prospects on weekends are pretty dire since the small *Trabants* and *Ladas* driven by Hungarians are usually packed with the drivers' families. Solo **women travelers** risk hassles, if nothing worse, so a few positively paranoid precautions are recommended. Establish the driver's destination before revealing your own; note how the door opens when you get in; never accept rides from two men; and keep an eye on the road signs.

BY HORSE OR WAGON

Hungarians profess a lingering attachment to the horse—their equestrian ally since the time of the great migration and the Magyar conquest—and the horseherds or *csikós* of the Plain are romantic figures of national folklore. Most native **horses** are mixed breeds descended from Arab and English thoroughbreds, crossed in recent years with Hanoverian and Holstein stock, and the adjective most commonly used to describe their character is "spirited" or "mettlesome."

Horseback riding tours, organized by *Pegazus Tours* (V, Károlyi M. u.5) and *IBUSZ* (V, Felszabadulás tér 5) in the capital, come in various forms. *IBUSZ*'s ten-day "Hungaria Riding Tour," every week from mid-April to the end of October, includes all transportation, meals, and accommodation. You spend six days in the saddle, covering 200–250km along one of six or eight different routes across the Balaton Hills,

the Danube Bend, or the Great Plain, accompanied by a guide. *Pegazus*'s eight-day tours are likewise varied and all-inclusive, but slightly less expensive than Hungaria tours. *Pegazus* also offers a rather bizarre expedition by **covered wagons**, which tourists drive and navigate across the puszta. Besides these, there are programs and instruction at **riding schools** (*Lovarda*): namely Alag, Üllő-Tornyoslöb, and Adyliget **in the vicinity of Budapest**; Taliándorog, Nagyvázsony, Nagyberek, Szentbékkálla, Szántódpuszta, Siófok, and Keszthely **around the Balaton**; Tata, Szombathely, Sárvár, Radiháza, Nagycenk, and Dunakiliti **in Transdanubia**; Visegrád on the **Danube Bend**; Szilvásvárad in the **Northern Uplands**; and Hortobágy, Bugacpuszta, Tiszafüred, Makó, and Szatymaz on the **Great Plain**. Ask *IBUSZ* for their "On Horseback" booklet, and check with local tourist offices if you're interested. The schools provide saddlery, but not riding clothes.

SLEEPING

The cost of accommodation is low to moderate by European standards, and finding a room to suit your tastes and budget shouldn't prove difficult.

Most towns have at least one hotel, the option of private lodgings, and quite often a campground or hostel within easy reach of the center. That said, however, the cheapest places tend to fill up during the "high" season (June–Sept), so it's wise to make **reservations** if you're bound for somewhere with limited accommoda-

tion. To secure the hotel of your choice in Budapest (see "Hotels and Pensions" in *Budapest*), reservations are best made in America, through travel agents, or by telexing yourself (hotel telex numbers appear in *Hotel Camping*). Once **inside Hungary**, you can use *Hungartours* (VII, Akácfa u:20) or *IBUSZ* (V, Károlyi M. u.17) in Budapest to reserve hotel rooms nationwide, or regional tourist offices to reserve hotels, hostels, or private rooms within their area (eg. *Mecsek Tourist* in Pécs will make reservations in Szigetvár, Siklós, and so on). Beds in college dormitories and a few campgrounds and hotels fall under the aegis of *Express*, whose main office in Budapest can make nationwide reservations; the provincial ones make local reservations only. You'll find their addresses, together with details of accommodation in towns and villages, in the free *Hotel Camping* booklet, which makes a useful supplement to this guide.

HOTELS

As the *HungarHotels* chain expands, three-star **hotels** (*szálló* or *szállóda*) have become commonplace; with deluxe four- and five-star establishments still confined to Budapest and major resorts; and humble one- and two-star joints almost extinct, even in provincial towns. Outside

> **Note**: Addresses of hotels, campgrounds, and so forth (including tourist offices for making reservations) appear under individual towns in the guide section.

Budapest and Lake Balaton (where prices are 30 percent higher), an average three-star hotel should charge around 1300Ft (roughly $24) for a double room with bath, TV etc; solo travelers often have to pay this too, since singles are rare. The same goes for four-star (upwards of 2000Ft) or two-star (downwards of 1000Ft) hotel rooms, assuming that you can afford or find them. Off-season travelers should note that **deluxe hotels in Budapest** slash their rates during winter. A similar rating system is used for **inns** (*fogadó*) and **pensions** (*penzió* or *panzió*)—often privately owned—which charge roughly the same as hotels. Found along highways and on the outskirts of towns, many are **motels** in all but name.

PRIVATE ACCOMMODATION

Private rooms in Magyar households are a cheaper way of staying near the center, and often quite appealling. Such accommodation (termed *Fiz*, short for *fizetővendégszolgálat*) can be arranged by local tourist offices for a small fee, which removes the burden of **registering with the police** in person; staying in a room obtained from the owner (who'll advertise *szoba kiadó* or *Zimmer frei*), you'll have to do it yourself. Ignore hustlers at railroad stations unless there's nothing else going. Once again, solo travelers are usually charged for a double; but with costs ranging from 300Ft (in provincial towns) to 700Ft (in Budapest or around the Balaton), the full rate can be bearable. Tourist offices rent sight unseen, but you can still exercise judgment when **choosing a room** by rejecting dubious-sounding locations. As a rule of thumb, a town's Belváros (inner sector) is likely to consist of spacious apartments with parquet floors, high ceilings, and a balcony overlooking a courtyard; whereas the outlying zones are probably charmless, high-rise *lakótelep*. Either way, your hostess (widows and divorcees are the biggest renters) will probably be helpful and then self-effacing, but a few words of Hungarian will make you seem less of a stranger. Use of the washing machine comes free, and some landladies will provide breakfast for a fee, although most leave early for work. For this reason, it's usually impossible to take possession of the room before 5pm; after that you can come and go with a key.

It's possible to rent whole **apartments** in some towns and resorts, while in western and southern Hungary regional tourist offices can arrange rural **farmstead accommodation** in old buildings converted into vacation homes with kitchen facilities (with license to go nude, in some cases). Both come more expensive than private rooms, but if there's a group of you, or you're traveling with children, they could prove to be just the thing.

HOSTELS

A cheaper option—spanning a range of surroundings and locations—is **hostels**, which go under various names. In provincial towns (where some occupy castles or historic mansions) they're called *Túristaszálló*, but in highland areas favored by hikers they go under the name of *Túristaház*. Both are graded "A" or "B" depending on the availability of hot water and the number of beds per room (which are best reserved through the regional tourist office); rates vary 60–120Ft per head, with minor student reductions. In addition to these, there's a string of (not particularly cheap) "hotels for young people," owned by the Youth Travel Agency *Express*, whose local offices also rent out vacant **college dormitories** during the summer. Known as *nyári* (summer) *túristaszálló* or *Épitőtábor* (if run by the Communist Youth League, *KISZ*), their location varies annually, but current details should be available from Express, on the spot. Opening dates vary too, so the open season between July 1 and August 11 is only approximate. A student card isn't always required, but it's worth buying one (see "Other Things" below) just in case. Beds normally cost between 80–150Ft, depending on the facilities; visitors staying more than two nights are usually asked to register with the local police. If you're flat broke during term-time, foreign students might let you crash on the floor in a university hall of residence (*diákszálló*).

COTTAGES AND CAMPSITES

Throughout Hungary, campgrounds and cottages come together in complexes where tourists of the world unite. **Cottages** (*üdölőház*) proliferate around resorts and on the larger campgrounds, and while some are reserved for members of trade unions (*SZOT*), others can be rented for 250–2000Ft, depending on their amenities and size (two to four persons). The first class cottages—with well-equipped kitchens, hot water and a sitting room or terrace—are excellent, while the most primitive at have least clean bedding and don't leak. **Campgrounds**—usually signposted *Kemping*—likewise range across the spectrum from "deluxe" to third class. The more elaborate places include a restaurant and shops—maybe even a disco—and tend to be overcrowded; second- or third-class sites often have a nicer ambience, with lots of old trees rather than a manicured lawn ineffectually shaded by saplings, and acres of campers and trailers. Expect to pay 80Ft, or twice that around jam-packed Lake Balaton. Solo campers lose out since fees are calculated on a basic ground rent, plus a charge per head and for any vehicle (eg. 40Ft + 30Ft + 30Ft), plus, for non-students, an obligatory *kurtaxe* which goes towards meeting the locals' rates bill. There are **reductions** of 25–30 percent during "low" season (before the end of May, and after the beginning of Sept) when fewer sites are open, and during the high season for members of the *FICC* (International Camping & Caravaning Club) and for people carrying a student card. **Camping in the open** is illegal—although many young Hungarians and East Germans do it, particularly in the highland areas where there are "rain shelters" (*esőház*). A free campground (closed by day) exists in Budapest's X district.

EATING AND DRINKING

Among the Eastern bloc countries, Hungary's abundance of food is exceptional: material proof of the "goulash socialism" which continues to amaze visitors from Romania or the Soviet Union. Hungarians are blasé about the range of foodstuffs, but not the spiralling prices; visitors from the West, however, can afford to eat and drink lavishly for (what seems to them to be) remarkably low prices.

For foreigners the archetypal Magyar dish is "goulash"—historically the basis of **Hungarian cooking** inasmuch as the wagon anticipated the motor car. The ancient Magyars relished cauldrons of *gulyás* (pronounced "gou-yash")—a soup made of potatoes and whatever meat or fish was available, which was later flavored with paprika and beefed up into a variety of stews, modified over the centuries by various foreign influences. Hungary's Slav neighbors probably introduced native cooks to yogurt and sour cream (vital ingredients in many dishes); while the influence of the Turks, Austrians, and Germans is apparent in the variety of sticky pastries and strudels, plus recipes which include sauerkraut or dumplings. Perhaps the main influence was that of France, which revolutionized Hungarian cooking in the Middle Ages and again in the nineteenth century—although nowadays you'd be hard pressed to find anything like *nouvelle cuisine* in a country whose cooking seems designed to thwart Weight Watchers.

BREAKFAST AND SNACKS

As a nation of early risers, Hungarians like to have a calorific **breakfast** (*reggeli*). Commonly, this includes cheese, eggs, or salami together with bread and jam, often accompanied by a shot of *pálinka* to "clear the palate" or "aid digestion" in rural areas. By 8am, cafés and snack bars are already functioning, and the rush hour is prime time for **Tej-bár** or **Tejivó**. These stand-up Milk Bars serve mugs of hot milk (*meleg tej*) and sugary cocoa (*kakaó*); cheese-filled pastry cones (*sajtos pogácsa*) and rolls (*sajtos-rollo*); envelopes of dough filled with curds (*túrós táska*), spongy milk-bread with raisins (*mazsolás kalács*), and other dunkable pastries.

Everyone is addicted to **coffee**. At intervals throughout the day, people consume tiny glasses of *kávé*—brewed super-strong, served black and sweetened to taste, a brew that can double your heart beat. **Coffee houses** were once the centers of Budapest's cultural and political life, hotbeds of gossip where penurious writers got credit and the clientele dawdled for hours over the free newspapers. Sadly this is no longer the case, but you'll find plenty of unpretentious *kávéház* serving the beverage with milk (*tejeskávé*) or whipped cream (*tejszínhabbal*) should you request it. Most coffee houses offer some pastries—although for these, you'll find much more choice in the patisseries (see below) which, of course, also serve coffee themselves. **Tea**-drinkers are a minority here—perhaps because the tea with milk (*tejes tea*) is so insipid, although the *tea citrommal* (with lemon) is fine.

A whole range of places purvey **snacks**, including the *Csemege* or **delicatessens**, which display a tempting spread of salads, open sandwiches, pickles, and cold meats, and are really superior take-outs (in a few, you can eat on the premises). Unfortunately, many delis (like Tej-bár) work using **the "kassa system,"** whereby customers order and pay at the *kassa* desk in return for a receipt which is then exchanged at the food counter. If your Hungarian is minimal, this can throw up a few surprises and misunderstandings. For sit-down nibbles, people patronize **bisztró** which tend to offer a couple of hot dishes besides the inevitable salami rolls; *snackbár*, which are superior versions of the same, with leanings in the direction of being a patisserie; and *büfé*. These last are found in department stores and stations, and are sometimes open around the clock. However their food can be limited to tired sandwiches and greasy sausages filled with rice (called *hurka* and *kolbász*), so it's often better to look elsewhere.

On the streets, according to season, toothless ancients preside over vats of *kukorica* (corn on the cob) or trays of *gesztenye* (roasted chestnuts); while fried fish (*sült hal*) shops are common in towns near rivers or lakes. *Szendvics*, *hamburger*, and *gofri* (waffle) stands are mushrooming in the larger towns, and there's even a *McDonald's* in Budapest. **Around resorts**, another popular munch is *lángos*: the native, mega-size equivalent of doughnuts, sometimes sold with a sprinkling of salt or a dash of syrup. Fruit, too, is sold on the streets (see the vocabulary below) and **in markets**, where you'll also find various greasy spoons forking out *hurka* and the like. Outdoor markets (*piac*) are colorful affairs which sometimes bizarrely feature rows of poultry sheltered beneath sunshades; in market halls (*vásárcsarnok*), people select their fish fresh from glass tanks, and their mushrooms from a staggering array of *gomba*, which are displayed alongside toxic fungi in a "mushroom parade" so that shoppers can recognize the difference!

No list of snacks is complete without mentioning **bread** (*kenyér*) which, as the old saying has it, is so popular that "Hungarians will even eat bread with bread." The white loaves produced by state bakeries are unsatisfyingly bland—hence the popularity of privately run *házi-kenyér* ("Home Bread") vans—but their brown (*barna*) and rye (*rozs*) bread—stocked by *Malomipari* shops and large supermarkets—is fine.

MAIN MEALS

Traditionally, Hungarians take their main meal at **midday**; so the range of dishes offered by restaurants is greatest for lunch (*ebéd*) rather than in the **evenings**, when Westerners expect to find all catering systems go for dinner (*vacsora*). It's important to remember this, and also the annoying fact that many places begin to close down the kitchen at 10pm, so that customers are turned away shortly afterwards—even on Hungary's national holiday, when a capitalist would weep to see the famished masses tramping from place to place being rebuffed by doormen. There are compensations, however, notably the bands of musicians that play in many restaurants during lunchtime and in the evening, whose violin airs and melodic plonkings of the cimbalom are an element of the "Hungarian scene."

All eating places display signs signifying their class, or *osztály* (*oszt.*). This categorization from I to IV is a fair guide to **comparative prices**, but doesn't necessarily reflect the quality of the food served. I've had some excellent meals in humble III *oszt.* joints, while it's possible that a restaurant's I *oszt.* rating derives solely from its flashy decor. Places used to tourists often have **menus** in German (English rarely), a language which most waiters and waitresses have a smattering of. By law, all eating places must provide two **set** menus (*napi menü*) at moderate prices; some also offer a low-priced student menu (*diák menü*) at lunchtime, which you might need an IUS/ISIC card to order. It's invariably more expensive to eat **à la carte**, where the choice is bigger, but the difference isn't outrageous. In an average II class restaurant, you can eat a three course meal and sink a few beers for 250–400Ft, while the set menu and a drink will cost about 150–200Ft. Service charges aren't usually included in the bill, and the staff rely financially on their customers **tipping** (10 percent of the total is customary).

DISHES AND TERMS

What follows is by no means a comprehensive list of Hungarian dishes, but by combining names and terms it should be possible to decipher anything that you're likely to see on a menu. Alcoholic and soft drinks are covered separately, as are desserts and pastries, which are best sampled in the ubiquitous *cukrászda*.

Basics, and how to order

bors	pepper	*kenyér*	bread	*só*	salt
cukor	sugar	*kifli*	croissant	*vaj*	butter
ecet	vinegar	*méz*	honey	*zsemle* or	bread rolls
egészségedre!	Cheers!	*mustár*	mustard	*péksütemeny*	
jó étvágyat!	Bon appetit!	*rizs*	rice		

Legyen szives ("Would you be so kind . . .") is the polite way of attracting a waiter's attention; while you can say *Kérnék . . .* or *Szeretnék . . .* ("I'd like . . ."), or *Kaphatok . . .* ("Can I have . . . ?") **to order**. Using these grammatical forms, Hungarians add a suffix (*-t, -et, -ot* or *-at*) to the item being requested, so that *vaj* becomes *vajat, kávé, kávét*, and so on.

Appetizers (*előételek*), soups (*levesek*), and salads (*saláták*)

bécsi hering-saláta	Viennese-style herring with vinegar	*gulyásleves*	meat, vegetable, and paprika soup
halmajonéz	fish with mayonnaise	*kunsági pandúrleves*	chicken or pigeon soup seasoned with nutmeg, paprika, ginger, and garlic
majonézes kukorica	sweetcorn with mayonnaise		
bakonyi betyárleves	"Outlaw soup" of chicken, beef, noodles, and vegetables, richly spiced	*lencseleves*	lentil soup
		meggyleves	delicious chilled sour cherry soup
csirke-aprólék	mixed vegetables and giblet soup	*palócleves*	mutton, bean, and sour cream soup
csontleves	bland bone and noodle consommé	*paradicsomleves*	tomato soup
bajai halászlé	fish and tomato soup	*szegedi halászlé*	Szeged-style mixed-fish soup
bableves	beans and meat soup—a meal in itself	*zöldségleves*	vegetable soup
burgonyaleves	potato, onion, and paprika soup	*alföldi saláta*	"Puszta salad"—sliced sausages in a vinaigrette dressing
gombaleves	mushroom soup		
(kalocsai) halászleves	spicy fish soup (with red wine)	*almás cékla*	dressed apple and beetroot slices

The names of other **salads** are easy to work out if you refer to the section on vegetables. **Cream** and **sour cream** feature in dishes whose name includes the words *tejszín, kem*, and *tejföl*.

Fish dishes (*halételek*)

csuka tejfölben sutve	fried pike with sour cream	*paprikás ponty*	carp in paprika sauce
fogas	a local fish of the pike-perch family	*ponty filé gombával*	carp fillet in mushroom sauce
fogasszeletek Gundel modra	breaded fillet of fogas	*pisztráng tejszín mártásban*	trout baked in cream
kecsege	sterlet (small sturgeon)	*rostélyos töltött ponty*	carp stuffed with bread, egg, herbs, and fish liver or roe
. . tejszínes paprikás mártásban	. . .in a cream and paprika sauce	*sült hal*	fried fish
nyelvhal	sole	*tökehal*	cod
		tonhal	tuna

Meat (húsételek) and poultry (baromfi) dishes

alföldi marha-rostélyos	steak with a rich sauce and stewed vegetables	*nyúl*	rabbit
bográcsgulyás	what foreigners mean by "Goulash"	*paprikás-csirke*	chicken in paprika sauce
		rablóhús nyárson	kebab of pork, veal, and bacon
borjúpörkölt	veal stew seasoned with garlic	*sertésborda*	pork chop
csabai szarvascomb	venison stuffed with spicy sausage	*sonka*	ham
		töltött-káposzta	cabbage stuffed with meat and rice, in a tomato sauce
cigányrostelyos	"Gypsy-style" steak with brown sauce	*töltött-paprika*	peppers stuffed with meat and rice, in a tomato sauce
csikós tokány	strips of beef braised in bacon, onion rings, sour cream, and tomato sauce	*vaddisznó borókamártással*	wild boar in juniper sauce
csirke	chicken	*virsli*	frankfurter
erdélyi rakott-káposzta	layers of cabbage, rice, and ground pork baked in sour cream—a Transylvanian specialty	**Terms**	
		comb	leg
		félig nyersen	underdone/rare
fasírozott	meatballs	*főve*	boiled
hortobágyi rostélyos	steak "Hortobágy style"; braised in stock, with a large dumpling	*jól megsütve*	well done (fried)
		jól megfőzve	well done (boiled)
kacsa	duck	*pörkölt*	stewed slowly
kolbász	spicy sausage	*rántott*	in breadcrumbs
liba	goose	*roston sütve*	grilled
máj	liver	*sülve*	roasted
marhahús	beef	*sült/sütve*	fried

Sauces (mártásban)

Many restaurants serve meat or fish dishes in rich **sauces**—a legacy of French culinary influence.

almamártásban	in an apple sauce	*kapormártásban*	in a dill sauce
bormártásban	in a wine sauce	*meggymártásban*	in a morello cherry sauce
gombamártásban	in a mushroom sauce	*paprikás mártásban*	in a paprika sauce
ecetestorma	with horse radish	*tárkonyos mártásban*	in a tarragon sauce
fehérhagyma mártásban	in an onion sauce	*vadasmártásban*	in a brown sauce (made of mushrooms, almonds, herbs, and brandy)
fokhagymás mártásban	in a garlic sauce		

Vegetables (zöldség)

bab	beans	*fokhagyma*	garlic	*paprika—édes* or *erős*	peppers—sweet or hot
borsó	peas	*gomba*	mushrooms	*paradicsom*	tomatoes
burgonya	potatoes	*hagyma*	onions	*sárgarepa*	carrots
(krumpli)	("spuds")	*káposzta*	cabbage	*spárgá*	asparagus
ecetes uborka	gherkin	*kukorica*	sweet corn	*uborka*	cucumber
fejes	lettuce			*zöldbab*	green beans

Fruit (gyümölcs) and cheese (sajt)

alma	apples	*málna*	raspberries	*füstölt*	a term covering several smoked cheeses, one of which unwinds like licorice laces
barack	apricots	*mandula*	almonds		
citrancs	grapefruit	*meggy*	morello cherries		
citrom	lemon			*karaván*	tasty smoked cheese
dió	walnuts	*mogyoró*	hazelnuts	*márvá}ny*	Stilton-like blue cheese
eper	strawberries	*narancs*	oranges		
füge	figs	*őszibarack*	peaches		
(görög) dinnye	(water) melon	*szilva*	plums	*trappista*	rubbery, Edam—type cheese
körte	pears	*szőlő*	grapes		

Hungarians have a variety of words implying fine distinctions among **restaurants**—in theory an *étterem* is a proper restaurant, while a *vendéglő* approximates the Western notion of a bistro—but in practice the terms are often used interchangeably. The Sixties saw the advent of *kisvendéglő*—basically smaller versions of bistros—which were originally used as youth hangouts; nowadays this title may also denote seedy, raucous dives in the vicinity of factories and stations, where single women are likely to attract unwelcome attention. The old word for an inn, *csárda*, applies to posh places specializing in certain dishes (eg. a "Fishermen's inn" or *halászcsárda*), restaurants alongside roads, or with rustic pretensions, besides the humbler rural establishments that it originally signified. At the bottom of the heap are *Önkiszolgáló* restaurants with **self-service**, mostly open 8am–8pm on weekdays. They're rock-bottom cheap and you can see the food while ordering it (removing the uncertainty inherent in menus or the *kassa* system), but the grubby decor and the prospect of lukewarm food outside of peak hours (midday and around 6–7pm) are both disadvantages.

When they can afford to be, Hungarians are enthusiastic eaters, so as a (presumably rich) Westerner you'll be asked if you want **appetizers** (*előételek*)—generally a soup or salad. However, nobody will mind if you just have one of the dishes offered as the **main course** (*ételek*) or, alternatively, take a soup and an appetizer and skip the rest. Bread is supplied almost automatically. On the same menu you'll normally find **drinks** listed under the heading *italok*.

OPTIONS FOR VEGETARIANS

Although carnivores can run riot, the outlook for **vegetarians** is poor. Aside from cooked vegetables (notably *rántott gomba*, mushrooms in breadcrumbs), the only meatless dishes are fried—literally "mirror"—eggs, *tükörtojás*, soft-boiled eggs (*lágy tojás*), scrambled eggs (*tojásrántotta*), and eggs in mayonaise (*kaszínótojás*). Even innocuous vegetable soups may contain meat stock, and the pervasive use of sour cream in cooking means that avoiding animal fat or by-products is difficult. However, greengrocers (*zöldségbolt*) and markets sell excellent produce which, combined with judicious shopping in *ABC* supermarkets (for legumes, granola, and more) should see you through. To be honest, though, Hungarians are amazed that anyone might forgo meat *willingly*.

CAKES AND ICES

Numerous **patisseries** (*cukrászda*) pander to the Magyar fondness for sweet things. **Pancakes** (*palacsinta*) **with fillings**—*almás* (apple), *diós* (walnuts), *fahej* (cinnamon), *mákos* (poppy seeds), *mandula* (almonds) or *Gundel*-style, with nuts, chocolate sauce, cream, and raisins—are very popular, as are **strudels** (*rétes*) made with curds and dill (*kapros túrós rétes*), poppy seeds (*mákosrétes*) or plums (*szilvás rétes*). Even the humble dumpling is transformed into a *somlói galuska*, flavored with vanilla, nuts, and chocolate, served in an orange and rum sauce. But the frontrunners in the rich 'n' sticky stakes have to be chestnut pureé with whipped cream (*gesztenyepüré*); chocolate soufflé (*kapucineres felfújt*); baked apple with vanilla, raisins, and cream (*töltött alma*); and the staggering array of **cakes**. *Dobostorta* (chocolate cream cake topped with caramel) and the pineapple-laden *ananásztorta* are only two; the average *cukrászda* displays a dozen or more types, all temptingly priced around 30Ft. If you're still not satiated, there's **ice cream** (*fagylalt*), the opium of the masses, sold by the scoop (*gomboc*) and priced low enough so that anyone can afford a cone. The most common flavors are *vanília, csokoládé, puncs, citrom,* and *kávé*; but mango, pistachio, and various nutty flavors can be found—see the fruit section for the Magyar names. And finally there's *metelt*—a rather unlikely-sounding but quite tasty dessert consisting of chopped sweet noodles, served cold with poppy seeds or some other topping.

WINE, BEER AND SPIRITS

Hungary's mild climate and diversity of soils is perfect for **wine** (*bor*), which is perennially cheap, whether you buy it by the bottle (*üveg*) or the glass (*pohár*). The main wine-growing regions surround Pécs, Eger, Kecskemét, Sopron, and Tokaj, and cover large areas of the Balaton and Mátra highlands. Standards are constantly rising as more farms try to win the right to label their bottles *minőségi bor* (quality wine), the equivalent of *appelation contrôlée*. By day, wine is often drunk with water or soda water, specifying a *fröccs* or a yet more diluted *hosszú lépés* (literally, a "long step"). **Wine bars** (*borozó*) are ubiquitous and generally far less pretentious than in the West; while true devotees of the grape make pilgrimages to the extensive **wine cellars** (*borpince*) that honeycomb towns like Tokaj and Eger.

Vörös bor or **red wines** can be divided into the light-bodied and the full-bodied types. Examples of the former are *Villányi burgundi*, *Vaskúti kadarka*, and *Egri pinot noir*, in the full-bodied category are *Villányi medoc noir*, *Tihanyi merlot*, *Soproni kékfrankos*, and the famous *Egri bikavér*, or "Bulls' Blood of Eger." **White wines** (*fehér bor*) are classified as sweet (*édes*) or dry (*száraz/furmint*). *Olasz risling* wines tend to be sweet, with the exception of the "Sand Wines" produced on the sandy soil between the Tisza and the Danube, which are dry. Other sweet whites include *Balatonfüredi szemelt*, *Akali zöldszilváni*, and the richest of the Tokaj wines, *Tokaji aszú*. In the dry category are three wines from the Badacsony vineyards, *kéknyelű*, *szürkebarát* and *zöldszilváni*; *Egri Leányka* from the Gyöngyös region; and two varieties of Tokaj, *furmint* and *szamorodni* (which means "as it's grown"). *Tököly* and *Pannonia* are sparkling wines.

Hungarians enjoy the ritual of **toasting**, so the first word to get your tongue around is *egészségedre* ("EGG-aish-shaig-edreh")—cheers! When toasting more than one other person, it's grammatically correct to change this to *egészségünkre* (Cheers to us!). Hungarians only consider it appropriate to toast with wine or spirits.

The latter are likewise cheap, if you stick to native brands of **spirits**. The best-known type of *pálinka*—or brandy—is distilled from apricots (*barack*), and is a specialty of the Kecskemét region; but spirits are also produced from peaches (*őszibarack*), pears (*körte*), and other fruits that are available. This is particularly true of *szilva*—a lethal spirit produced on cottage stills in rural areas, allegedly using plums—sold privately, and unashamedly, from toilets on the infamous "black train." Hungarians with money to burn order whisky (*viszki*) to impress—I saw a group inspecting a bottle of *J&B* with as much reverence as if it was a rare vintage—but most people find its cost prohibitive. Vodka isn't popular, despite the availability of excellent Russian *Stolichnaya* in *ABC*s. Possibly its reputation has suffered by association with the disgusting, yellowish Vietnamese vodka, bottles of which gather dust on supermarket shelves.

Bottled **beer** (*sör*) of the lager type (*világos*) predominates, although you might find brown ale (*barna sör*) and draft beer (*csapolt sör*). Western brands like *Tuborg*, *Wernesgrünner*, and *Gold Fassel* are imported or brewed under license at Nagykanizsa, and the famous old Austro-Hungarian beer *Dreher* has made a comeback. They're all more expensive than such humble Magyar brands as *Kőbányai*, excellent Czech *Urquell* Pilsen, and other socialist imports (eg. passable *NDK sör* from the DDR). In **beer halls** (*söröző*) you can usually get a small glass (*pohár*) or a half-liter mug (*korsó*) if desired.

SOFT DRINKS

Pepsi and Coke are available for those that like familiar **soft drinks**, but it's more fun trying out the cold juices available from street stands (see "Fruit," above). Fruit juices are for sale In supermarkets and *Vitamin Porta* shops; most *ABC*s also stock bottled *limonád*, mineral water (*ásvány víz*), soda water (*szóda víz*), and Hungarian *Kóla*.

ENTERTAINMENT

Music and dance are the best paths through the thicket of language that surrounds Hungarian culture, but they're not the only forms of entertainment. During the summer in particular, you'll find plays or films in foreign languages—or festivals where language is a minor obstacle—in the main towns and resorts.

GYPSY AND FOLK MUSIC

No visitor to Hungary should fail to experience **Gypsy music** or *cigányzene*, which is widely performed in restaurants during the evening, usually by one or two violinists, a bass player and a guy on the cimbalom—a stringed instrument that's struck with little hammers. *Mulatni* means "to be possessed by music," and the Gypsies have always venerated the range of sounds and emotions produced by the violin, the playing of which—*bashavav*—traditionally has magical associations. The sense of awe that great violinists used to inspire, and the bohemian life of these musicians, is well captured in Walter Starkie's book *Raggle Taggle* (see "Books" in *Contexts*). Hungarians are keen to make requests or sing along when the *Prímás* (band leader) comes to the table, soliciting tips; and foreigners are also likely to attract his attention, although it's fine to refuse with a *nem, köszönöm*. Nowadays, most musicians are townspeople and graduates of the *Rajkó* music school, rather than wandering, self-taught artists like János Bihari, Czinka Panna, and Czermak—a Magyar nobleman turned vagabond—who were legendary figures during the nineteenth century. But it's still common for sons to follow their forefathers' profession, as has Sándor Lakatos, the most famous violinist performing today.

Confusingly, this archetypically "Hungarian" music is neither Hungarian nor Gypsy in its origins. The music performed by Gypsies among their own communities (in Szabolcs-Szatmár county, for example) is actually far closer to the music of India and Central Asia, and inaccessible to outsiders unless they catch a concert by the Gypsy group *Kalyi Jag*.

Hungarian folk music (*Magyar népzene*) is different again, having originated around the Urals and the Turkic steppes over a millennium ago. The haunting rhythms and pentatonic scale of this "Old Style" music (to use Bartók's terminology) were subsequently overlaid by "New Style" European influences—which twentieth-century enthusiasts have discarded during the folk revival, centered around **Táncház**. These "Dance Houses" encourage people to build and learn to play archaic instruments; besides providing the site for **dances** which are usually fast and furious—particularly the wild, foot-stamping *csárdás*, or "tavern dance." Aside from Dance Houses, you can hear folk music at the Kecskemét and Nagykálló festivals (see below), the village of Decs on the lower Danube, and at concerts by **groups** like *Muzsikás* and the *Kalamajka* and *Sebö* ensembles (*együttes*). For a selection of folk records, see "Music and Records" in *Contexts*.

ROCK AND JAZZ

At resorts, the amps blare Western disco music rather than Hungarian **rock**, but it's easy to hear native bands in concert in Budapest and provincial towns. Those that don't merit notice in *Programme* magazine are advertised by posters or stickers specifying the type of *zene* (music) and the venue, usually a local *klub*. Since the Illés group braved Party disapproval and opened the door for "beat" musicians in the early Sixties, Hungarian rock has gone through its Seventies "supergroup" phase, epitomized by *Locomotiv GT* (playing a mix of styles from folk to heavy metal); thrown up the Abba-style *Neoton Family* and the winsome *Kati Kovács*; and spawned a host of new bands during the Eighties. Rock's "official" recognition just anticipated—and possibly depended on—the production of *István a Király*, the smash hit of 1983: a patriotic **rock opera** written by Bródy and Szörényi, Hungary's "Lennon and McCartney."

Although the Party clamped down on **punk** groups like *Beatrice* and *CPG*, their **new wave** (and less overtly political) successors have had an easier time of it. *Balaton, Europa Kiadó,* and *Trabant* have made it on to vinyl at the cost of a little self-censorship, and the Party's "softer" line is evident in the fact that *URH* (named after the police waveband) can play without being hassled. Groups like *Bizottság* (which moved into music from other arts), flourish in the small world of Budapest's avant garde alongside **"experimental"** or "Industrial Music" bands such as *KFT*. Outside Budapest, more **mainstream** tastes prevail. Current favorites include the poppy *Napoleon Boulevard*; *Dolly Roll*, with its infectious blend of Fifties R'n'R and the "Italian sound"; Robert Szikora's *R-GO*, which draws on Latin American music; Heavy Metalists *Ossian* and *V. Moto-rock*; and the country music parodists *Folk Celsius 100*.

Quite a few **foreign acts** visit Budapest, which even hosted an Amnesty International benefit concert with Bruce Springsteen and Sting heading the bill. Concerts by the Talking Heads, Queen, Tina Turner etc have been well publicized in the past, so anything scheduled during your visit should get similar treatment.

Jazz musicians like *Aladár Pege* and the *Benkó Dixieland Band* attract large crowds to the annual Tatabánya, Debrecen, Székesfehérvár,

Nagykanizsa, and Zalaegerszeg summer jazz festivals. Periodically, the *Hungarian Supergroup* brings together jazz and rock artists; while jazz musicians like the pianist György Szabados have built bridges towards classical music.

CLASSICAL MUSIC, OPERA, DANCE

Bartók, Kodály, and Liszt still enjoy the prime position in the field of **classical music**, but modern composers can be heard at the *Interforum* festival, staged at Keszthely every three years (scheduled for 1990). The "Budapest Spring" (March) and autumn "Music Weeks" (late-Sept to late-Oct), and the "Szeged Weeks" (July 20–Aug 20) are the landmarks of the concert-going year, which also features Haydn's and Beethoven's works (performed in the palatial surroundings of the Esterházy and Brunswick mansions); orchestral concerts at Veszprém and Diósgyőr castles; organ recitals in the main churches of Pécs, Buda, Debrecen, Eger, Miskolc, Szeged, and Tihany; and chorales in the Gothic churches at Köröshegy and Nyírbátor (mainly during the summer).

The reputation of the state **opera** continues to grow, with singers like Adrienne Csengery winning rapturous acclaim abroad. The Budapest Opera's **ballet** company is classically oriented, and most of the impetus for **modern dance** comes from the Pécs and Győr companies, choreographed by Imre Eck and Iván Markó. Both have a superb reputation (making it quite difficult to get tickets) and regularly visit the capital, as do foreign companies like the Bolshoi or Mongolian State ballet. For details of performances, and the addresses for making reservations, buy the monthly *Programme* magazine.

CINEMA

New **Hungarian films** are premiered at the annual Budapest Film Festival, staged over four days in early February. Performances are dubbed or subtitled for the benefit of foreign critics, and if you can wangle tickets it's a good opportunity to see films that you'll otherwise only be able to understand when they're shown abroad (for example, at film festivals in New York or L.A., or on television). His big-budget international productions *Colonel Redl* and *Mephisto* have made István Szabó well known (and wealthy)

abroad; but other talented **directors** chiefly concentrate on Hungary and a Magyar audience. Documentary film-makers like Pál Schiffer and Péter Gothár are by no means alone in their preoccupation with the flaws of Hungarian society, which has made for a lot of harrowing cinema. Subjects tackled by directors include abortion (Pál Zolnay), rape (Judit Elek), incest (Zsolt Kézdi-Kovács), lesbianism (Károly Makk) and Stalinism (Péter Bacsó, Márta Mészáros)— so it's hardly surprising that there's been a swing back towards fantasy, romance, and comedy in recent years. **Movies** are very popular, with all manner of foreign films screened at *filmszínház* or *mozi*, the majority of them dubbed into Magyar (indicated by *m.b.* or *Magyarul beszelő* on posters). Budapest movie theaters showing films in English are listed in *Daily News*. If tickets are sold out at the door (as might happen with a new release), ticket scalpers will usually be able to help you out.

FESTIVALS

The **festival year** kicks off with the **Mohács Carnival** of masked revellers re-enacting ancient spring rites and ritual abomination of the Ottoman Turks, on March 1, followed by the **Budapest Spring Festival** of music, drama, and dance. Newly restored as a national holiday, **March 15** now eclipses the Communist anniversaries of **Liberation Day** (April 4) and **Labor Day** (May 1) with speeches and torchlit parades, events best witnessed in Budapest. With the onset of tourists and fine weather, the summer months soon get crowded with events, most of which are listed in *Programme* magazine. You can see **historical pageants** at Szentendre, Veszprém, Tihany, Visegrád, Gyula, or Esztergom; and **equestrian shows** with a "rodeo" atmosphere and amazing displays of horsemanship at Nagyvázsony, Apajpuszta, Tamási, Szántódpuszta, Kisbér, and Hortobágy. The two-day Hortobágy Bridge Fair is an annual event whose finale coincides with Hungary's national day, August 20, which is also the climax of the **Szeged Weeks** of drama and music. Originally the name-day of Saint István, Hungary's patron saint, **Constitution Day** is marked by a Danube regatta and magnificent **fireworks** in Budapest; a **Flower Carnival** in Debrecen, and lesser displays in provinci towns. August is also the month of the *Téka Tábor* festival of **folk arts and music** at Nagykálló (exact dates vary) and the **Crafts' Fair** at Kecskemét (Sept 8–10). Budapest rings down the curtain with its **Autumn Music Weeks** (late Sept–late Nov), for as from 1989, the anniversary of the Bolshevik revolution will no longer be commemorated on November 7.

Saint István's relics attract multitudes of worshipers to the great Basilica in Pest but, with a few exceptions, **religious festivals** aren't widely observed in contemporary Hungary. The most obvious exception is Easter, when the churches and cathedrals are packed—particularly in Esztergom, the seat of Hungarian Catholicism. For reasons of spectacle rather than faith, I found the Orthodox (*Görög*) services more appealing. Orthodox believers commemorate their Serbian origins with a *kolo* dance outside the Preobrazhenska Church in Szentendre on August 19.

SPORTS

The hosting of the 1988 World Ice Skating Championships in Budapest confirmed Hungary's

place on the the international sports circuit, and other major **sporting events** are certain to follow. Already, there's an annual *Budapest Marathon* and the *Hungarian Grand Prix*. Full details of these, and national championships in everything from parachuting to canoeing are available from *IBUSZ*, regional tourist offices, and *Programme* magazine. Several pages of the weekly paper *Népsport* are devoted to **soccer** (*labdarúgás*) and most towns have a *stadion* and a team. These are also organized along "socialist" lines, with the railroad workers, miners, police, and army all fielding their own. Tickets are very cheap, as are facilities at local **sports halls** (*Sportcsarnok*).

Windsurfing (*szörf*) and **sailing** equipment can be rented (*kölcsönző*) at the main Balaton boat stations and Lake Velence, while **tennis** (*tenisz*) courts are often attached to the more upscale hotels in Budapest and the main resorts. Hungary's topography rules out any dramatic or lengthy slopes, but that doesn't stop enthusiasts from **skiing** in the Mátra Mountains and the Buda Hills. For **horseback riding**, see "Getting Around" above.

OPENING HOURS AND HOLIDAYS

During the week, most public buildings are open 8:30am–5pm, but the staff at lesser institutions usually take an hour off for lunch (around noon). Aside from shops, tourist offices, and *KEOKH* (detailed separately), the most obvious exceptions are museums, which almost always close on Monday. Otherwise, opening times are affected by the shift to and from summer time (see "Other Things" below), and by public holidays, when most things shut down. These are December 25–26, January 1, March 15 (the anniversary of the 1848 revolution), April 4 (Liberation Day), Easter Monday, May 1 (Labor Day), and August 20 (Constitution Day).

MUSEUMS

Museums are generally open Tuesday–Saturday 10am–6pm or 9am–5pm; and to make up for being shut on Monday, often stay open until

midday or mid-afternoon on Sunday, and have free admission over the weekends. In the case of significant exceptions to this rule, you'll find details in the guide alongside the relevant *múzeum*. Admission charges vary but rarely exceed 30Ft, and IUS/ISIC cards secure large reductions, or free entry in many cases. Hungary has about 600 museums, whose contents range from the crown jewels down to the dullest rag. Almost none of them have captions in any language but Hungarian, although important museums in provincial centers and the capital might sell catalogs in German, French, or English. When it comes to surmounting the language barrier, **Skanzens** are probably the most effective—fascinating ensembles of buildings and domestic objects culled from old settlements around the country, assembled on the outskirts of Szentendre, Nyíregyháza, Zalaegerszeg, and Szombathely, or preserved in situ at Öriszentpéter, Hollókő, and Csongrád, forming "Village Museums."

CHURCHES

Hungary's few remaining mosques (*djami*) now qualify as museums rather than places of worship, but getting into **churches** (*templom*) may pose problems. The really important ones charge a small fee to see their crypts and treasures, and may prohibit sightseeing during services (*szertartás*, or *Gottdienst* in German). In small towns and villages, however, churches are usually kept locked—open only for worship in the early morning and/or the evening (between around 6–9pm). A small tip is in order if you rouse the verger to unlock the building during the day; he normally lives nearby in a house with a doorbell marked *plébánia csengője*. Visitors are expected to wear "decorous" dress—that is, no shorts or halter-tops.

WORK AND STUDY

Teaching English is the main opportunity for working in Hungary, and Budapest in particular, where International House Language School (V, Bajcsy-Zsilinszky út 62) is probably the best place to inquire about giving classes in *Angol*.

Native speakers are definitely preferred, and since most of the teaching is at an intermediate or advanced level, you're rarely required to understand Hungarian. Wages, paid in forints, conform to Magyar rates, although some freelance teachers (working without permits) manage to command higher and/or hard currency payments from their private clients. It's also possible **to make arrangements in Britain**, where native-speaking sixth-formers, students or teachers (up to the age of 45) can apply for jobs at the annual English language summer camp in southern Hungary (3 weeks during July/Aug). Besides giving Hungarian 15–17-year-olds the chance to practice their English you're expected to organize sports and/or drama and musical activities—so previous experience in these areas is desirable. Board and accommodation is provided but applicants must pay for their own travel to Hungary; applications should be made to the *Youth Exchange Center*, Seymour Mews House, Seymour Mews, London W1H 9PE (☎01-486-5101) by the end of March.

Foreigners (aged 18–30) with previous experience of **workcamps** can apply to join various projects involving agricultural or construction work. Participants rise *early*, work six to eight hours and spend the afternoons and evenings pursuing various cultural, social, and sporting activities, five days a week; the official languages are English and Russian. Room and board is provided in student hostels, cottages or tents, and travel costs to the camp aren't included in the price. In certain camps participants can choose between pocket money or extra activities like an expenses-paid five- or six-day trip to Lake Balaton at the end of camp; in any case, a five-day trip around Hungary with free room and board and travel expenses is the traditional post-camp reward. Camps are normally organized in July and last for two or three weeks.

Applicants should contact *MIOT*, 1388, Budapest PO Box 72, Kun Béla Rakpart (☎37-38).

SUMMER COURSES

Eager to publicize their cultural achievements, build bridges across a divided continent, and earn foreign exchange, the Hungarians also organize **summer courses** in everything from folk art to environmental studies. Full details are contained in a booklet published in the spring, which can be obtained by writing to the Society for the Dissemination of Scientific Knowledge, H-1088

Budapest, VIII Bródy Sándor u. 16. The deadline for most applications is May 1, so it's advisable to write months in advance. Students are of all ages and come from countries as diverse as Vietnam, Switzerland, and Venezuela, so the chance to meet people is as much an attraction as the subjects being studied. These include photography (at Vác), Hungarian language and

culture (Debrecen), fine arts (Zebegény, see *The Danube Bend*), Esperanto (Gyula), Baroque recorder music (Sopron), jazz (Tatabánya), orchestral music (Pécs and Kecskemét), music-teaching by the Kodaly method (Esztergom and Kecskemét), folk art (Zalaegerszeg), and nature studies (Keszthely). Fees include room and board and various excursions and entertainments.

DIRECTORY

ACCENTS For technical reasons, street names on the maps in this book lack the proper accents given in the text.

ADDRESSES in Budapest begin with the city district in Roman numerals—XII, Hunyadi utca 4—which is also expressed by the middle two digits of the post code, eg. 1125. In the case of apartment buildings, the floor and apartment number are also given: III/21 means apartment 21 on the third floor. The most common abbreviations are *u.* (for *utca*, street) and *em.* (for *emelet*, floor). An *út* or *útja* is an avenue, a *tér* or *tere* a square.

BRING . . . any specific medication or spare parts that you're likely to need. Western magazines like *The Face* are much appreciated in trendy (*divatos*) circles. Passport-sized photos come in handy for season tickets, student cards, etc. Imported camera film is quite expensive, and 127 and *Polaroid* unavailable.

CAMPERS should bring a primus stove, which takes local *spiritusz*. Candles—*gyertya*—are sold in *ABC*s; buy lots if you're going on to Romania or

Bulgaria, since they're hard to find there, or are so badly made that they won't burn.

CIGARETTES are sold in tobacconists (*dohánybolt*), *ABC*s, bars, and restaurants. *Marlboro* and *Camel* made under license are cheaper than imports, but still more expensive than "native" brands like charcoal-filtered *Helikon* and *Sophianae*, or throat-rasping *Symphonia* and *Munkás*. Matches are called *gyufa*. *Tilos a dohányzás* means "no smoking," and applies to movie theaters, the Metro, all buses, trams, and trolleybuses.

CHILDREN (*gyerek*) qualify for reductions on most forms of public transportation (see "Getting Around"), and fifty percent off the cost of camping up to the age of 14. Separate visas aren't required for children under 14 who are included on their parent's passport. The best facilities and entertainments for kids are in Budapest and the Balaton resorts. Children are forbidden to ride in the front seat of a car. Most supermarkets stock baby food and *Libero* disposable diapers.

CONTRACEPTIVES *Fogamzásgátló* are available from pharmacies in the form of condoms; contraceptive pills (issued on prescription) come from the USSR or East Germany, and have worse side-effects than their Western equivalents.

ELECTRIC POWER 220 volts. Round, 2-pin plugs are used.

GAY MEN AND LESBIANS are emerging from the closet. Until recently, expression of their sexuality incurred social disapproval and police harassment (although the age of consent for lesbians and gay men is 18). But in May 1988, *HOMEROS-Lambda*, the socialist bloc's first organization for gay men and lesbians, was founded with government approval, suggesting that changes are underway. It's too early to judge the effect of *HOMEROS-Lambda*'s campaign for lesbian and gay rights, or the authority's response at the grass-roots level; both aim to fight AIDS, but the new law permitting compulsory blood-testing of "suspected" HIV-carriers hardly inspires confidence. Either way, Budapest is the most likely spot for developments. Reports from visitors would be welcomed for the next edition.

LAUNDRY Laundromats (*mosoda*) are rare, while at *Patyolat* you're unlikely to have your washing or dry-cleaning back in less than 48 hours. All supermarkets sell detergent.

NUDISM (often known by the German initials *FKK*) is gaining ground—with nudist camps outside Budapest, Szeged, Mohács, and Balatonberény, and nude sunbathing on segregated terraces at some pools—but you can't assume that it's permitted. However, a fair number of women do get away with going topless around the Balaton and on certain campgrounds—there's safety in numbers, it seems.

SHOPS AND SUPERMARKETS in larger towns are usually open 9am–7pm (8pm on Thurs) during the week; on Saturday until midday or 5pm. On Sunday and holidays, selected restaurants and *eszpresszó* sell milk, bread, and pastries.

Generally, supermarkets are called *ABC* and department stores *Áruház*, while shops are named after their wares: *húsbolt* (butchers), *italbolt* (liquorstore), *papírirószerbolt* (stationery store).

STUDENT CARDS entitle you to small reductions at hostels and campgrounds, free or reduced admission to museums, and significant discounts on international railroad tickets and *MALÉV* flights. *Express* offices in Budapest normally issue IUS or ISIC cards without asking for proof that you're a full-time student (photo required); only IUS cards get you discounts on international tickets.

SURNAMES precede forenames in Hungary, to the confusion of foreigners. In this book, the names of historical personages are rendered in the Western fashion—eg. Lajos Kossuth rather than Kossuth Lajos (Hungarian-style)—except when referring to buildings, streets, or other things named after them.

TAMPONS Try pharmacies for *tampon* or sanitary napkins (*egészségügyi vatta*).

TIME 6 hours ahead of EST, 9 ahead of PST; plus 1 hour during summer time (from the end of March to the end of Sept).

THE

GUIDE

CHAPTER ONE

BUDAPEST

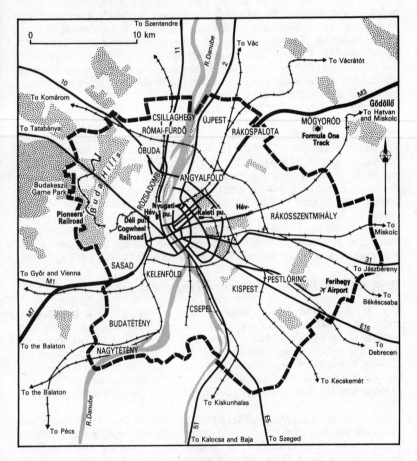

The importance of **BUDAPEST** to Hungary is difficult to overestimate, and no native of the city would appreciate being accused of doing so. Over two million people—roughly one fifth of the population—live in Budapest, and everything converges here: the roads and railroads; flights to Ferihegy (the only civilian airport); opportunities, wealth, and political power; industry, commerce, and the black market; state-approved cultural life, and the flourishing "underground" alternative. Like Paris it has a tradition of revolutions—in 1848, 1918, and 1956; buildings, parks, and avenues on a monumental scale; and a reputation for sophistication, hedonism, and parochial pride—in short, a city worthy of comparison with other great European capitals.

Surveying the city from the embankments or the bastions of Castle Hill, it's obvious why Budapest was dubbed the "Pearl of the Danube." Its grand buildings and sweeping bridges look magnificent, especially when floodlit or illuminated by a barrage of fireworks launched from Gellért Hill on Constitution Day. The inner city and the long nineteenth-century boulevards suavely combine Western fashions and advertising with totems of Soviet political culture, yet retain a distinctively Hungarian character which for visitors is highlighted by the sounds and appearance of the Magyar language, with its outlandish dactyls and bristling accents.

Through a combination of politics and geography, Budapest is currently the main point of contact between East and West. It's visited by millions of tourists from each side of the post-war European cleavage, who, when added together, actually outnumber the city's inhabitants. Budapest has a surfeit of fine sights, museums, and galleries, and while nightlife isn't quite as scintillating as in most western European capitals it's almost always affordable. Restaurants and bars abound, and there's a wide variety of entertainments, generally well publicized by the tourist board and accessible by efficient, cheap public transportation. Since people rise early the city begins closing down at 10pm, so at least you'll be full of energy and enthusiasm during the day, when residents interrupt their labors with breaks in patisseries and *eszpresszó* bars, or a long wallow in one of the capital's famous Turkish baths.

Orientation, Information, and Transportation

The Danube (*Duna*)—which is never blue—determines basic **orientation**, with Pest sprawled across the eastern plain and Buda reclining on the hilly west bank of the river. More precisely, one can refer to Budapest's 22 districts (*kerületi*), designated on maps and street signs by Roman numerals—eg. V, the Belváros or "inner city"; I, the Castle district; III, Római-Fürdő etc.—a system also used for addresses. The Belváros constitutes the city *centrum* and the hub of Pest, while Castle Hill is the historic focal point of Buda.

Most **points of arrival** are fifteen to thirty minutes from the center. *Keleti pu.*, *Déli pu.* and *Nyugati pu.*, the main **railroad stations**, are directly connected by Metro to Deák tér in the Belváros. Across the road from Deák tér Metro lies the **Engels tér bus station**, where the half-hourly shuttle from **Ferihegy airport** (leaving from Terminal 1; costs 20Ft) and buses from Vienna, Munich, Zagreb etc. arrive. Pest's **Népstadion** and **Árpád híd** bus terminals are farther out, but still on the Metro; while **hydrofoils** from Vienna dock right alongside the Belváros embankment. If you are arriving **by car** it makes sense to decide on a destination and route rather than simply follow the *centrum* signs towards a rendezvous with downtown one-way streets. Most main roads into Budapest are out of bounds, or only partially open, to **cyclists**, so send away for the cycling map listing permissible routes—available from the Hungarian Camping and Caravaning Club (VIII, Üllői út 6), or *IBUSZ* reps abroad—before leaving home.

There's always a long line to **check baggage** at the railroad stations. You'd do better to dump your stuff at a bus terminal's *ruhatár*, or hang on to it until you've found somewhere to stay. At the earliest opportunity, get hold of a proper map of the city; tourist offices supply small freebies, not much good, and might sell larger **maps** (50Ft), but the **Budapest Atlasz**—showing transportation routes, sights, and restaurants, and listing useful addresses— is streets ahead (63Ft from newsstands in Deák tér Metro, or some bookshops). Leaving aside the business of finding accommodation (see below), the main sources of practical **information** are the friendly polyglot women of **TOURINFORM** (V, Sütő u.2; 8am–8pm daily; ☎179-800), just around the corner from Deák tér Metro, and the "Listings" at the end of this chapter. To see what's on, check out the paper *Daily News*, *Programme* magazine, and this chapter's section on "Entertainments."

Getting Around

Running almost non-stop between 4:30am and 11pm, the **Metro** is the easiest way of getting around. Its three lines intersect at Deák tér, and there's little risk of going astray once you've learned to recognize the *bejárat*, *kijárat*, *vonal*, and *felé* ("entrance," "exit," "line," and "towards") signs. A yellow 5Ft ticket is valid for a journey along one line; you're supposed to punch another ticket when changing lines at Deák tér, but few people bother. Yellow 5Ft tickets are also valid for a single journey on **trolleybuses** (*trolibusz*), **trams** (*villamos*) and the **HÉV suburban railroad** (until the city limits; punch extra tickets thereafter). Rather than standing in line in a Metro station, it's quicker to buy a strip of tickets from street stands, tobacconists or news agents, which also sell blue 6Ft tickets, valid for a single journey on **buses**. *Autóbusz* with red numbers make limited stops, while the prefix "E" denotes buses running non-stop between terminals. Buses run every five minutes or so during the day (like trams and trolleybuses); and more or less hourly between 11pm and dawn along those routes with a **night service**.

A **day pass** cuts out ticket-punching, and could save money if you're traveling around town. Salespersons usually assume that the *Napijegy* is for today (*ma*), but sometimes ask whether it's to be validated for a future date. Relatively few outlets (eg. the *BKV* office in Kálvin tér Metro) sell them at time of writing, but hopefully they'll soon become widely available. The yellow ones (40Ft) are valid for travel on trams, trolleybuses, *HÉV* trains, and the Metro; the blue ones (48Ft) for all forms of public transit. There's a similar distinction between yellow (120Ft) and blue (185Ft) **two-week passes**, valid from the 1st–15th or the 16th–31st, and **monthly passes**, lasting from the 1st–5th, costing 180Ft or 280Ft (photo required). **Children** travel free up to the age of six, except on small river boats, where the limit is two years, with half-fares up to the age of ten. For further **information** on public transportation, dial 178-080.

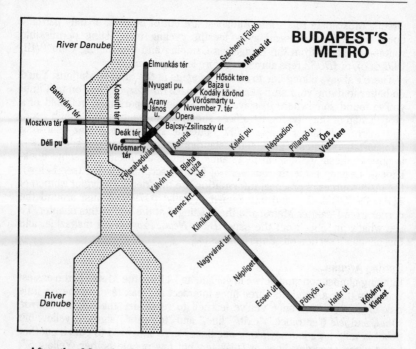

After the Metro's shut, you can safely rely on **taxis**, which are always metered. State-owned ones are the cheapest, but even a private (*magán*) cab shouldn't charge more than 250Ft ($5) for a ride across town. The main firms are *Radio Taxi* (☎776-766), *City Taxi* (☎533-633), *Buda Taxi* (☎294-000), and *Gabriel Taxi* (☎555-000). The first two accept reservations the day before (☎271-271 or 228-855).

Finding Somewhere to Stay

Although hotels might be out of your price range, private rooms, hostels, or campgrounds are easily affordable. Read the sections below covering each category and you'll see what your options are. The other trick is knowing **where to ask for accommodation**. Railroad stations, with long lines at the 8am–8pm *IBUSZ*, *Budapest Tourist* (for private rooms) and *Express* (for hostel beds) desks, and dubious scalpers and hustlers hanging about, are not the best places. For hotel inquiries and reservations, you should contact *HungarHotels* (V, Petőfi u.16/☎183-018), *Danubius Travel* (V, Martinelli tér 8/☎173-652), or Ferihegy airport's *Budapest Tourist* desk. Dozens of tourist offices (listed in *Hotel Camping*) can arrange private rooms; you'll always have to wait in line (*IBUSZ* on Felszabadulás tér is awful), but rarely for too long at the **24-hour** *IBUSZ* bureau (V, Petőfi tér 3) near the *Duna Intercontinental*.

Hotels and Pensions

To get the pick of **hotels** you must make **reservations** before leaving home
(see "Sleeping" in *Basics*); Budapest agencies (see above) have only limited
vacancies, with little scope for choice, during the summer and winter
seasons. Private bathrooms (but not air-conditioning) are universal, and most
places with three or more stars include breakfast, but there's still a broad
spectrum of ambiences, locations, and **prices**. In forint terms these climb
annually, yet reckoned in hard currency, the increases have been quite
modest so far. And whatever the inflation rate, comparative costs (between
different hotels) seem unlikely to change. Unless specified otherwise, prices
refer to double rooms.

Really **ritzy places** charge upwards of 5000Ft (3000Ft for a single, if one
exists). At the summit stands the *Atrium Hyatt* ($185) with its striking inter-
ior and views of the waterfront, followed by nearby *Forum* ($135), and the
reclusive *Thermal* and *Grand* on Margit Island ($115). The soulless *Novotel*
and *Buda Penta* ($110), set in ugly parts of Buda, have only modern conven-
iences to recommend them, but the *Hilton* ($100) is sited on Castle Hill, and,
like the *Duna Intercontinental*, overlooks the Danube.

One step down, in the 4000–5000Ft range, you'll find several refurbished,
traditional-style hotels. The *Royal* ($85), whose rooms face into a courtyard,
and the *Béke* ($95), near Nyugati station, are both on Pest's busy Great
Boulevard. But if you've got the money, it's more fun to stay at the famous
Gellért ($80), with its ornate baths and fin-de-siècle architecture, just beneath
Gellért Hill. Buda's *Flamenco* (II, Tas vezér u.7) and Pest's *Hungária* (VII,
Rákóczi út 90) are both slightly cheaper, but far **out of town**. Moving on to
hotels in the 3000–4000Ft bracket, the same applies to the *Stadion* (near
Népstadion), *Volga* (XIII, Dózsa Gy. út 65), and *Expo* (south of the
Lóversenytér) in Pest, or the *Olympia* (XII, Eötvös út 40) in the Buda Hills.
But the *Taverna* (V, Váci u:20), likewise priced around $70, is just off the
korzó, **in the heart of Pest.**

A dozen places charge between 2000–3000Ft, the most expensive being the
Nemzeti, a splendidly revamped nineteenth-century pile on the Great
Boulevard (VIII, József krt.4), with doubles for around $60. The modern
Emke, nearby, costs fractionally less, while the price comes down to $50 or
thereabouts for other establishments. To enjoy Pest's bustle and be **near the
shops**, you want the *Palace* or *Metropol* on Rákóczi út, or the *Astoria* (V,
Kossuth u.19) or *Erzsébet* (V, Károlyi M. u.11) in the Belváros. The *Orion* (I,
Döbröntei u.13) is close to **Castle Hill**, while the *Budapest* (II, Szilági E. fasor
47) has fine views, if nothing else. This can't be said of the *Park* (VIII, Baross
tér 10) or *Aero* (IX, Ferde u.1) in Pest, nor the *Wien* (XI, Budaörsi út 88) in
Buda; but the *Vörös Csillag* (XII, Rege út 21), *Rege* (II, Pálos u.2) and *Europa*
(II, Hárshegyi út 5) all gain from being **in the Buda Hills**.

Moderately priced hotels, with doubles for 1000–2000Ft (no singles), are
mostly well outside the center, but are nonetheless accessible by public transportation. Starting with Buda, one can reach the *Tot* (XII, Normafa út 54),
charging $32, by walking from Normafa stop of the Pioneers' Railway, or the
cheaper, tacky *Vénusz* from the Római–Fürdő *HÉV*-stop. A #49 bus from

Móricz Zs. körtér will get you near the *Számlak* (XI, Szakasits A. u.68), and Csillaghegy *HÉV* stop isn't too far from the *Minol* (III, Batthyány u:45), but it's some distance from Mártírok útja to the *Ifúság* (II, Zivatar u.1) in the backstreets. In Pest, the *Szot* (VI, Benczúr u:35) and *Medosz* (VI, Jókai tér 9) are five minutes' walk from the November 7. tér and Bajza u. Metro stops, respectively.

The **cheapest places**, charging under 1000Ft ($20), are prone to group-booking—reservations are essential for the *Citadella* (☎665-794) atop Gellért Hill, or the *Expressz* (XII, Beethoven u.9/☎753-082)—but vacancies should exist at **pensions**. In Buda, the *Sport Panzió* (II, Szépjuhászné út) is accessible by bus #22 from Moszkva tér, or on foot from the Ságvárliget stop on the Pioneers' Railway; it's a short walk from Csillaghegy *HÉV* stop to the *Strand Panzió* (III, Pusztakúti út 3/☎671-999); and a longer one from the Római-Fürdő stop to the *Lidó* (III, Nánási u.67/☎886-865), which lacks private showers, but has #134 buses from Flórián tér running to the door. All these charge between 140–500Ft ($3–7) for **singles**, slightly undercutting the *Täger–Trió panzio* (XI, Ördögorom út 20d/☎851-880), ten minutes' walk from the end of bus-line #8 in Buda's Sasad district. Of the two doubles-only pensions, the *Unikum Panzió* (XI, Bod P. u.13) has nicer surroundings than the dirt cheap *Depo Panzió* (IV, Törökbálint Pf. 3) in Újpest. To reach the *Unikum*, take bus #8 or #8A from Felszabadulás tér over to Buda, alight at Zolyomi út near Sashegy (Eagle Hill), and follow the signs.

Private Rooms and Apartments

Although solo travelers will almost certainly have to pay for a double, the chance of renting **private rooms** in downtown areas for only 500–700Ft ($10–15) a night seems irresistible. However, since tourist offices rent sight unseen for a minimum of three nights, it makes sense to guard against landing somewhere unpleasant. Your host and the premises should give no cause for complaint (both are checked out), but the location and ambience might. In my book, you can't beat those nineteenth-century blocks where spacious, high-ceilinged flats surround a courtyard with wrought-iron balconies and a tree growing up the middle—a feature of Pest's V, VI, VII, and VIII districts, and the parts of Buda nearest Castle Hill. Elsewhere—particularly in Újpest, Csepel or Óbuda—you're likely to end up in a box on the twelfth floor of a *lakótelep*. For checking the location of prospective sites and access by public transit, the *Budapest Atlasz* is invaluable.

Because many proprietors go out to work, you might not be able to take possession of the room until 5pm—if so, the tourist office will say. Some knowledge of Hungarian facilitates **settling in**; guests normally receive an explanation of the boiler system and multiple door keys, and may use the washing machine (which requires another demonstration). **Apartments**, rented out for 800–1600Ft a night, are perfect if there are several of you. They're not as common as rooms, but you should be able to find a tourist office with one on its books. Renting an apartment or room independently (say, from a hustler at a station), remember to comply with the rules on **registration** (see "Red Tape and Visas" in *Basics*).

Hostels

If you haven't got a tent, **hostels**—charging 80–120Ft ($2–3) a night, depending on the number of beds per room—are the cheapest option. Although *YHA* or student cards aren't always needed, it's worth buying one (see *Basics*) just in case. Short of calling early in the morning (☎665-794), there's little chance of staying in the *Citadella*, with its curved passages and breathtaking views of the city. But vacancies are more likely at other hostels, and if you're not fussy about their location, it's worth taking whatever the youth travel agency *Express* has to offer. Their head office (V, Szabadság tér 16) and branches in the railroad stations (8am–8pm) can confirm vacancies—if not make **reservations**—at hostels across the city, most of which operate in college dormitories during July and August; the exact dates and locations vary each year. *IBUSZ* might also get in on the act regarding two semi-permanent sites: *Strand* (III, Pusztakúti út 3; ☎671-999), next to the pension of the same name, operating from mid-April to mid-November; and the *SZOT Visegrád Üdülőhajó* on Margit Island (☎111-813), open March 15–November 1. At some hostels you're required to register with the local police after two nights' residence.

Bungalows and Campgrounds

Bungalows are a good deal for groups of three or four, if you divide the cost. A suite with kitchen, TV, terrace and separate rooms costs 1200–2000Ft ($25–40) in all; slightly less plush first class bungalows 800–1200Ft; second class ones (with a maximum of three beds) 500–800Ft; and a mere 250–500Ft buys a third class chalet. There are bungalows at the *Lidó*, *Strand*, and *Vörös Csillag* (see "Hotels and Pensions"); at Római-Fürdő and Tündér-hegy campgrounds (see below); and the awkward-to-reach place on the riverbank opposite Csillaghegy (IV, Üdülő sor 7; ☎891-114). You can normally make **reservations** through *Budapest Tourist* (V, Roosevelt tér 5; ☎173-555).

The majority of **campgrounds** are in the Buda Hills, more or less accessible from Moszkva tér. Bus #22 runs to *Hárshegyi*, near the Europa Hotel, bus #158 passes *Zugligeti* (or *Niche*) campground en route to its terminal just short of *Feeberg* (or *Tündérhegy*) on Szilassy út, while the *Caravan* site (XII, Konkoly u.18) can be reached by catching bus #90 from the Normafa stop on the Pioneers' Railway. Flat ground is scarce at all these sites, and the huge campground at *Római-Fürdő* (by the *HÉV*-stop of the same name in the III district) is no less crowded during the summer. Behind the latter, towards the Danube, you'll find a nicer, smaller campground at Rozgonyi Piroska u.21 (with a few rooms for rent).

The four sites in Pest are newer, if not improvised, and all within reach of Örs vezér tere Metro (line 2). Bus #100 will get you to *Expo Autós* near the Lóversenytér, the Pilis u. turn-off leading to *Rózsakert Camping* lies along the #45 and #46 bus route, and you can ride a #30 way up to *Metro Tenisz* (XVI, Csömöri út 222) in the Rákosszentmihály suburb. To dissuade tourists from sleeping rough in stations, a **free campground** (closed during the day, when anything left could well be stolen) operates near the Jászberényi út bridge during summer (bus #61 from Örs vezér tere). Most East German youths prefer to camp out in Keleti station, although the waiting room/ticket hall at Déli pu. is actually cleaner and warmer.

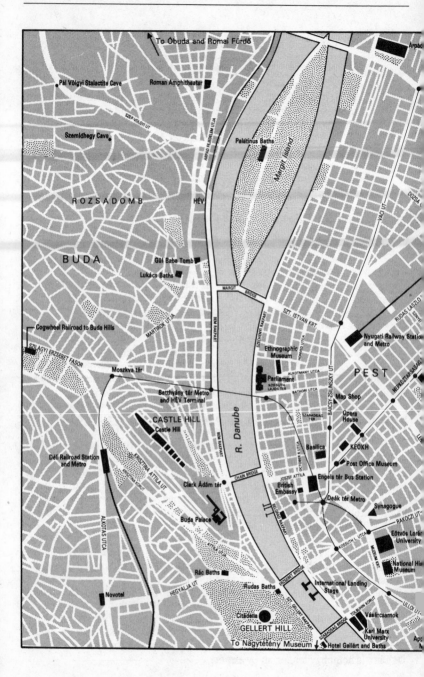

To Óbuda and Római Fürdő

Árpád

Pál Völgyi Stalactite Cave

Roman Amphitheater

Palatinus Baths

Margit Island

Szemlőhegy Cave

ROZSADOMB

HÉV

BUDA

Gül Baba Tomb

Lukács Baths

VÁCI UT

DOZSA

Cogwheel Railroad to Buda Hills

MARTIROK UTCA

BEM RAKPART

SZILAGYI ERZSEBET FASOR

MARGIT BRIDGE

SZT. ISTVAN KRT.

SZECHENYI RAKPART

Nyugati Railway Station and Metro

Moszkva tér

Ethnographic Museum

PEST

NADOR UTCA

BAJCSY ZSILINSZKY UT

Batthyány tér Metro and HÉV Terminal

Parliament
KOSSUTH LAJOS TER

ALKOTMANY UTCA

BATHORI UTCA

Map Shop

R. Danube

BEM RAKPART

CASTLE HILL

Castle Hill

SZABADSAG TER

Opera House

KEOKH

Déli Railroad Station and Metro

KRISZTINA ATTILA UT

KRISZTINA KORUT

Basilica

OKTOBER 6 UTCA

Post Office Museum

CHAIN BRIDGE

JOZSEF ATTILA

Engels tér Bus Station

Clark Ádám tér

British Embassy

Deák tér Metro

Synagogue

ALKOTAS UTCA

Buda Palace

BELGRAD RAKPART

RAKOCZI UT

ATTILA UT

KOSSUTH L UTCA

Eötvös Loránd University

Rác Baths

ERZSEBET BRIDGE

MUZEUM KRT.

National His Museum

HEGYALJA UT

Rudas Baths

International Landing Stage

Novotel

TO SOBEN KORUT

Vásárcsarnok

SZABADSAG BRIDGE

Citadella

GELLERT HILL

Karl Marx University

GELLERT RAKPART

App

To Nagytétény Museum

Hotel Gellért and Baths

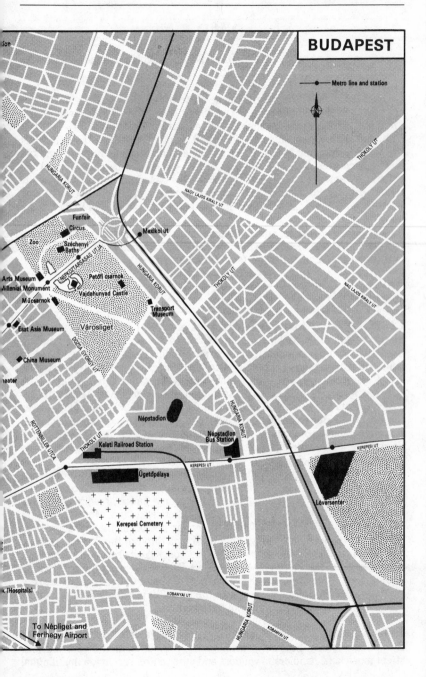

BUDAPEST

●── Metro line and station

BUDA

Seen from the embankments, **BUDA** looks undeniably romantic with its palatial buildings, archaic spires, and outsize statues rising from rugged hills. The
image conceals mundaner aspects, for Buda isn't all precipices and palaces,
but at times, in the right place, it can be appropriate. To experience Castle Hill
at its quasi-medieval best, come in the early morning before the crowds arrive.
Then you can beat them to the museums, wander off for lunch or a Turkish
bath, and return to catch street life in full swing during the afternoon. Most
parts of the Hill lapse back into tranquility around dusk, leaving the views to
lingering couples. The outlying Buda Hills—accessible by chair lift and the
children's Pioneer Railway—are obviously less visited during the week, while
Gellért Hill, the Rózsadomb, and assorted Roman ruins can be seen any time
the weather's fine, unless you'd rather sunbathe or have a dip in Buda's swimming pools. On the practical front, Buda has three campgrounds and two
useful railroad terminals. Trains for the Balaton and Transdanubia depart from
Déli station (Metro line 2), while regular *HÉV* services from Batthyány tér
enable you to reach Szentendre (see *The Danube Bend*) within an hour.

Castle Hill

CASTLE HILL (*Várhegy*) is Buda's most prominent feature, a plateau one
mile long laden with bastions, old mansions, and a huge palace, commanding
the Watertown. Its grandiosity and strategic utility have long gone hand in
hand: Hungarian kings built their palaces here because it was easy to defend,
a fact appreciated by the Turks, Habsburgs, Nazis, and other occupiers. A
war-torn legacy of bygone Magyar glories, it's been almost wholly reconstructed from the rubble of 1945, when Germans and Russians fought over
the hill while Buda's inhabitants hid underground, subsisting on cats and
scavenged horseflesh. Since then its decorative aspect has prevailed, and
barring a few fortunate diplomats who live on the Hill, the Castle district is no
longer involved in politics.

There are several **approaches** from Pest, starting with a breezy walk
across the Chain Bridge to Clark Ádám tér, where you can ride up to the
palace by *Sikló*, a renovated nineteenth-century funicular with capricious
automatic turnstiles (daily 7am–10pm). Otherwise, take Metro line 2 to
Moszkva tér, and a #116 bus from there; or get off at the previous stop,
Batthány tér, and start walking. Follow Fő utca through the Watertown until
you're below the spires, then one of the steep backstreets and stairways
(*lepcső*) which lead up to the Fishermen's Bastion, giving access to Trinity
Square—the heart of the Castle district. At this point visitors can go **touring
by horse-drawn coach**; it costs 400Ft, plus 100Ft per adult/50Ft per child,
and allows a passing look at most of the sights.

Trinity Square, the Mátyás Church, and the Fishermen's Bastion

By midday **Trinity Square** (*Szentháromság tér*) is crammed with tourists,
street musicians, handicrafts vendors and other entrepreneurs, a multilingual

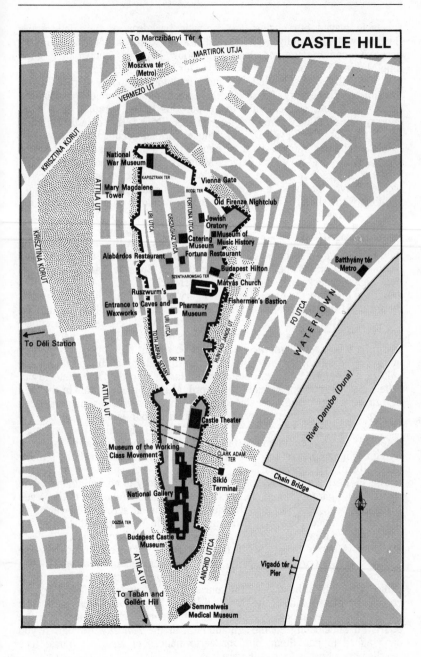

spectacle played out against the fantastic backdrop of the Fishermen's Bastion, with the wildly asymmetrical **Mátyás Church** (*Mátyás templom*) occupying center stage and stealing the show. Popularly known after "good king Matthias" but officially dedicated to Our Lady, the building is neo-Gothic run riot, with its brashly tiled roof and a multitude of toothy spires. Built in the nineteenth century, it's a superb recreation of the medieval spirit by Frigyes Schulek, grafted onto those portions of the original thirteenth-century church that survived the siege of 1686. Prior to that date the building was a mosque, the *Büyük Dzjami*, whose Turkish occupants whitewashed over the religious murals—so there's more than a hint of malice in one nineteenth-century fresco, which depicts Mátyás's father Hunyadi trouncing the Turks at Belgrade in 1456. It's almost lost amid the richness of the interior: painted leaves, animals, and geometric motifs run up columns and under vaulting, while shafts of light fall through rose windows onto gilded altars and statues with stunning effect. Specific sights include the **Loreto Chapel** beneath the tallest tower, various treasures in the crypt, and the iron-barred tomb of Béla III, who built the first proper palace on the hill. Though the medieval kings were crowned at Székesfehérvár (where Béla's tomb was discovered) a prior appearance at the church in Buda became customary— hence another nickname, the "Coronation Church."

In days gone by, the name day of Hungary's patron saint and first monarch Stephen (*István*) was celebrated here with a display of his "black mummified hand" and other holy relics, accompanied by a heraldic pageant. An equestrian statue of **King Stephen** stands just outside the church, commemorating this ruler who openly embraced Christianity, sought the Pope's recognition, and forced Catholicism onto his subjects, thus aligning Hungary with the culture of western Europe; a stern authoritarian who didn't hesitate to put rebels, pagans, and apostates to the sword. Much is made of this in the **Son et Lumière performances** staged in the church several evenings a week during July and August (buy tickets from the door in advance), but the "history of Hungary in lights and music" doesn't fully utilize the building's potential, and the commentary (assuming you attend a show in the right foreign language) sounds rather tacky. By contrast, the **choir** at Sunday Mass (10am) is magnificent.

The **Fishermen's Bastion** (*Halászbástya*) nearby is an undulating white rampart with gargoyle-lined cloisters and seven turrets (alluding to the seven Magyar tribes), which frames the view of Parliament across the river as its designer intended. Although fishermen from the Watertown district reputedly defended this stretch of the ramparts during the Middle Ages, Schulek's structure is purely decorative in function. By day it's besieged by diverse hustlers: artists crayoning rapidly, countrywomen selling embroidery from Kalocsa (and, occasionally, from Transylvania), and illegal money-changers, skilled at sleight of hand. Like the tourists they're surreally reflected by the copper and glass facade of the *Budapest Hilton*. This incorporates chunks of a thirteenth-century monastery and a select clientele which lounges in the courtyard anticipating candle-light dinners in the *Halászbástya* bar. If you can't afford to join them, outdoor performances of chamber music (see nearby notice boards for details) are free.

Streets and Caves

Though the Hill's appearance has changed much since building began in the thirteenth century, Uri utca, Fortuna utca, and Országház utca still follow their medieval courses, with Gothic arches and stone carvings half-concealed in the courtyards and passages of eighteenth- and nineteenth-century Baroque houses, whose facades are embellished with gracefully turned ironwork grilles. Diplomats and institutions occupy many of the old, brightly painted dwellings, others have been converted into "authentic Hungarian restaurants" with vaulted cellars and prices putting them beyond the average Magyar's pocket, and Buda's oldest inn, the *Red Hedgehog* on Hess András tér, has become a private residence. Practically every building displays a *Müemlék* plaque giving details of its history—for example, Hungary's first printing press stood on the premises of today's *Fortuna* restaurant.

More appropriately, there's the **Museum of the History of Music** in the former Erdödy Palace (Táncsics u.7) where Beethoven once stayed and Bartók had his workshop; the instruments and the lovely palace itself are the most attractive features of the museum (Mon 4–9pm; Wed–Sun 10am–6pm). Next door is the former prison where Lajos Kossuth and the writer Mihály Táncsics were held for nationalist agitation, from which Táncsics was sprung in 1848 by revolutionaries. The street was predominantly inhabited by Jews during the Middle Ages (when Italians, Germans, and French congregated in neighboring quarters), and at no. 26 the **Jewish Oratory** displays artifacts and gravestones from that era (April–Oct Tues–Fri 10am–2pm; weekends 10am–6pm). A fuller picture of their history emerges at the National Jewish Museum in Pest.

One block away you'll find **Fortuna utca**, named after the medieval inn at no. 4 which now contains the **Museum of Catering**. Here blackened *gulyás* cauldrons and a fearsome array of spits and cleavers mark the slow evolution of Hungarian cuisine from *bográcsgulyás*—the communal stew of the Magyar nomads—to the present day. During the Turkish occupation (1541–1686) the Hill's main thoroughfare—now called **Országház utca** (Parliament Street)— was the "street of the baths," *Hamam Yolu*. The Ottoman chronicler Tselebi noted numerous caravanserai, 34 mosques, four *djami*, three Dervish monasteries and over 100 tanneries in the Castle district, all of which have long vanished. However, medieval architectural features have survived at no. 18, 20 & 22, the *Alabárdos* restaurant and no. 9 (which incorporates niches with "lily-ended" traceries), and the quasi-Gothic **Mary Magdalene Tower** still lowers over Kapisztrán tér, albeit gutted and transformed into an art gallery. The square itself is named after **John Capistranus,** a fiery preacher who exhorted Hunyadi's troops to victory at the siege of Belgrade.

For more in a martial vein, visit the **National War Museum** on the Tóth Árpád promenade (which offers a nice view of Buda's western districts), where off-duty recruits rather the worse for booze stand lost in contemplation of casefuls of rifles and bayonets. Like the armor lumbering up the courtyard, it's the closest that this museum comes to the reality of war; upstairs, the brilliantly colored nineteenth-century hussars' uniforms and revolutionary banners merely highlight its "romantic" image. Other gun-toting conscripts guard the National Archives on Bécsi Kapu tér, known as the "Saturday" (market) square before its devastation in 1686. Given a new and somber cast in the eighteenth century, it was renamed after the chunky **Vienna Gate** that bestrides Ostrom utca, the steep descent to Moszkva tér (see "North of Castle Hill" below). It's worth detouring east of the *Bécsi Kapu* merely to see the *Old Firenze* **nightclub**'s blood-red carpet tiles and lavender stalactites.

Uri utca (Gentlemen's Street) has a plethora of medieval stonework sunk into its buildings, but the main attraction is underground. During the Middle Ages galleries almost 10km long were tunnelled between cavities and fissures in the bedrock and wells were dug, creating a network of **caves beneath the hill** to serve as shelters during wartime. These housed a make-shift hospital during the winter of 1944–45, and could be reached from one of the "safe houses" sheltering Jews from the Nazis. Nowadays part is given over to a dank **underground waxworks.** Not up to the standard of a Madame Tussaud's, the wax figures depict the goriest, most salacious events in Magyar history. There's also a bar that would like to be a club. The entrance is at no. 9; admission 170Ft (Tues–Sun 10am–6pm).

For a snack with snob value visitors favor **Ruszwurm's** *cukrászda*, founded a stone's throw west of Trinity Square in 1827. The patisserie's products are delicious and the decor is properly chintzy, but *Ruszwurm's* is too cramped and frenetic to make you want to linger over a strudel. To the south of Trinity Square the street widens as it approaches the palace, as if to presage gran-deur. Named Tárnok utca after the royal treasurers formerly resident here, its nineteenth-century inhabitants impressed John Paget with their "sedate-ness of air, and not unfrequently a pompous vacancy of expression." Visitors can marvel at dubious medieval pharmacopoeia and wince at eighteenth-century instruments for eviscerating and expurgating, displayed in the **Pharmacy Museum** (once the *Golden Eagle* apothecary), which might once have been applied to revellers who'd over-indulged at the *Arany Hordó*. This restaurant is one of the few buildings on the Hill to have kept its original *sgraffiti*—a bold red and orange checkerboard pattern covering the building's exterior. Tárnok utca ends in Dísz tér, where hussars once paraded (a custom recently revived for Constitution Day), and from here onwards ramparts and gateways buttress the hillside and control access to the palace grounds. On your left stands the **Castle Theater** where Beethoven performed in 1808, while straight ahead lies the scarred hulk of the old Premier's residence, the last outbuilding of the palace complex still to be restored.

Buda Palace

As befits a former royal residence the lineage of the *Budavári Palota* can be traced back to medieval times, and the rise and fall of various palaces on the Hill is practically symbolic of the fortunes of the Hungarian state. The earliest fortifications and dwellings hastily ordered by Béla III after the thirteenth-century Mongol invasion were replaced by ever more luxurious palaces occu-pied by the Angevin kings, who ruled in more prosperous and stable times. The zenith was attained by the palace of Mátyás Corvinus (1458–90), a Renaissance extravaganza to which European artists and scholars were drawn by the blandishments of Queen Beatrice and the prospect of lavish hospitality. The Turkish occupation—ended by a three month siege—left this in ruins, which the Austrian Habsburgs, Hungary's new rulers, leveled to build a palace of their own. From Maria Theresa's modest beginnings (a mere 203 rooms, which she never saw completed), the **Royal Palace** expanded inexorably throughout the nineteenth century, though no monarch ever dwelt here, only the Habsburg viceroy or Palatine. After the collapse of the empire, Admiral Miklós Horthy inhabited the building with all the pomp of monarchy until being deposed by a German coup in October 1944, not long before the three-month siege of Buda which once again resulted in total devastation.

Reconstruction work began in the 1950s and is virtually complete. Grouped around two courtyards, the somber wings of the Palace contain a clutch of museums and portions of the medieval structures discovered in the course of excavation—too much to see in one day unless you give it an unfairly cursory inspection. In any case frequent bouts on the grand terrace overlooking the river are essential if you want to avoid a bad case of historical overload.

Museums in the Palace

The **Museum of the Working Class Movement** in the northern wing gets into its stride after a slow start on feudalism. The iniquities of capitalist Hungary are vividly portrayed alongside relics of the revolutionary struggle: reconstructed prison cells and evictions, communist propaganda and Red Guard arm bands from 1919. Coverage of the Stalinist era and the 1956 Uprising is undergoing radical revision as history is rewritten—the Rákosi era is now totally condemned, and 1956 acclaimed as an "awakening of the people"—though museum catalogs (available in the foyer) may not have been updated yet. An exhibit on Stalinism in Hungary is planned for 1990; one exhibit will be the bronze ear of the Stalin Statue, recently purchased from the folks who knocked it off during the Uprising. Temporary exhibits on the ground floor reflect the museum's new license to criticize the regime in Romania, or the Warsaw Pact invasion of Czechoslovakia in 1968.

The **National Gallery** occupying the central and southern wings contains Hungarian art since the Middle Ages. In the main building Gothic stone-carvings, altars, and painted panels fill the ground floor, while nineteenth-century painting dominates the floor above. **Hungarian painting** really woke up in the 1880s, generating vigorous "schools" which are well represented here: genre painters; *plein air* painters like Pál Szinyei Merse; the *Barbizon group*; portraitists such as Miklós Barabás; and the dominant school of historical painting led by Lotz, Székely, Madarász, and Benczúr. The *Nagybánya Artists' Colony* founded in 1896 opposed all this academic art and made a big impact, securing them an entire floor in the museum alongside *József Rippl-Rónai*, the chief exponent of Hungarian Art Nouveau. The Baroque paintings and ecclesiastical sculptures in the southern wing were mainly confiscated from private collections, and for me at least were less appealing than the **children's section** on the top floor of the main building where, twice a week, some of Hungary's leading artists and performers participate in play groups and impart their skills.

Outside, beyond the ornate fountain where King Mátyás frolics among his hunting dogs, the treasures and vaults of the **Castle Museum** await visitors on the far side of the Lion Courtyard. Much of it is underground, in the marbled and flagstoned halls of the Renaissance palace (unearthed when rubble was sifted to a depth of 30m, and deftly incorporated into the reconstruction), giving Stephen Brook "the sensation of burrowing into the history of the city." Jeweled robes and banqueting ware, near-lifesize statues of knights and ladies, and carvings from the same rich red marble as used at Visegrád and Esztergom attest to the court's former splendor. In the Renaissance Room are relief portraits of Mátyás and Beatrice (whose coat of arms decorates the Beatrice Courtyard outside). Upstairs another exhibition—**Two Thousand Years of Budapest**—shows the evolution of Óbuda, Buda, and Pest by means of old prints, ceramics, and other artifacts. If you want explanations, though, a catalog is absolutely essential, since captions are in Hungarian only (as is the case in all the Palace museums).

Once terraced with vineyards, the southern end of the Hill supports a maze of paths, ramparts, and promenades, guarded by the **Mace Tower** and the *Lihegő Gate* leading into the Round Bastion. From 1961 until its closure in 1984, the **Youth Park** (*Ifjúsági Park*) on the hillside overlooking the embankment played a vital role in Hungarian pop culture, since practically every band of note either played here or aspired to do so. (Action has now shifted to the *Petőfi csarnok* in Pest.) From here you can either backtrack through the Watertown, or head south across what was once the Tabán district towards Gellért Hill, one of the city's landmarks.

Gellért Hill, the Baths, and the Watertown District

Tabán, formerly Buda's artisan quarter, has been practically eliminated by urban redevelopment, and barring the **Semmelweiss Museum** (see "Museums and Galleries" below) there's nothing to detain you here. Between the terraced lawns beyond, overpasses leading to Hegyalja út and the traffic pouring off the Erzsébet Bridge make a formidable obstacle—but press on, for liberation is in sight.

Or almost literally so, because from Tabán or the embankment you can't fail to see the vast Liberation Monument crowning the summit of **GELLÉRT HILL.** A craggy dolomite cliff rearing some 130m above the stone-faced quays, the *Gellérthegy* is named after Bishop Ghirardus, who converted pagan Magyars to Christianity at the behest of King Stephen. A statue of **Saint Gellért** bestrides a waterfall facing the Erzsébet Bridge, marking the spot where he was murdered in 1064—strapped to a barrow and toppled over the cliff by vengeful heathens following the demise of his royal protector. It's a short walk from Gellért's statue to Buda's oldest Turkish baths and the illustrious *Hotel Gellért* (see below), but I'd advise climbing the hill first, since the view from its summit is magnificent. You can reach the top by bus #27, leaving from Móricz Zs. körtér behind Gellért Hill, although anyone approaching from the embankment or the Castle district will find that walking up saves time, if not effort. The **panoramic view** of Budapest makes it all worthwhile: drawing the eye slowly along the curving river, past bridges and the monumental landmarks, beyond which lie the Buda Hills and Pest's suburbs merging hazily with the distant plain.

Every year on August 20, an amazing barrage of **fireworks** is launched from the hilltop **Citadella**, a low fortress built by the Habsburgs to cow Budapest's population with its guns in the aftermath of the 1848–49 revolution. When the "Compromise" with the Habsburgs was reached in 1867, citizens breached the Citadella's walls to affirm that it no longer posed a threat to them; nowadays the fort contains nothing more sinister than a few exhibits, a **tourist hostel**, and an overpriced restaurant (**discos** at the weekend). By entering through the gate marked "hotel" rather than the one labeled "Citadella Museum," you can gain free admission to the fortress and get a slightly different perspective on the Liberation Monument, which is too large to be properly appreciated when you stand directly below it.

Poised beside the Citadella, the **Liberation Monument** thrusts over 100 feet into the sky, a stark female figure holding aloft the palm of victory with Red Army men striking belicose poses around the base, mandatory viewing for Soviet tour groups which begin arriving here at 7am. The monument officially honors Soviet soldiers killed liberating Budapest from the Germans and *Nyilas* (Hungarian Nazis), although its history, not to mention the truth of "liberation" itself, rather differed from the version publicized today. Originally commissioned by Admiral Horthy, a reluctant ally of the Reich, in memory of his own son, the statue was adapted to suit the requirements of Hungary's Soviet liberators by its designer, Zsigmond Kisfaludi-Strobl. Much patronized by pre-war high society, he thereafter produced "Proletarian Art" for new masters and continued to prosper, known derisively as "Kisfaludi-Strébel" by his compatriots (*strébel* means "to climb" or "step from side to side"). The people's initial joy at being rid of the Nazis was rapidly dispelled as the Red Army raped and looted its way across Hungary. Once Communist rule became entrenched, mention of the very word rape was forbidden in the media; and a protest delegation of writers received a chilling rebuff from the Party leader, Rákosi. "What is there to write about? In Hungary there are, say, 3000 villages. Supposing the Russians violated, say, three women in every village. 9000 in all. Is that so much? You writers have no idea of the law of large numbers."

Descending the hillside through the playgrounds of Jubileumi Park, you'll see rough-hewn stone figures seemingly writhing from the massive portal of the **Gellért baths**, adjoining the **Hotel Gellért**. Since bathing details are given below, suffice it to say that the hotel has never been restored to the peak of Art Nouveau perfection attained before 1920, when it was comandeered by Admiral Horthy after his triumphal entry into "sinful Budapest" riding a white charger. The Admiral probably turned in his grave in 1987, when a nudist carnival was held here. Farther to the south, sprawling along the embankment, you'll see the **Technological University** (*Műszaki*

Egyetem). The halls of residence near the Petőfi Bridge serve as a **tourist hostel** during the summer vacation, and the students' union organizes **concerts and discos** at the **E-klub** (XI, Egri József u.1) and **R-klub**, to be found on the premises of like-numbered blocks.

Near the Erzsébet bridgehead, puffs of steam and cute little cupolas surmount the **Rudas baths** (*Gyógyfürdő*), an otherwise outwardly undistinguished building. Since it's for men only, women will have to miss out on Budapest's most atmospheric Turkish baths, the interior of which has hardly changed since it was constructed in 1556 on the orders of Pasha Sokoli Mustapha. Tselebi called it the "bath with green pillars," which still uphold the vaulted ceiling beneath which bathers wallow in an octagonal stone pool, watching other men or the steam billowing around the Rudas's shadowy recesses (there's a bit of a gay scene). On the other side of the Hegyalja út overpass, women have exclusive rights to the **Rác baths**, also built during the Turkish occupation, but largely modernized with the exception of its pool. For more details of both baths, see "Steam Baths and Swimming Pools" below.

The Watertown, the Chain Bridge, and Batthyány tér

If you've visited the places mentioned above, you'll already have seen something of the **WATERTOWN** (*Víziváros*) district, a wedge of streets between Castle Hill and the Danube. Originally a poor quarter housing fishermen, craftsmen, and their families, it became depopulated during the seventeenth century save for a few "Turkified Hungarians selling fruit," as the Mayor of Kassa noted in disgust, and gentrified when it was rebuilt in the nineteenth century. Today it's a reclusive neighborhood of old blocks and mansions meeting at odd angles upon the hillside, reached by alleys which mostly consist of steps (*lépcső*) rising from the main street—Fő utca—below. The southern end of the Watertown is marked by "Kilometer Zero" (a stone from which all distances from Budapest are measured), while its northern boundary is Batthyány tér (see below).

Just north of Kilometer Zero, in front of the *sikló* terminal, Clark Ádám tér handles traffic to and from Budapest's best loved monument, the **Chain Bridge**. Designed by W. T. Clark and built under the direction of **Adam Clark** (a compatriot but no relation), it was opened in 1849 having barely escaped destruction during the revolution which fulfilled the worst nightmares of the bridge's real instigator, Count **István Széchenyi** (1791–1860). A horse-fancying Anglophile with a passion for innovation, Széchenyi succeeded in making the nobility pay taxes to finance the building of the *Lánchíd*, overturning the ancient right of tax-exemption and establishing the precedent that the rich were bound to contribute to Hungary's development. Széchenyi died in an asylum having witnessed the brief triumph of Kossuth and revolution, his pet hates; but Adam Clark married a Hungarian woman and settled happily in Budapest. He also built the tunnel under Castle Hill which, Budapesters joked, could be used to store the new bridge when it rained. An apocryphal story has it that the sculptor responsible for creating the bridge's four lions omitted to give them tongues, and then cast himself into the river overcome by shame.

Walking northwards along Fő utca through the Watertown you'll pass an old Capuchin Church (no. 30) featuring Turkish window arches, followed by the spiky polychrome-tiled church on Szilágyi tér. A block or so beyond lies **Batthyány tér**, flanked by a market and busy with commuters and shoppers by day. Besides its **hangouts**—*Csarnok*, serving beer and wine; the more expensive *Casanova Bar*, a stop on the "Budapest by Night" tour; and the swish *Angelika* patisserie beside the Parish Church—the square abounds in transportation, with #86 **buses** to Flórián tér (see the following section), Metro connections with Pest and Déli station, and the terminal of the suburban **HÉV train** for Aquincum, Római-Fürdő, and Szentendre.

Farther north along Fő utca stands the **Király baths**, a contemporary of the Rác and Rudas, distinguishable by its four copper cupolas shaped like tortoise shells, which admits men and women on alternate days. Fő utca finally terminates at **Bem tér**, named after a Polish general who fought for the Hungarians in the 1849 War of Independence. Traditionally a site for **demonstrations**, it was here that crowds assembled in October 1956, prior to marching on Parliament bearing Hungarian flags with the hammer and sickle excised, hours before the Uprising. More recently, Bem Square has seen peace marches (1984), a demo against the dam at Nagymaros (1986), and the first "official" commemoration of the 1848 revolution on March 15, 1989; it's the place to be on significant anniversaries.

North of Castle Hill: Rózsadomb, Óbuda, and some Roman Ruins

Walking down from the Vienna Gate, past Ostrom utca's *Vörös Kaviar* restaurant, you'll emerge onto **Moszkva tér**, another major junction. Despite the flower-sellers and the kitschy **folklore show** at the *Trombitas-Kert* across the road, Moscow Square offers little incentive to stay, and with a Metro station and buses to Déli station and the Buda Hills, it's easy to get away.

Trams and buses (#56) head out along Szilágyi Erzsébet fasor, stopping at **Városmajor Park** where **chess** fans play beneath the elms, and at the terminal of the **cog-wheel railroad** (see "The Buda Hills" below), opposite the circular *Hotel Budapest*, known to locals as "the trash can." Another kilometer or so up the avenue stands a monument to **Raoul Wallenberg**, the "Righteous Gentile," who gave up a playboy life in neutral Sweden to help the Jews of Hungary in 1944. Armed with diplomatic status and money for bribing officials, Wallenberg and his assistants plucked thousands of Jews from the cattle trucks and lodged them in "safe houses" under Swedish protection ("Look, there goes another Swede," Jews joked to each other); maneuvering to buy time until the Russians arrived. Shortly after they did, Wallenberg was arrested as a spy and vanished into the Gulag; some believe that he's still there today. Reportedly, Kádár himself authorized the red marble **monument**—unveiled in 1987, just before Budapest hosted the World Jewish

Congress—and the article in *Magyar Hirlap* which acknowledged that Wallenberg's arrest had been a "mistake."

The Rózsadomb and Gül Baba's Tomb

To the north of Moszkva tér a colorful produce and **flower market** crams into the alleyways off Fény utca (opposite a good ice cream shop), while if you push up along Ezredes or Lövőház street you'll find **Marczibányi tér**, where a **craft market** with entertainment **for children** is sometimes held on Sunday. Advance notice of this is available from *TOURINFORM* or the columns of *Pesti Műsor*. Despite the grimy factories below Marczibányi tér and the smog-ridden Mártirok útja (Martyrs' Avenue) which dips around to meet the Margit Bridge, you're actually close to Budapest's premier residential area. Few can afford even the smallest of apartments on the **RÓZSADOMB** (Rose Hill), and a list of residents would read like a Hungarian *Who's Who*. Top Party *funcionárusok* live here (in the Rákosi era their homes had secret exits which enabled several *ÁVH* chiefs to escape lynching during the Uprising), Mercedes to Mercedes with forint millionaires; so too do wealthy film directors and the writer György Konrád, whose apartment is a meeting place for foreign journalists, Magyar nationalists, and reformers.

Tucked away in a hillside garden above Mecset u. (off Mártirok útja), the **tomb of Gül Baba** receives pilgrims from across the Muslim world. The small octagonal building is a shrine (*türbe*) to the "Father of the Roses," an esteemed Dervish who expired during a thanksgiving service in the Mátyás Church—then a mosque—before the Sultan's eyes. Carpets, examples of calligraphy, and Gül Baba's personal effects line the walls of the shrine, which appropriately stands in a rose garden (May 1–Oct 31, Tues–Sun 10am–6pm).

Óbuda

Slightly farther afield lies the district of **ÓBUDA**. This is actually the precursor of Budapest, contrary to the impression given by its old factories and new high rises, which hide the ancient ruins that remain. Its Roman founders built a legionary camp and a civilian town, Aquincum, which the Huns later took over and renamed Buda (supposedly in honor of Attila's brother). Under the first Hungarian dynasty, the Árpáds, Buda was an important town, but after the fourteenth century the Castle district eclipsed it, and the original settlement became known as Óbuda (Old Buda).

Starting from the Margit Bridge you can board a *HÉV* train to Aquincum (see overpage), zip up to the ruins on Flórián tér using bus #60 or #86, or walk northwards along the embankment for ten minutes to reach the **Komjádi swimming pool**. This is where Hungary's Olympic swimmers and water polo players usually train—Komjádi was a famous sportsman and coach—and, until a police raid in 1986, was also the main distribution point in Budapest for underground literature produced by the *samizdat* firm *ABC*. From the pool you can catch tram #17 to Kolosy tér, to catch the #65/#65A and #29 buses that run to the Pál-völgyi and Szemlőhegy **stalactite caves** (see below).

A small part of Óbuda blends gaudy Baroque with modern art and traditional gastronomy, only a minute's walk from the Árpád híd *HÉV* stop. Eyeball-throbbing **Op-Art paintings by Viktor Vasarely** decorate the former Zichy mansion, while **Fő tér** around the corner scores with its cobblestones and the famous *Sipos Halászkert* and *Postakocsi* **restaurants** (see "Eating and Drinking" in *Budapest*). In all weathers there are always several figures sheltering beneath umbrellas: life–sized **sculptures by Imre Varga**, whose other works can be seen next door to the *Vasmacska* restaurant on Laktanya utca, beyond.

Roman Ruins around Óbuda and Római-Fürdő

Óbuda has several Roman ruins although the largest site, Aquincum, is in the Római-Fürdő district. The weed-choked crumbling **amphitheater** at the junction of Nagyszombat and Korvin utca once covered a greater area than the Colosseum in Rome, and could seat 14–16,000 spectators. Farther north along Korvin utca (bus #6/#84) one can see lovely but fragmented hunting murals in the **Camp Museum** at no. 63, which also displays sunken baths, a few sarcophagi and other relics of the legionary camp once situated around Flórián tér. There, graceful columns stand incongrously amid a grassy plaza near the shopping center, and large chunks of the old **military baths** and other finds are huddled beneath the Szentendrei út overpass. About ten minutes' walk away, behind apartment no. 19 to 21 on Meggyfa utca, three blue canopies shelter the remains of the **Hercules villa**, named after the third-century **mosaic floor** beneath the largest canopy. Showing Hercules about to vomit at a wine festival, it was originally composed of some 60,000 stones, carefully selected and arranged in Alexandria before shipment to Aquincum. Another mosaic depicts the centaur Nessus abducting Deianeira, whom Hercules had to rescue as one of his twelve labors.

The legionary garrison of 6000 spawned a settlement of camp followers to the north which, over time, became a *Municipum* and later a *Colonia*, the provincial capital of Pannonia Inferior. The **ruins of Aquincum** lie a few kilometers north along the Szentendre road, easily visible from Aquincum station on the *HÉV* railroad, and followed by the remains of an aqueduct and another ampitheater near the *Római-Fürdő* (Roman Bath) stop, opposite a pool and campground. Enough foundation walls and underground piping survive to give a fair idea of the town's layout, although you'll need to pay a visit to the museum and use considerable imagination to envisage Aquincum during its heyday in the second to third century. A great concourse of people filled the main street, doing business in the Forum and law courts (near the entrance), and steaming in public baths. Herbs and wine were burned before altars in sanctuaries holy to the goddesses Epona and Fortuna Augusta, while fraternal societies met in the Collegiums and bath houses farther east. The **museum** contains oddments of the imperium—cake molds, a bronze military diploma, buttons used as admission tickets to the theater—and statues of gods and goddesses.

Like the Hercules villa and the Camp Museum, Aquincum is open from May 1 to October 31 (Tues–Fri 10am–2pm; Sat & Sun 10am–6pm).

The Buda Hills

Thirty minutes' journey from Moszkva tér, the **BUDA HILLS** provide a welcome respite from summertime heat in the city. While particular hills are often busy with people at the weekend, it's possible to ramble through the woods for hours yet see hardly a soul during the week. If your time is limited, the most rewarding options are the "railroad circuit" (see below) or a visit to **Budakeszi Game Park**. Take bus #22 from Moszkva tér to the Korányi Sanatorium stop, then follow the *Vadaspark* signs. Beyond a recreational forest and an exhibition center, the woods and fields are inhabited by red, roe and shovel-antlered fallow deer, wild pigs, mallards, pheasants, and other birds (daily, 9am–5pm).

The "railroad circuit" begins with a short tram (#18) or bus (#56) ride from Moszkva tér, at the **cogwheel-railroad** terminal opposite the *Hotel Budapest* on Szilaágyi Erzsébet fasor. Every half hour a small train clicks up through the peaceful **Szabadság-hegy** suburb, formerly known as "Schwab Hill" after its Swabian merchant founders. The current name, Freedom Hill, obliquely commemorates those who suffered during the Nazi occupation in the local *Hotel Majestic* (nowadays a residential building), when it was a Gestapo torture chamber. Outside the upper, Széchenyi-hegy terminal, cut through the park (folksy play equipment) at a good clip, and you'll arrive in time to buy tickets (12Ft) for the **Pioneers' Railway** (every 40min, 9am–6:30pm; 9am–5pm in winter). Built by youth brigades in 1948, it's a giant toy for kids who yearn to wear a *MÁV* uniform, wave flags, and salute; priggish fourteen-year-olds run signals, platforms and tickets, and the only adults on the staff are the engineers and drivers.

You can alight and start walking at several points along the way to Hűvösvölgy. There's a modest **ski run** at Normafa, while the summit of János-hegy (15min uphill from its station) offers a great **view** of the city. Below the summit, by the buffet, a **chair lift** (9am–5pm; 9:30am–4pm off-season;12Ft) reaches down into town, with #158 buses back to Moszkva tér. Budakeszi Game Park is also accessible by bus #22 from Ságvárliget, and **boars** (which prefer to roam during the evening and sleep by day) might occasionally be sighted in the forests above **Hárs-hegy**, the stop before Hűvösvölgy. Linked directly to Moszkva tér by #56 and #56E (non-stop) buses, **Hűvösvölgy** is the site of a small **amusement park**.

As in Poland and Russia cityfolk enjoy **mushroom hunting**, scouring the Buda Hills for diverse fungi which they take to special stalls where *gomba* experts distinguish the edible from the toxic ones (in the Vásárcsarnok and the market near Moszkva tér). If the local fungi don't attract you, **Hármashatár-hegy** still provides a fabulous **view** of Budapest from a different perspective, while from the western side of the hill **hang gliding** buffs launch themselves over the plain. Since Hármashatár-hegy lies at the end of the #129 bus route, which begins where bus #65 terminates, you can visit it before or after seeing the Pál-völgyi Cave, en route.

The largest and finest of Buda's **stalactite caves** is five stops from Kolosy tér in Óbuda (bus #65). The Hungarian Speleology Institute at III, Szépvölgyi út 162 runs guided tours of the **Pál-völgyi** labyrinth below (hourly, 10am–6pm, April–Oct; closed Mon), starting on the lowest level. Having seen rock formations like the *Organ Pipes* and *Beehive*, and *John's Look-out* in the largest chamber, you ascend a crevice onto the upper level, there to enter *Fairyland* before *Paradise*, overlooking the hellish *Radium Hall* 50m below.

Having seen this, you can ride on towards Hármashatár-hegy, or try to navigate through the backstreets towards the **Szemlőhegy** cave, whose walls bulge with pea-shaped formations and aragonite crystals resembling bunches of grapes. The cave (III, Pusztaszeri út 35; Wed–Mon 9am–4pm) can also be reached directly from Kolosy tér by taking bus #29 as far as the Pusztaszeri út turn-off.

Margit Island and Csepel Island

Located at opposite ends of the city, Budapest's two largest islands are poles apart. **MARGIT ISLAND** is an elegant tongue, green with oak trees and perfumed by flower gardens, where the wealthier folk have traditionally lolled around (before 1945, a stiff admission charge deterred the poor). Nowadays it's a favorite spot for courting couples, offering open-air **dancing** (near the Casino snack bar) and performances of **drama and opera** (on the stage near the water tower) during summer, as well as the chance to enjoy **nude sunbathing** on the single-sex terraces of the **Palatinus baths**. The *Thermál* and *Grand* **hotels**, filled with wealthy foreign invalids, are somewhat removed from the island's therapeutic tradition. Originally, lepers and outcasts were treated in a thirteenth-century convent—whose **ruins** can still be seen—where Béla IV confined his nine-year-old daughter, Margit, after whom the island is named; she was canonized for a lifetime of saintly deeds within the convent. The island is a fine place to get lost, yet is easily reached from Pest (Marx tér: bus #26, #26A) or Buda (Moszkva tér: tram #4, #6); although motorists can only approach Margit Island from the north, via the Árpád Bridge.

CSEPEL ISLAND, accessible by *HÉV* train from Boráros tér, is an entirely different animal: a dusty wedge of land 50km long, covered with market gardens, endless high-rise *lakótelep*, and the Tököl garrison of the Soviet army. The site of early copper smelting and Bronze Age graves, Csepel was suddenly transformed by **heavy industry** towards the end of the nineteenth century. The militant workers at the huge Manfred Weiss Iron & Metal Works soon earned the island its nickname "Red Csepel," and the post-war Communists made this Rákosi's parliamentary constituency. In 1956 it rapidly became one of the strongholds of the Uprising, with factory committees which maintained a strike for months after the suppression of all military resistance. Subsequent improvements in housing and amenities haven't addressed factory workers' major grievance, the iniquitous system of piece-work (*darabbér*), and though lone critics like Miklós Haraszti could simply be sent to jail in the 1970s, nowadays the authorities must beware of provoking more widespread opposition. As real wages drop, loss-making factories close, and workers quit the official SZOT **unions** in droves, the likelihood of industrial unrest grows. Should strikes occur, there's a potential cleavage of interest between Csepel's permanent residents and the many thousands of **migrant workers** housed in *Munkás-szálló*, who return on the "black train" at weekends to their families in the countryside.

Tourists rarely visit Csepel, one of the few parts of Budapest where women or obviously-rich foreigners might be at risk on the streets late at night.

PEST

PEST is busier, more populous, and vital than Buda: the place where things are decided, made, and sold. While Buda grew up around Castle Hill's forts and palaces, the east bank was settled by merchants, artisans, and laborers, surrounded by brick-works whose ovens—*Offen* to the original, largely German population—gave the growing town its name, which was later Magyarized to Pest (pronounced "Pesht"). Much of the architecture and general layout dates from the late nineteenth century, giving Pest a homogenous appearance compared to other European capitals. Boulevards, public buildings, and apartment houses were built on a grand scale appropriate to the Habsburg empire's second city, and the capital of Hungary, which celebrated its 1000-year anniversary in 1896. Now bullet-scarred and grimy or in the throes of restoration, these form the backdrop to life in the cosmopolitan *Belváros* (inner city) and the residential quarters, hulking gloomily above the street cafés, poky courtyards, and wine cellars where Pest's inhabitants socialize. There's plenty to see and do here, but the less tangible atmosphere is Pest's most attractive characteristic.

Beginning with the Belváros, the following sections describe fairly distinct areas of Pest, broadly defined by two semi-circular *körút*—the "Little" (*Kis*) and "Great" (*Nagy*) Boulevards—and long radial *út* leading to the railroad stations and city parks. The Belváros is small enough to explore on foot without much risk of getting lost, but transportation and a map (or at least a destination) are required once you go much farther than the Little Boulevard. As the meeting point of three Metro lines and several main avenues, Deák tér (see below) makes a good jumping-off point for such explorations.

The Belváros

Like the walled, medieval town of Pest—and with approximately the same boundaries—the **inner city** BELVÁROS (V district) is very cosmopolitan, consciously adapting to and reflecting foreign influences. For many centuries this owed much to Pest's predominantly German-speaking or Jewish population, consequently arousing the mistrust of provincial Hungarians (the more bigoted of whom referred to the city as "Judapest"). Charges of "alien cosmopolitanism" survived the nineteenth-century influx of Magyars and the fluorescence of Hungarian cultural and artistic life, so that right-wingers denounced the capital as "sinful" in 1919. Nowadays the area north of Felszabadulás tér positively revels in its international connections, with shops

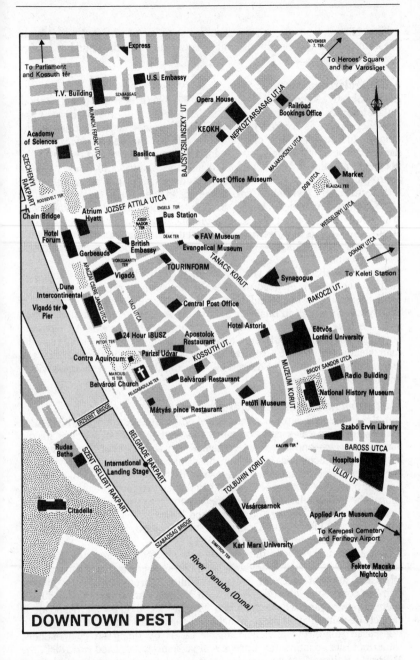

DOWNTOWN PEST

To Parliament and Kossuth tér

Express

U.S. Embassy

T.V. Building

SZABADSAG TER

Opera House

NEPKOZTARSASAG UTJA

Railroad Bookings Office

NOVEMBER 7. TER

To Heroes' Square and the Varosliget

KEOKH

MUNNICH FERENC UTCA

BAJCSY-ZSILINSZKY UT

MAJAKOVSZKIJ UTCA

Academy of Sciences

Basilica

Post Office Museum

DOB UTCA

KLAUZAL TER

Market

WESSELENYI UTCA

SZECHENYI RAKPART

ROOSEVELT TER

Chain Bridge

Atrium Hyatt

JOZSEF ATTILA UTCA

ENGELS TER

Bus Station

JOZSEF NADOR TER

Hotel Forum

Gerbeauds

VOROSMARTY TER

British Embassy

DEAK TER

FAV Museum

Evangelical Museum

DOHANY UTCA

To Keleti Station

TANACS KORUT

Vigadó

TOURINFORM

Synagogue

RAKOCZI UT.

ARPACS CSERE JANOS UTCA

Duna Intercontinental

VACI UTCA

Central Post Office

Vigadó tér Pier

Hotel Astoria

Eötvös Loránd University

24 Hour IBUSZ

PETOFI TER

Apostolok Restaurant

KOSSUTH UT.

MUZEUM KORUT

BRODY SANDOR UTCA

Radio Building

Contra Aquincum

Parizsi Udvar

MARCIUS 15 TER

FELSZABADULAS TER

Belvárosi Church

Belvárosi Restaurant

National History Museum

Petöfi Museum

Mátyás pince Restaurant

ERZSEBET BRIDGE

Szabó Ervin Library

KALVIN TER

BAROSS UTCA

Rudas Baths

BELGRADE RAKPART

SZENT GELLERT RAKPART

International Landing Stage

TOLBUHIN KORUT

Hospitals

ULLOI UT

Citadella

Vásárcsarnok

Applied Arts Museum

To Kerepesi Cemetery and Ferihegy Airport

SZABADSAG BRIDGE

DIMITROV TER

Karl Marx University

River Danube (Duna)

Fekete Macska Nightclub

selling Nikons and French perfume, posters proclaiming the arrival of Western films and rock groups, and streets noisy with the sound of foreign cars and languages.

Around Felszabadulás tér

Accessible by Metro line 3 or buses #7/#7A/#78 from Keleti station, **Felszabadulás tér** is more or less dead center, its approach from the Erzsébet Bridge is flanked by twin Clothild palaces, a last flourish of the empire. Just south of the bridgehead you'll see the deluxe *Mátyás Pince*, famous for its carp dishes and Sándor Lakatos's Gypsy band, while to the northeast are the *Belvárosi* nightclub and the *Egyetem*, Budapest's closest approximation to a gay bar. Opposite stands a slab of gilt and gingerbread architecture, the **Párizsi udvar**: home to an ice cream parlor and a big *IBUSZ* office, but chiefly known for its "**Parisian arcade**" adorned with arabesques and stained glass. The *Apostolok* restaurant on Kigyó utca, around the back, is likewise richly decorated, with paintings of saints and the "lost towns" of old Hungary, but it's cheaper to eat at the *Mézes Mackó* deli, a few doors along.

From Felszabadulás tér you can walk northwards into Pest's shopping district (see below), or head up Kossuth utca to meet the Little Boulevard. Until recently, women selling handicrafts from Székely region of Transylvania used to do business here in the **Astoria Metro** station, named after the *Hotel Astoria* on the corner, attached to which are an Art Nouveau beer hall and a **nightclub** frequented by cash-only prostitutes. Across the road stands the **Soviet Culture House**, a club for Russian officers and memsahibs, adjoining the Soviet Bookshop and the *Bajkál* restaurant, with a fine **tea room** upstairs.

The Korzó from Váci utca to Vörösmarty tér

But the immediate attraction has to be **Váci utca**, thronged with people strolling past its cafés and boutiques. It's part promenade—hence its old name, the *korzó*—and part Fifth Avenue. The crowds can get wearing and it's hardly the cheapest place to shop or drink, but there's no denying the energy, swank, and unabashed materialism that make Váci utca unique in the Eastern bloc. As far as **specifics** go, you'll pass two foreign language bookshops, the air-conditioned *Taverna Grill*, and a crowded *McDonald's* before reaching the *Pesti Theater* (no. 9), flanked by mock-Gothic fantasies, where twelve year-old Liszt made his concert debut, just beyond which there's the *Anna Terász*, a nice breakfast spot.

Barring such diversions the crowd flows onto **Vörösmarty tér**, breaking on a reef of portraitists to eddy about conjurers, violinists, breakdancers, and other acts, a few of which are truly dire. While children play in the fountains, over-16s congregate around the statue of **Mihály Vörösmarty** (1800–50)—a poet and translator whose hymn to Magyar identity, *Szózat* (Appeal), is publicly declaimed at moments of national crisis; in Romania the beleaguered Hungarian minority mark their anniversaries by doing so clandestinely. Underfoot lies continental Europe's first subway, opened in 1896: the **Millenial Railroad** (Metro line 1) that runs beneath Népköztársaság útja up to Heroes' Square. But **Gerbeaud's patisserie** is the most venerable institution on Vörösmarty tér, having been the favored haunt of Budapest's high society since the late nineteenth century. Its gilded ceilings and china, silverware, and starchy service recall la belle époque, and its clientele include Party bosses, film directors, matrons in furs, and chic literati, besides the more transient tourists. The cakes and ices are just as scrumptious but cheaper in the *Kis-Gerbeaud* annex that faces towards the **British Embassy** and **library** on Harmincad utca.

Various sidestreets and an *udvar* behind the *Taverna Grill* connect Váci Street with **Petőfi utca**, which carries all the traffic. Besides more shops, you'll find parking lots, a place to make **international phone calls** (no. 17–19), and the department of the **Central Post Office** (no. 13) where you would collect letters sent to you *poste restante*—all detailed under "Listings" (below).

Along the Embankment

Luxury hotels occupy most of the prime sites along the **Belgrád rakpart** embankment, and little of the original waterfront architecture remains. Starting just north of the Erzsébet Bridge you'll come upon **Március 15. tér**, a square commemorating March 15 when the 1848 revolution began and, more tangibly, the site of a small Roman ruin *Contra-Aquincum*, and the **Belvárosi Church**. Behind its grimy facade hide Renaissance niches, Baroque barrel-vaulting, and a *mihrab* from the time of the Turkish occupation, indicating the direction of Mecca. An adjoining square and statue honor **Sándor Petőfi** (1823–49), peasants' son, poet of the *puszta*, and revolutionary firebrand, whose *Nemzeti Dal* (National Song)—the anthem of 1848—and romantic death in battle made him a patriotic icon, still revered today. Petőfi tér is a traditional site for **demonstrations** in favor of *demokrácia* and national independence; in 1989, the Party bowed to popular feelings and restored March 15 as a national holiday. Walk northwards past the **24-hour IBUSZ bureau** (Petőfi tér 3) and you'll soon reach the **Vigadó**: a splendidly romantic concert hall, the name of which translates literally as "self-amused." Previous conductors at the Vigadó have included Franz Liszt (a Hungarian, whose surname means "Flour") and Gustav Mahler.

North of the **Vigadó tér pier** (for pleasure **cruises** and services to the Danube Bend), two deluxe hotels front directly onto **Roosevelt tér**. Assuming you don't cross the Chain Bridge to Buda or stop for a meal at the opulent *Szecsuán* restaurant, it makes sense to head up past the Academy of Science towards Parliament (see next page), or cut back across Attila út and József Nádor tér to reach Deák tér and the Little Boulevard.

Deák tér and Engels tér

Three Metro lines, two segments of the Little Boulevard and several avenues meet at **Deák tér** and Engels tér, giving rise to some confusion over addresses. You'll recognize the area by two landmarks: the dome of Saint Stephen's Basilica to the north, and a huge mustard-colored, mansard-roofed edifice to the east. Beneath this, in the Tanács körút section of the underground walkway, railroad buffs can grow maudlin over ornate fixtures and tiling, and yellow trams dating from the 1890s, in the **Metro Museum** (*FAV múzeum*). The entrance to the Metro proper lies across the main road, flanked by two rarely visited exhibits—the **National Evangelical Museum**, with relics and captions pertaining to the Lutheran or *Evángelikus* faith, to which around five percent of Magyars subscribe; and the *NDK Centrum*, which waves the flag for East Germany. On Sütő utca, running off between the two, **TOURINFORM** is the capital's best source of **tourist information**.

The **Engels tér bus terminal**, to the north, is equally useful if you're heading **for Transdanubia or the Balaton**, or **other countries**. On domestic routes it's usual to buy a ticket from the driver, whereas you need to reserve the day before, or earlier, for international services; see "Travel Details" for schedules and destinations. Engels tér is also the point of departure for buses **to Ferihegy Airport** (every 30min, 5am–10pm), and open-top *Omnibusz* **tours of the city**.

The following section begins with the government quarter and the two main avenues running north and northeast from Engels tér. The areas adjoining Deák tér to the southeast and south are covered afterwards.

Between the Boulevards

Emulating Baron Haussman in Paris, the architects who redesigned Pest in the late nineteenth century thought big, and were empowered to push their schemes through by imperial decree. Beyond the Belváros enclosed by the Little Boulevard, grand avenues run like canyons for kilometers between blocks of nineteenth-century housing or monumental public buildings, giving rise to certain distinctive areas like the government district or the Jewish quarter. Some of these lie just a few minutes' walk from the Belváros; to reach others, around the arc of the enormously long Great Boulevard, buses #12/#12A or trams #4/#6 are useful.

Parliament and Kossuth tér

Immediately north of the Belváros, narrow streets lined with somber administrative buildings lead towards the **government district**, only to have their gloomy progress interrupted by the verdant expanse of **Szabadság tér**. Flanked by the National Bank with its bas reliefs representing honest toil, and the equally imposing headquarters of Magyar TV, Liberty Square is also the site of the **US Embassy** where Cardinal Mindszenty sought refuge during the Uprising (no. 12), and the head office of **Express**, Hungary's Youth Travel Agency (no. 16). I'm inclined to suspect a sly joker in the public works department, since the one street that avoids Liberty Square yet still makes an undeviating line towards Parliament is named after Ferenc Münnich, whose expertise in civil repression (acquired with the *OGPU* during the Spanish Civil War) enabled the Party to "consolidate power" after the Hungarian Uprising. If the door of no. 15 is ajar, you can glimpse women sorting betting slips in the national *Totó Lotó* office; the *Terv eszpreszó* (no. 19) is a late night café/bar.

Continue northwards and Hungary's **Parliament building** (*Országház*) suddenly appears. Variously described as "eclectic" or "neo-Gothic" in style, it sprawls for 268 meters between the embankment and Kossuth tér, dominating the vicinity with a spiky facade embellished by 88 statues of Hungarian rulers. The symmetrical wings housing the Assemblies meet beneath a gigantic cupola 96 meters high, which can accommodate both chambers when they meet in ceremonial conclave. A vital force during the "Reform Era," Parliament had grown sluggish by the time its grandiose seat was built (in 1884–1902, according to Imre Steindl's plans). Under Fascism, opposition Members of Parliament learned to fear for their lives, while following the "Year of Change" in 1948, parliamentary politics became a mere echo of decisions taken by the Politburo and Secretariat of the Communist Party at *MSzMP* headquarters on Akadémia utca. Recently however, parliament has become a real decision making forum and the Communist Party (now officially defunct) surrendered its monopoly of power. As a consequence, there'll probably be fewer guided **tours** (see "Entertainments" below) than in the past, when Parliament only met four days every year.

Another sign of the times is the changing nature of demonstrations on **Kossuth tér**, a square dignified by statues of Lajos Kossuth and Prince Ferenc Rákóczi II, the sanctified heroes of the struggle for Hungarian independence. Inscribed on the plinth of Rákóczi's monument, the quote "The wounds of the noble Hungarian nation burst open!" refers to the anti-Habsburg war of 1703–11, but seems equally appropriate to the evening of October 23, 1956, when 100,000 Magyars filled the square chanting anti-Stalinist slogans at Parliament, and calling for the appearance of Imre Nagy, a popular "reform" Communist ousted by the Rákosi clique—the prelude to the Uprising that night. Thirty-three years later the wheel turned full circle as the new Republic of Hungary was proclaimed to an enthusiastic crowd from the same balcony that Nagy spoke, and the People's Republic of Hungary was officially consigned to the trash can of history. The removal of red stars from buildings and the return of the old emblem of royal Hungary – Saint Stephen's double cross – both symbolise this political watershed.

Barring a fine **Ethnographical Museum** (see "Museums and Galleries"), there's nothing of interest for several blocks north or east of Kossuth tér, so the trail heads back through Liberty Square towards Budapest's cathedral.

From Saint Stephen's Basilica to Marx tér

With its re-bronzed dome oxidized to a dull brown while builders shore up its facade, **Saint Stephen's Basilica** seems diminished for all its visibility over the billboards of Engels tér. Restorers have yet to reach the cavernous interior where shadows obscure the peeling frescoes and gilding, but hopefully it won't take as long as the actual construction of the Basilica; the architects, József Hild and Miklós Ybl, both died of old age before its consecration in 1905. The Basilica's dome, like that of Budapest's Parliament, is 96m high—a deliberate allusion to 896, the year of the Magyar conquest. On Saint Stephen's name day, August 20, his mummified hand and other **holy relics** are displayed to worshipers here, and on the 950th anniversary of his death they toured Hungary, where *Szent István* is still honored as the nation's founder and patron saint.

In the pantheon of Hungarian heroes there's a modest niche for Endre **Bajcsy-Zsilinszky**, the Social Democrat who opposed Szálaszi's fascists until he was arrested in Parliament (a statue on Deák tér captures the moment) and shot as the Russians neared Sopron. The avenue or *út* named after him has several useful places, accessible by Metro (line 3) if they're not within walking distance of Engels tér. On the right-hand side are the *Rétes* patisserie, the local branch of **Dunatours** (no. 17) and the *Habana* restaurant, with an outlet for **maps** at no. 37, farther up the avenue. You'll find the *International House* **language school** (no. 62) and the site of a future **US Consulate and Cultural Center** (no. 40) across the road. Halfway along the avenue, it's possible to catch tram #72 to the Városliget (see "Beyond the Great Boulevard" below) for a change of scene. Bajcsy-Zsilinszky út ends in a mess of over- and underpasses at Marx tér, overlooked by **Nyugati station** (see "Listings" below) and the glassy, terraced **Skála-Metró department store**. Founded as an association of Co-ops in 1973 to provide competition for the state-run *Centrum* chain, *Skála* has acquired other outlets by trading aggressively and issuing shares (called bonds) to raise capital.

Szent István körút, leading to the Margit Bridge, likewise reflects nascent Magyar capitalism. Along its length (which is safe to walk at night) are half a dozen more or less sleazy **bars** and fast food outlets, open till the small hours, plus the *Berlin* restaurant and the *Margit híd* **disco**.

Up the Avenue of the People's Republic to Heroes' Square

Of all the thoroughfares radiating from Engels tér, the Avenue of the People's Republic—**Népköztársaság útja**—is the longest and most re-named. Opened in 1884, it runs for two and a half kilometers up to Heroes' Square on the edge of the Városliget, a parade of grand buildings laden with gold leaf, stone dryads, and colonnades. Still known as Andrássy út by older folks, the avenue bore Stalin's name from 1949 until the 1956 Uprising. Its shops and sidewalk cafés retain some of the style that made the avenue so fashionable in the 1890s, when "Bertie" the Prince of Wales regularly drove down its length in a landau offering flowers to women passing by; the underground Millenial Railroad (Metro line 1) beneath it also dates from that time.

It's feasible to walk from Engels tér as far as November 7th Square, but if you're going any farther take bus #1 or #4 or the Metro. En route you'll pass the **Post Office Museum** at no. 3; the *KEOKH* bureau responsible for visa extensions (no. 12); and, on the left, the **Opera House**. Hungary's state opera was founded by **Ferenc Erkel** (1810–93), composer of the national anthem. It occupies a magnificent building designed by Ybl that was recently restored to its original glory. Tickets and reservations are available from the office around the corner (or from the bureau on Vörösmarty tér), and opera-goers are apt to patronize the *Művész* patisserie opposite, or the *Tokaj Borbár* next door. A couple of blocks beyond the Opera House on the right-hand side, international tickets and railroad timetables are sold at the **MÁV office** at no. 35, and delicious pastries and ices are available at the palmy *Párizsi cukrászda*.

The avenue meets the Great Boulevard at **November 7. tér**, an intersection still popularly known by its original name, the *Oktogon*, nowadays the site of an *IBUSZ* office and the *Abbázia* restaurant. Several places are worth noting between here and the Kodály körund, starting with the *Babszinház* **Puppet Theater** (no. 69) and ending with the *Vörös Sárkány* Chinese restaurant (no. 80), five doors back from which there's a sedate fin-de-siècle patisserie. Number 60, now the offices of a trading company, was once the most terrifying address in Budapest. Jews and other victims of the *Nyilas* were tortured here, and the specially equipped building was later occupied by the Communist *ÁVO*, which employed the same gadgets and many of the torturers. Capturing the building in 1956, insurgents found no trace of the giant meat-grinder rumored to have been used to dispose of corpses, but discovered masses of incriminating evidence.

The **Kodály körund** junction is named after the composer *Zoltán Kodály* (see "Kecskemét" in *The Great Plain*) who worked and died at no. 89, flanked by four neo-Renaissance palaces, one of them faintly graffitied with gold. From here on, plane trees run along the útja past Ferenc Hopp's **Collection of Eastern Asiatic Art** and mansions and villas, which peter out as you approach Heroes' Square.

Erected to mark the thousandth anniversary of the Magyar conquest, **Heroes' Square** (*Hősök tere*) is appropriately grand. Its centerpiece is the **Millenary Monument**, portraying Prince Árpád and his chieftains, half encircled by a colonnade displaying statues of Hungary's most illustrious leaders from King Stephen to Kossuth. You'll find two art museums, Városliget park, and Vajdahunyad Castle in the vicinity (described overpage), but before going to investigate, spare a thought for the **Stalin statue** that once stood nearby. As the arch symbol of foreign oppression it was torn down during the Uprising, dragged to Lenin körút, decapitated, doused with gasoline and then ignited, so that "flames came out of the mouth. The headless torso lay there for a week, and a constantly changing crowd surrounded it . . . hammering away to get bits for souvenirs." Since then the site has witnessed annual **parades** of banner-toting workers (May 1) and the armed forces (April 4, Liberation Day), but no genuine popular manifestations until June 1988, when 40,000 people marched from Heroes' Square to the Romanian Embassy, protesting against the planned demolition of villages in Transylvania (see *Contexts*).

Majakovszkij utca and the old Jewish Quarter

The VII district between Népköztársaság útja and Rákóczi avenue is mainly residential, composed of nineteenth-century buildings whose bullet-scarred, grimy facades conceal a warren of dwellings, wrought ironwork and leafy courtyards, interspersed with tiny workshops and wine cellars. Vladimir Mayakovsky, the punkish Russian poet who "trod on the throat of his own song" to serve the Bolshevik cause, gives his name to **Majakovszkij utca**—a street running parallel to Népköztársaság útja for an inordinate length, unlike the poet's terse, militant verses. Formerly known as Király utca and noted for its brothels (where, Leigh Fermor was told, "any man could be a cavalier for five pengöes"), the street and those around it are now the place to find antiques, secondhand shops (*bizományi*), and outlets for cheap and stylish, slightly flawed (*alkami*) shoes and clothing.

A number of sidestreets lead southwards towards Pest's old **Jewish quarter**, which fans out behind the Synagogue trailing a string of cheap **restaurants** along Dob utca. Specific "sights" here are few, but practically every apartment building on Síp, Rumbach, and Kazinczy streets contains a rundown yet beautiful courtyard with stained-glass panels enscribed in Hebrew characters, and sad memorial plaques naming those who perished on the "Death March" to Hegyeshalom and in the camps of Auschwitz and Bergen-Belsen. Bullet holes in the walls are a grim reminder of the "autumn that bled" in 1944, when Nazi squads rampaged through the ghetto leaving Jewish corpses piled up in the streets, and Hungarian gentiles walked by, averting their eyes. While the Zionist underground prepared for escape or last-ditch insurrection, the Wallenberg group (see "North of Castle Hill" above) used legalistic maneuverings and bribery to gain time. Unable to thwart the murderous Nyilas gangs led by Minorite priests and aristocrats, they still managed to forestall the final SS assault on the ghetto, planned as Russian troops were encircling the city.

On the corner of Wesselényi and Dohány utca, just off the Little Boulevard, restorers are hard at work on the main **Synagogue**, whose dramatic Byzantine-Moorish architecture had grown cracked and filthy from prolonged neglect. The restoration is largely funded from abroad, not least by the Hungarian-Jewish diaspora, with Tony Curtis (born of Twenties immigrants) spearheading the drive. Depending on its progress, you'll be able to see at least part of the *zsinagoga* complex, and certainly the **National Jewish Museum** (Mon & Thurs 2–6pm; Tues, Wed, Fri & Sun 10am–1pm; closed on the Sabbath). Here, torahs and other magnificent Judaica dating back to the Middle Ages, or the cultural fluoresence of the nineteenth century are opposed by a harrowing Holocaust exhibit, the memory of which casts a chill over the third section, portraying Jewish cultural life today. Its current resurgence owes something to the World Jewish Congress of 1987, held in Budapest, which boosted the confidence of the 80,000-strong community, previously reticent to proclaim itself in a country where anti-semitic prejudices linger.

Other notable places in the VII district include **Klauzál tér**, the site of two privately owned restaurants (*Étkezde*) and another **Skála supermarket**; the **map shop** at Nyár u. 1 just off Rákóczi út; and two discreet **gay bars**. The *Emke* lies 100 meters north of the Great Boulevard junction, while the seedier *Diófa* is at Dohány u.38.

Muzeum körút, Üllői út, and the City Market

South of the Synagogue you can turn east and go window **shopping** up **Rákóczi út** (see "Shops and Markets") to **Keleti station**, accessible by #7,#7A or #78 bus; or continue following the Little Boulevard as it begins curving towards the Szabadság Bridge. **Múzeum körút**—the section running as far as Kálvin tér—resembles Népköztársaság útja in miniature, with its trees, shops, and grandiose stone piles. Past the natural sciences faculty of **Eötvös Loránd University**, remains of the **medieval walls** of Pest can be glimpsed in the courtyards of no. 17 & 21, and a series of *Antikvárium* selling old books and prints cluster nearby.

From the steps of the **National History Museum**, Petőfi stirred up a crowd of students and apprentices, and first declaimed the *National Song* with its rousing refrain: "Choose! Now is the time! Shall we be slaves or shall we be free?" Inside, the museum is divided into two sections—before and after the Magyar conquest—of which the latter is definitely more interesting. All the captions are in Hungarian only, so buying a catalog for each section is essential. While I was more impressed by the amazing carved pews from Nyírbátor and the tent of the Turkish general, the most prestigious exhibit is undoubtedly the **Coronation Regalia**, reputedly the very crown, orb, and scepter used by King Stephen. Although the crown, described by Brook as resembling "a soufflé," most likely belonged to one of Stephen's successors, the regalia is nevertheless esteemed as the symbol of Hungarian statehood. Kossuth buried the regalia in Transylvania rather than let the Habsburgs possess it, and fascists took it to the US in 1945, where the treasure reposed in Fort Knox until its return to Hungary in 1978.

Narrow Bródy Sándor utca, running alongside the museum to the north, seems an unlikely place for a revolution to start. Yet one did outside the nondescript **Radio Building** (no. 5), when *ÁVO* guards fired upon students demanding access to the airwaves, an act which turned what had been peaceful protests on October 23, 1956 into a violent uprising against the secret police and other manifestations of Stalinism. Street fighting was especially fierce around **Kálvin tér**, where insurgents battled tanks rumbling in from Ferihegy and the Soviet garrison on Csepel Island; it's something of a miracle that the plush reading room of the **Szabó Ervin Library** survived unscathed on the corner of Baross utca.

Don't bother with **Üllői út** unless you've got a destination in mind, since this grimy thoroughfare of ponderous neo-Classical and "vaguely Art Deco" apartment blocks runs for miles out to the Airport and Debrecen highways. Although it's a minute's stroll from Kálvin tér to the **all-night bar** *Pepsi*, the plush *Kaltenberger* cellar lies several blocks back from the Ferenc körút Metro, past Budapest's **Applied Arts Museum**. Layers of soot obscure the rich Zsolnay earthenware, porcelain, and yolk-colored tiles covering the portico and facade of this vast "neo-Byzantine monstrosity," designed by Ödön Lechner in a mixture of Art Nouveau and Turkic folk styles. The interior—modeled on the Alhambra in Granada—tends to overwhelm exhibits, which are mostly on a temporary basis. You might find anything from Transylvanian enamel ware to Finnish glass, or Tibetan scrolls and prayer rugs collected by the explorer Sándor Kőrosi Csoma (see "Museums and Galleries"), so it's worth checking out.

Points farther out, beyond the Great Boulevard, are covered below, but since the *Színpad Centi* (no. 45) lies just past the junction it would be churlish not to mention its **mime shows**. The building occupies the former site of the Kilian barracks, whose garrison was the first to join the 1956 insurgents; and this became the headquarters of Colonel Pál Maleter and teams of teenage guerrillas who sallied forth from the maze of passages surrounding the *Corvin Cinema* to lob Molotov cocktails at Soviet tanks.

Tolbuhin körút, which leads from Kálvin tér to the Szabadság Bridge, is notable chiefly for the *Vásárcsarnok*, Budapest's main **market hall** (Mon 9am–5pm; Tues–Thurs & Sat 6am–6pm; Fri 6am–7pm). A dusty mock-Gothic facade conceals a lofty wrought iron pillared hall, filled with colorful produce and rich smells. Fish swim in tanks awaiting buyers at the back of the hall, near stalls festooned with strings of crimson and scarlet paprika. In 1984 it was here that Mrs. Thatcher endeared herself to the locals by haggling ("I'm a housewife and mother too, you know") and doing a walkabout, a rare phenomenon in the Eastern bloc before the advent of Gorbachev. In the back-streets outside you'll find flower sellers and cheap workers' cafés; while with a student card it should be possible to gain admission to discos and gigs at the **MKKE klub** of **Karl Marx Economic University**, located between Dimitrov tér and the embankment. These generally take place in one of the subsidiary blocks at the southern end of Ráday utca or, less frequently, in the courtyard of a building on Zsil utca; ask around.

Beyond the Great Boulevard

There's no reason to cover every *kerület* **beyond the Great Boulevard**, but a few places deserve a mention, if not a visit. Most of them are best reached by Metro, for traveling from one to another by surface transportation can be awkward.

City Park and the People's Stadium

The **VÁROSLIGET**, or City Park, starts just back of Heroes' Square. Across the boating lake you'll see **Vajdahunyad Castle** rearing up among the trees, an extraordinary sight to behold. Built in 1896 for the Millenary Exhibition, the building is a "stone catalog" of architectural styles, incorporating a replica of the Chapel at Ják in western Hungary and two Transylvanian castles (One of the originals, the Hunyadi Castle in Romania, gives its name to the building). Facing the entrance to the **Agricultural Museum** in the main building—a place to make vegetarians blanch and everybody else yawn—sits the hooded statue of "Anonymus," who chronicled the times of King Béla III. In the southeastern corner of the park, mothballed steam engines filled with excited kids stand outside the **Transport Museum**, where nostalgia buffs will enjoy the antique cars and the earthbound can admire pictures of Bertalan Farkas, Hungary's first man in space courtesy of the Soviet Union. Between here and Vajdahunyad Castle you'll find the **Petőfi Csarnok** where **films, flea markets, and discos** are staged at weekends (see "Entertainments" below), while on the opposite side of the park are the **Széchenyi baths** (see "Steam Baths and Swimming Pools" below) and the **zoo, circus,** and **amusement park** (see "Listings" below).

You can reach the **NÉPSTADION** district by Metro from Deák tér (line 2), or by bus from the neighborhood of the Városliget (take #20/#30 down Dózsa György út, or #55 around the once-fashionable part of the Hungária körút). Népstadion's namesake, the 173,000-seat **People's Stadium**, serves as a venue for major **soccer** matches and **rock concerts** (for example,

Springsteen and Sting for human rights in 1988), which are advertised in *Daily News* and *Programme*; lesser events occur in the park or the smaller *Kisstadion*. Budapest's *Sportcsarnok* (see "Listings") is the place for skating and diverse **indoor sports**. En route from the Metro to any one of these, you'll see the **Népstadion inter-city bus terminal**, covering areas east of the Danube (see "Listings" below).

Abhorred by early puritanical Communists, **horse racing** and betting on the turf still exists in several Eastern European countries. Until recently, Magyar betters had to be satisfied with trotting races at the *Ügetöpálya* alongside Kerepesi út, starting at 2pm on Saturday and Sunday and at 4:30pm on Wednesday and Thursday. However, it's now possible to watch flat racing at the new *Lóversenytér* north of Budapest's EXPO Center; races are held on the same days at 2pm and 4pm. Bus #95 or trolleybus #80 from either Népstadion or Keleti Station will get you to the trotting track, but to reach the flat racing course at X, Dobi István u.10 it's easier to catch a #100 bus from the Örs vezér tere Metro terminal. The Hungarian Derby and other races are advertised in *Népsport*, *Daily News*, and *Programme*.

Cemeteries, Lowlife, and Seeing Stars

It's worth mentioning three of **Budapest's Cemeteries** if only for their historical associations. Some way into PESTLÖRINC Cemetery, a new memorial marks the **grave of Imre Nagy**, who was secretly executed in 1958 for his actions as Premier during the Uprising, and buried beneath plot 301 surrounded by murdered colleagues. Thirty-one years later they were exhumed and ceremonially reburied (June 16, 1989) as the Party prepared to acknowledge 1956 as a "popular awakening." By a twist of fate, Nagy's successor and betrayer **János Kádár** expired (July 6) hours before the Supreme Court posthumously acquitted Nagy of "counter-revolution." Now Kádár lies amid the **Pantheon of the Working Class Movement** in the spruce part of KEREPESI cemetery, near the tomb of **László Rajk**, his predecessor as Minister of the Interior in 1949. Kádár obtained Rajk's "confession," for which Rajk was shot—and then honorably reburied as a "party martyr" seven years later. Nearby are florid **nineteenth-century mausoleums**, some equally contoversial in their own day. Kossuth, who revolted against the Habsburgs; Batthyány, whom they executed for rebellion; and Deák, who engineered the *Ausgleich* between Hungary and the empire, are buried here; so too the great *diva* Lujza Blaha, the "Nightingale of Budapest." One can reach Kerepesi by bus #33 or tram #23/#24 from Baross tér, and buy a brochure locating the VIP tombs there. Devotees of **Béla Bartók** might make a pilgrimage to the FARKASRÉTI Cemetery in Buda's XI district, where the composer's remains were ceremonially reinterred on July 7, 1988 following their return from America.*

Between Kerepesi út and the József körút, the **VIII district** can have a seedy aspect. Although smartly dressed folk attend performances at the

---

*Bartók spent the last five years of his life there after fleeing Hungary's "regime of thieves and murderers" in 1940. His will forbade the erection of monuments in his honor back home so long as any street was named after Hitler or Mussolini.

Erkel Theater on Köztársaság tér, the area around Rákóczi tér and Bérkocsis utca is something of a **red light district,** and risky for women after nightfall. The Communists shut down all licensed brothels in 1950, and compelled many of the prostitutes to undergo "re-education through labor" at Dunaújváros, but they gradually drifted back into Budapest during the Sixties, at the same time as *digozok* or "amateurs" emerged to cater to the influx of Yugoslav and Italian tourists. Today there's a great divide between "hard currency," or cash-only prostitutes earning high fees and frequenting Belváros nightclubs, and the women of the VIII district, who cater to Hungarians and might service a man for the price of a bottle of pálinka.

Finally, a brief mention of the outer reaches of Üllői út, accessible by Metro line 3. There are weekly **discos** in the **Semmelweiss Medical University** (*SOTE*) high rise, near the Nagyvárad tér stop, while Budapest's second-largest park, the **NÉPLIGET,** has a **Planetarium** and a **Laser Theater** (see "Entertainments" below), 100 meters from the Népliget Metro.

Museums and Galleries

Almost invariably, Budapest's museums are open from Tuesday to Sunday, 9am–5pm or 10am–6pm. Admission is free or half price with a student card; no entry charges are made at weekends. Besides the places described in the text (on Castle Hill, Rózsadomb, and Deák tér; the Transport, Applied Arts, and Jewish museums; Óbuda's Roman ruins), the city's other museums include:

Ethnographical Museum (V, Kossuth tér 12) A diverse collection of Eskimo furs and kayaks, African instruments and barkcloth, totems and wonderfully carved Melanesian masks. Definitely worth a visit.

Museum of Fine Arts (Heroes' Square) Depending on the process of restoration you can see halls containing Egyptian funerary relics, Greek and Roman ceramics, and paintings and drawings by thirteenth- to twentieth-century European masters. Among the latter, big names include Rembrandt, Dürer, Leonardo, Bloc, Chagall, Rodin, Renoir, Picasso, and Toulouse-Lautrec.

Imre Varga Museum (III, Laktanya u.7) A sense of humor pervades these sheetmetal, iron, and bronze effigies of famous personages, fetchingly displayed indoors and outdoors. Varga is Hungary's foremost living sculptor.

Viktor Vasarely Museum (III, Fő tér 1) Eyeball-throbbing Op-Art paintings by a founder of the genre, perhaps short on imagination for all the meticulous illusionism. Exhibited in the former Zichy mansion.

Museum of Eastern Asiatic Art (Népköztársaság útja 103) Small but fascinating collection of Japanese and Indian silks, puppets, ivory, and the like, trawled by Ferenc Hopp on his many voyages east.

Tibetan Artifacts Beautiful scrolls, prayer shawls, and paintings of Buddhas gathered by **Sándor Körösi Csoma** (1784–1842), who tramped on foot to

Tibet, spent many years there and compiled the first Tibetan–English diction-ary (also on show). This exhibit changes its venue: try the Applied Arts, Fine Arts or Ethnographical museums.

China Museum (VI, Gorkij fasor 12) Closed when I inquired. Reputedly contains Chinese ceramics and bronzes; maybe worth a visit.

Kicselli Museum (III, Kicselli u:108) Historical paintings of Budapest and a nice selection of pictures by nineteenth- and twentieth-century Hungarian artists.

Post Office Museum (Népköztáraság útja 3) Blunderbusses and thigh-boots testify to mailmen's hard life during the eighteenth century. Hungarian stamps galore, an amusing compressed-air mail tube, and push-button displays of *Magyar Posta* in the telecommunications age.

Stamp Museum (VII, Hársfa u.47) More stamps, strictly for philatelists. (Wed 10am–6pm; Sat 10am–3pm; Sun 10am–2pm).

Nagytétény Museum (XXII, Csókási u.9) A long ride on bus #3 from Móricz Zs. körtér to see antique furniture in a rundown stately home.

Semmelweiss Medical Museum (I, Aprod u.1–3) Medical instruments through the ages, plus objects belonging to **Ignac Semmelweiss**, known as the "savior of mothers" for his discovery of the cause of puerperal fever, a disease up until then usually fatal for pregnant women.

If you're interested in Hungarian literature and can tolerate unintelligible captions, four **Literature Museums** and memorial rooms (*emlékszobá*) deserve a mention. **Sándor Petőfi** and **Attila József** are reverentially recalled at V, Károlyi u.16 and IX, Gát u.3; while **Endre Ady**—who many Magyars consider the greatest poet of the three—is commemorated at V, Veres u.4–6. **Nyugat** (West), the journal that published the Village Explorers and virtually every writer of note during the Twenties and Thirties—except for Attila, who the editor, Mihály Babits, hated—is the subject of another museum (Városmajor u.48) near Moszkva tér. As to the remaining half dozen museums, don't bother.

Budapest has a score of galleries, some fly-by-nights on Castle Hill, others long-established venues for **exhibitions of contemporary Hungarian art** or foreign artwork touring the country. The most prestigious are the *Műcsarnok* on Heroes' Square, the *Vigadó* beside the embankment, and the *Csontváry* on Vörösmarty tér. Artwork at the *Studió* (V, Bajcsy-Zsilinszky út 52), *Csók* (V, Váci u:25), *Derkovits* (Lenin krt.63), *Paal* (Rákóczi út 57B), and *Mednyánszky* (Tanács krt.26) galleries is more likely to be for sale, but prices are still prohibitive. However, many of these places sell **prints and posters** at affordable rates, and the Castle History Museum stocks a fine range of cheap facsimile **engravings** of old Hungarian towns. These make nice souve-nirs, as do some of the reproduction **postcards** sold by a shop beneath the mustard-colored pile on Deák tér—if you can find them amongst all the nudie cards and calendars.

Steam Baths and Swimming Pools

The best way to immerse yourself in Hungarian history is to wallow away an afternoon in one of Budapest's **thermal baths** (*Gyógyfürdö*). For 2000 years people have appreciated the relaxing and curative effects of the mineral water from the Buda Hills, currently gushing at a rate of about 70,000,000 liters per day, at temperatures of up to 80°C. The baths at Aquincum (and by implication, the custom of bathing) declined with the Roman empire, but interest revived after the Knights of Saint John built a hospice on the site of the present Rudas baths, and Elizabeth—the canonized daughter of Andrew II—cured lepers in the springs at the foot of Gellért Hill. The Turks consolidated the habit of bathing, since as Muslims they were obliged to wash five times daily in preparation for prayer. Nowadays, with the decline of coffeehouses as social centers, certain baths have become popular sites for tête-à-têtes between literary and artistic personages; some Hungarians go there just to spot the famous faces.

I felt like an initiate in a ceremony at the *Király Gyógyfürdö*, one of several **Turkish baths** which function in virtually unchanged form: dressed in the ritual apron, and ushered through a relentless sequence of hot and icy pools and the hands of a beefy masseuse before dropping onto the bed for the (wisely recommended) twenty minutes of recovery. The heat *is* exhausting, so plan nothing more rigorous than a good meal for the following two hours. A basic *gyógyfürdö* ticket—costing 30–70Ft—covers three hours in the pools, *szauna*, and steamrooms (*gözfürdö*), while supplementary tickets costing 20–30Ft are available for the tub baths (*kadfürdö*), mud baths (*iszapfürdö*), towels (*törülközö*), and *masszázs*. The latter is incredibly vigorous and refreshing and the masseurs and masseuses deserve a tip, for they work long hours on a near constant stream of clients for only 3000Ft a month. **Specialist treatments** for chronic disorders—cardiac, locomotor, gynecological and others—are offered by balneological clinics adjoining the baths, but referral to these is undertaken centrally, by *Danubius Travel* (V, Martinelli tér 8; ☎173-652).

The **Rudas Baths** (I, Döbrentei tér 9; ☎754-449) near the Erzsébet Bridge were built by Pasha Mustapha in 1566, and the interior strikingly resembles a chapel. Conspiratorial vaulted cloisters surround a sunken octagonal pool, at the top end of which once sat those *beys* anxious to avoid contamination by lesser mortals who arrived to sluice off the filth of lucre after haggling in the caravanserai which occupied the nearby river bank at that time. The Rudas has an adjoining swimming pool and offers drinking cures for stomach and respiratory complaints; all for **men only** and hence something of a gay venue.

The same springs feed the **Rác Baths** (Hadnagy u.8–10; ☎758-373), which squat beneath the Erzsébet Bridge overpass on the edge of the former Tabán district. Named after the Serbians or Rác people who lived here centuries ago, it has been much remodeled since the fifteenth century, but the octagonal pool ordered by Mustapha still remains (women only). The **Király Baths** farther to the north (Fő u.84; ☎153-000) are one of the friendliest establishments, open **for men** on Monday, Wednesday and Friday, and **for women** on Tuesday, Thursday and Saturday. Its nineteenth-century owners and namesake, the German König family, erected a trim neo-Classical facade which hides the dim warren of domed chambers dating from Mustapha's time.

The **Gellért Baths**—below the hill and adjoining the hotel of the same name—were built in 1913 and have a snob reputation which makes the staff as pompously aloof as the architecture. Perhaps it's a left over from the Thirties, when debutantes danced upon a glass floor laid over the pool, flood-lit from below, or because these days it's full of foreigners paying prices that Hungarians can't afford. If the thermal pool, flanked by carved pillars and lions' heads spouting mineral water, or the mud baths and **outdoor pool with artificial waves** don't appeal, at least take a peek at the feast of majolica tiles and mahogany in the foyer.

The pensioners who play chess seated in thermal pools lend a surreal touch to the **Széchenyi Baths** in the Városliget (Állatkerti krt.11). Hopefully, the restoration of the once-elegant baths founded by the geologist Zsigmondy Vilmos (who discovered the spring in 1895 and is commemorated by a statue near the entrance) should soon be completed. The triumph of figuring out the convoluted route to its contemporary, the **Lukács Baths** (II, Frankel Leó u:25–29), is quickly dispelled by the general dinginess and stench of sulfurous waters. Here is the National Institute for Rheumatology and Physiotherapy and, unofficially, the favorite winter haunt of the capital's gay men. However until restoration is completed, it might leave you scratching at some unwelcome souvenirs.

The **opening hours** of all the above are 6am–7pm, while baths other than the Rác, Rudas and Király have mixed pools and single-sex annexes for saunas, etc. In addition there are numerous **lidos**, notably the *Komjádi Béla* (III, Árpád fejedelem útja 8), the *Csillaghegyi* (III, Pusztakúti u.3), and the *National* on Margit Island. There, you'll also find the *Palatinus*, where **nude sunbathing** is possible on single-sex terraces (a habit that's also spreading to the Csillaghegyi baths, though without official sanction).

Eating and Drinking

Hungarians relish—and rarely separate—**eating and drinking**: at their best, keenly sensitive to the nuances of atmosphere, cuisine, and conversation; at their worst, gorging as if to efface the memory of subsistence diets or hunger (a fact of life for many people before the Sixties). Magyar cooking naturally predominates in Budapest, but the capital has a fair number of places devoted to foreign cuisine, and it's easy to get "international" dishes and fast food. Many restaurants feature **music** (and sometimes dancing) in the evenings, so **bars** are probably better suited for a quiet drink and likely to be cheaper, too.

Prices are usually displayed and by Western standards **costs** seem very reasonable indeed. Though your budget might preclude regular meals at Gundel's, it's likely to stretch to at least one binge in a top-flight place providing you're otherwise forint-conscious. Soups and salads are invariably cheap, and you'll save money by filling up with a meaty *bográcsgulyás* rather than a succession of snacks and pastries. The following categories—restaurants (for eating), taverns and brasseries (for drinking), and patisseries (for non-alcoholic drinks and a sweet tooth)—are pretty arbitrary, since all restaurants serve alcohol and all bar-type places some food, while *eszpresszó* feature both, plus coffee and pastries. Likewise, the order of places listed under each heading only roughly reflects the spectrum of prices (most expensive ones first).

If the place of your choice doesn't have a menu in German (which most waiters understand) or English, the **food and drink vocabulary** in *Basics* should suffice for **ordering meals**. Simply pointing to dishes on the menu (*étlap*) or on neighboring tables might result in some surprises.

Restaurants

Second class restaurants generally offer the widest choice of meals around midday, but in deluxe and first class establishments where reservations and formal dress are required, the range is greatest during the evening. By law all restaurants must provide a set *napi menü* (soup, main course, and dessert) priced lower than a combination of these ordered à la carte, and some also offer "tourist menus" or a rock-bottom "student menu" for about 80Ft. As an approximate guide to prices, the following list is broken into three categories. **Deluxe & first class restaurants** charge 500–1000Ft for a set three-course meal (including a glass or carafe of wine) and 400–850Ft for one of the richer main dishes chosen à la carte. Second class restaurants form a spectrum of **cheaper possibilities**: set meals can be priced as high as 500Ft (120–400Ft for a main course) or as low as 80Ft for the fixed menu (30–100Ft for a substantial single dish). At the lower end of that scale, prices may equal or even undercut **self-service joints**.

Deluxe and First Class Restaurants

Gundel, XIV, Állatkerti krt.2 (☎221-002). Named after the famous nineteenth-century restaurateur who founded it on the edge of City Park. The Zsolnai room is decorated with brilliant ceramics from Pécs. 9am–4pm & 7–10pm.

Fortuna, I, Fortuna u.4 (☎756-857). An elegant tavern on Castle Hill, specializing in pork cutlets *Budavári* or *Kedvessy* style, and *Gyulásleves* made with beefsteak. Dancing in the bar.

Bellevue, in the *Hotel Duna*, with a floor show, dancing, and a magnificent view of the river. In the same building there's also a deluxe *Csárda* with Hungarian dishes, wines, and music, and the elegant "international-style" *Rendezvous* restaurant. The latter is open for breakfast; all three function from 7pm until midnight.

Forum Grill, Barbecues and home-made pasta dishes prepared before your eyes between 4pm–2am. The *Hotel Forum* also contains the *Silhouette* restaurant. Noon–3pm & 6–11pm.

Étoile, XIII, Pozsonyi út 4 (☎122-242). The intended ambience is French, with accordian music in the evenings and specialties like hunter's style hare and trout with roasted almonds. Mon–Sat noon–3pm & 6pm–midnight; the club functions from noon until midnight.

Szecsuán, V, Roosevelt tér 5 (☎172-407). Luxurious Chinese restaurant where diners should expect to pay no less than 1000Ft. each for a spread. Mon–Thurs 11am–3pm & 7pm–midnight; Fri & Sat until 1am.

Astoria, V, Kossuth u.19 (☎173-411). Once a rendezvous for spies and journalists, the restaurant is nowadays overshadowed by the adjacent nightclub, renowned as a spot for rich foreigners and expensive prostitutes to meet.

Régi Országház, I, Országház u.17 (☎750-650). The "Old Parliament" is lodged in historic premises on Castle Hill, and boasts private rooms, a wine-cellar, and *Gypsy and Schrammel bands*. Daily 11am–1am.

Szászéves, V, Pesti Barnabás u.2 (☎183-608). Founded in the mid-nineteenth century, the "Hundred Years" restaurant is equally noted for its beautiful decor and game in wine and flambé dishes. Reservations are essential, particularly for garden tables.

Kárpátia, V, Károlyi M. u.4–8 (☎173-596). Likewise richly decorated in the Renaissance style, with limited seating. Magyar, Slovak, and Transylvanian recipes feature on the Carpathian menu.

Mátyás Pince, V, Március 15. tér 7 (☎181-650). First-class establishment with a slightly cheaper brasserie, both open until 1am. Sándor Lakatos, the doyen of *Gypsy violinists*, performs here. House treats include Dorozsma carp and Bridegroom's soup. Arrogant waiters.

Margitkert, II, Margit u:15 (☎354-791). Refurbished nineteenth-century establishment, with a garden, near Gül Baba's tomb. The Maître du métier specializes in old Hungarian recipes and meats roasted over charcoal; music by Lajos Boros's *Gypsy band*. Noon–midnight.

Vadrózsa, II, Pentelei u.12 (☎351-118). Fondue dishes and charcoal grills, served in a flower-filled garden. Daily 5pm–midnight; closed Mon.

Ménes Csárda, V, Apáczai Csere u:15 (☎170-803). Specializes in pork fillets with various garnishes. Noon–midnight (2am in high season), with *cimbalom music* in the evenings.

Arany hordó, Tárnok u.16. A restaurant, brasserie and wine-cellar occupying sixteenth-century premises on Castle Hill; exorbitant for Magyars but most tourists should find it affordable. Daily 10am–midnight.

Alabárdos, I, Országház u.2 (☎560-851). Vastly overpriced, indifferent food; the restaurant boasts medieval furnishings and a roaring open fire as the centerpiece.

Pest-Buda, I, Fortuna u.3 (☎360-768). One of the quieter places on Castle Hill; pricewise, roughly on a par with the others. Daily 4pm–midnight.

Cheaper Possibilities

Aranyszarvas, I, Szarvas tér 1. Just south of Castle Hill, its forte is game dishes; venison and boar dishes take an hour to prepare. *Schrammel music* every evening until closing at 1am.

Vendéglő a Vörös Postakocsihoz, IX, Ráday u:15 (☎176-756). Also at the pricier end of the spectrum, as you'd expect of a mahogany-paneled restaurant with a Maître du métier. Once the haunt of Gyula Krúdy, a famous writer, epicure, and toper, who relished dishes like bone marrow on toast, bacon stew with egg-barley, and beef and horse-radish soup. Daily 9am–11pm; Sun 9am–4pm.

Hungária, VII, Lenin krt.9-11 (☎221-648). An overpriced tourist-trap trading on its pre-war reputation as a haunt of writers and VIPs, rebuilt after its devastation during the Uprising. Daily 7am–10pm.

Emke Csárda, VII, Lenin krt.2 (☎220-689). Decked out with painted furniture, lace, and flowery murals in the "Kalocsa style," this csárda often hosts *IBUSZ*'s "Hungarian Evening," complete with a *Gypsy band* and a "folklore show" after 9pm. Costs reflect this.

Berlin, V, Szt. István krt.13 (☎316-533). Generous portions of Germanic and Magyar delicacies, with music by József Radics's *folk ensemble* in the main restaurant, open until midnight. There's also a beer cellar on the premises and a nightclub of sorts across the way (see below).

Vörös Kaviar, I, Ostrom u.19. Caviar at 500Ft. a shot, with blinis, chicken Kiev, beef stroganoff, and other Russian favorites for 100–400Ft. On the road from Moszkva tér up to the Vienna Gate.

Japan, VIII, Luther u.4–6 (☎143-427). A new, upscale restaurant with a Japanese chef, Yasushige Kikuchi, serving Sabu Sabu, Suki Yaki, Tokyo steak, and Sake. Open until midnight, on a sidestreet running between Rákóczi út and Köztársaság tér.

Sipos Halászkert, III, Fő tér 6 (☎888-745). Bearing the same name as a famous fish-restaurant founded in 1930 (see below), this upscale and touristy version has a garden. Music by *László Oláh's Gypsy band*. Noon–midnight.

Postakocsi, III, Fő tér 3 (☎351-159). An old coaching inn on the other side of the square, serving traditional Magyar haute cuisine.

Kis Kakukk, XIII, Pozsonyi út 12 (☎321-732). Superb venison and fowl dishes, plus all kinds of other Magyar specialties, but no music.

Vasmacska, III, Laktanya u.3–5 (☎887-123). Fish, poultry, and beef dishes. Around the corner from the *Postakocsi*, next door to the Varga Museum.

Napoletana, V, Petőfi tér. Pizzas, spaghetti and the like, make this a popular place with tourists. Just along from the 24-hr *IBUSZ* bureau and the *Duna Intercontinental*.

Capri Pizzeria, I, Krisztina krt.41. Italian and Austrian beer, inside the *Hotel Buda-Penta* (11am–11pm). Two cheaper pizzerias are listed below.

Szofia, V, Kossuth tér 13. Despite its name, this place to the north of Parliament offers few Bulgarian dishes, but the drab decor and surly service strike an authentically Sofian note.

Trombitas, II, Retek u.12 (☎351-374). A garden restaurant with a "folklore show" in the evening (200Ft admission), just off Moszkva tér.

Híd, IX, Ferenc krt.17 (☎337-994). Near the Petőfi Bridge. Booths on the ground floor and a gallery hung with paintings by Haranghy upstairs. Mainly fried meat dishes. 9am–11pm.

Vörös Sárkány, VI, Népköztársaság útja 80 (☎318-757). Chinese food, with a mixture of regional dishes (Cantonese, Szechuan etc), some of which don't come off very well. Noon–3pm & 6pm–1am.

Művész, XIII, Vígszínház u.5 (☎110-235). Good food, popular with artists from the Vígszínház Theater.

Royal, VII, Lenin krt.49. Hungarian and French cooking, accompanied by *Gypsy music*. Good value lunches in the *Hársfa Room*.

Lúdláb, VII, Lenin krt.39. Light music, open late. Closed Sun.

Hársfa, II, Vörös Hadsereg út 132 (☎164-002). Garden restaurant offering "hunters' suppers," accompanied by *Schrammel music* in the evenings. Daily noon–midnight, closed Mon.

Berliner Rathauskeller, VII, Dob u.31 (☎221-834). German-style place with *Schrammel music*. Entrance on Kazinczy utca. Daily noon–midnight.

Szeged, XI, Bartók út 1 (☎666-503). *Csárda*-style fish restaurant near the Hotel Gellért, with obtrusive *violin and cimbalom music*. Some like the place, others hate it. Daily 11am–1am.

Sipos Halászkert, on Lajos u, near the Roman Amphitheater (☎686-480). At the "Old" (*regi*) restaurant meals are equally good, but cheaper. Scruffier than its modern counterpart, with **Gypsy music** and a jolly atmosphere; undiscovered by tourists.

Matrózcsárda, IX, Alsórakpart. Likewise into fish dishes, as well as frogs and snails. Good food. Summer terrace on the Pest embankment, near the Szabadaság Bridge, within earshot of heavy trucks.

Öreghalász, IV, Árpád u:20 (☎694-192). Another second class fish restaurant with *Gypsy music* and singing. Mon–Fri 10am–midnight, Sat & Sun 10am–1am.

Fesztival, VI, Népkötársaság útja 11. *Gypsy music* and *dancing* during the evening, and hearty meals at reasonable prices. Mon–Sat 10am–1pm, Sun 10am–9pm.

Habana, VI, Bajcsy-Zsilinzsky út 21 (☎121-039). Believe it or not, this soothing hacienda-style establishment with its rum cocktails and *pollo* dishes used to be a dark and violent strip joint in the VIII district. Thoroughly recommended nowadays. Noon–midnight.

Thököly, XIV, Thököly út 80 (☎225-444). Delicious Transylvanian food, served piping-hot on a pleasant patio, or in the Renaissance-style interior, to the accompaniment of *Gypsy music*. Real value for money, to get there take bus #7 or tram #67 from Baross tér. Noon–midnight.

Bajkál, V, Semmelweiss u.1–3. Whether the Russian and regional dishes have improved is for you to discover; the restaurant (beside the Soviet Culture House) was closed for a total renovation during my last visit. Previously, the *Bajkál* tea rooms upstairs had been its best feature.

Mama Rosa I, Ostrom u.31. A reasonably priced pizzeria just downhill from the Vienna Gate.

Szicilai Ételbár, I, Fő u:40. A slightly cheaper option for Italian food, and another alternative to the overpriced restaurants on Castle Hill.

Pizza Udvar,VI, Bajcsy-Zsilinszky út 27. Handy if you want a pizza in Pest.

Horgásztanya I, Fő u.27. Mainly into fish, and likewise on the Watertown's mainstreet. Good food, but check your bill for errors. Noon–midnight.

Karczma Polska-Kis Royal, XII, Márvány u.19 (☎566-851). Polish nosh and drink, served outdoors during summer. Located off Alkotás utca, several blocks south of Déli Station.

Bukarest, XI, Bartók út 48 (☎666-580). A chance to enjoy cuisine that's restricted to the élite in Ceauşescu's Romania. Good value, but the premises—which include a brasserie and disco—are rather soulless. Popular with African students for some reason.

Aranyfácán, XII, Szilágyi Erzsébet fasor 33. Cheap, unpretentious Slovakian restaurant, with food revolving around liver, pork, or chicken, and a charming waiter, Juri.

Kislugas XII, Szilágyi E. fasor 77. Farther out along the avenue, a Serbian garden restaurant with a lugubrious cimbalom player.

Kis Papa, VII, Akácfa u.38 (☎422-587). Typically Hungarian food and atmosphere; reasonably priced.

Ezerjó, XIV, Állatkerti krt.3. Another outdoor spot, near the Széchenyi baths. Overpriced third-rate food and tacky music; a definite miss.

Csiki, IX, Angyal u.37 (☎136-627). A small place with a summer garden in Pest's Ferencváros district, featuring Transylvanian food and *Gypsy music* in the evenings. Noon–11pm.

Sirály, V, Bajcsy-Zsilinszky út 7. Handy, should hunger strike you on Engels tér. Daily 11am–midnight.

Arany Pince Vendéglő VII, Dob u.4. Recommended for its excellent cheap meals and the nice cellar premises. Mon–Sat 11am–11pm.

Hanna, VII, Dob u:35 (☎421-072). A humble kosher restaurant secreted in a courtyard of the Jewish quarter. Daily 11:30am–4pm, closed Sat.

Kiskacska Vendéglő VII, Dob u.26. A totally unkosher workers' eatery across the street.

Bohém Tanya Vendéglő VI, Paulay E. u.6. Another really cheap neighborhood joint, rightly called Bohemian, in a backstreet off Engels tér.

Góbé, VIII, József krt.28. The "Rascal" specializes in mutton dishes.

Kádár Étkezde, VII, Klauzál u:10. A small privately owned family restaurant just off Klauzál tér—good for lunch. Mon–Sat 11:30am–3:30pm.

Rézkakas Vendéglő V, Veres Pálné u.3. Likewise good value.

Fast food, Self-service, and Snack Bars

McDonald's, V, Régiposta u.2. Currently the sensation of Budapest, with non-stop lines from 9am–9pm, resulting in litter strewn about the once-pristine *korzó*.

Taverna Grill, V, Váci utca. Not far away, a pricier fast food joint with longer hours and slightly more varied fare (including pastries and bagels, sold from a stall).

Top Pipi Grill, V, Münnich F. u.22. In a similar vein but smaller. Daily 10am–6pm.

Anna Terássz Equally suitable for reading the papers over breakfast indoors, or observing life on Váci utca outside; but alcoholic drinks are costly.

Iázes Sarok, V, Bajcsy-Zsilinszky út 1. If you don't mind standing up, a nice place to breakfast on open-faced sandwiches, coffee, and juice, situated on the edge of Engels tér.

Badacsony, VIII, Üllői út 6. A gloomy self-service outlet for *Debreceni bogdány* cutlets and macaroni à la Milanese. Mon–Fri 10am–4:30pm, Sat & Sun 10am–3pm.

Halló, VII, Majakovszkij u.65. Pork chops stuffed with liver or pork steaks with mushrooms and spuds are house specialties. Self-service. 6:30am–9:30pm.

Torkos, IX, Mester u.12. Modern place where you watch the grills being prepared. Good range of salads.

Iázek utcája, VII, Lenin krt.49. Hamburgers, Hungarian and Mediterranean dishes, and a summer palm garden. The name means "Street of Tastes." 11:30am–8:30pm.

Unió, VIII, József krt.6–8. Basic self-service canteen, said to cook a mean *Szegedi* chicken goulash. Daily 6:30am–9:30pm.

Central, VII, Tanács krt.7. Big canteen just off Deák tér; very busy at lunch time. A place to sit outside and watch life on the Little Boulevard.

Lotto, VII, Rákóczi út 57. Cheap, basic Önkiszolgáló 200m from Keleti station. The bookshop opposite sells hiking maps.

Önkiszolgáló, XII, Alkotás út 7–9. Over the road and just uphill from Déli station. Daily 7am–9pm.

Taverns, Brasseries, Winecellars, and Beer Halls

It's difficult to draw the line between **taverns and brasseries** but the city has plenty of both, mainly in Pest. Foodwise the emphasis is on grills, roasts, or stews, and busy places are likely to resent visitors who are only interested in drinks. If this applies to you, it's better to look for **beer halls** (*söröző*), **wine bars, or wine cellars** (*borozó, borbár,* or *bor pince*). Szent István krt. has a few that keep **late hours**, but most places close around 10:30–11pm. As a rule of thumb, the farther from Pest's shopping district or Castle Hill, the lower the prices. Discovering **really cheap dives** for yourself adds to their appeal, and for this I'd suggest looking behind the Vásárcsarnok, around working class districts like Újpest or Csepel, or in the backstreets of the Jewish quarter.

Halászbástya, Reservations, smart clothes and a well-filled wallet are necessary to enjoy this nightspot occupying the lowest cloister of the Fishermen's Bastion, with its spectacular view of the waterfront.

Pepita Oroszlán, V, Váci u:40. A quiet place to drink above a reasonably priced restaurant at the unfashionable end of Váci utca, near the Eötvös Club. 11am–11pm.

Apostolok, V, Kigyó u.4–6. Just behind the Párizsi udvar, this splendidly Art Nouveau-cum-Gothic establishment is also a restaurant, making it difficult to just drink at peak times. Painted panels in one room depict the "lost towns" of the Kingdom of Hungary.

Háry, VIII, Bródy S. u:30a. A fairly upscale cellar-brasserie with *Gypsy music*, a wide range of wines, and rich food. 4pm–1am.

Bécsi, V, Eötvös L. u.8. Goes for a Viennese ambience (if not quite Viennese prices) as its name suggests. Viennese-style decor, Austrian beers, meat soup, Wienerschnitzel, and *gemütlich*.

Raabe Diele Bierkeller, V Szent István krt.13. Located beneath the *Berlin* restaurant, so you're encouraged to partake of a snack like *Berliner Eisbein* or stuffed turkey breast with cauliflower while a duet provides *Schrammel music* in the cellar. 4:30pm–midnight. The **Nirvana Bár** across the alleyway has overpriced drinks and a floor show that's in dubious taste. Daily 10pm–4am.

Kaltenberger, IX, Üllői út 37. A liveried doorman sets the tone for this smartly appointed beer cellar, a joint venture by Skála-Coop and the Kaltenberg Brewery. Good roasts and service. Entrance on Kinizsi utca; open until 11pm.

Söröző a Két Pisztolyhoz, IX, Tompa u.6. Another beer-hall of recent origin, boasting grills including flambéed "Robbers' meat" on a spit.

Bécsi, XIII, Sallai u.18. Austrian beers and snacks, just north of Szent István krt.

Tüköry, V, Rosenberg házaspár u:15. Notable for its *harp music* (Mon, Tues & Fri), meals and draft Pilsner. Mon–Fri 9am–midnight, closed Sat & Sun.

Krúdy, VIII, Krúdy u.19. Archetypal cellar-bistro with *Gypsy music*.

Erzsébet, VII, Lenin krt.48. A well-established brasserie on the Great Boulevard, divided into booths.

Lővér étterem, VI, Majakovszkij u:100. Besides its banqueting hall, brasserie, and wine-cellar (stocked with products of the Sopron region), the "Huntsman" also has a bowling alley.

Bowling Brasserie, XII, Alkotás u.63–67. With four automatic bowling lanes and Austrian beers, a kind of synthesized home away from home for German or American business types, or anyone else who cares to enter the *Hotel Novotel*. Mon–Fri 11am–11pm, Sat & Sun 11am–midnight.

Krisztina, XII, Krisztina krt:25. For roasts, snacks, and draft Wernesgrüner beer.

Wernesgrüner Söröző, Two more outlets for this bevy can be found at II, Bem rakpart 49 (on the Buda embankment) and V, Sörház u.7. (near Pest's Eötvös Club).

Taverna Borpince, V, Szabadsajtó út 5. Devoted to northern dishes and Eger wines (not just *Egri bikavér*).

Montmartre Brasserie, VI, Népköztársaság útja 47. Baguettes, Kronenburg beer and French music.

Pipács Bár, V, Aranykéz u.5. All-night tourists 'n' hookers bar, one block east of the Duna Intercontinental. As you'd expect, it's relatively expensive. 10pm–5am.

Gösser Söröző V, Régiposta u.4. Rather short on atmosphere for all its pub furnishings, Western music, and Gösser beer.

Tuborg Söröző Much the same goes for this set-up, which is next door to the *Central* self-service joint on Tanács krt.

Pepsi Bár, VIII, Üllői út 5. A dark little spot to swill cheap drinks until 5am, three minutes' lurch from Kálvin tér.

Bastyá Borozó, I, Székely u.2–4. A reasonably priced wine bar in the Watertown, featuring piano music. Daily 9am–10pm, closed Sat.

Tokaj Borbár, VI, Népköztársaság útja 20. The place for opera-goers to tipple Tokaj wines. Daily 9am–10pm.

Trojka, VI, Népköztársaság útja 28. Due to be reopened as a beer hall.

Pragai Wenczel Söröző VII, on Rákóczi út, between Blaha Lujza tér and Keleti pu. Good Czech food and beer.

Körúti Söröző VIII, József krt.85. Something of a student hangout, and good value whether you're eating or drinking.

Fregatt, V, Molnár u.26. Designed as an "English pub," which it partly resembles; Holsten beer and Fifties & Sixties *rock music*. Mon–Fri 10am–midnight, Sat & Sun 5pm–midnight.

Borsodi, V, Honvéd u.18. Two blocks east of Parliament, this humble place dispenses beer and hearty recipes from the Borsod region.

Dóm Söröző V, Szent István tér 2. A cheap bar near the Basilica.

Gresham Borozó, V, Merlég u.4. Just around the corner from the Szecsuán restaurant.

Villany Borozó, V, Gerlóczy u.13. Quiet bar in the backstreets off Tanács krt.

Te + Én, II, Bem rakpart 30. Café/bar with cocktails, a pool table and a youthful clientele; its name means "You & I."

Metropol, VII, Rákóczi út 58.

Numero Uno, IX, Gustav utca 9.

Patisseries, Coffee Houses, Tearooms, and Ice Cream

Daily life in Budapest is punctuated by the consumption of black coffee drunk from little glasses, and for anyone who can afford it, a pastry or ice cream. Together they make a quintessentially Central European interlude, although nowadays less prolonged than before the war, when Budapest's numerous **coffee houses** (*Kávéház*) were social clubs, home and haven for their respective clientele. Free newspapers were available to the regulars—writers, journalists, and lawyers (for whom the cafés were effectively "offices") or posing revolutionaries—with sympathy drinks or credit to those down on their luck. Today's *cukrászda* or **patisseries** generally have less mystique and more variety; ranging from stand-up places to establishments with Belle Époque decor and smoothly deferential service. Those listed below are the most atmospheric or famous; the majority also serve tea, a beverage best sampled in one of Pest's **tearooms**. Street vendors and many patisseries sell **ice cream** (*fagylalt*), but for the sheer range of flavors and the view of life on Felszabadulás tér you can't beat the *Jégbüfe* occupying one wall of the Párizsi Udvar.

Gerbeaud's, The flagship of the fleet, also known as *Vörösmarty*'s after its location on Vörösmarty tér. Tourists and wealthy Hungarians favor the elegant salon facing the square, where a coffee and a *torta* will set you back around 80Ft; the same rich pastries are cheaper in *Kis Gerbaud* around the corner, a less sumptuous annex. Daily 9am–9pm.

Atrium Terrace, Adjoining the *Atrium Hyatt*. Touristy but undeniably well-situated for breakfast, pastries or ice cream when the weather's fine. 6am–10pm.

Intermezzo, Likewise a summer terrace overlooking the Danube, with standards, clientele, and prices reflecting its attachment to the *Duna Intercontinental*. 9am–11pm.

Hauer cukrászda, VIII, Rákóczi út 49. Performances of the *Mignon Cabaret* on Fri (from 8:30pm until midnight depending on the duration of impromptu skits); tickets available from Népköztársaság útja 18, or perhaps at the door (☎142-002). Otherwise known for its cream- and fruit-filled pastries.

Lukacs, VI, Népköztársaság útja 70. The cakes are as good as Gerbeaud's but cheaper, the premises more somber than Belle Époque, with the dark patina of old woodwork. Daily 8am–9pm.

Müvész, VI, Népköztársaság útja 29 (same hours). Likewise posh; patronized by opera-goers more frequently than by the artistic clientele its name implies.

Angelika, I, Batthyány tér 7. A haunt of poets and writers beside the parish church of the Watertown district. 10am–10pm.

Gyöngyszem IX, Tolbuhin krt:15. Notable for its summer garden and piano music in the evenings; located on Kálvin tér. 8am–11pm.

Omnia cukrászda, VIII, Rákóczi út 67. Morello cherry cake and the oddly named *Lúdláb torta* (goose-foot cake) are specialties. Mon–Sat 8am–10pm, Sun 10am–8pm.

Pálma, VII, Lenin krt.36. In the first class category like all the above. Known for its creams in glasses and *parfait* specialties. 8am–10pm.

Korona, Dísz tér 16. A popular tourist trap on Castle Hill lacking in character despite being the venue for literary evenings. Daily 10am–9pm.

Ruszwurm's, Szentháromság tér 7. Excellent cakes, served production-line fashion to folks taking a break from sightseeing on Castle Hill, who crowd its diminutive interior. 10am–8pm.

Hungária Kávéház, VII, Lenin krt.9–11. As with the restaurant, now more of a tourist trap than a rendezvous for artists and writers. 7am–10pm.

Astoria Kávéház V, Kossuth u.19. Another annex to the hotel, furnished in the style of a traditional Pest coffee-house.

Híd, IX, Ferenc krt:15. Cosy place next door to the restaurant of the same name, serving cakes prepared on the spot. Daily 7am–10pm.

Rákóczi, VII, Rákóczi út 40. Dance music and late hours (until 2am); Chestnut purée (*gesztenyepure*) and a cake called *Eva torta* are both specialties.

Szimfónia, IX, Üllői út 65–67. Features *dance music* from 6pm–midnight.

Párizsi, VI, Népköztársaság útja 37. Palmy stand-up patisserie with a tempting range of French ice cream. Just beyond the *MÁV* office.

Diabetikus cukrászda, XI, József krt.71. Pastries and sweets prepared *for diabetics*. Located on the Great Boulevard (bus #12 or tram #4/#6).

Bajkál Tearoom, V, Semmelweiss u.1–3. Closed while the Russian restaurant below has a refit. Previously, the tearoom had a relaxed atmosphere and a fine range of brews. 7am–11pm.

Rétes, V, Bajcsy-Zsilinszky út 15. Cheap cakes and ices, eaten standing up.

Entertainments

Eating out could fairly be classified under **entertainments** such is the prevalence of music at restaurants, so apart from the options covered below you should bear in mind the places previously listed. Since full details of the **Budapest Spring Festival** (March) and the **Autumn Music Weeks** (from late Sept to late Oct) are available from *TOURINFORM* and publicized in *Daily News* and *Programme*, it's enough to say that the cream of Hungary's artists and top international acts make both star events in the capital's cultural year. There's hardly less in the way of concerts and the like during the summer months, and on **Constitution Day** (Aug 20) the population lines the embankments to watch a **Danube regatta** and, around 8pm, a fantastic display of **fireworks** (best seen from the Szabadság Bridge, but get there early to secure a place; for other **parades** see "Between the Boulevards" above). Finally, aspiring film critics should enjoy the four-day **Budapest Film Festival** which premiers (subtitled or dubbed) Hungarian and foreign pics. The attendant razzmatazz falls short of more profligate displays in Hollywood or Cannes, but the main difference is the weather, for at the beginning of February Budapest is blanketed with snow.

For Kids . . . and Adults

From Klauzál tér's scaled-down assault course to the folksy wooden see-saws and swings erected on Széchenyi-hegy in the XII district, there are **children's playgrounds** all over Budapest. Adults could combine a visit to Jubilemi Park on Gellért Hill with some sightseeing, or extract a series of childish diversions from **the Városliget** with its mock castle and old trains. Vidám Park **amusement park** nearby has a score of cheap rides, although some of them might seem pretty tame to progeny raised on western amusement parks. Farther along the road are the state **circus** and a **zoo** that's probably best avoided (see "Listings" below). While the **Waxworks** on Castle Hill (see "Castle Hill" above) could be just the thing for kids going through a gory phase, the choice of **museums** (see "Museums and Galleries" above) is probably best left to them.

The **Planetarium** near the entrance to the Népliget offers a variety of sensory experiences. Most tourist offices have a leaflet detailing seven or eight programs at the **Laser Theater** (☎344-513/ext.24), ranging from films of Genesis in action to music by Mussorgsky—all accompanied by lasers—not to mention the amusingly tacky *Lézerotika*, which avoids serious porn by substituting "green luminous pencils" whenever "the photographs and music fail to express the torments of the senses." Unsurprisingly, the Laser Theater has pushed astronomical shows into the background, although by prior arrangement (☎138-280) groups are treated to György Csaba's *Starry Rhapsody*, accompanied by a lecture on Magyar folk cosmology in the appropriate language. If you'd rather actually squint through a telescope, the *Uránia Observatory* (I, Sánc u.3b; ☎869-233) offers the chance to do so 6–10pm on clear nights.

The **Marcibányi tér Crafts Fair** (held on intermittent Sunday mornings as advertised in *Programme* and *Daily News*) has something for everyone: music, mime, and puppet shows, crafts demonstrations, and dancing—either inside the Cultural Center or on the square itself—plus a **childcare center.** From nearby Moszkva tér (see "North of Castle Hill" above) you can ride the **cog-wheel and Pioneers' Railway** up into the **Buda Hills,** wander around and then return to the city by **chair-lift** (see "The Buda Hills" above). Breezier still are the **riverboat cruises,** mostly organized by *IBUSZ*. Sightseeing boats charging 300Ft per head leave every hour 11am–6pm from the *Kossuth* boat-restaurant, moored north of the main Vigadó tér pier. This serves as the point of departure for ninety-minute pleasure cruises (at 10am, 3pm, 5:30pm & 8pm Mon–Fri; 11am on Sat & Sun), or rented twelve-person boats (2200Ft per hour). You can also go sightseeing by motorboat, starting from the *BKV* station alongside Petőfi tér at 9am. Disco and folklore cruises are covered below.

If the *Petőfi Csarnok* or *MOM* (see below) have nothing suitable for children, you could take them to a dance club or one of Budapest's two **puppet theaters**. Morning and matinée performances are for kids, while the evening's masked grotesqueries or renditions of Bartók's *The Wooden Prince* and *The Miraculous Mandarin* are intended for adults. Tickets and programs are available from the *Bábszínház* themselves, located at VI, Népápköztársaság útja 69 (☎215-200), and on Jókai tér. Thanks to the *Táncház* movement, most local Cultural Houses (*Művelődési Ház*) have **children's dance clubs** on Saturday afternoons or Sunday mornings, which foreigners are welcome to attend—just ask at the nearest center (addresses listed at the back of the *Budapest Atlasz*).

Guided Tours and Organized Nightlife

Readily available, free brochures detail the various **guided tours** offered by *Budapest Tourist* (V, Roosevelt tér 5; ☎173-555), *Omnibusz* (V, Engels tér; ☎172-511) or *IBUSZ*. You should make reservations in advance for evening programs (or the day before; see "Excursions from Budapest" below), but on other tours it's okay to pay at the assembly point, which is usually Engels tér bus terminal. Prices are normally reckoned in Deutschmarks, so the equivalent costs in dollars, below, are only approximate.

Since the Waxworks, Buda Hills, Gellért Baths, and city landmarks can all be visited at less expense on your own steam, I can't see the attraction of the "Hall of Fame," "Buda Hills," "City of Baths," or "Sightseeing by coach". But as the only way of seeing the building's splendid interior, it's worth considering a **tour of Parliament,** combined with a visit to the Mátyás Church ($8), or the National Gallery ($12). Tours start at Gate XII at 11am and 2pm unless they're cancelled because Parliament is in session.

IBUSZ **"Folklore evenings"** cost $32 per head inclusive of a meal and drinks. Two-hour folklore **cruises** depart from the Vigadó pier at 7:30pm every evening except Monday and Sunday (June 15–Sept 30), and on terra firma you can sign up for the "Goulash Party." If its name suggests fifty foreigners pigging out while quaintly-costumed musicians accompany some ghastly entertainer clasping a giant, imitation paprika plant to her bosom— well, that's more or less what transpires. The show at the *Trombitás* restaurant on Moszkva tér is livelier and much cheaper (200Ft)—but then dinner and drinks aren't included.

There's a much better program at the **MOM Cultural Center** (XII, Csörsz u.18; bus #4 from Engels tér or Clark Ádám tér), where visitors are encouraged to join in the whirling and stamping, which can be fun if you're in the mood. Events commence at 8:45pm, and tickets are available from the Municipal Cultural Center (XI, Fehérvári út 47; ☎811-360), *IBUSZ* or Budapest Tourist. Both the latter can also arrange a visit to *Cats, Les Misérables* (or whatever the latest attraction is), or a program which includes topless showgirls at *Maxims*, dancing at the *Casanova Bár*, and Gypsy music and bean soup on Castle Hill as a climax. **Budapest by Night** costs around $50, the **Theater Evening** $12–20.

Clubs, Gigs, and Táncház

Most young Magyars shun Budapest's premier **nightclubs** like a plutonium cocktail, dismissing them as "full of tourists and hookers." Certainly, the price of drinks is higher than anywhere else and the ambience has a palpable tackiness—but neither of these are necessarily deterrents. Admission charges can be as low as 80Ft at hotel nightclubs like the *Horoszkóp* (I, Krisztina krt:45), *Astoria* (V, Kossuth u.19), and *Joker bár* (II, Szilágyi E. fasor 47), which are liveliest between midnight and 4am. Admittance to the glittery world of *Maxims* (VII, Akácfa u.3; ☎227-858) and the *Moulin Rouge* (VI, Nagymező u.17; ☎124-492) requires advance reservations and costs rather more; the show combines elements of a James Last-style big band and a cabaret. At *Pipacs* (V, Aranykéz u.5) and the *Casanova* piano bar (I, Batthyány tér 4) the action is interpersonal, accompanied by slow dance music or the odd spot of disco beat. It's worth popping into Castle Hill's *Old Firenze* (open until 3am) merely to see the wonderfully kitschy decor—an improvement on the airport-lounge style *Fekete Macska* (IX, Knézits u.1; ☎170-496; until 1am).

Insofar as Budapest's youth scene has a single focus, the **Petőfi Csarnok** in the Városliget (☎424-327) is it. Despite its resemblance to the back of a supermarket, all sorts of **events** happen here: concerts, flea markets (Sat & Sun 9am–2pm), movies (Sun–Thurs 8:30pm) and most of all the Saturday night *Starlight Disco*, billed as Eastern Europe's largest. The 40–80Ft admission charge is pretty standard at Budapest **discos**, which open and fold often enough to make any list of them outdated within a couple of months; to identify those currently active, check the fliers around Váci u. and Felszabadulás tér. With the exception of Sunday evening's *Alternativ Disco* at the Vörösmarty Culture House (VIII, Golgota u.3), specializing in heavy metal and punk, most DJs play very loud "sampling" or last year's pop hits. Only two spots are open every night: the basement *Margit híd* (V, Szt. István krt.1; until 4am) and the Go-Go dancing *Rómaitó* (until midnight behind Római-Fürdő campground).

One needs a passport or ID card to enter discos at **student clubs**, where refreshments are limited to soft drinks (though it's possible to smuggle in a bottle of spirits). On the Buda side of town you'll find the *Kandó Kollegiumi klub* (III, Becsi út 104–108; Fri until 1am) and three places associated with the Technological University. Both the *R*- and the *E-klub* (XI, Egri József u.1; Fri & Sat 8–2pm) are named after outlying college blocks, just around the corner from the *Új Vár klub* (XI, Irinyi József u.42), which swings on most summer evenings. Across the river in Pest, Karl Marx University's *MKKE-klub* hosts a *Kalypso* disco on Tuesday, Thursday, Friday, and Saturday nights, and other events might occur in the courtyard of the block on Zsil utca, or at the bottom end of Ráday utca, farther to the south. Rather than fall for the *Disco Arato* on the corner of Felszabadulás tér and Váci utca (Fri–Sun 7pm–1am), hunt down the *Belvárosi Ifjúsági Ház* (V, Molnár u.8) or the *Eötvös klub* (V, Irányi u.29), both active on Friday and Saturday. On off nights of the week, there could be discos at the Telecommunications Youth Club (VII, Csengery u:10; Mon from 6:30pm) and the *SOTE klub* of Semmelweiss Medical University, near the Nagyvárad tér Metro (Thurs from 8pm).

By contrast with the *Young Artists' Club* (VI, Népköztársaság útja 108) with its plush premises and subsidized buffet, where visitors require a member to sign them in, **other clubs** fly by night, making transience part of their appeal. While these places advertise themselves by little posters on the lamposts around Felszabadulás tér, other events rely upon word of mouth—jazz **cruises** (from the Vigadó pier) or a secretive gig by a group in disfavor with the authorities, for example. Most discreet of all is the capital's **lesbian and gay scene**, revolving around the *Egyetem*, *Emke* and *Diófa* bars (see "Majakovszkij ucta" above) and certain baths (see "Steam Baths and Swimming Pools" above).

Fear of incurring official displeasure used to haunt **cabaret**, so that *Mikroszkóp* (VI, Nagymező u.22-24/☎313-322) went in for peckish—as opposed to biting—political satire. Nowadays, however, virtually all taboos have disappeared, but you won't be able to appreciate most of the new cabaret acts without speaking Hungarian. But the show at the *Hauer Cukrászda* (VIII, Rákóczi út 49), where actors and literati perform skits before an audience replete with the establishment's rich pastries, is tailored to tourists (Fri 8:30–10:30pm).

Although the *Kassák klub* (XIV, Uzsoki út 57) features **jazz** buffets on Wednesday and Sunday evenings from July 15 onwards, you'll have to check the posters and *Daily News* regarding **rock concerts**. Generally, new or "suspect" groups play the transient clubs, bands with their foot in the door (see *Basics*) the *E-klub* or the *Petőfi Csarnok*, and really big **foreign acts** merit an athletic stadium. To date, the *Népstadion* and *MTK Stadion* (VIII, Hungária krt.6) have served as venues for a Human Rights concert with Springsteen and Sting topping the bill; Joe Cocker, Talking Heads, Tina Turner, Elton John, Kiss, and Queen; and even Julio Iglesias (a long-awaited Black Sabbath concert was cancelled after the band played Bophuthatswana). As a rule, **tickets** can be obtained through the Central Booking Office (VI, Népköztársaság útja 18) or *Philharmonia* (V, Vörösmarty tér 1).

Lastly there's **folk music and dancing**, centered around "Dance Houses" or **Táncház**, which began as a reaction to foreign pop, but also to the kind of stereotyped folk art promoted during the 1950s. They aim to revive old Magyar instruments, tunes, and dances and get people *involved* in the process—a folkier-than-thou attitude isn't encouraged. You're welcome to attend the gatherings, which usually occur one evening a week around 8pm–midnight (the 50–100Ft admission fee contributes to new instruments and costumes). You can compare Magyar folk music and dances at the *Eötvös* and *Kassák* clubs (Wed & Thurs respectively), Almássy tér's *Téka Táncház* (Fri) or the *Kalamajka Táncház* on Molnár u. (Sat) with Greek and South Slav styles at the *Mahart klub* (V, Vigadó u.2; Fri from 7pm). Don't pass up a chance to hear the Young Gypsy Orchestra and Dance Company should they perform anywhere.

Opera, Ballet, Mime, and Classical Music

A box at the magnificently plush *Opera Ház* on Népköztársaság útja costs little over $8, so treat yourself to a grandiose gesture in keeping with the style of the place. Hungarians prefer their **opera** "old style," with lavish sets and costumes and histrionic performances which they interrupt with ovations after particularly bravura passages. Operas by Mozart, Verdi, Puccini, Wagner, and native composers are staged throughout the year, while during the Spring and Autumn festivals six to eight new productions are premiered. The most recent contemporary Hungarian opera to tour the West earned high praise for its lead singer, Adrienne Csengery, but little for its composer. You'll find the **box office** around the corner on Dalszínház u. (Tues–Sat 10am–2pm, 2:30–7pm, Sun 10am–1pm, 4–7pm).

The National Opera is also renowned for its **ballet** company, which fruitfully combines native and Russian choreography. Each year Budapest receives a visit from at least one premier company like the Bolshoi, if not exotic acts such as the Mongolian State Troupe, which appear at the *Erkel Theater* (VIII, Köztársaság tér; ☎330-540), commonly also a venue for **modern dance**. Győr's company always sells out when it comes to Budapest, but you shouldn't have too much difficulty getting tickets for the **mime** show at the *Színpad Centi* (Üllői út 45), or for performances of *Mandragora*. The latter is an adaption of Machiavelli's racy story, which is enacted by the Dominó Mime Ensemble in the precincts of Buda Castle (tickets from I, Úri u.62).

To inquire about performances of **classical music**, pay a visit to *Philharmonia* on Vörösmarty tér, which handles **reservations** in Budapest and the provinces (rock concerts included). Don't miss virtuoso performers like the cellist Miklós Perényi and the pianists Desző Ránki and Zoltán Kocsis (whose names will be given back to front, Hungarian style). The *Vigadó*, where Liszt, Brahms, and Dvořák once conducted, is the grandest venue, followed by the *Academy of Music* (VI, Liszt tér 1/☎420-179) whose Main Hall presents orchestral and chamber music on a more or less daily basis, while the more intimate Chamber Hall is generally used for performances of contemporary works. Smaller concerts may also take place in the Mátyás Church, the Erkel Theater, the *Pesti Rondella*, and the courtyard of the *Budapest Hilton* during summer and the festivals. *IBUSZ* organizes evening-trips to Martonvásár during the Beethoven Season of concerts (see *Lake Balaton and the Bakony*) for $10 a head.

Films and Plays

During the summer *Daily News* runs a column listing **films** in English, showing at the capital's movie theaters. Some of them are last year's hits or flops; others are American B-Movies dating back to the Forties. If you're hot on languages or prepared to sit through incomprehensible dialogs, the range of viewing can encompass Magyar *film noir*, Polish (*Lengyel*) sex comedies, Soviet (*Szovjet*) Westerns, or East German (*NDK*) cops 'n' robbers films— Budapest's movie theaters show them all. **Theater** makes slightly fewer concessions to the tourists, but throughout summertime and the two festivals there's a good chance of something that transcends the language barrier. Likely venues include the open-air *színház* on Margit Island, Városmajor Park, and the courtyard of the *Hilton Hotel* on Castle Hill. For details see *Daily News* or *Programme*.

Spectator Sports

The **Hungarian Grand Prix**, first held in 1986, now occurs every August. The **Formula 1** track, 20km northeast of the capital near MOGYORÓD, can be reached by the Hatvan road (M3), or special services provided during the Grand Prix—namely buses from the Árpád Bridge or trains from Keleti pu. to FÓT (then buses from there). Alternatively, board a Gödöllő-bound *HÉV* train at the terminal near Örs vezér tere (Metro 2) and alight at the twelfth stop, SZILASLIGET, which is 1800m northeast of the racetrack's entrance "C." Tickets (ranging in price 300–3000Ft.) and program details are available from *IBUSZ* or Budapest Tourist.

Some time during the spring (generally April) the **Budapest Marathon** takes place. The route runs from the Népstadion to Római-Fürdő and the event is thoroughly publicized and televised. Locals seem to get more excited about **soccer**, covered in *Népsport* and the sports sections of *Daily News* and *Programme*. International matches are held in the Népstadion, league games at smaller stadiums across the city. *Ferencváros* (named after the IX district where their stadium is located) is one of the city's leading clubs; their fans, alas, have a growing reputation for rowdiness and violence. For information about **horse-racing**, see "Beyond the Great Boulevard" above.

Shops and Markets

When it comes to shops, Budapest is streets ahead of other Eastern bloc capitals and several blocks behind the West; instead of food lines there are lines outside McDonald's and the Adidas shop. Váci utca, pin-up girl posters and Madonna-style jewelry aside, much of the merchandise and the stores themselves seem like Seventies left-overs—but don't let this deter you from **shopping**, which can yield some real bargains and be fun if you take breaks between combing department stores (many of which have snack bars). It's often worth investigating boutiques in poky courtyards off the main avenues, but avoid shopping on Saturday, when supermarkets are invariably crowded and most of the smaller shops are closed.

Shopping for Food

Whether you opt for the glossy *Skála-Metró* or a plebian *ABC*, **supermarkets** are the most accessible (and frequently the cheapest) source of food. Health foods like granola and dried fruits are making an appearance, but most travelers rely heavily on the cheese and salami counters, where you can order by the *deka*; *harminc deka* (300 grams) seems about the right quantity. Supermarkets are also good places for value-for-money souvenirs—wine, 40cl. bottles of spirits and tins of "Pride of Szeged" paprika. Outside regular **hours** (Mon–Fri 9am–7pm, 8pm on Thurs; Sat 9am–1pm) your best bets are the stores on Flórián tér, Kálvin tér, or Blaha L. tér, open till 3pm on Saturday; or the *Csarnok* on Batthyány tér, functioning until 5pm and from 7am–1pm on Sunday.

Shopping for **fruit and vegetables** it's wise to eschew the lead-tainted street-barrows in favor of *gyümölcs* and *zöldség* shops or the new *Vitamin Porta* outlets (V, Régiposta u.2 and VII, Rákóczi út 27a) that charge higher prices for out-of-season and imported produce (pineapples and bananas are luxuries here). Alternatively, track down one of Budapest's **markets**, known as *vásárcsarnok* or *piac* depending on whether they're held indoors or outside. Besides the well-known *Vásárcsarnok* on Tolbuhin krt. (see "Between the Boulevards" above), there's an equally atmospheric market hall between Rosenberg házaspár and Vadász utca, two blocks east of Liberty Square (open from 6:30am Mon–Fri; 7am–2pm on Sat; until 7pm on Wed). You'll find lively *piac* just off Moszkva tér; on Garay tér (a few blocks from Keleti Station) and Élmunkás tér (Metro line 3); at XIV, Bosnyák tér; and near Szent István tér in Újpest (popular with countryfolk). Opening **hours** are usually Monday 6am–5pm; Tuesday to Thursday, and Saturday, 6am–6pm; Friday 6am–7pm, but Élmunkás tér and the Fehérvári út market in the XI district also function on Sunday mornings. There's an **all-night** produce stall on Moskva tér.

Clothing and Accessories

With the exception of CCCP T-shirts, most of the stuff in Váci utca's **boutiques** is too passé or expensive to be worth considering, but there are bargains to be had elsewhere in Pest. Although you'll probably dislike much of the merchandise in places listed below (whose stocks have doubtless changed since our visit), when you finally hit upon something to your taste there's a good chance that it'll cost half—or even a third—of what you'd pay back home. This particularly applies to the five **department stores** (*áruház*) on Rákóczi út, where racks of trash can obscure stylish coats and quilted jackets.

On the same avenue you'll find street vendors, and a shop at no. 18, selling cheap **sunglasses** and **T-shirts** (*Békőt*, at Oktober 6. u.6 in the Belváros, is another source). The best place for **women's clothing** is probably *Éva* (Rákóczi út 33), particularly for reasonably priced sundresses, skirts, and jackets. For those with a couple of thousand forints to spare, two boutiques in the backstreets south of Kossuth utca specialize in silk clothing: *Péter* (V, Magyar u.1) and another branch of *Éva* (V, Váci u.57). Discontinued items could end up at the *Ádám & Éva* shop (V, Münnich F. u.5), but the *bizományi* and *alkami* outlets on Majakovszkij utca are usually more rewarding for **discount** clothes and footwear. Within the Belváros, **handbags** (from *Csángó*, Petőfi u.4) are cheaper than back home, though **shoes** (Tanács krt.16; *Corso Cipo*, Kossuth u.6) and **fashion jewelry** (*Sikk Divatszalo* facing the Post Office on Petőfi utca; *Black Mici*, Tanács krt.16) cost about the same.

Until *Ádám* (branches all over Pest) improves its **menswear** there's not much alternative to department store clothing or jeans (available everywhere). Two exceptions to this state of affairs are *Ciao Rigazzo*, selling cool menswear at Italian prices (V, Kossuth u.4), and *Tropical*, purveying tropically intense jackets and shirts (VI, Népköztársaság útja 46).

Records and Tapes

Whether you're in search of Beethoven conducted by von Karajan or Bruce Springsteen's latest, **records and tapes** are excellent value, retailing at half or one third of their Western price. Pricewise, there doesn't seem to be much difference between *zeneműbolt* ("musical culture") or *hanglemez* ("sounds") shops in the Belváros—on Petőfi and Váci u. and Vörösmarty tér—and those on Rákóczi út. Classical or World Music enthusiasts might also strike it lucky at the cultural centers of the USSR (V, Semmelweiss u.1–3), Czechoslovakia (V, Tanács krt:15), Bulgaria (on Népköztársaság útja), and the DDR (on Deák tér). The basement *Tropical Hanglemez* (V, Vadász u.19; Mon–Fri 1–6pm) specializes in reggae, cult groups, and **secondhand** oldies of all kinds.

At V, Fehérhajó u.5, near *TOURINFORM*, one can listen to the **Musical Collection of the Szabó Ervin library**.

Books and Newspapers

If you're looking for novels, coffee-table **books**, or Hungarian authors in foreign languages, the *Könyvesbolt* at Váci u.32 has the best range. It's also often crowded with tourists, so you might find it easier to browse at other bookshops—at Váci u.33, Petőfi u.2, Vörösmarty tér 4 and inside the Párizsi udvar. *Antikvárium* or **secondhand** bookshops at Váci u.28 & 75, Múzeum krt:15, Károlyi u.3, and on the corner of Deák tér and Bajcsy-Zsilinszky út, might yield the occasional find, but most of the books are in Magyar or German. However, collectors of antique volumes and prints can have a field day.

By contrast with other Eastern bloc capitals, where the only **Western newspapers** available are *L'Unita* or *The Morning Star*, Budapest permits the sale of the staunchly conservative *Times* (from England) and *International Herald Tribune*. The most up-to-date editions (one to two days old) arrive at the *Atrium Hyatt* and other top hotels before they hit the newsstands inside the Párizsi udvar and the Deák tér subway. For a change of tone (where you'll feel you should be having tea in England), visit the **library at the British Embassy** on Harmincad utca, open to readers (Mon–Fri 10am–12:45pm, 2:30–5:15pm). Unfortunately, even long-staying tourists aren't allowed to take books out, but the range of material that's available for perusal will expand with the inauguration of an **American Cultural Center** (Bajcsy-Zsilinszky út 40) at some future date.

Crafts and Antiques

Kalocsa embroidery, Herend china, and other "traditional" modern craftsware is marketed for high prices in dozens of shops on Castle Hill and Váci utca, and it's only the vendors of quilts and samplers from Transylvania that are prepared to bargain. In **antiques** shops east of Petőfi u. and Majakovszkij u., however, this is quite feasible; but with pre-war and Habsburg bric-a-brac so popular, you shouldn't expect to discover some unappreciated treasure. What you can hope to find is old silver, jewelry, glass, or china at an unexorbitant price.

Budget travelers should feel happier at **craft markets**, where woodcarvings or Szekszárd pottery (to name but two items) can be surprisingly cheap. If the Marczibányi tér fair (see "For kids" above) isn't on, consider taking the HEV out to SZENTENDRE, which has good craft markets most summer weekends, rather than risk disappointment at the often lackluster Petőfi Csarnok market (Sat & Sun 9am–2pm). Or investigate Budapest's sleazy *Ecseri* **flea market**, which sells everything from bike parts and Nazi-style boots to nineteenth-century peasant clothing and hand-carved pipes (I even saw an unwanted bust of Stalin!). Bargain hard and avoid being taken for a West German—they're always overcharged. The Ecseri lies along Nagykörösi út in Pest's XX district, reached by bus #54 from Boráros tér. (Mon–Fri 8am–4pm, Sat 8am–3pm). You might also run into antiques or crafts at the **Polish markets** which sometimes occur at ÉRD and GYÁL on the outskirts of Budapest. Mostly, however, these are orgies of tag sales, bartering and moneychanging (Accessible by "local" trains from Déli and Józsefváros station).

Excursions from Budapest

Given the frequency of buses and trains, there are dozens of feasible **excursions from the capital** to be made. Independent travelers should peruse the subsequent chapter introductions, explaining transportation from Budapest, which is also summarized in "Travel Details" at the end of each chapter. The more expensive alternative is to join trips **organized by IBUSZ or Omnibusz** (May 1–Oct 31, unless specified otherwise); because prices are reckoned in Deutschmarks, costs in dollars given below are only approximate.

Excursions **to the west bank of the Danube Bend** are mainly by bus. *IBUSZ*'s standard tour of Szentendre, Esztergom, and Visegrád leaves Engels tér at 9am on Tuesday, Friday, and Saturday (or on Sat only between Nov 1–April 30). At around $38, it's more expensive than *Omnibusz*'s tour of the same by open-topped omnibus ($30), which likewise includes lunch in Szentendre; the omnibus leaves Engels tér at 10am on Saturday and Sunday (July 1–Sept 30). A visit to the Village Museum, an inn and various galleries, followed by a jig around town by hansom cab, constitutes *IBUSZ*'s "Nostalgia Programme" in Szentendre; starting at Engels tér on Thursday at 9am, it costs $38. The same buys you a tour of the Bend by boat, with sightseeing and wine-tasting in Szentendre, and a brief walk in Visegrád. Boats depart from the Vigadó pier at 8:30am on Wednesday and Saturday.

Day excursions **to the Balaton** are also popular. The basic $48 tour includes sightseeing at Tihany and Badacsony, meals, wine-tasting, and a jaunt on the lake; buses leave Engels tér on Monday and Thursday at 8am, so you're advised to book the day before. This also applies to "Vintage in the Badacsony" ($60), with lunch, a boat ride with champagne, and all the grapes and wine that you can consume (departs Sat at 9am from Sept 1 to Oct 31). A $35 overnight wine-sampling binge in Cserkeszőllő is available from *Omnibusz* (between late-Sept and mid-Oct only), which also runs a two-night gastronomical and folklore program in Szarvas, for $45 (late-July to late-Aug only). If you don't feel up to the train journey and buying tickets, *IBUSZ* can arrange outings **to the Beethoven Concerts at Martonvásár** ($10) during the summer (see *Lake Balaton and the Bakony*). Finally, there are three **folklore/equestrian tours**, to Lajosmizse near Kecskemét ($50); Kalocsa and Solt ($60); and Tök, following a visit to the ruined thirteenth-century **Romanesque Church at Zsámbék** ($33).

Listings

Airlines Mostly in the Belváros. Tickets on *MALÉV* flights can be reserved at Váci u.1 (☎184-33) or Roosevelt tér 2. Foreign agencies are listed on p.25 of the *Budapest Atlasz*.

Airport Ferihegy, southeast of the city beyond Üllői út, is best reached by taxi or the half-hourly bus shuttle from Engels tér (20Ft). Terminal 1 (☎572-122) is used by foreign airlines and the Paris flights of *MALÉV*, which otherwise operates from Terminal 2 (☎579-123).

Amusement Park (*Vidám park*) Near the Circus on the edge of the Városliget; no Disneyland but plenty of things to ride. Daily April–Sept 10am–8pm, Sept–March 10am–7pm.

Banks Most OTP branches are open Mon–Fri 9am–4pm, but changing money and Traveller's Checks is easier at almost any tourist office (**24-hour service** at V, Petőfi tér 3). For information about receiving money transferred from abroad ring 389-133 or inquire at Alagút u.3 in the I district.

Barbers (*Férfi fodrász*) There's one near the *Tuborg Söröző* on Tanács krt.

Bicycle shops *Keravill* (VIII, József krt.41 & VII, Thököly út 2); *Mobil* (VI, Bajcsy-Zsilinszky út 59). Try Antal Szalai (VII, Wesselényi u.56; ☎215-826), József Fülöp (XIV, Erzsébet királyné útja 14; ☎635-619) or Zoltán Káraki (VII, Dózsa Gy. út 6; ☎411-183) for bike **repairs**.

Bus terminals The most useful are *Népstadion* (Metro line 2; ☎187-315) serving areas east of the Danube; *Engels tér*, in the Belváros, for buses to Transdanubia, Ferihegy Airport and foreign countries (☎182-122); and *Árpád híd* (Metro line 3), covering both banks of the Danube Bend. Destinations and schedules are given in "Travel Details."

Camping and Caravaning Club (IX, Kálvin tér 9;Mon–Fri 8am–4pm; ☎177-248). Can supply canoeing maps of the Danube, advise on equipment and arrange reductions for FICC members.

Car rental *IBUSZ/Avis* V, Martinelli tér 8 (☎184-158) and V, Petőfi tér 3 (☎185-707); *Fötaxi/HERTZ* VII, Kertész u.24–28 (7am–7pm daily; ☎221-471); *Volántourist* IX, Vaskapu u.16 (☎334-783); Ferihegy Airport (8am–8pm daily); and from most deluxe hotels.

Car repairs *Fiat* models at XII, Boldizsár út; *Ford & Mercedes* at XIII, Révész u.1–5 & 11; *Opel* at XX, Láva u:20; *Peugeot & Renault* at XI, Bicskei út 3; *Volkswagen* at XIII, Szabolcs u.34 and III, Mozaik u.3. For **repair information** try *AFIT* (Váci u.46B/☎409-560), for **spare parts** VII, Dózsa Gy. út 36. Ring 260-688 for the Magyar Auto Klub's **breakdown service** (7am–7pm daily) and 327-834 for 24-hour **tow-away**.

Circus (*Nagycirkusz*) On the north side of the Városliget. A good show, with a brilliant Cuban tightrope walker, notwithstanding the unnatural animal acts. Ring 428-300 for details of performances (Wed–Sun). ·

Dry cleaning Flórián tér shopping center, Párizsi u.1, Majakovszkij u:15 and the Skála-Metró department store. **Laundries** (*Patyolat*) take a minimum of 24 hours.

Embassies/consulates Austria VI, Benczúr u.16 (☎229-467); Bulgaria Népköztársaság útja 115 (☎220-836/824); Canada II, Budakeszi út 55 (365-728); China VI, Benczúr u.17 (☎224-872); Czechoslovakia XIV, Népstadion út 24 (☎636-600); Denmark II, Vérhalom u.12–6 (☎152-066); West Germany II, Ady u.18 (☎150-644); DDR XIV, Népstadion út 101–103 (☎635-275); Israel (currently represented by the Swedish consulate, see below); Netherlands XIV, Abonyi u.31 (☎228-432); Norway XII, Határór u:35 (☎665-161); Romania XIV, Thököly út 72 (☎426-941); Sweden XIV, Ajtósi sor 27A (☎229-800); UK V, Harmincad u.6 (☎182-888); USA V, Szabadság tér 12 (☎119-629); USSR Népköztársaság útja 104 (☎318-985); Yugoslavia VI, Dózsa Gy. út 92A (☎429-953).

Emergencies Ambulance: ☎04; Police: ☎07; Fire service: ☎05.

Hairdressers (*Női fodrász*) usually work from 7am–8pm on weekdays and until mid-afternoon on Sat. There's a cheap one at V, Münnich F. u.17.

Hospitals and Dentistry The *Városi Kórház*, V, Baross u.69–71 (☎690-666); for teeth the *Szájsebészeti Klinika, Stomatológiai Intézet* (VIII, Mária u.52/☎330-189); specialist clinics around *Klinikák* between Baross u. and Üllői út.

Embassies can recommend private, foreign language-speaking doctors and dentists.

Insurance *Állami Biztosító* (X, Üllői út 1) for information and policies, claims to XI, Hamzsabégi út 60.

International calls are best made from the **telephone and telegram bureau,** V, Petőfi u.17–19 (Mon–Fri 7am–9pm; Sat 7am–8pm; Sun 8am–1pm) or, more expensively, from deluxe hotels. If you run into problems dialing direct from a phone booth, try the international operator (☎09) or foreign language information service (☎172-200).

Lost property For items left on public transit, VII, Akácfa u.18 (Mon, Tues, Thurs 7am–4pm, Wed & Fri 7am–6:30pm; ☎226-613); otherwise Engels tér 5 (Mon 8am–6pm, Tues & Thurs 8am–5pm, Fri 8am–3pm; ☎174-691). Lost **passports** should be reported to *KEOKH* (VI, Rudas u:45/Mon 8am–4:30pm, Tues–Fri 8:30am–noon), and any found will be forwarded for collection there.

Motoring information The *Magyar Auto Klub*, II, Rómer Floris u.4A (☎152-040 & 666-040); *Fővinform* for traffic conditions in Budapest (☎171-173); *Útinform* (☎222-238) for national conditions.

Naturism is catching on with the support of the *Naturisták Egyesülete* (XIII, Kárpát u.8), a Naturist Union which runs a nudist camp at the DÉLEGYHÁZA LAKES, 40km southeast of Budapest (take route 51 or a train from the Józsefváros terminal). Closer at hand, nude sunbathing is permitted on the single-sex terraces of Margit Island's Palatinus baths, and just about acceptable on the fringes of the pool at Csillaghegyi.

Pharmacists 24-hour service on Felszabadulás tér; other branches open nights are advertised in the windows of other pharmacists. For herbal remedies try *Herbária*: VIII, Rákóczi út 49 and V, Bajcsy-Zsilinszky út 58.

Photomats Passport-sized photos available from V, Dorottya u.9; VIII, Somogyi B. u.18 (Mon–Fri 9am–6pm); the *KEOKH* office at Népköztársaság útja 12; or on the 3rd floor of the Corvin department store on Blaha Lujza tér.

Photographic equipment sold at Váci u.12; Párisi u.13; Szent István krt.3; Tanács krt.14, and Rákóczi út 34, most of which are in the Belváros.

Post Offices Main office/*poste restante* V, Petőfi u.13 (Mon–Fri 8am–6pm/ Sat 8am–2pm); 24-hour *postas* at VI, Lenin krt:105 and VIII, Baross tér 11c, near Nyugati and Keleti station, respectively.

Railroad stations More details of trains from each *pályaudvar (pu.)* appear in "Travel Details," but here's a résumé of destinations and practical matters. Basically, *Keleti pu.* is the point of departure for expresses to Miskolc and Békéscsaba, and Austria, East and West Germany, Switzerland, France, Czechoslovakia, Poland, Romania, the USSR, Yugoslavia, and Bulgaria. *Nyugati pu.* handles traffic for Szeged, Debrecen and Nyíregyháza, and additional services to Romania, Czechoslovakia and the DDR; while *Déli pu.*, chiefly serving Lake Balaton and Transdanubia, gets the most crowded during summer. Few visitors use *Józsefváros pu.* (south of Kerepesi Cemetery) to reach the western Great Plain or Délegyháza. Half a dozen services to Romania and/or Bulgaria make brief stopovers at *Kőbánya-Kispest* (Metro line

3) or the *Zugloá* station (bus #7 from Felszabadulás tér), but on these lines it's difficult to get the required seat reservations. Reservations and **international tickets** for other lines should be purchased 24–36 hours in advance, preferably at the *MÁV* booking office, VI, Népköztársaság útja 35 (Mon–Wed 9am–5pm,Thurs–Fri 9am–7pm; ☎228-049) where lines are shorter than at *Nemzetközi-jegy* (international tickets) counters in the stations. Budapest also has three **suburban HÉV lines**, running from Batthyány tér to Szentendre; from Örs vezér tere to Gödöllő; and from Boráros tér to Csepel Island.

Radio *Radio Danubius* (100.5, 103.3 & 102 MHz VHF) for pop, tourist information, and DJ patter. *Radio Petőfi* broadcasts the news in English (11am) and German (10:27am) on weekdays, and on Sat at 11:57am and 10:27am. Other broadcasts in foreign languages are advertised in *Daily News*.

Sports Indoor sports facilities and ice skating in the *Sportcsarnok*, near Népstadion soccer stadium. Tennis courts for hire at II, Nagykovácsi út (Mon–Fri 8am–2pm). Contact *Pegazus Tours* (V, Károlyi u.5/☎171-562) about horseback riding at the Petneházy school (II, Feketefej u./Tues–Sun 9am–7pm). You can also shoot pool at the *Eden Billiard Club* (I, Ostrom u.18; Mon–Fri 5pm–1am) or skittles at the *Bowling Brasserie* (XII, Alkotás u.63–67). During winter, it's possible to ski at Normafa and Jánoshegy in the Buda Hills. Various types of **equipment** can be rented from II, Török u.2; VI, Jókai tér 7 and VIII, József krt.67.

Zoo (*Állatkert*) Just north of the Városliget (May–Sept, 9am–dusk; closed Wed). Károly Kós's Turkish and Transylvanian style buildings look nice, but aren't fit accommodation for bird or beast. However, a long overdue renovation is currently underway.

festivals

Winter
The latest Magyar and foreign pictures get a showing at the four-day **Film Festival** at the **beginning of Feb**.

Spring
Music, drama and other events during the **Spring Festival** in **March**. Military parades and the like to commemorate Liberation Day on **April 4**. Floats, processions and speeches to mark International Workers' Day on **May 1**.

Summer
A Danube Regatta at noon and fireworks around 8pm on **Aug 20**, **Constitution Day**.

Autumn
From **late Sept to late Oct**, the Budapest **Music Weeks**. After years of being branded "counter-revolutionary," the Hungarian Uprising may well become an honored anniversary (**Oct 23**).

travel details

For reasons of space, these are limited to the most obvious destinations and routes.

Express trains
Aside from these daily *gyorsvonat* there are also numerous slower trains, listed in the

"Travel Details" of subsequent chapters. The following services are usually quicker than *Volán* buses.

From Déli Station to Balatonfüred (*Göcsej Express*; 2hr); Balatonszentgyörgy (*Kanizsa*; 2hr

45min); Dombóvár (*Somogy*, 2); Győr (*Ciklámen*, *Lővér*, 2); Pécs (*Baranya*, *Mecsek*, 3); Siófok (*Kanizsa*, 1hr 45min); Sopron (*Ciklámen*, *Lővér*, 3hr 30min); Szombathely (*Bakony-Őrség*, *Savaria*, 3hr 30min); Zalaegerszeg (*Göcsej*, 4).

From Keleti Station to Békéscsaba (*Csaba*, *Körös*, 3); Debrecen (*Tokaj*, 3hr 45min); Miskolc (*Borsod*, *Rákóczi*, *Tokaj*, 2).

From Nyugati Station to Debrecen (*Hajdú*, *Szabolcs*, 3); Kecskemét (*Napfény*, *Szeged*, 1hr 15min); Szeged (*Napfenány*, *Szeged*, 2hr 15min).

Intercity Volán buses

From Engels tér to Lake Balaton and Transdanubia: Balatonfüred (Mon–Fri 4:40pm, Sat 1:40pm); Dunaújváros; Győr (Fri–Sun 8:30am); Harkány; Hévíz (Mon–Sat 9:40am); Kaposvár; Keszthely (Mon–Fri 2pm); Pécs; Siklós; Siófok (8am & 12:40am daily); Sopron (7:40am & 2:50pm daily); Szekszárd; Székesfehérvár (10:40am daily, Mon–Fri 1:40 & 6:40pm); Szombathely (6am daily, Wed 8am); Veszprém (Mon–Fri 7:20 & 8:40am, Sat–Sun 9:40 & 11:40am, 12:10 & 1pm); Zalaegerszeg (Mon–Fri 5pm).

From Népstadion to Northern Hungary and the Great Plain: Baja (4 daily); Balassagyarmat (hourly); Békéscsaba (1 daily); Eger (9); Gyöngyös (15); Jósvafő for the Aggtelek Caves (1 daily at 6am); Kalocsa (7 daily); Kecskemét (15–20); Kiskunfélegyháza (8–10); Lillafüred (1); Mátrafüred (10); Siófok (1); Szeged (5); Vác (hourly).

From Árpád híd to the Danube Bend: Dobogókő; Dömös; Esztergom via the Bend (hourly) or Dorog (every 30min); Pomáz; Szentendre (hourly); Vác (every 30min); Visegrád (hourly).

International trains

Although destinations should remain the same, the departure times of express services below will doubtless change—so double check. Reservations are required on all routes, but it may not be possible to obtain them on trains leaving from Kőbánya-Kispest. This also applies to services from Zugló Station, which sometimes handles international traffic (though not at time of writing). The Vienna-bound Weiner Waltzer often runs late, so reserve sleepers on from Austria in Budapest. Also bring drinks, as the buffet staff overcharge quite shamelessly.

From Déli Station: *Adriactica* (to Zagreb & Rijeka; departs around 12:10pm); *Lehár* (Vienna; 6:30pm); *Maestral* (Zagreb, with connections for Split; 12:35pm).

From Keleti Station: *Arrabona* (Vienna; 7am); *Báthory* (Warsaw; 8pm); *Budapest–Moscow* (Kiev & Moscow; 11:15pm); *Dráva* (Zagreb, with connections for Venice & Rome; 6am); *Meridian* (Belgrade & Sofia 3:45pm; Bratislava 1:45pm); *Orient Express* (Vienna & Paris 9:45am; Bucharest 9pm); *Polonia* (Belgrade 6:25am; Katowice, Częstochowa & Warsaw 11:20pm); *Puskin* (Kiev & Moscow 11:40pm; Belgrade & Athens 12:50pm); *Rákóczi* (Košice & Propad Tatry; 6:10am); *Saxonia* (Prague & Dresden; 6:25pm); *Sofia–Berlin* (Berlin; 5:40pm); *Varsovia* (Bratislava, Warsaw & Gdansk; 5:25pm); *Wiener–Waltzer* (Vienna & Basel, with connections for Paris or Venice; 4:25pm).

From Kőbánya-Kispest Station: *Mamaia* (Cluj, Brașov & Constanța 10:20am; Prague 1:10pm); *Nord–Süd* (Cluj, Brașov, Ruse & Burgas 8:25am; Warsaw 11pm); *Trakia* (Cluj, Brașov & Varna 5:35am; Prague, Dresden & Berlin 9:20pm); *Transdanubium* (Brno & Prague 9:50pm; Timișoara, Ruse & Burgas 8am); *Vitosha* (Prague, Dresden & Berlin 7:45pm; Brașov, Ruse & Sofia 3:30am).

From Nyugati Station: *Amicus* (Prague; 8:25pm); *Balt–Orient* (Prague & Berlin 1:45pm; Bucharest 6pm); *Budapest–Chop* (6am); *Budapest–Leipzig* (9:25pm); *Hungaria* (Prague & Berlin; 7:45am); *Metropol* (Prague & Berlin; 5pm); *Nesebar* (Timișoara, Ruse & Varna; 12:20am); *Pannonia* (Bucharest & Sofia 6am; Prague & Berlin 11:45pm); *Tisza* (Kiev & Moscow; 8:15pm).

International buses

Here too, it's essential to verify departure schedules and make reservations.

From Engels tér to *Banská Bystrica* (Tues 4:30pm; Dec 13–March 21 only); *Bratislava* (6:25am daily); *Dubrovnik* (Mon 5:45am until Sept 26); *Dunajskastreda* (Mon, Wed, Fri & Sun 6:50am); *Galanta* (Tues, Thurs & Sun 6:50am); *Graz* (Wed 4:30pm; Sat 4:30pm from July 2–Sept 31); *Helsinki* (Wed & Fri 11am; July 1–Aug 27); *Komarnó* (6:50am daily; Wed 6:45am); *Kraków* (Wed 6:45am); *Levice* (Mon–Wed, Fri & Sun 6:30am; Wed, Thurs & Sat 4pm); *Lovran* (Fri 8pm until Sept 21); *Lučenec* (Wed 5pm); *Munich* (Thurs 6:30); *Nitra* (Wed & Sun 6:30am); *Opatija* (Fri 8pm until Sept 21); *Rimavska–Sobota* (Mon, Wed & Fri 6:10am);

Rovinj (Sat 8pm until Sept 24); *Rožňava* (6:10 daily); *Samorin* (Wed & Fri 6:50am); *Semmering* (Fri & Sun 6am); *Stockholm* (twice a month from June 21–Jan 17); *Subotica* (6:10 daily); *Tatranská Lomnica* (Sun 6am; April 2–Dec 18); *Venice* (Tues 6:30am until Sept 27); *Vienna* (7am daily; Fri 8am until Sept 2; Sun 3pm from July–Sept 16); *Zakopane* (Wed 6:45am); *Žilina* (Sat 4pm; June 4–Dec 17).

Hydrofoils to Vienna

From the Belgrád rakpart: Between April 1–26 and Sept 30–Oct 25, Mon, Wed & Fri at 9am. Between April 29–Sept 29, daily at 8pm (plus a 1pm service between July 1–Sept 1). The journey takes 5hr 30min.

MALÉV international flights

From Ferihegy Airport to Adelaide (1 weekly); Amsterdam (10); Athens (4); Atlanta (5); Barcelona (7); Basle (7); Beijing (7); Belgrade (2); Berlin (33); Bordeaux (10); Boston (7); Brussels (6); Bucharest (5); Chicago (5); Cologne (7); Copenhagen (8); Dresden (8); Dublin (6); Dusseldorf (14); Frankfurt (14); Geneva (7); Genoa (9); Hamburg (7); Hanover (7); Istanbul (6); Leipzig (12); Leningrad (6); Lisbon (7); London (7); Los Angeles (4); Luxembourg (7); Lyon (11); Madrid (6); Manchester (6); Marseille (7); Melbourne (5); Miami (6); Milan (7); Montreal (5); Moscow (37); Munich (14); New York (7); Oslo (9); Paris (11); Philadelphia (3); Prague (12); Rome (8); San Francisco (3); Stuttgart (7); Sydney (6); Toronto (6); Venice (5); Vienna (9); Warsaw (15); Washington (3); Zurich (14).

TELEPHONE CODE
BUDAPEST ☎1

CHAPTER TWO

THE DANUBE BEND

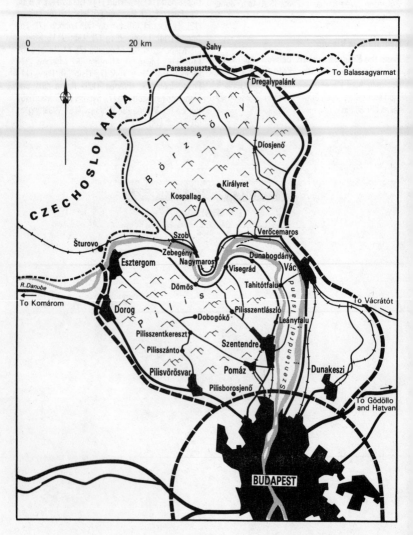

To escape Budapest's humid summers, people flock to the **Danube Bend** (*Dunakanyar*) north of the city, whose **scenery** was described by Bernard Newman as "one of the grandest" stretches of the 2000-mile river, "only outdone by the Kazan Gorge." Entering the Carpathian Basin, the Danube widens hugely, only to be forced by hills and mountains through a narrow, twisting valley—almost a U-turn, the "Bend"—before parting for the length of Szentendrei Island and flowing into Budapest. The **historic towns and ruins** of Szentendre, Esztergom, and Visegrád can be seen during a long day excursion to the west bank, but with the chance of **hiking** or **horseback riding** in the neighboring Pilis and Börzsöny highlands, it would be a shame not to linger.

Though increasing changes are being wrought by tourism, a greater threat to the Bend has been averted; in 1989 the government finally bowed to public opinion and ceased work on the hydro-electric dam at Nagymaros (see "Nagymaros and the Dam" below)—a victory for environmentalists and a milestone along the road to democracy.

THE WEST BANK

By building a line of *castrum* to keep the barbarians on the far side of the Danube in the second to third century, the Romans unwittingly staked out the sites of the future castles of Magyar kings, who had to repulse the Tartars, and the most tourist-ridden places along **the west bank** today. If crowds bother you, pick a day when *IBUSZ* isn't running **day excursions** (see "Excursions from Budapest" in *Budapest*), but remember that all the museums are shut on Monday. Baroque **Szentendre**, one hour's journey **by HÉV train** from Batthyány tér in Budapest, is the logical place to start; though with hourly **buses** from the capital's árpád híd terminal, you could travel directly to Visegrád (2hr) or Esztergom (2hr 30min). Services from Szentendre are equally frequent, so having seen the medieval ruins of **Visegrád** it's easy to push on up to **Esztergom**, the heart of Hungarian Catholicism.

Traveling **by boat** can be fun, but few travelers are laid back enough to last the five hours from Budapest to Esztergom. It's better to sail only part of the way, say between Visegrád and Esztergom (2hr), or the capital and Szentendre (1hr 30min). The 7:30am boat terminates at Szentendre, but subsequent services from Budapest's Vigadó tér pier continue upriver as far as Leányfalu (departing at 8:30am), Visegrád (10am), or Esztergom (2pm), calling at each west bank settlement en route. Boats for Vác (see "The East Bank" below) use a separate channel, the *Váci Duna ág*. Should you board the wrong boat, or feel like a change of scenery, there are regular car ferries between towns on opposite banks. Esztergom is also accessible **by train** (from Nyugati station) and by buses which take the quicker, un-scenic Dorog route. Sites in **the Pilis range** can be reached by bus from Esztergom, Szentendre, or Budapest's árpád híd terminal, though services are pretty irregular.

Szentendre

Having cleared the bus and HÉV terminals and found their way into its Baroque heart, visitors are seldom disappointed by **SZENTENDRE**. Ignoring the outlying housing projects and the rash of *Nosztalgia* and *Folklór* boutiques in the center, "Saint Andrew" seems a friendly maze of houses painted in fall colors, secretive gardens, and alleys leading to hilltop churches—the perfect spot for an artists' colony, which it is. Before the artists moved in during the 1900s, Szentendre owed its character largely to Serbian refugees from the Turks, who arrived in two waves. Their townhouses—now converted into galleries, shops, and cafés—form a set piece around **Fő tér**, a stage for musicians, mimes, and other **events** (every weekend from the end of June) and the place to embark on sightseeing tours by horse-drawn coach (150Ft). On August 20, the square also hosts a **pop concert**, in marked contrast to the **Serbian festival** held the previous day outside the Preobrazhenska Church.

The **Blagovestenszka Church**—whose iconostasis by Mikhail Zivkovič suggests the richness of the Serbs' artistry and faith—is first stop on the heritage trail, while just around the corner at Vastagh Gy. u.1 stands the wonderful **Margit Kovács Museum**, displaying the lifetime work of Hungary's greatest ceramicist, born in 1902. Her themes are legends, dreams, love, and motherhood, and the sculptures and reliefs never fail to delight visitors, though sadly her work is not very well known abroad. You will find that Szentendre is stuffed full of **galleries**, with three on Fő tér alone. The *Műhely* (Workshop) exhibits contemporary work, though most is rather tacky; next door is a gallery devoted to the drawings and paintings of **János Kmetty**, while across the square at no. 6 **the Ferenczy family** of artists gets full exposure. Károly, the father, pioneered Impressionism in Hungary, while his children Noemi and Beni branched out into textiles and bronzeware.

Climb one of the narrow *lépcső* above Fő Square in order to gain a fine view of Szentendre's steeply banked rooftops and gardens from the hilltop **Templom tér**, where frequent **crafts fairs** are held in order to help finance the restoration of the Parish Church. Opposite this, paintings whose fierce brush strokes and sketching were a challenge to the canons of neo-Classicism during the 1890s hang within the **Béla Czóbel Museum**, beyond which the spire of the **Serbian Orthodox Cathedral** pokes above a walled garden dark with trees. To see its iconostasis, by Vasilje Ostoic, you will have to rouse the sexton living in the house marked *plebánia csengője*, who can also open up the strongroom containing **ecclesiastical treasures** (5, Engels utca). But you should save some enthusiasm for the Village Museum (see below), since there's an excess of galleries. Listed in roughly descending order of interest, they exhibit **folk art** (Rákóczi u.1); outdoor **sculptures** (Ady u.7); work by former and current members of the Artists' Colony (Vörös Hadsereg út 51 and Vastagh Gy. u.2–5); the Barcsay Collection (Dumsta u:10); and eroded **Roman stonework** at 1, Dunakanyar körút.

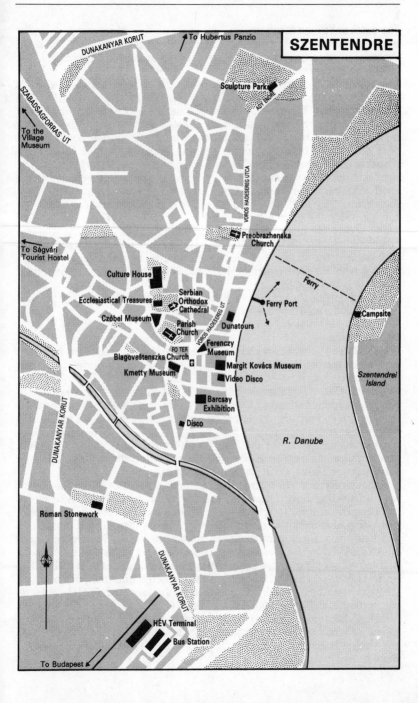

The outdoor Village Museum

By taking a bus from stand eight at the terminal some miles out along Szabadságforrás út, you can reach Szentendre's *Szabadteri Néprajzi Múzeum* or **Village Museum**. (Tues–Sun 9am–5pm, April 1–Oct 31). Though only two "regional units" are presently complete, the museum is intended to eventually include reconstructed villages from all over Hungary, and already it's a fascinating place. Downhill from the entrance is a composite village from Szabolcs-Szatmár county, culled from isolated settlements in the Erdőhát region (see *The Great Plain*). The brochure on sale at the gate points out the finer distinctions between humble peasant dwellings like the house from Kispalad, and the cottage from Uszka formerly occupied by petty squires, that rises amongst the barns and the woven pigstys (which could be erected on the spot). Rural carpenters could execute highly skilled work, as you can see from the circular "dry mill," the wooden belltower from Nemesborzova, and the carving inside the church from Mandok (on a hilltop). The second village "unit" seems far more regimented, originating from the ethnic German communities of the *Kisalföld* (Little Plain) in Transdanubia. Neatly aligned and whitewashed, the houses are filled with nick-nacks and embroidered samplers bearing homilies like "When the Hausfrau is capable, the clocks keep good time."

A stand outside the entrance sells good pancakes; walk 100m up the main road to find the stop for buses back into town.

Practicalities

While fast-food joints and **restaurants** are concentrated around the terminals and the center, **accommodation** is mainly in the north of town. The *Party* and *Danubius* hotels on Ady utca are the most expensive option, followed by the *Coca Cola* (Dunakanyar körút 50) and *Hubertus* (Tyukosdűlő 10) pensions, and then whatever **Dunatours** can arrange in the way of rooms. A lot of people end up *camping*, either on Szentendrei Island or on Pap Island to the north of town (accessible by ferry or bus, respectively). For travelers with transportation, heading for the Pilis, it's also worth mentioning two hostels, several miles out: *Ságvári Endre* and *Kőhegyi*. Reservations for both can be made through *Dunatours* in Szentendre or Budapest.

Although **ferries**, leaving from the pier nearest Dunatours, are the coolest way of **traveling north**, buses are quicker and more frequent. A new road has been constructed to relieve congestion on road 11 between Szentendre and Visegrád (which runs over the hills via Pilisszentlászló), but most buses still take the embankment route, as follows. Just after Szentendre comes **LEÁNYFALU**, a leafy resort (first popularized by writers like Zsigmond Móricz) with a **strand** and **campground** and ferries to POCSMEGYER on **SZENTENDREI ISLAND**. Leányfalu's villas merge with those of Tahitófalu, the next settlement, which has one foot on the mainland (**TAHI**, with two campgrounds and a *Fogadó*) and the other (**TÓFALU**, where the architect Mihály Pollack once resided) on Szentendrei Island, plus dozens of private rooms for rent. Continuing northwards, the land begins to rise, with orchards and vineyards flourishing around DUNABOGDÁNY, just before the Danube Bend heaves into sight . . .

Visegrád

When the hillsides start to plunge and the river twists, keep your eyes fixed on the mountains to the west for a first glimpse of the Castle of **VISEGRÁD**—"its upper walls stretching to the clouds floating in the sky, and the lower bastions reaching down as far as the river," still almost as it appeared to János Thuroczy in 1488. At that time, courtly life in Visegrád was nearing its apogee, and the palace of Mátyás and Beatrice (described to Pope Sixtus IV as a "*paradiso terrestri*") was famed throughout Europe, although the involuntary residence here of Vlad the Impaler must have soured the atmosphere somewhat during the previous decade. After the Turkish occupation Visegrád declined, turning into the humble village that it is today, but the basic layout of the Citadel on the hill, joined by ramparts to Soloman's Tower and the Water Bastion below, hasn't altered significantly since the thirteenth century, when Béla IV began fortifying the north against a recurrence of the Mongol invasion. The royal palace, however, disappeared, and until János Schulek unearthed one of the vaults in 1934, many doubted that it had ever existed.

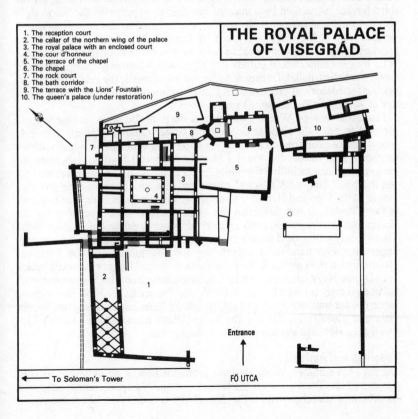

1. The reception court
2. The cellar of the northern wing of the palace
3. The royal palace with an enclosed court
4. The cour d'honneur
5. The terrace of the chapel
6. The chapel
7. The rock court
8. The bath corridor
9. The terrace with the Lions' Fountain
10. The queen's palace (under restoration)

THE ROYAL PALACE OF VISEGRÁD

Entrance

← To Soloman's Tower

FŐ UTCA

The Ruins of Visegrád

Now almost totally excavated, the **ruins of the Palace** are spread over four levels or terraces behind the gate of 27, Fő utca. Originally founded by the Angevin king Charles Robert, the Palace was the setting for the Visegrád Congress of 1335, attended by the monarchs of Central Europe and the Grandmaster of the Teutonic Knights, who failed to agree upon responses to the growing Habsburg threat, but managed to consume vast quantities of victuals, including 10,000 liters of wine. Nothing remains of Charles Robert's Palace, but the *cour d'honneur* built for his successor Louis, which provided the basis for subsequent building by Sigismund and later Mátyás Corvinus, is still to be seen on the second terrace. Its chief features are the pillastered Renaissance loggia and two panels from the *Hercules Fountain*; the upper story—which was made of wood, heavily carved and gilded—having long ago disappeared.

A legend has it that Beatrice, desiring to rule alone, eventually poisoned Mátyás, so a chalice with toxic contents might have passed between the King's and Queen's suites, which once stood beneath an overhang on the third terrace, separated by a magnificent chapel. Reportedly, the finest sight was the garden above the bath corridor, embellished by the *Lion Fountain*. A perfect copy of the original (carved by Ernő Szakál) bears Mátyás's raven crest and dozens of sleepy-looking lions for which the fountain is named, but is no longer connected to gutters and pipes which formerly channeled water down from the Citadel. During summer (as advertised), the ruins provide the setting for **historical pageants** and/or films intended to recreate the splendor of Visegrád's Renaissance heyday.

From the decrepit **Water Bastion** just north of the main landing stage, a rampart ascends the slope to **Soloman's Tower** (*Salamán torony*): a mighty hexagonal keep buttressed by concrete slabs, near which lies a ruined *castrum* on Sibrik Hill. Inside, the tower's **Mátyás Museum** houses finds from the excavated palace including the white Anjou Fountain of the Angevins and the red marble "Visegrád Madonna" carved by Tomaso Fiamberti (the probable maker of the Lion and Hercules Fountains). Visegrád's most dramatic feature is the **Citadel** on the mountain top, which served as a repository for the Hungarian crown jewels until a maid of honor treacherously stole them. Though only partly (and rather crudely) restored, the Citadel is still mightily impressive, commanding a superb view of Nagymaros and the Börzsöny Mountains on the east bank. You can reach it by the "Calvary" footpath which begins near Nagy Lajos utca, or by catching a bus (from the Mátyás statue on Salamán-torony u.) which follows the scenic Panorama út. From the parking lot on the summit, one road leads to the luxury *Hotel Silvanus* (. . ."mit Tennisplatz und disco"), the other to the **Nagy-Villám observation tower**, where you'll get a view that stretches into Czechoslovakia.

Lodgings and Activities

During high summer you might have problems finding **somewhere to stay**. Check out the Tourist Hostel (Salamán-torony u.5), a small campground with bunkhouses (Széchenyi u.7), the *Elte Hostel* (Fő u.117), and private rooms

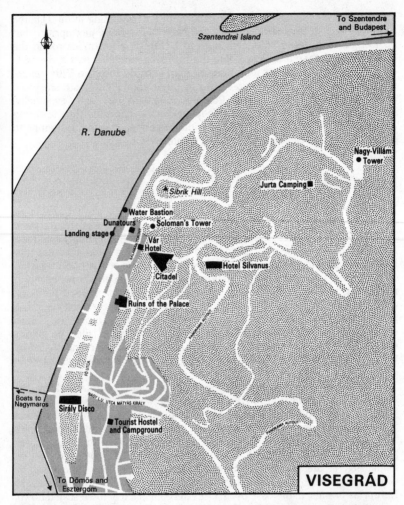

VISEGRÁD

(from Fő u:107, Széchenyi u:10 and *Dunatours*) before conceding defeat to *Jurta Camping*—with cabins and a restaurant like a Mongol stockade—or the *Hotel Silvanus*, both of which are expensive and only half-accessible by bus from below. Although **Dunatours** (Fő u.3) can arrange **pony trekking** in the Pilis Hills, most visitors venture no farther than the *Vár* and *Fekete Hollo* fish **restaurants** along the promenade, or the *Sirály* **disco** (8am–2pm Mon–Sat). For an evening's fun, the *Sirály* or summertime disco **cruises** (which leave the main landing stage as advertised) are much better value than the over-priced jazz-piano joint (by day an eszpresszó) at 30, Fő utca.

Besides regular **buses**, and three boats a day for Esztergom and Budapest (sailing from the main landing stage), a small **car-ferry** crosses from

Visegrád to Nagymaros every forty minutes or so. Swimming in the Danube continues despite the earthworks of the Nagymaros Dam, just upriver, but for a salubrious *strand* you need to go to **DÖMÖS**, a few miles round the Bend. Half-smothered in vegetation, the township straggles past a riverside campground and signposts indicating the start of **trails into the Pilis range**. By following the Malom tributary two to three kilometers upstream you'll reach a path that forks right (for the *Rám precipice* and, eventually, Dobogókő) and left (for the Vadallo Rocks beneath the towering *Prédikálószék*—a 641m crag that only the experienced should attempt to scale). Both hikes can be accomplished within a few hours.

Esztergom

Beautifully situated in a crook of the Danube facing Czechoslovakia, enclosed by glinting water and soft hills, **ESZTERGOM** is dominated by its great Basilica, whose dome is visible for miles around. The sight is richly symbolic, for although the royal court abandoned Esztergom for Buda after the thirteenth-century Mongol invasion, this has remained the center of **Hungarian Catholicism** since 1000, when Stephen (who was born and crowned here) imposed Christianity. Historically, Esztergom's Primates wielded temporal authority and the Church, like the *Natio*, represented the ancien régime—two powerful reasons for the Communists to fear them. During the Rákosi era Cardinal Mindszenty and hundreds of priests were jailed on phony charges, but efforts to liquidate the faith of 6,000,000 Magyars failed, and by the Seventies the Party was acknowledging that religion had a valid place in society.

Nowadays it tries to harness the patriotic spirit commanded by the Catholic church (which forms the oldest link between Hungary and Western Europe) by making concessions—as in 1988, when the anniversary rites of Saint Stephen's death were televised, 60,000 Magyars attended the Pope's "Mass for Eastern Europe" in Austria, and a **Papal visit** to Hungary was promised (possibly for 1990). Equally relevant to Esztergom, and just as tantalizing, is the prospect of **Soviet troop withdrawals**, announced by Gorbachev at the UN. If six tank divisions are withdrawn from Eastern Europe as promised, the base north of Esztergom is likely to be scaled down; a smaller camp beneath Peace Square, near the Basilica, was already being demolished during my last visit.

Around Town

Esztergom's focal point is the largest **Basilica** in Hungary; 118m long, 40m wide, capped by a dome 71.5m high. Though Kühneland and Packh supervized the initial construction, it was József Hild who completed the building in 1856. Its nave is on a massive scale, clad in marble, gilding, and mosaics, with a collection of saintly relics in the chapel to the right as you enter. Archbishop Tamás Bakócz, who commissioned the red marble **chapel** (with an altar by Florentine craftsmen) opposite, had designs on the Papacy, but ruined his chances when the crusade that he launched turned into the great peasant uprising of 1514. Visitors require a ticket to visit the **crypt** resembling a set from an old horror movie, with giant stone women flanking the stairway that descends to Archbishop Boehm's glass-encased mummy, and gloomy vaults full of prelates' tombs. The **treasury** (*kincstar*) entrance is north of the altar, and having seen its overpowering collection of bejewelled crooks and chalices, it's almost a relief to climb the seemingly endless stairway to the **belltower** (*harangtorony*) and cupola which, like the treasury, also require admission tickets. Pigeon droppings and grafitti decorate the bell-

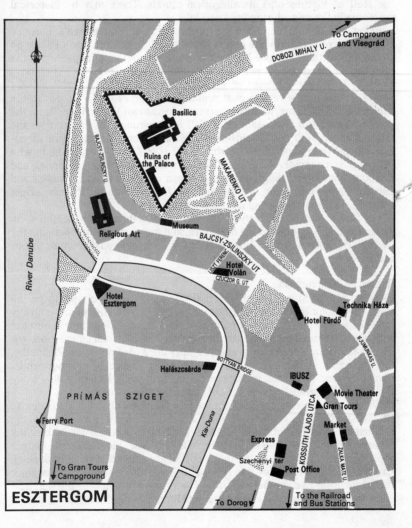

room and the heat is stifling inside the **cupola**, but all this is forgotten the moment you step outside and see the magnificent view.

On the same craggy plateau you'll find the **ruins of the medieval palace** once occupied by Béla III, the widowed Queen Beatrice, and sundry Archbishops. According to Djelalzade's boastful account, the Turks "knocked down idols in the churches and destroyed the symbols of infidelity and error" when they sacked Esztergom in 1543, but left intact the wheel and "narrow copper tube" which ingeniously piped up water from the Danube. Today, you can visit the remains of a **chapel** with a rose window and interior Byzantine-style frescoes, Beatrice's suite, and the study of Archbishop Vítez—known as the **Hall of Virtues** after its allegorical murals. There may be **historical pageants** in the ruins during June and July.

Below, the sound of choirs floats through the **Watertown**'s Baroque streets, where **religious art** gets a showing in the old Primate's Palace on Berényi utca (there's a nice *Vendéglő* at no. 4, nearby), and mementos of the poet **Bálint Balassi**, who perished while fighting the Turks on Esztergom's walls in 1594, are exhibited at 63, Bajcsy-Zsilinszky út. Bajcsy-Zsilinszky slopes around past several decent **restaurants** (the *Fürdő* for economy, the *Alabárdos* for its Transylvanian roast) into **downtown** Rákóczi tér. Here, the poky *Galeria Disco* (9pm–4am Fri & Sat) is just around the corner from the movie theater, with posters advertising Saturday and Sunday night **disco-cruises** to Visegrád plastered nearby. See *IBUSZ*, *Gran Tours*, or the **tourist office** on Széchenyi tér—a pleasant square with pavement cafés, *Express*, and the post office—regarding **concerts** of organ or choral music. If violins and fish are more your scene, try the outdoor *Halászcsárda* on **Prímás sziget** ("Bandleader island")—a popular spot with tourists.

The flamboyant, Moorish-style *Technika Háza* on Ifújmunkás utca, an open-air **market** halfway down Zalka Máté utca, and museums commemorating the Danube (Kölcsey u.2) and Mihály Babits (on Előhegy) could count as **minor attractions**.

Rooms and Moving On

Esztergom's rundown Tourist Hostel (Dobozi M. u.8) seems set to go the way of the notorious medieval *Baldhead Inn*, so private **rooms** are probably the cheapest option. It's easy to compare prices at the various tourist bureaus with *Express*'s rates for dormitory beds, since the four offices are close by. The *Hotel Volán* is fractionally cheaper than the *Fürdő* on Bajcsy-Zsilinszky, the *Esztergom* stylish and expensive. There's a choice of **campgrounds**. *Gran Tours*, on the island, is best reached on foot; while *Vadvirág*, 3km along the road to Visegrád, lies near the tail-end of the #6 bus-route.

With more frequent services from the **bus terminal** on Zalka Máté utca, to Budapest (via Dorog is quickest) and Komárom, it's not worth walking to the railroad station. Most of the Pilis range (see below) is accessible by bus, but hikers often start from **Vaskapu** in the hills 3km east of town; reserve beds in the *Túristaház* at Széchenyi tér 15 (or *IBUSZ* at Lenin körút 55 in Budapest). **Crossing into Czechoslovakia** is possible if you already have the visa; since the bridge from Esztergom to ŠTUROVO was never rebuilt after the war, travelers cross the Danube by a wallowing **car-ferry** (hourly during daylight).

The Pilis Range

Whether you describe them as mountains or hills, the **PILIS RANGE** (*Pilis hegység*) offers scope for **easy hiking** and a succession of fine views. The Pilis is directly accessible from Esztergom, Szentendre, and the árpád híd terminal in Budapest by bus, or you can hike up by various routes—for example, from Dömös to Dobogókő by way of the Rám precipice (see "Visegrád" above). If you're planning any walking, obtain a **map** that shows paths (*turistaút/foldút*), caves (*barlang*), and rain shelters (*esőház*) throughout the highlands.

Dobogókő, in the shadow of 756m-high Pilis-tető, is the only proper resort, and the deluxe *Hotel Nimrod* charges accordingly. The hostel is cheaper but liable to be full, so advance reservations (from *Dunatours*, V, Bajcsy-Zsilinszky út 17 in Budapest) are recommended. Roughly half the buses to Dobogókő pass by Kovács Canyon, where an ancient but still functioning lime kiln marks the start of **Pilisszentkereszt**. No trace remains of the Cistercian Monastery founded here during the Middle Ages, when the Pilis was a royal hunting ground. Other tourist hostels (marked *th.* on maps) exist in the southern Pilis: *Stromfeld Aurel*, one and a half kilometers north of **Pilisborosjenő**, and *Csikovári*, west of Pomáz.

Many of the inhabitants of **POMÁZ** are of Serb or Croatian extraction, giving a different flavor to the local Táncház, where the **Vujicsics Ensemble** meets. Named after its founder, Tihamer Vujicsics, who died in 1975, the Ensemble plays **South Slav music**. If you hear of a concert (which might be advertised in Szentendre), Pomáz is easily reached by HÉV train or bus from Budapest or Szentendre.

THE EAST BANK

The **east bank** is less monumental than its counterpart (**Vác** is the only sizeable town), but all things considered, visitors should be amply compensated by the scenery around **Zebegény** and **Nagymaros**. Like other settlements nestled beneath the craggy, wooded **Börzsöny range**, they're the starting points for well-marked trails opening up the possibility of encounters with wildlife in the highlands.

Getting There, Dunakeszi, and Vácrátót

Starting **from Budapest**, you can reach anywhere along the east bank within an hour or two by train from Nyugati station, or bus from the árpád híd terminal. The slower alternative is to sail from Budapest's Vigadó tér pier to Vác (2hr 30min), or on to Nagymaros, Zebegény, and Esztergom; the boat departs at 7am on weekdays, 6:45am at weekends.

Two sites might possibly induce you not to head straight for Vác. **DUNAKESZI**, just outside the capital, is the home of the **Alag Riding School**, patronized by Budapest's diplomatic corps. Less illustrious mortals may join the cross-country rides (held weekly during Sept, Oct, and Nov) providing that they have some equestrian experience and that they book in advance—for details, contact *Pegazus Tours* in Budapest (V, Károlyi M. u.5/ ☎171-552) or the *Magyar Loverseny Vallalat* in Dunakeszi (☎41-656). You will find a trailer-**campground** beside the Danube, north of *Dunatours* on Barátság út.

At **VÁCRÁTÓT** you can visit the lovely **botanical gardens** founded by a nineteenth-century Count Vigyázó, who subsequently bequeathed them to the Hungarian Academy of Sciences. Trains leaving Nyugati station around 7:20, 9:30, & 11:30am take one and a quarter hours to reach Vácrátót, which is also accessible by bus or rail from Vác. Services along the branch line from Vácrátót to Aszód (12:30am & 2:40pm) enable you to change lines and head north **towards Balassagyarmat** in the Cserhát Mountains.

Vác

The inexorable roll and swell of the Danube swept away the discouraging picture of **VÁC** conjured up by my Budapest friends, colored by the town's once notorious, though now long-defunct, prison. *IBUSZ* (Széchenyi u.14) are currently busy polishing up a more respectable past, and though you're unlikely to spend more than an afternoon here, they can direct visitors to the *Tabán panzió* or arrange private **lodgings.** Orientation is fairly simple, since Széchenyi utca runs from the **railroad and bus terminals** up to Marcius 15. tér in the center, and from there Bartók u. leads westwards to the **waterfront**.

Barring the concealed entrance in the middle of the tér which leads to a medieval **wine cellar** where you can drink to the accompaniment of Gypsy music, Vác's Belváros is characterized by worthy buildings and relics of ecclesiastical zeal. Hungary's first Institute for the Deaf and Dumb occupies the former Bishop's Palace at no. 6, while patriarchal justice is symbolized on the central gable of the Town Hall (no. 11) by two prostrate females, one bearing the Hungarian emblem, the other the Migazzi coat-of-arms. **Bishop Migazzi** was the moving force behind Vác's eighteenth-century revival, an ambitious prelate who also served as Archbishop of Vienna. When Empress Maria Theresa proposed to visit Vác in 1764 he planned theatrical façades to hide the town's dismal housing, but settled for commissioning Isadore Canevale to design an incongruous **Triumphal Arch** on Köztársaság út, from which Habsburg imperial heads—including Maria Theresa's—grimace a stony welcome.

The arch flanks one windowless face of **Vác Prison**, hung with plaques commemorating Communists killed here during Admiral Horthy's regime, though none bear witness either to the political prisoners tortured during the Rákosi era, or their dramatic mass escape in 1956. Thrown into panic by reports from Budapest where their colleagues were "hunted down like animals, hung on trees, or just beaten to death by passers-by," the *ÁVH* donned civilian clothing and mounted guns on the rooftop, fermenting rumors amongst the prisoners, whose hopes had been raised by snatches of patriotic songs overheard from the streets outside. A glimpse of Hungarian flags with the Soviet emblem cut from the center provided the spark: a guard was overpowered, locks were shot off, and the prisoners burst free amid the bluster of machine-gun fire.

Rather than retrace your steps along Köztársaság útja, dip down behind the prison to the **riverside promenade**—its three sections named after the composer Liszt and the poets Ady and József—which runs the length of town. On Liszt sétány the *Halászkert* serves delicious spicy fish dishes, while beyond lies a flashy indoor swimming pool. From Ady sétány, Rév köz climbs up to the Trinity statue which lends its name to Szentháromság tér. Skip the monastery and church of the Piarists (a Catholic order founded during the sixteenth century) to visit the **market** behind them, or turn right for Konstantin square and the museum.

Squat, ugly, and impressive only in size, the neo-Classical **Cathedral** dominating the square is more a sign of Migazzi's worldliness than an invitation to celestial heights. Gigantic Corinthian columns topped with crumbling statues guard the entrance to an interior thankfully brightened by Maulbertsch's frescoes—particularly the exuberant *Meeting of Mary and Elizabeth* above the altar. It's worth looking, too, at the exquisitely embroidered chasubles and intricate gold filigree in the **treasury** before crossing over to the gardens surrounding a former palace, which open onto Vak Bottyán tér. From here a short walk along Múzeum u. leads to the **Local History Museum** (Tues–Sun 10am–noon, 1–5pm). The pre-Turkish era is reduced to a sorry collection of broken masonry, silver coins from Vác's fourteenth-century royal mint, and some lovely, though fragmented, mosaics. Other displays document the development of craft guilds and the 1848 revolution with Hungarian captions, and there's also weaponry and paintings of nineteenth-century markets to look at.

Moving On

From Vác, it's possible to catch a bus or train (5–7 departures daily) northwards through the Börzsöny to Balassagyarmat, enabling you to spend the night in sleepy Diósjenő (see below). Buses to other **villages in the Börzsöny** follow such roundabout routes that hitching or walking might be a quicker means of getting there. The more frequent buses and trains traveling **up the east bank** stop at every settlement en route to Szob, while riverboats call at Verőcemaros, Nagymaros, and Zebegény (see below). Not content with his work in Vác, Migazzi plumped for another Baroque church and a summer mansion at **VERŐCEMAROS**, a nondescript village with two cheap hotels, the *Béke fogadó* and a *panzió* at árpád u.65—and a memorial museum in the home of the late ceramicist Géza Gorka. One train stop farther north at *VERŐCEMAROS-FELSŐ/KISMAROS*, an **International Youth Camp** run by Express rents cottages, tent space, and sporting equipment from behind the terminal of the *Kis-vasút*, a **miniature railroad** leading up to Királyrét in the Börzsöny (described at the end of this chapter).

Nagymaros and the Dam

A quietly prosperous village with an air of faded grandeur (nobles lived here in the age of royal Visegrad), **NAGYMAROS** seems an unlikely focus for years of environmental protest, let alone a rift with the Czechoslovak government. The cause isn't Nagymaros itself, where the one record shop's mediocre funk and a drunk's ejection from an *italbolt* used to count as major disturbances, but a short way upriver, the site of earthenworks and access roads.

A joint venture by the Czech and Hungarian governments of the early 1980s, largely financed by Austria (where a similar scheme was thwarted by environmentalists), the **Gabčikovo-Nagymaros Hydro-electric Barrage** was intended to harness 200km of river, diverting it for 25km, and tapping it for energy with two dams. Whereas the Czech dam at Gabčikovo on the upper Danube is almost finished, work at Nagymaros was suspended in May 1989 after five years' **opposition** by *Duna Kör* (Danube Circle), and finally abandoned in November of the same year. The ensuing diplomatic tiff over financial liability is yet another obstacle to progress on the real issue: cleaning up a sick river, which requires the cooperation of all the Danubian countries.

The dam aside, Nagymaros's claims to attention are muted. The Gothic church by the **railroad station** had a facelift in the eighteenth century; whitewashed houses straggle up the hillside; and social life centers around the pastry shops and leafy squares. From the station, duck under the bridge to reach the main road; then turn right for the **campground** (2km away on the riverbank, with cottages), or head on up the main backstreet. One kilometer uphill, the path divides at a parking lot—one fork heads south to Hegyestető, where you can enjoy a **panoramic view of the Bend**, the other heads up **into the Börzsöny**. There, one can sojourn amongst the beech woods at the *Törökmező* hostel: 5km away by footpath (marked with blue signs), or slightly longer if you follow the Panoramaút road. Beds should be reserved in advance at *IBUSZ* in Budapest (V, Lenin krt:55).

Zebegény, Szob, and Crossing into Czechoslovakia

At **ZEBEGÉNY** the Danube turns south before taking the Bend. The scenery here has attracted painters since **István Szőnyi** (1894–1960) first put brush to canvas, and his house at Bartók út 7 is now a **museum** and the venue of an annual summer **International Art School**, offering two- to four-week courses in sculpture, ceramics, enamelling, graphics, and painting. If you're interested, write early for a prospectus, since the deadline for applications is May 1. There's no accommodation (take the boat across to Visegrád or Esztergom or use the Nagymaros campground) unless you're willing to walk for a few hours up to the Törökmező Hostel, which is also accessible from Nagymaros.

Depots, dust, and dead-end depression sum up most frontier posts, and **SZOB** is no exception. Tourists rarely come here (and, again, there's no accommodation), but for chance visitors the **Börzsöny Museum** (Hámán u.14) is ready with peasant costumes, carved tombstones, and a piece of the petrified primeval tree found at Ipolytarnoc (which is distributed amongst half a dozen provincial museums).

Anyone planning to take a local train across from Szob **into Czechoslovakia** must acquire a visa from the Czech consulate in Budapest beforehand, as must motorists, who have to cross the border farther to the northeast, at **PARASSAPUSZTA** (open 24 hours). Czech border guards have a reputation for stringent customs searches and turning away "punk" or "hippy" travelers—whether they mellow as the winds of *glasnost* reach Prague remains to be seen. The road from Szob follows the Ipoly River demarcating the frontier—where a pimply guard accosted me with, "Hey baby, passport!"—before joining route two at Parassapuszta; **DRÉGELYPALÁNK**, a neighboring village, is on the Vác–Diósjenő–Balassagyarmat line (trains roughly every two hours).

Walking in the Börzsöny

The **BÖRZSÖNY RANGE** sees few visitors despite its scattering of hostels and forest footpaths, and the abundance of rabbits, pheasants, and deer, watched by circling eagles. Though the frontier zone should be avoided, it's otherwise feasible to camp rough here, but most of the following sites offer some kind of accommodation. Would-be walkers should buy Cartographia's *Börzsöny-hegység* map, which shows paths and the location of *túristáház*. The only peak you need climbing experience to scale is **Mount Csóványos**, at 939m the highest in the Börzsöny, which hikers usually approach from the direction of **DIÓSJENŐ**. A **campground** here with chalets lies 1km from the village and twice that distance from the railroad station; both trains and buses for Diósjenő depart from Vác around five to seven times daily.

An alternative route into the mountains begins at KISMAROS near Verőcemaros beside the Danube (see "Vác" above), whence narrow-gauge trains trundle more or less hourly up to **Királyrét** from 7:30am to 10:30pm. Supposedly once the hunting ground of Beatrice and Mátyás, this "Royal Meadow" is now the site of a forking path; one trail (marked in red) leads 3km to the **Magas-Tax hostel**, the other to the "Big Cold" peak, **Nagy Hideg**.

This latter has excellent views and its own tourist hostel, the starting point for walks to Mt. Csóványos and two villages. The route marked by blue squares leads westwards to **NAGYBÖRZSÖNY**, a wealthy town during the Middle Ages, but ruined by the depletion of its copper, gold, and iron mines, nowadays merely a humble logging village with a **thirteenth-century Romanesque church** as its sole relic of past prosperity, and no accommodation for visitors. The path with red markings runs south from Nagy Hideg down to **KOSPALLAG**, another rather dreary village, redeemed only by a cheap hostel with felt-trimmed boar hides in its restaurant, and a bus service to Vác until 9pm. But things improve beyond the Vác-Szob junction below the village, where the path wanders through the beech woods to a lovely open meadow graced with a solitary tree and the first view of the Danube. Cutting southwest across the meadow puts you back on the path to the **Törökmező** hostel—a largish place with tennis courts and a restaurant that's popular with motorists following the Panorama-út—or you can head west towards Zebegény when the path divides by the exercise camp in the woods. This leads eventually to a parking lot at the junction of paths to Hegyes-tető and Nagymaros.

festivals

Summer

During **June and July**, **historical pageants** at ESZTERGOM and VISEGRÁD (as advertised).

SZENTENDRE celebrates its Serbian roots with *Kolo* performances on **Aug 19**, with a televised festival of folkdancing, jazz, and pop on **Aug 20**.

travel details

Trains

From Budapest to Esztergom (12 daily; 1hr 15min); Szentendre (every 15–30min; 45min); Váctrátót & Vác (2 daily).

From Esztergom to Budapest (9; 1hr 30min); Komárom (3; 45min).

From Vác to Diósjenő (30min) and Balassagyarmat (2hr), 5–7 daily.

From Vácrátót to Aszód (3; 1hr 30min).

From Esztergom to Visegrád, Szentendre and Budapest (hourly); Komárom (every 1hr 30min).

From Szentendre to Visegrád and Esztergom (hourly, or more frequently).

From Vác to Budapest (hourly); Diósjenő (5–7 daily); Kospallag (every 1hr 30min); Szob (every 20–40min).

From Visegrád to Budapest (hourly); Dömös and Esztergom (every 20–40min).

Buses

From Budapest *árpád híd* terminal to Esztergom via the Bend (every 1hr 30min) or Dorog (every 30min); Dobogókő (1–3 daily); Vác (every 30min); Visegrád (hourly). From *Népstadion* terminal to Vác (hourly).

Ferries

From Budapest to Esztergom (2 daily; 5hr); Szentendre (5; 1hr 30min); Vác (1; 2hr 30min); Visegrád (3; 3hr); Zebegény (2; 3hr 45min).

From Esztergom to Budapest (2; 4); Štúrovo (hourly); Szentendre (2; 2hr 45min); Vác (2; 2hr).

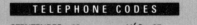

TELEPHONE CODES	
SZENTENDRE ☎26	VÁC ☎27
VISEGRÁD ☎26	

CHAPTER THREE

LAKE BALATON AND THE BAKONY

F
ew Magyars would subscribe to the old romantic view of **Lake Balaton** as the "Hungarian sea," but, despite rising prices pushing out natives in favor of Austrians and Germans, it is still very much the "Nation's Playground." Vacation resorts line the lake's southern shore, almost wholly given over to the pleasures of guzzling, swimming, and sunbathing, and with **Siófok** as the prototype, one place is much like another. Nature only reasserts itself at the western end of the lake, where the Zala River flows through the reeds to **Kis-Balaton**, a bird reserve. The northern shore is equally crowded, but waterfront development has been limited by reedbanks and cooler, deeper water, giving tourism a different slant. Historic **Tihany** and the wine-producing **Badacsony Hills** offer fine sightseeing, while anyone whose social life doesn't take off in **Keszthely** can go soak themselves in the thermal lake at **Hévíz**. It helps not to be taken for an Austrian or West German, whom many locals rip off, and despise for what many consider obnoxious, money-waving behavior.

The lower prices around **Lake Velence**, midway between the Balaton and Budapest, have made this the preferred destination for Magyar and East German vacationers. Close by is **Martonvásár**, where Beethoven concerts are held in the grounds of the Brunswick mansion during summer. And while you're visiting the Balaton, it would be a shame not to see the romantic-looking Belváros and "Bory Castle" at **Székesfehérvár**, or something of the hills that roll picturesquely into **the Bakony**. A wine-producing region dotted with small villages and ruined *vár*, dominated by the towns of **Veszprém** and **Sümeg**, the Bakony is nowadays exploited as a military training ground, and for its mineral wealth at **Tapolca**.

APPROACHING THE BALATON

There are various ways of **approaching the Balaton from Budapest**, and much depends on which shore you're aiming for. Most **trains** from Déli station to Siófok call at Lake Velence, Székesfehérvár, and the main settlements along the southern shore before veering off towards Nagykanizsa at Balatonszentgyörgy. From mid-July to late August *MÁV* even runs **steam trains** between Siófok and Fonyód (1hr), and from Déli pu. (leaving at 8:40am) to Siófok (10hr!). Services from Budapest to Balatonfüred are like-

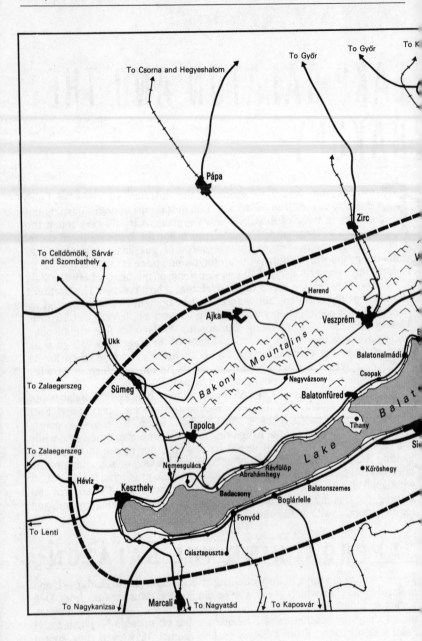

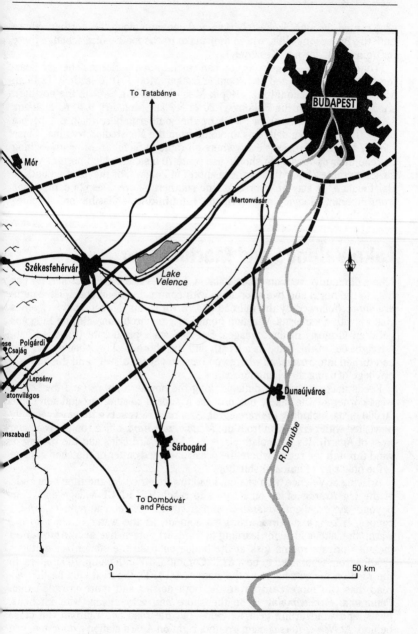

wise routed through Székesfehérvár, and continue along the northern shore until the Badacsony Hills, where they make tracks for Tapolca (change there for trains back down to Keszthely).

From Budapest's Engels tér you can catch **buses** to Székesfehérvár (leaving at 10:40am daily, and at 1:40pm & 6:40pm Mon–Fri); Keszthely (2:40pm Mon–Fri), and Balatonfüred (4:40pm Mon–Fri; 1:40pm Sat) on the northern shore; Veszprém in the Bakony (7:20 & 8:40am Mon–Fri; 9:40 & 11:40am, 12:10 & 1pm Sat & Sun); or Siófok on the southern shore (8am & 12:40pm daily). There's also a daily bus to Siófok from the Népstadion terminal. Since the M7 highway bypasses everywhere en route to Siófok, **motorists** wishing to keep their options open should use route 70 instead, which permits you to switch to route 71 (for the northern shore) at Polgárdi or the junction outside Balatonaliga, or stay on course for the southern shore. Despite competition from itinerant Magyars and Germans, **hitchhiking** is feasible on all routes except the M7.

Lake Velence and Martonvásár

Like a diminutive version of the Balaton, **LAKE VELENCE** (*Velencei-tó*) has hills to the north and two shorelines with contrasting characters. The southern shore (followed by the railroad and rd.70) is busy, brash, and welcomes visitors with open arms. Vacation homes are mushrooming, closing the gaps between formerly distinct villages; fast-food stalls proliferate (the fried fish, "straight out of the lake," is a treat); and the shore is slowly being enclosed and turned into *Strandbad* where you have to pay for a swim and the dubious privilege of using the changing rooms.

Reeds make swimming difficult along the northern shore (and the southwest corner of the lake), but provide a superb nesting ground for some 30,000 birds, including the rare egret. As a **nature reserve** the area can only be visited with permission from the *Madárrezervátum* office (on the road just west of Agárd). It's a desolate place, filled with bird cries and the wailing of wind through the reeds, where the occasional reed-cutter or thatched cottage is the only sign of human habitation.

Arriving at Velence train station, head towards the lake and then bear right at the big *Express* office on Fő utca to reach **VELENCE** village and, 2km beyond, the excellent *Panorama* campground. Here you can rent (*kölcsönző*) canoes, **bikes**, and **windsurfing** equipment; as the water is shallow and warm, the lake is ideal for learning to windsurf. Alternative **accommodation** includes private rooms (ask at the house opposite the station) or cottages (200Ft) from what used to be a *KISZ* Communist Youth camp, 100 meters up the road on the same side as the station. **AGÁRD**, the next stop on the railroad, has two more **campgrounds**, both noisier and more crowded than Panorama. *Park-camping* is on the shore and very cheap, with kitchens, boats, and windsurfing gear for rent—but the road and railroad run close behind. At *Nemes Kócsag* campground, right on Agárd station's doorstep, you can rent little stoves by the hour and obtain private rooms.

Velence **nightlife** is limited to the *Disco Arató* (behind *Express*)—a bar until 10pm, after which you pay not too much to boogie on until 3am—and the *Lido* restaurant opposite Velence station, which features reasonably priced eats and nightly performances by local headbangers.

Situated to the north of the lake, the **Velencei Hills** are sparsely populated and have well-marked paths for hikers. From the hilltops most of the views are uninterrupted and pastoral, though at Mészeg-hegy—just east of Pákozd village—looms a heap of World War II hardware and an obelisk commemorating the first battle of the 1848 War of Independence. You will find a *balászcsárda* by the lake, with Gypsy music and tour buses. There are fairly regular **buses from Velence** to Székesfehérvár, Balatonfüred, and Siófok in the Balaton region, and to Pusztaszabolcs and Dunaújváros in Transdanubia.

Martonvásár

A fifteen-minute train ride from Velence to **MARTONVÁSÁR** transports you into quite another era. Follow the road opposite the railroad station to reach a neo-Gothic castle where Hungary's first nursery school was opened by **Teréz Brunswick**, and where **Beethoven** was a frequent guest. Rumor has it that Josephine Brunswick was the "immortal beloved" to whom Ludwig addressed his love letters, and that the Moonlight and Appassionata sonatas were inspired by his sojourns at Martonvásár. Whatever the truth, a small Beethoven museum contains manuscripts and personal belongings, and on summer evenings **performances of his symphonies** by the State Symphony Orchestra are held on an island in the middle of the park, beneath a great bower of beech and sycamore. Armed with mosquito repellent and a couple of bottles (there's a bar-buffet in the grounds) you can watch the sun set and hear the soaring music, if necessary catching the last train back to Budapest (around 11:30pm on Sat). **Tickets**, available on the spot or from *Philharmonia* (V, Vörösmarty tér 1) in Budapest, cost 100–300Ft; the cheapest ones are fine.

Székesfehérvár

Reputedly the site where Árpád pitched camp and founded his dynasty, **SZÉKESFEHÉRVÁR** was probably the earliest Hungarian town. (The name, meaning "seat of the white castle," is pronounced "SAIKesh-fehair-var"). It was later changed to Alba Regia by King Stephen, who made it his capital and the center of his campaign to Christianize the Magyars. The Turkish occupation destroyed Alba Regia, and modern Székesfehérvár owes its character to two events: its eighteenth-century resurgence under the Habsburgs, during which the Belváros was constructed; and the final German counter-attack in 1945, which ravaged the suburbs but ironically cleared the way for new industries and an encircling girth of *lakótelep*.

Around the Belváros

From the railroad station, follow Lenin út northwards until it becomes Népköztársaság útja, an avenue delineating the longest side of the roughly triangular Belváros, which occupies approximately the same area as the great castle once did. The Romkert adjoining Népköztársaság útja is an obvious first stop, an open air museum containing fragmented medieval masonry, bordered by a stretch of the original town wall. Opposite are Stephen's tomb and the ruins of the Coronation Church where 38 Magyar rulers were crowned and eighteen buried, originally designed by Italian architects to rival Saint Mark's in Venice. With its schools, salt-house, markets, and mint, well fortified and surrounded by marshes, Alba Regia prospered even after the royal seat was moved to Buda; but fell in 1543 to the Turks, who plundered and then blew up the Church and Basilica.

The **István Király Museum** on Gagarin tér deftly incorporates archaeological finds into a series of rooms comprising a historical record from geological beginnings to the present day, including some examples of eastern Celtic pottery. To the west of the Romkert lies **Szabadság tér**, the center of Székesfehérvár's revival under Maria Theresa, a gracious setting for *Albatourist* (no. 6), a squat Bishop's Palace built with stones from the Basilica, and a severe Franciscan church. Ecclesiastical piles are ranged north and south of here: a Baroque Cathedral raises twin spires over Arany J. utca, dwarfing the town's single Gothic monument, Saint Anna's chapel, while a Rococo church and monastery stand together on Marcius 15. utca, with *IBUSZ* on the corner. This pastel-colored street is so perfectly preserved that you almost expect to see crinolined ladies emerging from the ornate eighteenth-century *Fekete Sas* pharmacy (now a musuem). Nearby on Bartók tér, a gallery displays the work of **István Csók** (1865–1961), a painter first associated with the Nagybánya School who fell under the influence of Vuillard and Bonnard in Paris, and returned to Hungary to practice *plein air* painting. He later joined the *MIENK* group's opposition to "narrative" painting, insisting that art should be "purely pictorial" and concerned with the visual experience.

Bory's Folly

The town's best sight, however, is out in the eastern suburbs, beyond the computer and TV factories which nowadays underpin Székesfehérvár's economy. Accessible by bus from Marx tér, **Bory's Castle** (*Bory Vár*) is a bizarre product of matrimonial obsession, an eclectic structure combining features of Scottish, Romanesque, and Gothic architecture, built of reinforced concrete, ceramics, and stone by a group of students directed by the sculptor Jenő Bory. The rooms and courtyards are filled with statues and paintings of Ilona Komocsin, Bory's wife and favorite model, whose memory the castle enshrines. Although the overall effect of Ilona's multiple images is slightly morbid, it's a marvelous place to wander around.

Practicalities

The **tourist offices** on Szabadság tér, Ady u. and Rákóczi u. all arrange private rooms (usually in the high-rise zone); it'll be cheaper **accommodation** than in the *Alba Regia* or *Velence* hotels, though only a shade below the cost of a double in the *Hotel* (József u.42) or the *Két Góbé* "Two Rascals" pension at 4, Gugásvölgyi utca. Even cheaper beds exist—but may be occupied—in the *Török Udvar* hostel at Jókai u.2, while *Express* (Rákóczi u.4) does its best to fill college dorms during summer.

The *Ósfehérvár* (Táncsics u.1) and *Velence* (Marcius 15. u.) are both upscale **places to eat and drink**, open until midnight and featuring music in the evenings; locals seem to prefer the *Kis Kulacs* (at the corner of Lenin and Vörös Hadsereg útja) or *Szabadság* (Vörösmarty tér) restaurants. The *Ezerjó* on Gagarin tér is a nice wine bar. For self-catering or cheap snacks, investigate the **market** just north of the **bus terminal** on Piac tér. Other things you might need to buy can probably be found in the big *Fehérvár* **department store**, whose once-silvery exterior so impressed a group of visiting Soviet journalists that they concluded that it had to be *pokazuka*—"for show." Hopefully you shouldn't need the **pharmacy** on Vörös Hadsereg útja or the **hospitals** farther west beyond the Sergélyesi út junction.

Traveling on from Székesfehérvár

Unless you're bound for foreign parts (see below) or Dunaújváros, there are basically three routes out of Székesfehérvár, negotiable by *Volán* bus or rail. En route **to Siófok**, antiquarians might care to catch a bus from SZABADBATTYÁN (a halt for local trains, but not services from Budapest) to TÁC, 5km south along rd.70, where signs point towards the **Roman ruins of Gorsium**, an Aquincum-style restoration of the town raised by Hadrian to the rank of a city, later abandoned and plundered for building material. But otherwise there's nothing worth remarking upon before Siófok (see next page).

If you're heading for northern Transdanubia, the route **through the Vértes** range is a scenic one. Kisbér-bound trains call at BODAJK (*fogadó* and hostel, reservations through *Albatourist*) and the village of CSÓKAKŐ (off rd.81), where a ruined hilltop castle on the outskirts offers tremendous views; followed by **MÓR**, the starting point for **walks** in the Vértes. Distinguished by two former *kastély* on its main square, Mór is known for its **wine**, available for sampling at a **Wine Museum** opposite the tourist hostel on Ezerjó u. (there's also a pension on Kodály utca). Since trains continue northwards towards Komárom, you'll need to change at KISBÉR to reach Győr (see *Transdanubia*), which rd.81 enters via a fiendish knot of overpasses.

Traveling **towards Veszprém in the Bakony** (see "Approaching Veszprém" below) by bus or railroad, **VÁRPALOTA** appears through a haze of lignite smoke. Emissions from the *November 7* Power Plant and an aluminum foundry are quietly falling as acid rain upon the Bakony's forests, the **castle** in Várpalota's center, and a **Roman wier**, constructed of gigantic stones, which stretches brokenly for almost 1km near the suburban swimming resort of PÉTFÜRDŐ rooms are cheap at the *Palota* on Szabadság tér, for surely few wish to stay here, despite the lure of an **eleventh-century circular chapel** with a mushroom-shaped cupola, which graces ÖSKÜ (9km west by bus or railroad).

You need to reserve seats the day before on **international trains** from Székesfehérvár to Leipzig (the *Favorit*, leaving at around 8:15pm), Vienna (*Kálmán Imre*; 4:35pm), or Zagreb (*Dráva* 7am; *Maestral* 1:30pm).

LAKE BALATON

With 197km of shoreline to exploit, **LAKE BALATON** is the apple of *IBUSZ's* eye, a place as geared to the tourist industry as the Nógrád Basin is to coal mining. Since 1945, when private villas and hotels became trade union vacation homes (*üdülőház*), certain **resorts** have become the recognized perks of sections of society—with workers from the Kaposvár sugar factory getting their two weeks at Balatonboglár, members of the Writers' Union retreating to a more salubrious place in Szigliget, and Party *funkcionárusok* enjoying the exclusiveness of Balatonvilágos. More footloose and youthful visitors started flocking to the Balaton in the mid Sixties, when private life was removed from the Stalinist strait-jacket; while in the Seventies, the private house-building and room-renting boom began, fuelled by the "New Economic Mechanism" and an influx of tourists from the West.

Balaton isn't to everyone's taste, but it certainly tries to be. While the southern shore is unabashedly hedonistic (without being "naughty"), places along the northern shore boast of historic monuments, cultural events, and scenic landscape. **Tennis, riding, and water sports** are easily arranged, and most resorts have a disco (often inside the classiest hotel) or two for **nightlife**. Hotels cost about the same as in Budapest, with private **rooms** 300–700Ft per head, depending on whether you use a private-sector bureau, *IBUSZ*, or *Siótour*, or rent directly from the householder (usually the cheapest option; look for *Zimmerfrei* signs). Most **campgrounds** operate between May 1 and September 31, but for precise details pick up a *Camping Hungary* map or *Hotel-Camping* brochure. From June to August, auxiliary campgrounds open to handle the overflow from the main sites near each resort. Balaton campgrounds are Hungary's most expensive—though some sites drop their prices out of season—so the savings incurred by having FICC membership or a student card are significant.

Along the southern shore and between Balatonalmádi and Badacsony on the opposite bank, trains are the easiest way of **getting around**; buses link Tihany and Balatonfüred, Badacsony and Keszthely, and Veszprém and Siófok; while **ferries** criss-cross the lake. **Organized tours** are available from *Siótour* (see sections on "Siófok", "Balatonfüred", and "Keszthely"), while **ferries** sailing between various points around the lake provide the breeziest, cheapest excursions of all.

The Southern Shore from Siófok to the "Little Balaton"

Approaching **the southern shore** from the direction of Budapest by train, you'll catch your first glimpse of the Balaton at BALATONVILÁGOS. One of the lushest, least commercialized resorts, built on wooded cliffs and along the shore, this is reserved for Party officials. Unlike vacationers at other resorts, they have something that could properly be called a beach; elsewhere, the strand is an expanse of lawn terminating in a concrete embankment with quays and diving boards.

Siófok

SIÓFOK is the largest port on the southern shore: a plebian, open-armed place that pioneered the incorporation of video-discos into its traditional nightlife of wine bars and gypsy bands. A string of high-rise hotels—their communal beach is like a sardine can—casts another shadow on Siófok's pre-war reputation as a center of quiet elegance, of which a token reminder is the Petőfi sétány, the central promenade: leafy, lined with sedate villas and terminated by a rose garden in Dimitrov Park. Fő utca is the town's modern axis: full of bustle but unremarkable, save for the *Fogás eszpresszó*'s selection of pastries. From the **bus and train stations** it runs past the post office, shops, and the meteorological tower on Szabadság tér to **Siótour** (no. 174); and then to an excellent indoor **market** and an *ABC* on the west bank of the Sió canal.

Emperor Galerius initiated the first canal and locks to regulate the level of the lake in 292, but things were busiest during the Turkish occupation, when a fleet of 10,000 men was stationed here. Before steamboats were introduced (as usual, by Count Széchenyi), crossing the lake could be a hazardous business, as you can imagine from some of the vessels displayed in the **Beszédes József Museum** (Sió út 2). Named after a hydraulic engineer, it traces local aquatic history including the building of the **concrete embankments**, which give the southern shore a sterile appearance but prevent flooding—and outlines future plans for the Balaton.

If this fails to hasten your steps to **the harbor** and a getaway ferry (services to Tihany, Alsóörs, Balatonfüred, and Balatonföldvár), excursions and **accommodation** are plentiful. The cheapest hotel, *Touring*, is out on the west road; the Altálános school on Fő tér is a hostel from July 1 to August 20; or there are several campgrounds on Siófok's outskirts. "Golden Beach" (*Aranypart*) is a misnomer for the concrete and grass embankment stretching eastwards to **BALATONSZABADI**, with three campgrounds: *Kék-Balaton*, nearest to Siófok but wedged between the road and railroad track; *Gamasza* (July–Aug only); and *Ifjúsági* practically on the shore.

Siótour can arrange **sports** equipment and coach **excursions** to Székesfehérvár and Gorsium, Veszprém, Herend, Tihany, Hévíz, or Mezőszilas (for a **horse show** and Puszta-ish rites); **pleasure cruises**; parties at Nagyberek Farm or the Highwaymen's Bakony csárda; or a display of **folk dancing** at Siófok's cultural center. Come evening, **bars and discos** bashfully appear around the waterfront. At Siófok, you can board **international trains** to Zagreb (the *Dráva* or *Maestral*, leaving around 7:40am & 2:15pm); Prague, Dresden, and Leipzig (*Favorit* 7:30pm); or Vienna (*Kálmán Imre* 4:30pm). There are also *Volán* **coaches** to Bratislava, Semmering, and Vienna.

Between Siófok and Fonyód

BALATONÚJHELY begins west of the Sió canal, but merged with **BALATONSZÉPLAK** in 1949 to form *Ezüstpart Camping* (with free kitchens) and the *Strand* site (offering bicycles for hire by the hour; 200Ft per week). Blink as you pass through **ZAMÁRDI**, the next settlement, and you'll miss it—which isn't a great shame. Red signs lead from the station to **Szamárkő** ("Donkey rock"), thought by archaeologists to be a sacrificial site of the ancient Magyars, and claimed by some Christians to bear the hoof-print of Christ's donkey; while the **Tájház** displays peasant pottery, tiled ovens, and old agricultural equipment. Otherwise Zamárdi offers the standard beach 'n' bars set-up, with *Auto-camping* I and II on the shore road, and *Siótour* at Kossuth u.12. Neighboring **SZÁNTÓD** has the expensive *Rév camping* (high season only) and a **car-ferry to Tihany** on the northern shore.

BALATONFÖLDVÁR is in a similar vein but on a larger scale. Swimming began here at the turn of the century, and now thousands come to amble from snack bar to snack bar. It's a tedious terrain, of carefully laid parks and concrete vacation complexes, though the *Magyar Tenger* campground down by the *Hotel Neptun* is surprisingly pleasant. A 4km stroll brings you to **KŐRÖSHEGY**, where **chamber-music concerts** are held on summer evenings in a fifteenth-century church, beyond which the hills resound with the choruses of mating **deer**.

The boundary of **BALATONSZÁRSZÓ** is marked by a cemetery containing the grave of the poet **Attila József**, whose anarchic verses now endear him to society at large. Dismissed by his literary peers (Babits, the editor of *Nyugat*, persistently thwarted his career) and rejected by his lover and the Communist Party, the impoverished poet threw himself beneath a local freight train in 1937, having spent his last days in a house that's now a memorial museum (József u.7). Balatonszárszó also has a tourist hostel (Fő u.3) and *Tura* campground, open from May 26–August 31 and June–July, respectively.

BALATONSZEMES, crowned by the ruined ramparts of Bagolyvár Castle, offers a **Post Office Museum**, cheap double rooms in the *Lido Fogadó* (from April to Sept), and several **campgrounds**. Of these, *Express* is usually full, so try the *Lidó*, expensive but on the beach, *Auto* on Fő utca, or the overcrowded *Vadvirág* development west of town. Three formerly volcanic hills bear the burden of **BOGLÁRLELLE**, a settlement now merged with Balatonboglár. Cemetery Hill (Temetőhegy) hosts art exhibits during summertime, while Vár-hegy is topped by a spherical **look-out tower**, commanding a sweeping view from Keszthely to Tihany. **BALATONLELLE**, nearer to Siófok, has an outdoor theater in the grounds of a mansion at Kossuth u.2, the setting for **folk-dancing** performances, and an antiquated smithy at Szabadság út 52. Its campground is by the harbor, *Siótour* operates from Szent István út, and you can rent **bicycles** on Vasúti sétány. Balatonboglár has two reasonably priced hotels: *Hullám* (Dózsa Gy. u:55) and *Platán* (Hunyadi u.56).

Fonyód, Nagyberek, and the Kis-Balaton

FONYÓD grew up between the Sipos and Sándor hills and subsequently spread itself along the lakeside, so the symmetry of its setting is best appreciated from the far shore. A built-up strand and bleak modern architecture make this an unlikely setting for the grand passion that inspired Fonyód's **"Crypt Villa."** Raised above a red marble crypt with room for two, this was built by a grieving widower who lived there in seclusion for many years, and is now undergoing restoration as a "sight" for a place otherwise bereft of curiosities. Should you want **to stay**, the cheapest options are *Liget*, in Fonyódliget 1km east of the center, or *Napsugár* cottage-campground in Fonyódbélatelep, another suburb to the west of town. Fonyód's main station is a flying stop for the *Favorit*, *Dráva*, and *Maestral* **trains to Prague and Dresden or Zagreb**.

Between Fonyód and BALATONFENYVES, reclaimed swampland now belongs to the **NAGYBEREK** state cooperative farm, where forestation and irrigation work since the 1950s has produced fewer benefits than expected and simultaneously spoiled the rich breeding ground for fish. **Horseback riding** can be arranged nearby at **CSISZTAPUSZTA**, where drilling for oil unexpectedly yielded **warm springs** instead of "black gold," and the waters—reputedly good for relieving rheumatic diseases and tension—may be reached by **narrow-gauge railroad** which begins at Balatonfenyves and runs around the farm. Beyond Fonyód the lake is very shallow and partially banked by reeds, making it the least tamed stretch of the southern shore. You'll see whole tribes of swimmers de-camping to large rafts anchored offshore, armed with crates of beer and piles of lángos.

BALATONMÁRIAFÜRDŐ and **BALATONKERESZTÚR** are both pretty quiet: a café by the Balatonmáriafürdő-alsó station sells great ice cream, while Balatonkeresztúr has a cheap hostel occupying one of the Festetics family's former mansions (Ady u.26). **BALATONBERÉNY** features a **nudist beach**, the inexpensive *Kocsag Fogadó*, and arguably the best campground on the southern shore. From here, reeds stretch all the way to the Zala River through the **KIS-BALATON** (Little Balaton) **nature reserve**, a nesting ground for rare birds which can only be visited with prior permission from the Conservation office in Budapest (XII, Költő u.21) or Veszprém (Tolbuhin u.31).

Moving on, you can reach Keszthely (see below) by bus or train from Balatonszentgyörgy, or catch a ferry from Balatonmáriafürdő across to Balatongyörök on the northern shore.

The Northern Shore as far as Balatonfüred

To reach Balaton's **northern shore** by road from Budapest, turn off rd.70 just ouside Balatonaliga and follow the shoreline round through **BALATONKARATTYA**, a suburb of Balatonkenese distinguished only by the dead trunk of the *Rákózi fa*—a tree where the honored freedom fighter (see *The Northern Uplands*) is said to have tied his horse—and *Piroska* campground, a pleasant place at the bottom of a steep hill. **BALATONKENESE** is larger, with a Baroque church and **peasant houses** along Bajcsy-Zsilinszky, Kossuth, and Fő streets; while above the settlement are **caves** dug into the clay banks by refugees from the Turks (hence their name, the Turkish holes), which continued to be inhabited by poor people until the end of the last century.

BALATONFŰZFŐ, site of a large and smelly nitro-chemicals plant, doesn't merit a stop, but beyond Fűzfő bay you reach **BALATONALMÁDI**, the first town on the northern shore. A resort since 1877, it's now modern looking, with only the Chapel of Saint Job—originally part of Buda Castle—built into its Catholic church (decorated with mosaics by Károly Lotz) to engender historical interest. The *Hotel Aurora* dominates the skyline; *Kék-Balaton* (József A. u.27), and to a lesser extent the *Tulipán* on Marx tér, are cheaper alternatives. There are also cottages on József utca, private rooms for rent from *IBUSZ* at Petőfi u.21, and a campground (with another one in the suburb of Vörösberény, named after the red, sandy soil). Ferries and trains continue around to **ALSÓÖRS**, formerly a mining village where the rock was used to make millstones. Although it's insuffecent reason to linger here, there's an odd remnant of the Ottoman occupation at Petőfi köz 7: a Gothic manor house once inhabited by the local Turkish tax collector, distinguished by a turban-topped chimney (a sign of wealth in the days when smoke left most houses through a hole in the roof). Although Alsóörs has *Kemping* and *Autos strand*, neighboring **CSOPAK**—with private rooms (reservations through Blaha u.5) and a reputation for its *Olaszrizling* and *Furmint* wines—is a nicer place to stay.

Balatonfüred

Seventeenth-century chronicles tell of pilgrims descending on **BALATONFÜRED** to "camp in scattered tents" and benefit from the mineral springs here. Nowadays some 30,000 people come every year for treatment in the town's sanatoria. A busy harbor and skyscraper hotels dominate Balatonfüred's approaches, but **the center** has a sedate, convalescent atmosphere, typified by the embankment promenade, Rabindranath Tagore sétány, named after the Bengali poet who came here in 1926 and planted a tree in gratitude for his cure. Other celebrities followed his example—the origin of the sétány's memorial grove—and some are remembered in the Pantheon beside the Trade Unions' Sanatorium on Gyógy tér (Health Square), onto which the promenade opens. Here you can drink the Kossuth spring's carbonic water at a columned, pagoda-like structure in the center of the square. Four other springs feed the hospital (which treats around 10,000 people annually), and the adjoining **mineral baths** on the eastern side. Excavated villas suggest that the Romans were the first to use the waters to treat stomach ailments and, when mixed with goats' milk whey, as a cure for lung diseases.

On the western side of the square stands the late-eighteenth-century **Horváth House**, one of the first inns in a land where inn-keeping developed tardily, and then largely thanks to the Swabians. Magyars tended to consider such work beneath them: Petőfi complained that his landlord wouldn't utter a word of welcome until he had been paid, and served food "as if by the special grace of God"; while another nineteenth-century traveler reported that his host wore spurs to emphasize his gentlemanly status, and was "capable of giving his guests a good hammering or throwing them out" on impulse. Patronized by leading writers and politicians during the Reform era, the Horváth Inn is now a uranium miners' sanatorium.

Beyond this lies Blaha Lujza utca, named after Hungary's answer to Gracie Fields, the "Nightingale of Budapest," who spent her summers in a villa at no. 2, and maybe had her tea—as one still can—at the *Kedves cukrászda* (next to **Balatontourist Nord**) across the road. Nearby Jókai utca is likewise named after someone whose sojourn testified to the spa's efficacy. The novelist **Jókai** came to Balatonfüred at the age of 37, half-expecting to die from a serious lung infection, built the villa which now stands as a **memorial house** so that he could return each year, and lived to the ripe age of 84. Beyond the railroad tracks, the street becomes Ady utca; an ironic juxtaposition of names, since the poet Ady died of syphilis at the age of 42. Farther along you'll find Balatonfüred's original center, where Siske and Vázsonyi utca, near a Calvinist church, are dotted with houses in the traditional local style; and there's a touch of village atmosphere about the **market**, held near Arácsi út.

Balatonfüred's cheapest hotels are the *Aranycsillag* (Zsigmond u.1), *Erdei* (Koloska u:45), and *Panorama* (Kun u:15); all a shade more expensive than private **accommodation** from Balatontourist Nord or *IBUSZ* (just off Petőfi utca, the main road encircling the center). The campground on the eastern outskirts, named after the 27th Reunion of the Federation of Camping & Caravaning Clubs, made me wish that they'd stopped meeting after the twenty-sixth time: loudspeakers bombard campers with details of **excursions**, and harassed staff may snarl *sprich Deutsch*! should you attempt a request in broken Magyar. Buses #1 and #2 run via Jókai u. from the campground to the **railroad station**, while **buses** following Széchenyi utca (rd.71) out of town are usually bound **for Tihany**, which is also accessible **by ferry**. (Other boats sail to Siófok on the southern shore). Heading eastwards, the railroad skips Tihany peninsula, going by way of Aszófő (good campground) and Örvényes; while from Balatonfüred there's also a bus service **to Nagyvázsony** (see "Approaching Veszprém" below) in the Bakony.

Tihany

A rocky peninsula that was declared Hungary's first national park in 1952, **TIHANY** is historically associated with the Benedictine order, fishing folk, and ferrymen, and the redoubtable castle (no longer in existence) that withstood 150 years of Turkish hostility. Buses from Balatonfüred follow the road along the peninsula's undeveloped eastern side—no beaches, but plenty of people fishing—past the main harbor ranged beneath the old quarter, and down to *Tihanyi rév*, the tourist complex beside the quay for boats to Balatonföldvár and Szántód. The historic center of Tihany sits above the harbor where the ferries from Siófok and Balatonfüred pull in; you'll find it by pursuing winding steps up between a screen of trees, like thousands of other people who come to rubberneck around the "Pearl of the Balaton." Overcrowded and overpriced it may be, but the luster hasn't entirely gone.

In days gone by, Tihany's tone was set by the **Benedictine Abbey**, established here at the request of Andrew I to be a beacon of enlightenment for his supposedly beknighted subjects, and founded—true to the biblical injunction—upon a rocky promontory overlooking the Balaton. The king's body still lies in the crypt of the **Abbey Church**—the only one of the Árpád line to remain where buried—but the building overhead is Baroque, for the original church succumbed to wars and time. Inside are virtuoso woodcarvings by Sebestyén Stulhoff, who lived and worked in the monastery for 25 years after his fiancée died, and is said to have preserved her features in the face of an angel, which kneels to the right of the altar of the Virgin. The frescoes painted a century later by Lodz, Székely, and others exemplify the "narrative" school which dominated Hungarian fine arts before the World War I. Floodlit during the evenings, the church is a magnificent setting for **organ concerts** on Tuesday and Wednesday during the summer.

The adjoining monastery now contains a **museum** displaying Balaton landscapes, and an interesting collection of costumes, implements, and musical instruments gathered from far-flung communities in the *taiga* beneath the arctic circle and in the Ural mountains—the **Finno-Ugric tribes** from which the Magyars originated. Until linguistic and ethnographic investigations were undertaken by János Sajnovics (1733–85), Antal Reguly, and others, it was assumed that Hungarians were descended from the Huns; a theory revived in recent years following the decipherment of inscriptions on the Nagyszentmiklós "Treasure of Attila" (see *The Great Plain*), which show a remarkable similarity with old Hungarian. In the museum basement are Roman altars, a mosaic pavement, and bits from the Paulite Monastery at Nagyvázsony. Just for the record, the foundation deed of Tihany is the earliest document to include Hungarian words among the Latin—a source for pride, it seems.

Quaint adaptation à la Szentendre abounds, from the rip-off restaurant occupying the monastery stables to the Fishermen's Guild Museum down on Pisky promenade, where **folkloric performances** are staged in the courtyard. Around Petőfi and Csokonai street, **houses** are built of gray basalt tufa, with windows and doors outlined in white and porticoed terraces, including the **tourist office**. Even without a map it's easy to stumble upon *Belső-tó*, one of the peninsula's two **lakes**, whose sunlit surface is visible from the Abbey Church. From its southern bank, a path runs through vineyards, orchards, and lavender fields past the Aranyház **geyser cones**—funnels forced open by hot springs—and down to Tihanyi-rév, a hive of tourism. Routes heading eastwards from Belső-tó and Tihanyi-rév wind up at **Csúcs Hill** (232m), whose observation tower gives a **panoramic view** of the Balaton; while farther inland lies the "Outer" lake, *Külső-tó*, drained in 1809 but refilled since 1975, when it became a bird sanctuary.

Otherwise, people eat and drink (mainly in **Tihanyi-rév**) and take to the water, paying to swim at the peninsula's southern tip, although there are other strand, interspersed by secluded, reedy stretches of shoreline. Hotels in Tihanyi-rév are exorbitant, so the neighboring campground, or private rooms (from Petőfi u.4 in the old town) are the only forms of **accommodation** unless you want to base yourself in one of the shoreline resorts west of the peninsula.

West Towards the Badacsony

For 30km west of Tihany **the shoreline** is infested with vacation homes and nondescript resorts; perhaps it's worth stopping if you hit upon a beach or campground to your taste, but generally there's nothing special. At **ÖRVÉNYES**, beyond **ASZÓFŐ** (good campground, hard currency only), an **antique watermill** (*műemlék malom*) still operates—acclaimed as a conservation triumph by the tourist board, although in the 1950s almost 200 similar mills were demolished on the Party's orders to clear the way for larger, state milling collectives. Its carved bins, loft, and workings are interesting, but there's little life before **Killiántelep International Youth Camp**, west of BALATONUDVARI (with its own *v.m.* train halt). During the busy summer months, advance reservations (especially of the cheap two- and four-bed cottages) are advisable—and possible through any of the country's *Express* offices—while on the spot, you can rent boats, bicycles, and windsurfing boards. **BALATONAKALI** is known for its *Akali muskotály* white wine, and presumably by a host of Czech nationals, for whom the Vasúti campground is reserved, while Westerners use the *Strand*—a huge and stony site on the beach east of the station—or the *Holiday* site next door, which has a buffet and more shade. Private accommodation bureaus at Kossuth u.17, Petőfi u.4, and outside the railroad station.

A fortress-like miners' rest home guards the road to BALATONSZEPED, with a pension at Arany u:10 and *Virius* campground east of the station. Similar directions apply to the overpriced, hot water-less *Napfény* campground in RÉVFÜLÖP, a settlement offering two restaurants, a disco, and a ruined thirteenth-century sandstone church to break the monotony of vacation homes. Beyond a few private rooms, ÁBRAHÁMHEGY lacks tourist facilities, and for this reason is a good place to stop and swim.

The Badacsony

A coffin-shaped hulk with four villages prostrated at its feet, backed by dead volcanos ranged across the Taploca basin, **THE BADACSONY** is one of the Balaton's most striking features. When the land that later became Hungary first surfaced, molten magma erupted from the seabed, and cooled into a great semi-circle of **basalt columns**, 210m high, which form the Badacsony's southeastern face. *Kökapu*, the Stone Gate, cleaves the northeast side—two natural towers flanking a precipitous drop. The rich volcanic soil of the mountain's lower slopes has supported vineyards since the Age of Migrations, when the Avars buried grape seeds with their dead to ensure that the afterlife wouldn't be lacking in **wine**. Nowadays growers own their plots—small and lovingly tended—but being collectivized, must sell two-thirds of their harvest to the state wineries which blend *Badacsonyi Szürkebarát, Kéknyelű, Zöldszilváni*, and *Olaszrizling*.

Developments are clustered around the southern tip, where you'll find a **tourist bureau** behind *Badacsony v.m.* **station**, above the quay where **ferries** from Révfülöp, Boglárlelle, Fonyód, and Szigliget dock. From there, the trail up Lábdi út is marked by locals selling wine and careering jeeps taking drunken tourists up to the former Bormúzeum, a large basalt hall now serving as an expensive "peasant" restaurant festooned with the obligatory strings of paprika and a "Gypsy" band. Farther uphill there's a nicer restaurant in the house once owned by Sándor Kisfaludy, who lauded the Balaton's beauties in verse; his wife Rózsa Szegedi's house is now a local **museum**. Lábdi út ends at the **Rose Rock** (*Rózsakő*), of which it's said that if a man and woman sit upon it with their backs to the Balaton and think about each other, they'll be married by the end of the year.

Walking up through the beechwoods to the Kisfaludy look-out tower is a fairly tame, Sunday stroller's route, well trodden as far as the famous **Stone Gate**, where people gape and ooh-aah before returning to the jeeps and wine bars. To escape the crowds, try the 4km **hike to Gulács-hegy**, a perfectly conical hill farther north near the Nemesgulács railroad halt for trains en route to Tapolca, with the impressive *Szent György Hill* on the other side of the tracks (see "The Bakony" below). Private rooms from *miniTOURIST* (Park u.53), or at the campground (with a small beach, five minutes' walk westwards from the tourist office) are good accommodation options, followed by the hostel (Park u.7) and *Harsona Penzió* (Szegedi R. u.37). However, there's a better campground at BADACSONYÖRS (the train stop after Ábrahámhegy), which faces the pleasant **Folly arboretum** of pines and cedars from all over the world, viewable with permission from the owners.

After Badacsony the railroad veers northwards up to Tapolca in the Bakony (see below). Though you can switch **trains** there and ride back down to Keszthely, it's easier to continue around the southern shore **by bus**.

Around Keszthely

Approaching Keszthely by rd.71, the small **SZIGLIGET** peninsula beneath the Kamonkő cliffs looks less dramatic than when viewed from an incoming ferry. Entwined with a branch road, it supports the restored **ruins of a fortress** commissioned by Pannonhalma Monastery in the wake of the Mongol invasion. It's accessible by a footpath starting behind the small white church sited on the highest spot in the village. Below the fortress is a lush park, with a former castle inside that serves as the vacation resort of the Writers' Union. Non-members may look around the grounds only with permission; the hoi polloi can camp beside the paying beach at BALATONEDERICS, a place otherwise merely notable as a train halt and the junction for rd.84 to Sümeg. BALATONGYÖRÖK, the next settlement, is still half a village of white-porticoed, thatched houses, with a campground on the beach hiring windsurfing gear. The **panorama** from Szépkilátó (which means "beautiful view") encompasses Szent György Hill, the castles atop Csobánc (see "Basalt hills and Tapolca" below), and Szigliget, the Badacsony and—across the lake—the twin peaks of Várhegy in Fonyód. After this comes VONYARCVASHEGY, with a campground and the outdoor *Fészek* Vendéglő, merging into GYENESDIÁS (campground on Madách út and a bad beach), followed by the suburbs of Keszthely.

Keszthely

A tradition of free thinking, dating from the eighteenth century, gives **KESZTHELY** a sense of superiority over other resorts, and you don't have to believe boasts that "the authorities are nervous of us" to feel a difference. Cultural life isn't synonymous with tourist entertainment, and Keszthely's Belváros and strand somehow absorb thousands of visitors gracefully, without looking bleak and abandoned out of season. With some good bars and restaurants, the Festetics Palace to admire, and a thermal lake awaiting bathers at Hévíz, nearby, Keszthely is the Balaton's best hangout.

On **arrival**, consider finding accommodation (see below) before making for the center, which is roughly ten minutes' walk from the ferry dock by the main strand (follow Tanácsköztársaság útja), or the railroad station at the bottom end of Mártirok útja, where some inter-city buses terminate. Most, however, drop passengers on Fő tér, downtown, halfway along the main drag, Kossuth utca.

Walking up from the railroad station you'll pass the **Balaton Museum**, whose exhibits depict the region's zoology, ethnography, and archaeology—the latter with artifacts dating back to the first century AD, when roadbuilding Roman imperialists disrupted the lifestyle of local Celtic tribes. The *Béke*, two blocks north along Kossuth utca, is the best place to dine out, but there are other restaurants fore and aft of Fő tér, an ambiguous square with a much-remodeled Gothic church fronted by bus stops, which counts as **the center**. From here onwards Kossuth utca is given over to cafés, vendors, street musicians, and strollers, a cheerful procession towards the *Festeticspalota*.

Founded in 1745 by Count György, the **Festetics Palace** grew to embrace a library, chapel, and archive, and from the nineteenth century onwards attracted the leading lights of Magyar literature (now recalled by memorial trees) as Hungary's first public forum for criticism. The building's highlights are its gilt, mirrored ballroom and the **Helikon Library**, a masterpiece of joinery and carving by János Kerbl, containing rare books in diverse languages. Chinese vases and ornately tiled ovens jostle for space with portraits of the family racehorses and dachshunds, whose pedigrees are proudly noted, but are overwhelmed by the pelts and heads of tigers, bears, and other animals shot by Count Windishgrätz. Seven generations of aristocratic ease ended in 1945, when the state opened a detention center for boys here; as a museum, the building is now open 9am–5pm daily (30Ft admission).

György's most useful contribution was an agricultural college, or Georgikon, the first of its kind in Europe, and the forerunner of today's **Agrártudományi University**, a green and daffodil-yellow building sited halfway along Széchenyi utca. On Bercsényi utca, two blocks west, stands the original **Georgikon**, a cluster of white buildings where the first students lived and worked together, now displaying dairy and viticulture equipment; cartwright's tools, old Ford tractors and suchlike. Visiting hours are 10am–6pm, April to November.

Keszthely's **waterfront** has two moles (one for swimming, the other for ferries) thrusting into the lake, a slew of parkland backed by plush hotels and miniature golf courses, and dozens of fast-food joints and bars catering to the folks in bathing suits who amble and flirt around the *strand*. Like the other "beach" farther south along the shore (between the two campgrounds), this is open 8:30am–7pm. After closing time action shifts to the Belváros, with a **disco** in the Theater Club (Mon & Thurs from 8pm) and **restaurants** working at full steam. The most popular tourist spots are the *Gösser* on Fő tér and

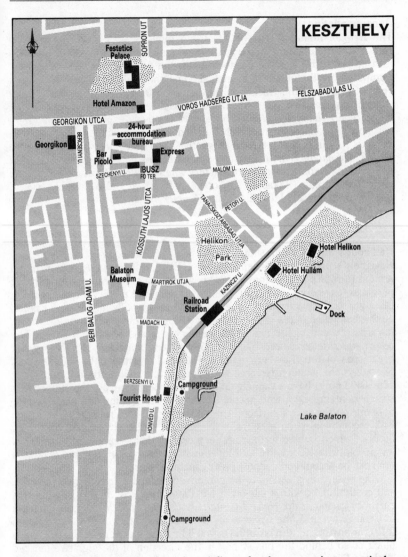

the *Kert* on Széchenyi utca, featuring violin and soft pop music respectively; *Béke*, 200m south along Kossuth utca, is favored by locals for its outdoor setting and cheaper meals. On Szabad nép utca, one block north of Széchenyi utca, the *Bár Picolo* is a friendly student hangout serving Czech Urquell beer. Until the next *Interforum* **festival of modern music** in 1990, when Keszthely will once again be overrun by avant garde composers, *IBUSZ* and *Zalatourist* are offering a "**Betyár Party**" with "highwaymen" and a knee-slapping floorshow over dinner, for around $12.

Accommodation

The *Helikon* **hostel** at Honvéd u.22, ten minutes' walk from the railroad station (bear left behind the bus park into Madách utca, then take the second turn on the right) has the cheapest beds, but vacancies can't be expected. Campers have the option of a small site just south of the station, between a cement plant and the tracks, or the big *Castrum* **camping** ground, hiring windsurfing gear on its own strand, one-and-a-half kilometers along the shore. The *Helikon* and *Hullam* **hotels** are relatively expensive, and with no certainty of rooms at the moderately priced *Amazon* outside the Palace gates, **private lodgings** are a better alternative. You can shop around between *IBUSZ*, *Locomotiv Tourist*, *Zalatour*, and other **tourist offices** near Fő tér; as a rule, double rooms cost more (700Ft) when obtained through the private enterprise bureau (Bakacs u.12), open 24 hours. It's also possible to rent directly from householders displaying *Zimmer frei* signs.

Hévíz

Half-hourly buses from stand #2 outside the station will take you past Keszthely's *kertváros* (garden city) to **HÉVÍZ**. This famous spa is based around Europe's largest **thermal lake**, whose waters were used for curative purposes, as well as for tanning leather, throughout medieval times. During the eighteenth century they were subjected to scientific inquiry and salubriously channelled into a bath-house erected by Count György, around which, towards the end of the nineteenth century, a grand resort developed. The resort was briefly favored by crown princes and magnates like those other great spas of the Habsburg empire, Karlsbad and the Baths of Hercules. Nowadays the wooden terraces surrounding the *Tófürdő* **baths** (8am–5pm; admission 60Ft) have a vaguely fin de siècle appearance, but the ambience is strictly contemporary, with people sipping beer or reading newspapers while bobbing on the lake's surface in rented inner tubes. Prolonged immersion isn't recommended on account of the slightly radioactive water, 70,000,000 liters of which bubble forth from deep craters daily—supposedly beneficial for people with locomotive and inflammatory disorders, of whom 2000 at a time can be accommodated in Hévíz's sanatoria.

Otherwise, Hévíz seems to be comprised of fodder troughs, rest homes, and costly hotels, with a late-night bar (9pm–3am; closed Wed) and a hard currency casino in the *Hotel Thermal*. Should you wish **to stay**, it's cheaper to try at Zrínyi u:15, the *Gyöngyvirag* (Felszabadulás tér) or *Piroska* (Kossuth u:10), or any of the **tourist offices**; you'll find the main one at Rákóczi u.8, a block or so behind the bus station in the direction of the high-rise marked "Balaton Füszert."

Moving On

Buses from Hévíz run to the Badacsony (dep. 4:20pm on weekdays, 2:40pm at weekends), Győr (4pm), Pécs (3:40pm), Székesfehérvár, and Budapest, but for other destinations it's easier to start **from Keszthely**. Services from the town's Fő tér reach Nagykanizsa (6 daily), Sümeg (2), Veszprém (5), Szombathely (2), and Zala (4), with early-bird departures for Sopron (5:20am) and Győr (4:50am), and a bus *to Prague* (10pm) June 17–September 26. Buses from the station terminal run to Balatongyörök (6 daily) and overnight to Budapest (3:45am). **Ferries** sail twice daily (8am & 2pm) for the Badacsony and Tihany, two hours and four and a half hours journey, respectively. The railroad around the lake's curve to Balatonszentgyörgy (change there for Nagykanizsa) is really only a continuation of the mainline down from Tapolca and Sümeg—which provides the easiest means of reaching the Bakony. **Cyclists** might enjoy the tree-lined road following the River Zala through ZALASZENTGRÓT—there's a picturesque bridge and manor and a good restaurant, the ill-named *Grót Étterem*, towards Zalaegerszeg, Szombathely, or Sárvár. On the road to VASAR, oxen and horse-drawn carts are more common than cars.

THE BAKONY

The Bakony range cuts a swath across central Transdanubia, as if scooped from the ground to provide space for the lake, and piled as a natural embankment behind the lowlier Balaton hills. Abundant vineyards testify to the richness of the volcanic soil and, more recently, mineheads to the mineral wealth beneath it. With dense woods and narrow ravines, this was the "Hungarian Sherwood Forest" during the centuries of warfare and turmoil, and also the setting for a dozen castles, the finest examples of which stand at **Sümeg** and **Veszprém**, while others—brooding, Gothic ruins—decorate peaks as far afield as Csobánc and Nagyvázsony. Siófok's tourist board organizes day trips to Veszprém and the porcelain center of **Herend**. Or you can get away from everything **walking** in the Bakony, providing you steer clear of military land. During fall, pink crocuses spangle the meadows between Sumeg and the Balaton, and huge sunflower fields and leguminous, red-podded trees abound near Sárvár.

Basalt Hills and Tapolca

Behind the Badacsony a succession of **hills** (*hegy*) range northwards towards the Bakony, offering the chance of **hikes** through woodland up to Szent György-hegy, Csobánc, and other heights. Basalt columns looking like petrified dwarves known locally as "organ pipes" ripple the side of **Szent György-hegy**, a hill near the *Nemesgulács v.m.* halt along the railroad between Badacsony and Tapolca, which can also be reached as an extension of the hike from the Stone Gate to Gulács Hill (see "The Badacsony" above). From its summit on a clear day distant Sümeg is visible, and just a few kilometers east rises **Csobánc-hegy**, its peak crowned by a ruined castle which women once defended against the Turks. Since 1970, when public petitions roused the state to declare these hills a conservation area, reforestation and orchard-planting have partially alleviated the damage caused by sixty years of ruthless quarrying for basalt, during which one peak, the Holáp, was completely decapitated.

Farther north, the town of **TAPOLCA** has become a profitable blot on the landscape with the development of bauxite mining and aluminum processing. This is the subject matter of Tapolca's **Bakony Bauxite Museum**, opened on Miners' Day in 1981, but is hardly enthralling stuff. Mining operations have sadly necessitated the damming of the **Tavas Caves** (source of underground springs that feed the Mill Lake, *Malom-tó*, in central Tapolca), so that for the next fifteen years, only the smallest, least interesting caves can be visited; the entrance is on Kisfaludy utca, where there's a tourist hostel at no. 1. Tapolca itself, though the neo-Classical Belváros centered around Malom-tó is nice enough, has nothing to keep you. Instead, use the town's **transport links** to move on down to Keszthely or up to Sümeg by train, or catch a bus towards Veszprém, which should call at Nagyvázsony (see below) along the way.

Sümeg

SÜMEG is a nicer town to visit than Tapolca, and despite its two fine historic monuments, seems far less tourist-oriented and pretentious than Tihany. Possibly the most impressive and certainly the best restored of the many fortresses built around the Balaton region, **Sümeg Castle** is lodged high upon a conical limestone massif, a unique Cretaceous outcropping among the basalt of the Bakony. The citadel to the south, built during the thirteenth century, provided the basis for successive fortifications—including the outer wall and gate tower—which kept the Turks out, but succumbed to the Habsburgs in 1713, when the struggle for independence, led by Rákóczi, collapsed. The complex of living quarters and defensive structures was restored between 1959 and 1964, and its history is recalled by exhibits displayed in the oldest tower. It's well worth the climb for the views alone. On the road uphill, Vak Bottyán utca, you'll find a cheap hotel, the *Tourist*, and an old stables mounting a display of saddles, "jiggling woggles," and other such objects.

Much of **the town** dates from the eighteenth century, when Sümeg was the seat of the Bishops of Veszprém, whose residence at 10 Szent István tér is now a school, still decorated with stone figures but starting to crumble badly. Like the porticoed birthplace of the poet Sándor Kisfaludy (whose belongings are on show inside), and the seventeenth-century church commissioned by Bishop Széchenyi, it pales in comparison to the **Church of the Ascension**, which contains probably the finest **frescoes** ever executed by *Maulbertsch*, the prolific Austrian court painter. With a team of assistants, he was able to cover the whole interior within one and a half years, mainly in Biblical scenes, but also with advertising. Along the rear wall are portraits of his main patron, Bishop Biró, together with local gentry and noblewomen, while on the wall facing the choir are depictions of the building itself and a church in Zala, which Biró also sponsored. Apropos of Biró, it was another Hungarian, Lászlo Biró, who invented the ballpoint pen, or biro, as it's commonly called in Europe.

Other forms of **accommodation** are available at the *Kisfaludy* hotel and through the tourist office, both on Kossuth street. Most **transportation** heads northwards. Traveling up that way by railroad, you can switch trains for places in Transdanubia at UKK, BOBA, and CELLDÖMÖLK—three oddly-named but otherwise undistinguished junctions that enable you to reach Zalaegerszeg, Vesprém, and Szombathely or Győr respectively. Rd.84 heads off for Sárvár and Sopron, meeting route 8 (from the Austrian border to Veszprém and Székesfehérvár) near the village of "John's house," Jánosháza.

Approaching Veszprém

The somnambulant atmosphere of the Balaton gives way along the road **between Balatonfüred and Veszprém**, some 15km away, as low-flying helicopter gunships make their appearance from a base in the hills above SZENTKIRÁLYSZABADJA. Around this part of the Bakony you can't miss the **Soviet Forces Temporarily in Hungary**; here since 1945 on a "provisional" basis, hence the joke "long, longer, provisionally." The recently announced troop withdrawals make no mention of **nuclear weapons**, an officially taboo subject here; for while Hungary was never obliged to accept SS-20s during the early 1980s, "tactical" missiles and bombs have been stored in the Bakony since the 1960s. Most Hungarians are resigned to their presence, and any resentment is more likely caused by the soldiers themselves, although their behavior rarely matches that of a Soviet tankman in 1986 who, responding to bar-room taunts that the USSR-Hungary football match had been "fixed," stole a tank from his camp outside Veszprém and returned to bulldoze the *vendéglő*.

A nicer, though much less direct way of **approaching Veszprém** is to go **via Nagyvázsony**, sited along the Tapolca–Veszprém road (and accessible by bus from Balatonfüred). Buses to Nagyvázsony pass the ruined *Zadorvár*, secreted in a wood between Pécsely and Barnag. **NAGYVÁZSONY** itself is a sleepy market town, enlivened annually by three or four **days of show-jumping and jousting** (at the end of July), held in the grounds of **Kinizsi Castle**. Begun in the fifteenth century by the Veszenyis, this was given by King Mátyás to Pál Kinizsi, a local boy who made good as a commander—being reputedly so strong that he wielded a dead Turk as a bludgeon to slay 100 enemies—and was later buried in the red marble fortress chapel. Fine views and cheap beds may be had here in the *Vár túristaszálló*; for sustenance, the *Kinizsi* restaurant is more prominent, though more expensive and less lively than seedier bars along the main street.

Approaches **from the west** run past Herend and Nemesvámos (see below); the route **from Várpalota** is covered above (see "Travelling on from Székesfehérvár"). Traveling by rail **from Szombathely**, Celldömölk, Boba, or **Székesfehérvár**, much of the scenery is marred by industry or trampled underfoot by *Honvéd* conscripts doing their basic training, but the route down **from the north**, following the Cuha Valley, is a picturesque one (see next page).

Veszprém

Cobbled together by a maze of streets which twist up the interlying valleys, **VESZPRÉM** stands upon hills prone to abrupt halts above the fine panorama of the ancient Bakony forests. Notwithstanding its perfectly restored Castle Hill, redolent of a millenium of ecclesiastical influence, and the parks and orchards that green the town, Veszprém has its gritty side; with smoke spewing out from the chemical factories, and local people shocked by the recent closure of the Veszprém Construction Company under Hungary's new bankruptcy laws.

Entering the town from the west, over Valley Bridge, there's a glimpse of Veszprém's castle en route to **the center**, where sights and activities cluster about boomerang-shaped Népköztársaság and Bajcsy-Zsilinszky avenues, which join the incoming highways. You can walk there from the **bus terminal**—past the **market** onto Ferenc tér, and then along the pedestrian mall, Kossuth utca—or take a bus from the **railroad station** beyond the northern suburbs, alighting by the big Áruház store just east of Szabadság tér. From this square, graced by Attila's statue, to its triangular neighbor Vörös Hadsereg tér, where the Red Army memorial serves as a begging-spot for Gypsy children, the surrounding architecture is floridly Baroque and Rococo—painted in bright pinks, blues, and the shade known as "Empress Theresa yellow" (which she ordained as the color scheme for all public buildings throughout the Habsburg empire). At the top end, the swish plastic *Elefánt bisztró* ensnares tourists seeking the dead-end street which leads to the **Firetower**, or *Tűztorony*. Its lower section is medieval and formed part of the castle, while the upper stories, dome, and balcony were added in the nineteenth to twentieth century, together with a mechanical set of bells which plays a traditional recruiting tune every hour on the hour.

The Castle area (*Várhegy*) occupies a plateau, like its counterpart in Buda, and though it contains only one street, its appearance and antecedents are impeccable. True, the *Heroes' Gate* is a bombastic monument of the reactionary Thirties; but in the **museum** just behind it, and along Tolbuhin út, both state money and public reverence are lavished upon a romantic past of bejewelled bishops and saintly kings. Here, the Archbishop of Salzburg established a Christian bridgehead among the pagan subjects of Prince Géza; here too were crowned Gisella, the wife of Hungary's first king, and her successors, giving Veszprém the title of the "Queen's town." **Saint Michael's Cathedral** on Trinity Square boasts of similar lineage, although the building itself has been razed and resurrected half a dozen times. Its current incarnation (dating from 1907–10) is neo-Romanesque, with only a Gothic crypt to show for its origins. Behind the Cathedral, Saint György's chapel is a mere fragment beneath a glass dome, but **Gisella's chapel** to the south (likewise, Tues–Fri, May–Oct) contains Byzantine-influenced frescoes, albeit slightly damaged since her residence was demolished in order to build the adjoining U-shaped Bishop's Palace. In the former Franciscan church opposite the Cathedral you can view wooden votive statues, chasubles and so forth, to the sound of mournful, taped Mass; while at the end of the promenade, monuments to István and Gisella overlook the Bakony hills and the graceful Völgy-híd bridge over the Séd Valley. During summer, the Castle district is the setting for open-air **concerts**.

Retrace your steps to Szabadság tér, where commercial life gravitates towards Kossuth utca (Post Office, **Express**, and **IBUSZ**) and the market, just as movie theaters, theaters, and groups of students inhabit the university district extending to the south. A short walk past County Hall brings you out into Lenin tér, flanked by Kálvária Hill and a building housing the **Bakony Museum**, whose best exhibits are the Roman mosaics unearthed in a villa at Balácapuszta, southeast of town, and artifacts pertaining to the Bakony's *betyár*, or highwaymen.

The **Chemical Technical University** is situated on the far side of the park, through which Lenin sétány leads farther south to the *Sport bisztró*, a popular place with **students**, serving cheap, filling food. By inquiring here, at Express, or the student hostel (*diákszálló*) opposite the university, you should be able to obtain dormitory beds from June through August; cheaper **accommodation** than in the *Hotel Veszprém* (Budapesti u.6), the *Erdei* motel on Kitten berger u. in the valley, or a private room from *IBUSZ* (Kossuth u.6). The nearest campground is at Kárdárta, a village along rd.82 north of town.

Veszprém's *divatos* set frequents the *Marica kávéház*, where a late night café/disco operates on the top floor of the twenty-story building opposite Szabadság tér; another, cheaper hangout is the *Vadasztanya kisvendéglő* on Attila utca, out towards Nagyvázsony. Less intoxicating **pursuits** include sports at the complex southwest of the university; viewing movies or plays (in the center); and walking in the Séd Valley. Along the riverbank west of the *Völgy-híd* viaduct (which carries rd.8) is an old watermill; to the south lie the *Erdei Motel*, a **Village Museum**, and a ghastly zoo.

Through the Bakony to Szombathely or Győr

Leaving aside the places already covered in this chapter, you have a choice of destinations when it's time to move on. **Westwards towards Szombathely**, both rd.8 and the railroad pass through Herend, while by road it's only 5km to **NEMESVÁMOS**, the site of an old **Bakony inn**, the *Vámosi csárda*. Ignore the odd modern fixture and today's clientele, and it's possible to imagine the csárda's appearance at the end of the nineteenth century: servants hurrying from the tap-room with its huge casks into the cellar, where swineherds, wayfarers, and *betyár* caroused seated upon sections of tree trunk. Poor though most were, Bakony folk were proud of their master-less lives among the oak forests, esteeming the *kondás*, with his herd of pigs, and the highwaymen who robbed rich merchants. These latter called them-selves *szegénylegények*—"poor boys"—of whom the most audacious, Jóska Savanyú, claimed the tavern as his home.

HEREND, 10km farther west, is the site of a **porcelain** factory. Established in 1839, its products were to nineteenth-century Central Europe what Delftware or Miessen china were to more northerly countries. The craftswomen's talents which won international prizes and the acclaim of monarchs are still in evidence—judging by stuff on display in the **factory museum**—and Hungarians are proud of this tradition. One friend told me of a woman "so rich and snobbish that when she threw tantrums, she only smashed Herend china!" Following Herend, the scenery deteriorates around AJKA, but 6km beyond DEVECSER (where the railroad turns northwards towards Celldömölk) there's a great view of the Bakony from a look-out tower near SOMLÓVÁSÁRHELY. In clear weather Mt. Kőris (713m) and even the Austrian Alps may be visible. Sárvár and Szombathely—the most feasible destinations when traveling west—are described on pages 144 and 147.

Alternatively, you can head **northwards towards Győr** by rd.82 or the railroad, both of which roughly follow the course of the River Cuha. ZIRC, 23km north of Veszprém, has a Baroque church with *Maulbertsch altar paintings* on Népköztársaság útja, while 17km to the west by bus, BAKONYBÉL lies at the foot of **Mount Kőris**, the Bakony's highest peak. There's cheap accommodation in Zirc (on Rákóczi tér) and Bakonybél (at Fürdő u.59), and opportunities for walking in the surrounding mountains, should you decide to stop. Continuing northwards, the ruined castle on a steep hill at CSESZNEK permits a fine view of the region, and while trains stop some distance away (at Porva-Csesznek), the railroad journey is itself a scenic one, winding between cliffs, over bridges, and through tunnels along a line built in 1896. Before reaching Győr, trains stop at **Pannonhalma**, the site of Hungary's greatest Benedictine Monastery (for details of both, see *Transdanubia*).

Heading down **towards southern Transdanubia** is awkward by public transportation from Veszprém. By a three-stage railroad journey (changing trains at Lepsény, and then Dombóvár) it should be possible to reach Pécs within seven to eight hours, but it might be quicker to catch a bus from Veszprém to Siófok. Trains from there take less time to reach Kaposvár, a short distance from Dombóvár where you switch again for the final leg down to Pécs (see *Transdanubia*).

festivals

Summer

Chamber music at KŐRÖSHEGY, organ recitals at TIHANY, Beethoven's symphonies at MARTONVÁSÁR, and open-air concerts in VESZPRÉM's castle district at intervals throughout **June, July, and August**. In the last few days of July there's a festival of **show-jumping** and **jousting** at NAGYVÁZSONY.

travel details

Trains

From Budapest to Balatonfüred (13 daily; 2–2hr 30min) and Siófok (hourly; 2hr) call at Székesfehérvár en route (15–20 daily; 1–1hr 30min).

From Balatonfenyves to Csisztapuszta (6 daily; 45min).

From Balatonfüred to Budapest (hourly; 2–2hr 30min).

From Balatonszentgyörgy to Nagykanizsa (10 daily; 45min).

From Székesfehérvár to Balatonfüred (hourly; 30min–1hr); Komárom (6 daily; 1hr 15min–1hr 45min); Siófok (hourly; 30min); Szombathely (7 daily; 2hr 30min–3hr 45min); Veszprém (10; 45min).

From Tapolca to Celldömölk (5; 1hr 15min); Sümeg (9; 1hr 30min); Szombathely (2; 1hr 30min).

From Veszprém to Győr (4; 2hr 30min); Szombathely (6; 1hr 15min–2hr 15min).

Buses
From Badacsony to Keszthely (hourly).

From Balatonfüred to Nagyvázsony (5–6 daily); Tihany (frequently); Veszpréem (roughly every hour).

From Keszthely to Hévíz (every 15min); Szombathely (hourly); Zalaegerszeg (hourly).

From Lake Velence to Balatonfüred; Dunaújváros; Pusztaszabolcs; Siófok; Székesfehérvár (all roughly every hour).

From Tapolca to Nagyvázsony; Sümeg; Veszprém (the last two hourly, or more frequently).

From Veszprém to Herend; Nemesvámos; Siófok (all regularly).

International Trains
From Fonyód to Dresden (1 daily); Leipzig (1); Zagreb (2).

From Siófok to Dresden (1); Leipzig (1); Prague (1); Vienna (1); Zagreb (2).

From Székesfehérvár to Dresden (1); Leipzig (1); Prague (1); Vienna (1); Zagreb (2).

International buses
From Keszthely to Prague.

From Révfülöp to Vienna.

From Siófok to Bratislava; Semmering; Vienna.

Ferries
Besides the following services (departing every hour or two) there are ferries linking each port with others on the same shore.

From Alsóörs to Siófok.

From Badacsony to Balatonboglár; Balatonmáriafürdő; Fonyód.

From Balatonboglár to Révfülöp; Badacsony.

From Balatonmáriafürdő to Badacsony; Balatongyörök.

From Fonyód to Badacsony.

From Siófok to Alsóörs; Balatonfüred; Tihany.

From Szántódrév to Tihany-rév.

From Tihany to Siófok.

TELEPHONE CODES

ALSÓÖRS ☎86	BALATONSZEMES ☎84
BALATONAKALI ☎86	BALATONVILÁGOS ☎84
BALATONKARATTYA ☎80	CSOPAK ☎86
BALATONALIGA ☎84	KÖRÖSHEGY ☎84
BALATONALMADI ☎86	SIÓFOK ☎84
BALATONFÖLDVÁR ☎84	SZÉKESFEHÉRVÁR ☎22
BALATONFÜRED ☎86	TIHANY ☎86
BALATONFŰZFŐ ☎80	VÁRPALOTA ☎80
BALATONSZABADI ☎84	VESZPRÉM ☎80
BALATONSZÁRSZÓ ☎84	ZAMÁRDI ☎84

CHAPTER FOUR

TRANSDANUBIA

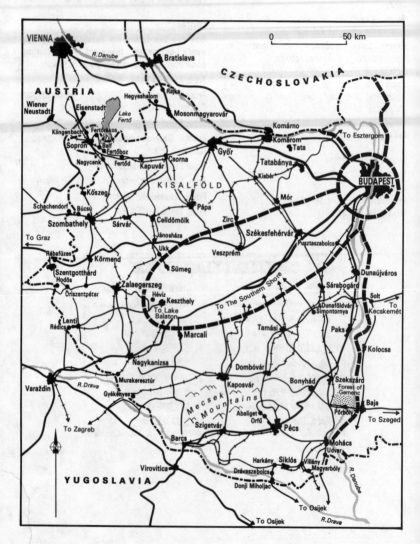

Traveling from Vienna to Budapest it's easy to gain a poor impression of **Transdanubia**—the *Dunántul*—from the monotonous *Kisalföld* (Little Plain) or the industrial dreck around Tatabánya. What you don't see in passing is lakeside Tata, Győr's antique waterfront, Sopron's cobbled streets, deer in the Forest of Gemenc, or the rolling hills of the Mecsek region.

More than other regions in Hungary, the *Dunántúl* is a patchwork land, an ethnic and social hybrid. Its valleys and hills, forests, and mud flats have been a melting pot since Roman times: settled by Magyars, Serbs, Slovaks, and Germans; torn asunder and occupied by Turks and Habsburgs; and, within the last 150 years, transformed from a state of near feudalism into what the Party describes as a "developed Socialist society." Though **Szombathely** with its Temple of Isis and other ruins has the most to show for its Roman origins, all the main **towns** display evidence of this evolution. **Castles** (*vár*) are at the heart of them: survivors of the centuries of warfare that decimated medieval culture, leaving only a few superb churches—for example at **Ják** and **Velemér**—and living evidence in the form of **Pannonhalma Monastery**. Around each weathered vár stands a *belváros*, with rambling streets and squares overlooked by florid Baroque and the odd Gothic or Renaissance pile. **Tata, Kőszeg,** and **Győr** provide fine examples of the genre; so too does **Sopron**, the most archaic, and **Pécs**, which boasts a Turkish mosque and minaret.

Sopron, Szombathely, and Pécs host major summer **festivals** of classical music, drama, and folk; but the most interesting event is the masked *Busó Carnival* at **Mohács** in March. During summer, concerts are also held in two unique settings—the **Esterházy Palace at Fertőd** and the rock chambers of **Fertőrákos**–both close to Sopron and **Nagycenk**, where you can ride antique **steam trains** on the Széchenyi railroad. At the monthly **market** in Pécs, you'll sense the peasant roots underlying many Transdanubian towns, whose sprawling *lakótelep* house recent immigrants from the countryside. In the oil town of **Zalaegerszeg**, a village museum commemorates the old life and farmsteads of the Göcsej region, while **Dunaújváros** is entirely the product of brute labor and Five Year Plans.

NORTHERN AND WESTERN TRANSDANUBIA

Imagine drawing a line from Budapest to Zalaegersezeg. Exclude the Bakony highlands, Székesfehérvár, and Veszprém (which are dealt with in Chapter Three), and what's left above the line is **northern and western Transdanubia**. Approaching from Graz and Vienna in Austria, it's possible to cross the frontier near **Szombathely, Kőszeg,** or **Sopron**—the main sites of interest in the west—but most people venture into Transdanubia via the E15 highway or the railroad between Vienna and Budapest. The highway, and trains from Budapest's Déli station, pass through **Győr**, which is the junction for trains going through to Sopron or Szombathely, and is linked by road and rail to **Komárom** (a point of entry from Czechoslovakia) and **Tata**. The latter lies just off the E15, and like **Pannonhalma Monastery** between Győr and Veszprém, is worth the detour.

Tatabánya and the Vértes

Following the Budapest–Vienna route, **TATABÁNYA** is inescapable: an ugly mining town surrounded by ravaged countryside. The town's only "sight" can be glimpsed from a train carriage window, perched on a mountaintop overlooking the grimy sprawl. The giant bronze **Turul statue** was erected to commemorate the thousandth anniversary of the Magyar conquest in 1896, and symbolically clutches the sword of the ancient Magyar tribal chieftain, Árpád, in its talons.

There are only two reasons to stay in this drab, polluted town: the Tatabánya **Jazz Festival** (sometime in the summer) or to go **walking in the Vértes**. This modest range is virtually the only high ground in northern Transdanubia, an advantage that the warlord who raised **Vitány Castle** plainly couldn't resist. Nowadays, the ruined *Vitányvár* lends a somber cast to a crag 5km south of Tatabánya's *felsővasútállomas* station. You can also walk there from VÉRTESSOMLÓ village, accessible by bus from town. Legend has it that the cowslips that grow around here during April are able to guide you towards hidden treasure.

Accommodation in Tatabánya's *Újváros* district includes a costly hotel, private rooms from *Komturist* (Győri út 12), *Nomád* campground (Tolnai út 14), and a hostel in Jubileumi Sportpark (reservations from Tóth B. u.3). The *Varsovia* express **train to Bratislava, Warsaw, and Gdansk** stops briefly in Tatabánya's main station around 6:15pm.

Tata

A small, sleepy town interlaced with canals and streams, **TATA** derives much of its charm from its **lakes**. **Öreg-tó** is a delight, surrounded by slender trees and spires and the pillared *Lovarda* riding school. The eastern embankment, Tópart utca, leads past a late-night grill/disco, a statue of the "Tata mermaid," luxuriant gardens and a now-defunct mill to the **Castle** at the northern end of the lake. Once a fortress and then a royal hunting lodge, this was kicked around by the Turks and Habsburgs, despite its ivy-covered ramparts and moat, which has been dredged by Soviet conscripts (Tata is a small garrison town) and now serves as a fish farm. In the reconstructed half of the castle, a **museum** displays Roman miniatures, weird ceramics, and the spectacular pottery of Domokos Kuny, a local craftsman.

Öreg-tó is higher than streets surrounding it to the north, and the water is guided down through lockgates and canals. Previously, almost twenty **mills** (*malom*) were grouped around the lake, and there's the derelict shell of one just east of the castle. Below, and farther along Bartók utca, another old mill

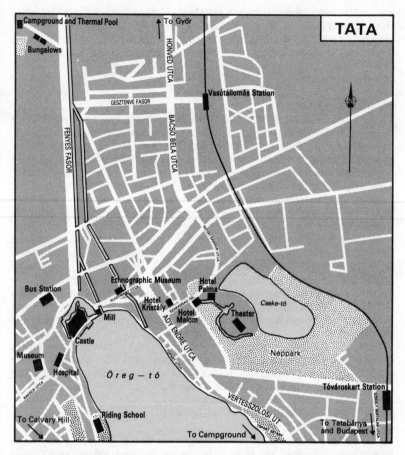

building (Alkotmány u.2) contains an **Ethnographic museum** devoted to the German communities of the Little Plain. As always the **costumes** are best: the men wearing knee-high army boots and braided black and stovepipe hats, the women swathing their layers of petticoats and ruffles with embroidered shawls.

Ady Endre út, Tata's charmless main street, runs between Öreg-tó and the smaller lake—called just that, **Cseke-tó**. Just north of the Miklós Mill (no. 26), Szabadság tér meanders off towards the **park** surrounding Cseke-tó, passing two cheap hotels. Perhaps to compensate for its lack of size and swans, the lake offers opportunities for **fishing**, while there's a swimming pool, theater and fake ruined church (cobbled together from Roman and Benedictine stonework) in the park. Another area to ramble lies southwest of the castle—the hilly quarter between November 7 tér and Kossuth tér, mostly built in the eighteenth century to the plans of Jakob Fellner. Along the way, at the foot of Rákóczi utca, a **museum** displays lifesize plaster copies of Hercules and Laocoön, Roman statues in the Louvre, and that prize of archaeological piracy, the Elgin marbles. At the top of the hill stands leafy Kossuth tér, behind which back alleys wind towards **Calvary Hill** with its bleak crucifixion monument and a blackened observation tower looming above patches of urban wasteland.

Practicalities

Twin sets of **railroad stations** and campgrounds are located some distance from the center of Tata. From the main *vasútállomás* in the north of town, buses #1 and #3 run down into the center, the latter terminating at the **campground/cottage** complex on Gesztenye fasor (Chestnut Avenue) 500m short of the **thermal pool**. Alternatively, you can catch bus #5 from the smaller *Tóvároskert* station to Kossuth tér, or reach the other campground on the banks of Öreg-tó by following Székely B. u. to its end, turning right and walking to the highway at the finish of Lumumba utca, where you'll see the site signposted over the road.

The **tourist office** stands nearly opposite the mill and *Hotel Kristály* on Tata's main street; private **rooms** or the *Hotel Malom* cost somewhat less; the *Pálma* roughly 200Ft more. Rowing boats (*csónakázás*) and pedal boats (*vízibicikli*) can be hired on Öreg-tó embankment, where the grill/disco on Tópart u. is perhaps the best place **to eat**, although the *Vár Étterem* on November 7 tér is quieter. For those with money to burn, there are more expensive hotels and bars in the **REMETESÉGPUSZTA** suburb (bus #4) out of town.

From the *Pályaudvar* north of the castle there are two or three **buses** every day to Komárom, Budapest and Győr (see below), which tend to be quicker but more crowded than **trains** to the same destinations. There's also a daily bus **to Bratislava**, leaving at 7:45am from stand #11.

Győr

Few towns look enticing from a bypass or railroad siding, and **GYŐR** (pronounced "Dyur") isn't one of them. The waterfront Belváros, Győr's glory, is obscured by heavy industries like the giant *Rába* truck and tractor combine, and is separated from the rest of the city by Tanácsköztársaság útja. This grimy wind-tunnel of an avenue is named after Hungary's brief experience of the 1919 Republic of Councils ("all power to the soviets"), whose leader, Béla Kun, later fled to the USSR and died during Stalin's purges. Revolutionary *tanács* also wielded power during the 1956 Uprising, when Győr's monumental Town Hall was occupied by a regional Provisional National Council, chaired by Antal Szigetti, which pressed the Nagy government to act faster on Soviet troop withdrawals.

You'll pass the Town Hall and come upon the Avenue of the Republic of Councils beyond Lenin Bridge, which leads from the main **bus and railroad stations** towards the center.

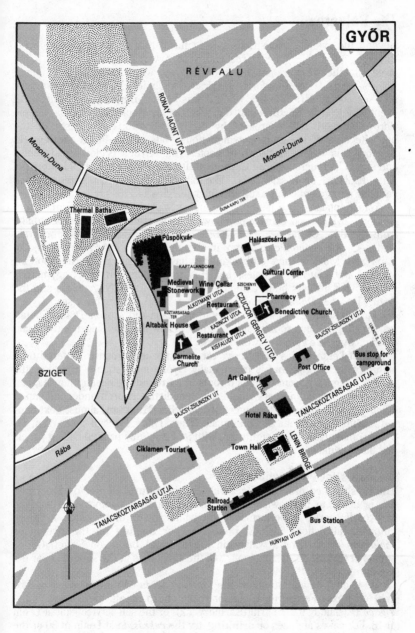

GYÖR

RÉVFALU

Mosoni-Duna

RÓNAY JÁCINT UTCA

Mosoni-Duna

Thermal Baths

DUNA-KAPU TÉR

Püspökvár

Halászcsárda

KÁPTALANDOMB

Cultural Center

Medieval Stonework

Wine Cellar

SZÉCHENYI TÉR

Pharmacy

ALKOTMÁNY UTCA

Restaurant

CZUCZOR GERGELY UTCA

Benedictine Church

KÖZTÁRSASÁG TÉR

KAZINCZY UTCA

Altabak House

BAJCSY-ZSILINSZKY UTJA

LUKÁCS S. U.

Restaurant

KISFALUDY UTCA

Carmelite Church

Post Office

Bus stop for campground

SZIGET

Art Gallery

LENIN UT

TANÁCSKÖZTÁRSASÁG UTJA

BAJCSY-ZSILINSZKY UT

Hotel Rába

Rába

Ciklamen Tourist

Town Hall

LENIN BRIDGE

TANÁCSKÖZTÁRSASÁG UTJA

Railroad Station

Bus Station

HUNYADI UTCA

The Belváros

Beyond the avenue, pedestrians-only Lenin út thrusts into the old town—
throwing off cobbled alleys (*köz*) that lead towards the Rába River. Many
streets to the west are narrow and shadowy, with overhanging timbered
houses—the stage setting for a conspiracy (and indeed, the Communist Party
met secretly at Sárlo köz 15, when it was banned during the Thirties). All
eventually lead to **Köztársaság tér**, a square overlooking the Rába, largely
Baroque though still buttressed by surviving **bastions** of a castle on the
opposite side of the square, which house bits of **medieval stonework**.
Beyond it is **Káptalan-domb**—Chapter Hill—Győr's ecclesiastical center
and site of its much restored **Cathedral**. Its star feature is the gilded bust of
King Ladislas, or László (who, like István, was also canonized), which
contains a fragment of his skull and thus qualifies as a holy relic.

From Káptalan-domb it's only a minute's walk to **the waterfront**, where
women hawk fish on Duna-kapu tér while their menfolk watch proceedings
from the door of the nearest *borpince* or *italbolt*. Since the Danube grain
trade—Győr's economic mainstay in the nineteenth century—stopped, the
Rába and Mosoni-Duna embankments have become a favorite spot for
anglers and courting couples, but this may change if the Nagymaros-
Gabčikovo dam gets built. Critics of the scheme (see "Nagymaros and the
Dam" in *The Danube Bend*) claim that as the Danube rises, Győr's
discharged sewage will wash back into the Rába and Mosoni-Duna tributaries, creating a dangerous health hazard. Meanwhile, the Sziget and Révfalu
districts **over the river** are worth a brief look.

East of Lenin út lies **Széchenyi tér**, a sun-baked expanse centered on a
statue of the Virgin, that is traditionally Győr's main square. Eye-like attic
windows regard it from the steep roofs of surrounding, peeling houses, and
black-garbed grandmothers attend the Benedictine church under the super-
cilious gaze of lounging teenagers. The **Patika Museum**, almost next door
to the church, functions as a pharmacy (Tues, Thurs, Fri 9am–5pm; Wed, Sat
2–5pm) that also attracts sightseers with its beautifully painted ceiling panels
and fine cabinet work.

Diversions and Practicalities

The brashly tiled *Művelődesi központ*, Győr's **cultural center** on Széchenyi
tér, is home to the town's superb **modern dance** company, under Ivan
Márkó. If there's a performance on while you're there, catch it. More
mundane attractions include **boat trips** or **angling** on the river (see
Ciklámen Tourist), or a wallow in the **thermal baths** on Sziget. Győr's
soccer team can be worth a look, too; the stadium is in the suburbs near the
campground.

You should be able to afford the *Matróz Csárda* or the *Halászcsárda* (for
fish) off Rózsa Ferenc utca, but for really cheap **meals** there's always the
Vigadó (Kisfaludy u.2), a grill (Kazinczy u.2), or the self-service joint at Lenin
út 13. For cakes and ices or **drinking**, try the *cukrászda* at Lenin út 30 or the
Vár-borozó cellar on Alkotmány utca. Other things include a **foreign-**

language bookshop (Kisfaludy u. 7), the **zoo** near the campground, an **art gallery** (Lenin út 33), and the **hospitals** and **police** headquarters (for visa extensions) around Felszabadulás út, south of the bus terminal. If 2000Ft-a-night **hotels** are your thing, skip the high-rise *Rába* in favor of the *Klastrom* (Aradi vértanúk útja 2), with all modern conveniences inside a former priory of the Carmelite Order. Taking other options in descending order of cost, there are three **pensions** (Tessedik u.27, Csaba u.22 & Kiss u.4); the hotel on the campground; private **rooms**, or beds in the *KTM Kollégium* (Ságvári u.3), from *Ciklámen Tourist*; and finally *Kiskút-ligeti* **campground**. Equipped with mosquitos and cottages, this can be reached by boarding bus #8 next to the playground on Tanácsköztársaság útja, opposite Lukács Sándor u.

Moving on, the obvious destination to the west is SOPRON (see next page), which is easy to reach by train. If you're heading there, however, it's still worth making a detour to **Pannonhalma Monastery**—described below—which lies along the way to VESZPRÉM (see *Lake Balaton and the Bakony*). As for **international connections**, Győr has more or less daily *Volán* buses to Galanta and Trnava in Czechoslovakia, and four trains. Providing you get seat reservations, and already have the necessary visas, you can reach Bratislava, Prague, Dresden, or Berlin on the *Meridian*, leaving Győr around 3:30pm; Vienna on the *Arrabona* (8:45am), or *Lehár* (7:50pm); or Bratislava, Warsaw or Gdansk using the *Varsovia* (7:15pm). For details of local border crossings, see below.

Pannonhalma Monastery

Thrusting skywards from the summit of Saint Martin's Hill, **PANNONHALMA MONASTERY** makes an imposing presence after the low-lying Kisalföld, as was surely intended when **the Benedictine Order**, with the support of Prince Géza, founded an abbey here in 969. Known as the church militants, the Order helped King Stephen to unify the anarchic pagan Magyars into one unified Christian state; rebuffed a Tartar invasion from behind its abbey's fortified walls; and grew more powerful for centuries until its suppression in 1787 by Emperor Joseph II. Re-established by Joseph's successor, the Benedictines thereafter confined themselves to prayer and pedagogy, founding schools which still function today.

Manifesting different styles and varying degrees of antiquity, the buildings are grouped around several courtyards with thirteenth-century cloisters. The **Basilica** is likewise Gothic in origin, with a finely carved portal and marble sepulchers containing the bones of two abbots and a princess. Medieval codices and incunabula are displayed in the 300,000-volume **library**, where you can see a portrait of the legendary Stephen (István) and, for the linguistically-minded, the first document to include Hungarian words—55 of them—amongst the customary Latin. During the summer, there are **organ recitals** at Pannonhalma.

Ciklámen Tourist (Vár u.1) can arrange private **rooms** if the hostel or campground (Fenyvesalja u.9) are full.

Mosonmagyaróvár and the Border

Guide books normally mention **MOSONMAGYARÓVÁR** because of its small **castle** (now a college) and the twisting River Lajta with its seventeen bridges, or the parade of Baroque edifices along Lenin utca; and a veil is usually drawn over the event which briefly made the town notorious, and still haunts the memory of inhabitants over the age of forty. On October 25, 1956, two days after the Uprising began in Budapest, some 5000 men, women, and children held a peaceful demonstration that the *ÁVH* fired upon without warning as it approached the town hall, killing more than 100 people. Although the officer responsible was recently tracked down in peaceful retirement, and might now belatedly be prosecuted, the few tourists that stop here emerge from the local history **museum** with its colorful folk costumes (Lenin u.135) undisturbed by any mention of it.

The *Hotel Minerva* is hardly extortionate, but you'll pay less at the *Fekete Sas* (no. 93) or *Lajtha* hostel (no. 119) on Lenin utca. Avoid the *Magyar Autóklub* campground.

Crossing the Border

Close by runs the border, which used to be wired and mined, and guards were authorized to shoot would-be escapers (the fate of the lesbian heroine of a Károly Makk movie). Since the barbed wire was cut down in the spring of 1989 (segments were later sold abroad as "relics of the Cold War"), thousands of citizens from East Germany and other socialist countries have escaped to Austria via Hungary. Numbers soared as word of successful attempts spread, and it became known that Hungarian border guards were now forbidden to open fire. On one occassion, a picnic party of 660 people just strolled across the border. Because of this, travelers in border areas may be asked to prove their nationality to plainclothes security men or uniformed guards. Providing you're polite and your visa's in order there shouldn't be any problems.

Hungarians themselves don't need to sneak abroad illegally. The special red passports required to travel west became progressively easier to obtain during the 1970s, until the government issued a new *Vilég* (World) passport, valid for visiting any country, a few years ago. Nowadays, most Magyars travel westward as often as they can afford to, if only to shop in Vienna (though new customs taxes have put a crimp in the once-thriving trade in consumer goods).

At any hour of the day or night motorists can drive across **from Rajka or Hegyeshalom into Czechoslovakia or Austria**. There are infrequent "local" trains to like-named stations, but these are miles from the checkpoints on the roads (and, obviously, strangers wandering around are suspect). Leaving Hungary at Hegyeshalom by road, however, the Austrian *Grenzepolizei* are well-mannered and even prepared to tolerate hitch-hikers starting just behind the *zoll*. But their Czech counterparts are notorious for searching, questioning, and sometimes turning back, "punks" or "hippies", and even the squeaky clean aren't admitted without **visas**. Get them before you leave home, or from the Czech consulate in Budapest (allow seven working days); visas are *not* issued at the border.

Sopron

With its 115 monuments and 240 listed buildings, **SOPRON** can legitimately claim to be "the most historic town in Hungary" despite the drab modernity that greets visitors outside the railroad station. Walk a few hundred meters up Mátyás Király utca, however, and you'll see why. North of Széchenyi tér, Lenin körút encircles a horseshoe-shaped Belváros that's full of antique buildings, most of them refreshingly unmonumental. Note that **museums** here are open 9am–5pm and closed on Tuesday unless specified otherwise.

The Inner Town

Templom utca is as nice a street as any to follow into the Belváros, leading to Orsolya tér where the cobbles sink towards a central orb of stone. Look

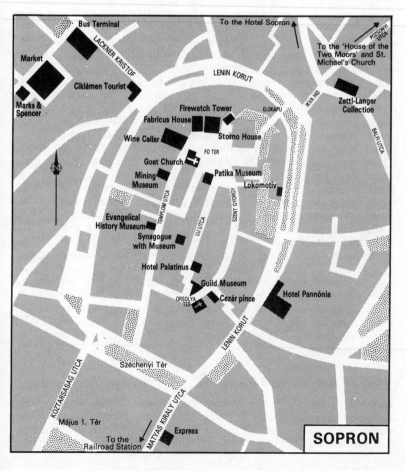

around and you'll see Renaissance edifices dripping with loggias and carved protrusions, a Gothic church exhibiting Catholic artifacts, and a **Guild Museum** dealing with local crafts' traditions. But there's more atmosphere in the **Cezár Pince**, a cellar with oak butts and leather-aproned waiters, serving local wines and platters of *wurst*, redolent of Habsburg times (9am–9:30pm).

Despite its name and the presence of the *Holsten Söröző* and *Palatinus* hotel, **Új utca** (New Street) is one of the town's oldest thoroughfares, a gentle curve of arched dwellings painted in red, yellow, and pink, with chunky cobblestones and pavements. At no. 22 stands one of the **synagogues** that flourished when the street was known as Zsidó (Jewish) utca; its near-desertion and a Judaica collection serve as mute reminders that Sopron's Jewish community survived the expulsion of 1526 only to be decimated during World War II.

During my last visit, the northern end of Új utca and the tourist hostel there were both closed due to excavations, so you might have to backtrack and exit by Templom utca. This street has two **museums**, covering evangelical history (10am–1pm, closed Tues & Wed) and mining (at no. 2), but the main source of interest is **Fő tér**, up ahead. A parade of Gothic and Baroque drawn up around a Trinity Statue crawling with cherubim, the square is partly overshadowed by the **Goat Church**—so called, supposedly, because its construction was financed by a goatherd whose flock unearthed a cache of loot. The Renaissance **Storno House**, once visited by King Mátyás and Count Széchenyi, now exhibits Roman, Celtic, and Avar relics, plus mementos of the composer Liszt, while the ground floor serves as the *Corvin Pizzeria*. If you can't gain admission to the "whispering gallery" in the **Fabricus House**, then the old pharmacy, now a **Patika Museum**, is worth a brief look.

North of the square rises Sopron's symbol, the **Firewatch Tower** (*Tűztorony*), founded upon the stones of a fortress built by the Romans, who established the town of *Scarbantia* during the first century AD. Though sentries—who in times past were expected to play music for the townsfolk while they stood guard—are no longer posted, the tower (Tues–Sat 9am–6pm) still offers a stunning **view** of Sopron's narrow streets and weathered rooftops. Offered the choice of Austrian citizenship in 1921, the townsfolk voted to remain Magyar subjects and erected a "Gate of Loyalty" at the base of the tower to commemorate this act of patriotism. Walk through it and you'll emerge onto **Előkapu** (outer gate), a short street where the houses are laid out in a "saw-toothed" pattern and "errant burghers" and "gossiping, nagging" wives were once pinioned in stocks for the righteous to pelt with rotten food.

On **Lenin körút** beyond, boutiques seem to have supplanted two minor monuments: the colorfully-tiled *Arany Sas* pharmacy and the former *White Horse Inn* where Haydn stayed when he wasn't enjoying the hospitality at Fertőd (see below).

Outside the Belváros

Ikva híd (crossing a narrow stream which flooded noxiously in the nineteenth century) points towards a couple more sights. Atmospheric Balfi utca leads directly to the privately owned **Zettl-Langer collection** of porcelain, earthenware and weaponry at no. 11 (10am–noon daily), while Pozsonyi utca wends uphill past the "House of the Two Moors" to the partially Gothic Church of Saint Michael, whose gargoyles leer over the Chapel of Saint Jacob decaying in the graveyard. Nearby stand the cross-less tombstones of Russians killed liberating Sopron from the Hungarian Nazi puppet-government, which massacred hostages like the Member of Parliament Bajcsy-Zsilinszky, and any Jew or suspected Communist that came along, before fleeing to Austria with the Coronation Regalia in April 1945.

The killing grounds were the **hills** outside town, nowadays given over to vineyards and locals fond of **walking**. To the southwest are the sub-Alpine *Löverek* (bus #1 or #2), with paths leading up to the TV mast and lookout tower atop Károly-magaslat, where you can gaze across the *Bürgenland*. Inhabited by bilingual folk engaged in viticulture, the region was divided between Hungary and Austria (which got the lion's share) after the collapse of the Habsburg empire—an amicable divorce settlement, it seems, since nobody complains about it today.

Finally, there's the so-called **Fool's Castle** (*Taródy-* or *Bolond-vár*), which is said to be as much fun as Bory's folly in Székesfehérvár (see *Lake Balaton and the Bakony*). I didn't have time to check it out, but the tourist office gave the following directions. Ride bus #1 to the domed *Fedett uszoda* outside town; walk 50m back and turn down the second street on the left, and then take a left at the end to reach the *vár*. Alternatively, take a taxi (☎14-089).

Other Things

The town is at its liveliest during the **Festival Weeks** (roughly June 22–July 14), when various places host folklore displays, rock theater, and concerts, details of which are available from *Ciklámen Tourist*. For what it's worth, Sopron has the distinction of possessing the only branch of England's famous **Marks & Spencer** department store in the Eastern bloc, which sells clothes for US dollars. Along the way from the bus terminal you'll pass stalls whose vendors might suggest that you buy them something from Marks & Spencer in exchange for one of their wares at a knockdown price; such deals are worth considering.

Places for sampling **local wines** like *Kékfrankos* and the white, apple-flavored *Tramini* include *Stefánia* (Szent György u.12) and two cellars, the abovementioned *Cezár* and the *Gyógygödör* on Fő tér. On the same square you can enjoy pizzas outside the Storno House; the "Corvinus"—ham garnished with pineapple, tangerines, and cherries—is delicious. Aside from hotel **restaurants** the best options are on Lenin körút—ranging from the popular *Vörös Étterem* and *Vendéglő* (no. 25 & 63) to the spit-and-sawdust *Finom Fatalok* grill—and around Széchenyi tér. Új utca's *Holsten Söröző* (open until 10pm) dispenses beer and disco-beat. Elsewhere, try the local *Alpsei* beer.

With the exception of *Lokomotiv*, responsible for organizing trips on the **Széchenyi steam train** (see below), any of Sopron's **tourist offices** can arrange **private rooms**—use *IBUSZ* on the körút if you arrive after 4pm, when *Ciklámen Tourist* shuts. They're cheaper at the *Kállai* pension (Ferencz J. u.66) or any of Sopron's **hotels**, of which the *Pannonia* and

Sopron are marginally less expensive. During July and August there's a possibility of **dormitory beds**, probably located at Damjanich u.9 (in a side street opposite *Ciklámen Tourist*) or the Jereván high school; but contact *Express* first. With the **hostel** (Új u.8) currently closed, the remaining alternative is **camping** or a cottage at the *Lövér* site (bus #12 hourly from Május 1. tér). Should you need one, **visa extensions** are granted at the police HQ next door to *Volántourist* (closed Sat & Sun).

Moving on and discounting the nearest sites, covered below, the most obvious destinations are Szombathely (best reached by afternoon train) and Kőszeg (easily accessible by bus), though there are also two or three buses for Balatonfüred, Keszthely, and Veszprém. Around 6am, noon, 5pm and 6:20pm, special GYSEV trains leave Sopron's *Déli* station for Wiener Neustadt and Vienna. The schedules of *Volán* buses to **Austria** (which cross at KLINGENBACH, open 24 hours) are more irregular. Services for Vienna leave on Monday (9:25am & 6pm), Wednesday (8:56am & 6pm), Thursday (6pm), Friday (8:50am, 9:25am & 6pm) and Saturday (8:56am, 9:25am, 5:55pm & 6pm); check the timetable regarding buses to Eisenstadt, Forchtenstein, Neunkirchen, Oberpullerdorf, Purbach, Semmering, or Krumbach. Travelers with the requisite visa may also catch a weekly bus (Wed 6:30am) to Bratislava in **Czechoslovakia**.

The Quarry at Fertőrákos, the Esterházy Palace, and Széchenyi's Railroad

Plenty of buses run from Sopron to BALF, where wealthy convalescents attending the spa stay in the Baroque Wossinszky mansion, but it's the less regular services from stand 7 that run all the way to **FERTŐRÁKOS**. The village presumably gets its name ("Cancerous slough") from the monumental **quarry** produced by centuries of chalk-mining, whose giant chambers and pillars skewed at odd angles form a Cyclopean labyrinth like one of the mythical pre-human cities imagined by H.P. Lovecraft. **Concerts** are performed here during the Sopron Festival Weeks, but otherwise there's no reason to linger once you've seen the quarry (8am–7pm, May–Sept; earlier closing during off-season), unless to stay at the **tourist hostel** (Fő u.141). *Ciklámen Tourist* can book concert tickets and beds.

Twenty-seven kilometers from Sopron (hourly buses from stand 5, except on Sun), lies a monument to one of Hungary's most famous dynasties: the **ESTERHÁZY PALACE** at **FERTŐD**. With its 126 rooms fronted by a vast horseshoe courtyard where Hussars once pranced to the music of Haydn, Esterházy's resident maestro, the palace was intended to rival Versailles. Highlights of the **guided tour** include salons of blue and white Chinoiserie, paneled, gilded rooms lined with mirrors, and a hall where **concerts** are held beneath a splendid fresco of Hermes, so contrived that from whichever angle one views it, his chariot seems to be careering towards you across the sky. And, of course, there's also a room full of **Haydn memorabilia**.

Originally of the minor nobility, the **Esterházy family** began its rise thanks to Nicholas I (1583–1645), who married two rich widows and sided with the Habsburgs against Transylvania during the Counter-Reformation, thereby being elevated to Count. The palace itself was begun by his grandson, Nicholas "the Ostentatious," who inherited 600,000 acres and a Dukedom in 1762. Whereas his father, Paul, had been content to publish a songbook, *Harmonia Celestis*, Nicholas II boasted "Anything the Kaiser can do, I can do better!," and spent 40,000 gulden a year on pomp and entertainments. After 1945 the family was expropriated and "un-personed," but not eliminated; today, one descendant drives trams in Vienna, while two others (from a separate branch of the family) are respected figures back home: the writer Péter Esterházy and his cousin, Marton, center forward on the national soccer team.

Individual **rooms** are usually full (see *Ciklámen Tourist* first), but if you argue hard enough the staff should grudgingly unlock the hostel in the east wing of the palace. For food and drink, try the place opposite the main gate, or the restaurant and supermarket on Fertőd's main street.

It's also possible to stay at the *Gloriette* hostel at FERTŐBOZ, en route to Fertőd, a village where the steam train turns around and returns to **NAGYCENK**, site of the **Széchenyi family mansion** (*kastély*). Less arriviste than the Esterházys, the family is best remembered for István, the prime mover behind the building of Budapest's Chain Bridge (see *Budapest*). Though politically conservative, Széchenyi was obsessed with modernizing Hungary—especially its communications—and to this end initiated the taming of the River Tisza and the blasting of a road and navigable passage through the Iron Gates of the Danube. A keen Anglophile and a passionate convert to steam–power after riding on the Manchester–Liverpool express, Széchenyi invited Britons to build Hungary's second line of track from Budapest to Vác—designed to carry **steam trains**, not the horse-drawn carriages used on the first railroad line to Pozsony. Fittingly, you can ride on one today, a 100-year-old beauty that chugs along the 3km **Széchenyi Museum Railroad** between Nagycenk and Fertőboz. The train—crewed mainly by Young Pioneers—runs roughly every hour from 9am–5pm, and there are fairly regular buses to Sopron. Should you decide **to stay**, a room in Széchenyi's mansion costs around 2000Ft; a double in the *Hársfa Fogadó* (Kiscenki út 1) one fifth of that.

Kőszeg

Skirting the lurking dog patrols and watchtowers along the border, buses also make the 50km journey to **KŐSZEG**, south of Sopron. Notwithstanding the summer blitzkrieg of German tourists which briefly arouses avarice and excitement here, Kőszeg is basically a small, quiet town where people are friendly and honest enough to leave fruit for sale (and the takings) standing unguarded in the streets. Buses #1, #1A, and #1Y from the **train station**, or a short walk from the **bus terminal**, will take you to Köztársaság tér: site of two hotels and three **tourist offices**. The Gothic Church of the Sacred Heart points its diamond-patterned spires aloft, while twin saints flank the alley to the archway of the **Heroes' Tower**—a product of the nostalgia for bygone glories that gripped Hungary in the Twenties and Thirties. This in turn guards **Jurisics tér**, the cobbled main square, surrounded by eye-catching old buildings, a Town Hall embellished with oval portraits of worthies, and a fancifully painted Renaissance façade above the espresszó bar at no. 7, among them—which put the Pharmacy and Local History **museums** into the shade.

The Turks complained that Kőszeg's **Castle** was "built at the foot of a mountain difficult to climb; its walls wider than the whole world, its bastions higher than the fish of the Zodiac in heaven, and so strong that it defies description." Since the castle is actually rather small, with nary a mountain in sight, the hyperbole is probably explained by its heroic defense during the **siege of 1532**, when a tiny garrison under *Miklós Jurisich* defied an army of 100,000, thus foiling the Ottomans' advance on Vienna. Relics of the siege are exhibited in the castle which, come evening, turns into a **disco-bar**.

For around 800Ft you can stay at the *Írottkő* or *Strucc* **hotels** on Köztársaság tér, or the *Kóbor Macska* pension at Várkör 100. You'll pay slightly less at the Express **Hotel Park**, in the Liberation Memorial Park west of town, but for significant savings one must opt for private **rooms** (from Savaria Tourist or *IBUSZ*), or tourist **hostels**. There's one on Szabó-hegy (Tailor's Hill), southwest of Kőszeg, accessible by bus #2; however, the *Vár* hostel outside the castle is better placed, providing you don't mind the brass band in a hall across the square. Restaurants are either attached to hotels or, in the case of workers' cafés, on the approaches to the main square. There's a **beer garden** at the junction of Schneller utca and Várkör, on the northern edge of the Belváros.

Szombathely

SZOMBATHELY ("Saturday market") is western Hungary's largest, liveliest town, and two local jokes cast some light on its modern history. The Austrian who asked his buddy, "Fancy a beer? Right, get your passport," epitomizes the hordes that drive across in their Mercedes and BMWs to have their hair and teeth fixed and shop in the country they've nicknamed "the discount store"; while the "short and the long joke" refers to Szombathely's large Soviet garrison. "The short joke is that the Russians are leaving, the long one that they're going one by one." In truth, most of the conscripts are confined to barracks for the three years that they're posted here; memories of the Russians who fraternized with local people during the first days of the Uprising have led to the rule that only officers can wander around town. Local people may grouse about their "fraternal allies" and rich Austrians, but they're happy to overcharge them in the markets and tune into fashions and TV emanating from across the border. One suspects that the townsfolk might have reacted similarly during ancient times, when trade and legionnaires flowed through here along the Roman Amber road, and foreign idols followed in their wake, notably the Egyptian goddess Isis, whose temple still stands here today.

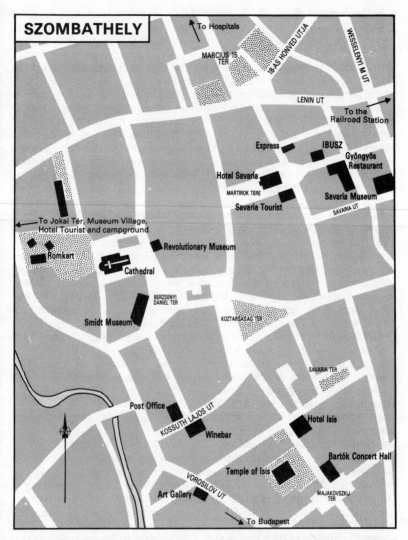

SZOMBATHELY

To Hospitals

MARCIUS 15 TER

18-AS HONVED UTJA

WESSELENYI M UT

LENIN UT

To the Railroad Station

Express

IBUSZ

Gyöngyös Restaurant

Hotel Savaria

MARTIROK TERE

Savaria Museum

Savaria Tourist

SAVARIA UT

To Jokai Tér, Museum Village, Hotel Tourist and campground

Revolutionary Museum

Romkert

Cathedral

BERZSENYI DANIEL TER

Smidt Museum

KOZTARSASAG TER

SAVARIA TER

Post Office

KOSSUTH LAJOS UT

Winebar

Hotel Isis

Bartók Concert Hall

Temple of Isis

VOROSILOV UT

Art Gallery

MAJAKOVSZKIJ TER

To Budapest

From the **railroad station**—the junction for trains to Sopron, Kőszeg, Veszprém and southern Transdanubia—buses #3, #5 and #16Y follow a meandering route to **the Belváros**, itself rather haphazardly laid out and dotted with buildings from the time of Empress Maria Theresa. The **Savaria Museum** starts with unearthed mammoth tusks and works through to **Roman times**, represented by a number of baths, columns, and reliefs of mythical figures which are less impressive than those in the **Romkert**, situated near the bus terminal.

In the Romkert stands the **Temple of Isis** or *Iseum*, a battered structure built in the late second century. One of three such temples extant in Europe, it's centered around a sacrificial altar which the rising sun illuminates, and decorated with a pantheon of deities. Reliefs depict Isis riding the dog Sothis, Victoria holding palm leaves, a glum-looking Fortuna-Abundantia, and Mars-Harpokrates. The custom of daily Isis-worship at sunrise originated in Egypt, where the goddess was believed to be the Pharaoh's mother and the Pharaoh to be Horus who, in a variant of the myth, was the son of an incestuous union between Isis and her brother Osiris, and avenger of his father's murder by Seth, another brother. Carried to Rome by Greek traders, the cult was supressed by Tiberius, but then legalized in the first century when an Iseum was built at Pompeii. Nowadays the temple provides the backdrop for Szombathely's Savaria Festival (see below), and is open to sightseers between 8am–6pm from May to October.

Nearby on Majakovszkij tér, Szombathely's newest **art gallery** exhibits the work of two proletarian painters. **Gyula Derkovits** (1894–1934) was a member of the **Group of Eight** (*Nyolcak*) of committed socialist artists who "declared war on the importance of impressions, sensations and moods; on disorder and denial of values, on all those ideologies and styles of art that begin and end with the 'I'." Living amongst the working class—his subject matter—Derkovits strived to rid his art of "every element of illusion", moved towards Cubism and studied at the Nyergesújfalu Free School during the heady days of the Soviet Republic. The crushing of the 1919 revolution left him desolate, as can be seen from *The Last Supper*, where Christ—with Derkovits's features—sits amidst a group of weary workmen. **István Dési Huber** (1895–1944), regarded as Derkovits's successor, was of working class origin, a goldsmith by trade. He abandoned Naturalism for Cubism to express his Marxist beliefs and together with Derkovits and others in *Nyolcak*, struggled against the dominance of the "School of Rome" (modeled on Italian fascist art) during the Thirties.

The square is also the site of Szombathely's former Synagogue, a lovely piece of neo-Byzantine architecture similar to the one in Pest, which is now the **Bartók Concert Hall** and music college. Here, as at other Hungarian universities and colleges, entrance is determined by competitive examination, and student grants vary according to parental income and academic performance. As stipends rarely match the cost of rent, many students live at home, and all depend on extra money from their parents.

Like Bory's Castle in Székesfehérvár, the **Smidt museum** (Hollán Ernő u.2) represents the fruits of a life-long obsession, for as a boy, Lajos Smidt scoured battlefields for souvenirs and collected advertisements and newspapers. After qualifying as a doctor he diversified into furniture and pictures, and the destruction of many items during World War II only spurred him to redouble his efforts during retirement; until finally, he founded this museum. It's quirky enough to warrant a visit, unlike the **Museum of the Revolution** (Alkotmány u. 2) which has the usual monolingual mass of documents, portraits, flags, and exhortations to struggle. Far better—if you're still keen to sightsee—is the outdoor **Village Museum** (*Falumúzeum*), sited just beyond the campground and accessible by bus #5 from the railroad station. Reconstructed here are eighteenth- and nineteenth-century farmsteads culled from 27 villages in the Őrseg region, furnished with all the necessities and knick-knacks, an architectural progression from log cabins to timber-framed wattle and daub dwellings.

Practicalities

Szombathely's **Savaria Festival** features folk ensembles and Hungary's best classical musicians and opera singers, and usually culminates in a performance of Mozart's *The Magic Flute*, with its aria *Isis and Osiris*. The festival takes place during June, and **Savaria tourist** (Mártírok tere 1) or *IBUSZ* can furnish full details of the program and reserve tickets. Like *Cooptourist* in the vicinity, both agencies rent private **rooms**, while *Express* can probably arrange dormitory beds (quite likely in the college at Nagykar utca 1–3). These are far cheaper than Szombathely's hotels, of which only the *Tourist-B* (north of Jókai park) charges under 1000–2000Ft for a room, but roughly the same price as the cottages for rent at the **campground** (take bus #5). Pink Floyd-ish music gets an airing in the beer garden in Jókai park—the town's youth hangout, situated south of a swimming pool and boating lake. If you feel like splurging, any of the big hotel restaurants can oblige, while the cheapest **places to eat** are the self-service joint on Mártírok tere and the *Gyöngyös* restaurant on Savaria utca.

BÚCSÚ, 14km west of town, is a 24-hour road **crossing into Austria**, and there's a daily train from Szombathely to Graz which leaves around 4:30pm. Travelers with Czech visas might find the *Volán* bus service **to Bratislava** useful. Ják, Körmend, and the Őrség villages are accessible by **local buses**; most **trains** head eastwards through Sárvár to CELLDÖMÖLK and PÁPA (the junctions for Sümeg, Tapolca, the Balaton, and Győr), or south towards ZALAEGERSZEG and Nagykanizsa (the latter for connections to southern Transdanubia). Heading south into Zala county, the road and railroad pass through EGERVÁR—a small village with a fortified *Kastély* serving as a hostel.

Ják, Sárvár, Zalaegerseg, and Villages in the Őrség

JÁK, 14km southwest of town, has Hungary's finest **Romanesque church**, adorned with benign lions, eleven saints in niches, and other intricate stone carvings about its portal. Cloisters included, the church is far more impressive than the scaled-down replica in Budapest's City Park, although you have to pay 20Ft for light to view Ják's frescoes (whose significance the English-speaking priest will explain if he likes you). The tourist office outside sells books on the surrounding area, but there's nothing else to see—and nowhere to stay—in the village. However, there's a hotel (Bercsényi u.24) and private **rooms** (reservations at Rákóczi u.11) in **KÖRMEND**, 16km away, where a former Batthyány mansion provides a spot of color.

SÁRVÁR ("Mud Castle") was founded in the twelfth century, and enjoyed two centuries of prestige as a center of Reformation culture under the **Nádasdy family**, whose fortified **palace** designed by Italian architects is the town's sight. To get there, take bus #1 or #1Y from the railroad station, or walk east along Lenin utca from the bus terminal. Within the *vár* (closed on Mon) you'll see Dorffmeister frescoes of Old Testament episodes, allegories of art and science, and murals depicting the triumphs of Ferenc Nádasdy, the "Black Knight." While Ferenc was away at war his wife **Erzsébet Báthori** began torturing servants, a habit that grew stronger following his death, when she moved to Castle Čachtice in Transylvania. Belatedly tried *in camera* for the murder of six hundred women, **the "Blood Countess"** was secretly imprisoned to prevent the noble Nádasdy and Báthori families being "disgraced by the murky shadow of this bestial female," and the **museum**—which displays the treasures that weren't carted off to Vienna to punish Ferenc for rebellion in 1670—barely mentions this blot on the Nádasdy escutcheon.

Although the *Hotel Thermál* is ultra costly, there's more reasonably priced **accommodation** at the *Plátán* guest house (which buses pass en route to the castle), or the *Vadász Kastély* by the campground (bus #1Y to the end). Alternatively, inquire about private rooms at *Savaria Tourist* (Várkerület 33), which also gives the rundown on training or shows at Sárvár's **riding school**.

Zalaegerszeg

ZALA, as everybody calls it, is no place to arrive on a rainy Monday: despite the futuristic TV tower featured on all the tourist brochures, the town's museums are its main interest. Modern Zala with its costly sports arena and drab *lakótelep* depends on oil—the subject of the **Olajipari Museum**. Rigs, models, and more convey an idea of the development of the industry since the Thirties, but for a clue about the workforce and its origins, go next door to the **Village Museum**, a fascinating collection of dwellings from the **Göcsej region** where most of Zala's inhabitants come from—complete with mill and orchards. Traditionally, the Göcsej was so poor and squalid that no one would admit to being a part of it, and inquirers were always hastily assured that its boundaries began a few miles on, in the next village. Nowadays Göcsej villagers spend their weeks working and sleeping in hostels in Zala, returning home on weekends; some have bought apartments in town and are saving up for a vacation home in the hills.

Both museums can be reached by bus #1A from Rákóczi út, close to Szabadság and Marx square, Zala's center. You'll find oily Göcsej cheese and other local produce in the **market** to the north, and a museum of Göcsej **folk costumes** on the main square adjoining the exhibition of **sculptures by Zsigmond Kisfaludi Strobl** (1884–1975). The son of a sculptor, Zsigmond enjoyed early success with his busts of British Royals, religious figures, and a Lady Plunkett. After 1945 he adroitly switched to producing glorified Workers, earning himself medals, further wealth, and the nickname "Step from Side to Side." See the show and have a laugh.

Rooms at the *Aranybárány* (Széchenyi tér 1) can go for as little as 500Ft or as much as 2000Ft, while the *Balaton* hotel is uniformly expensive. If you

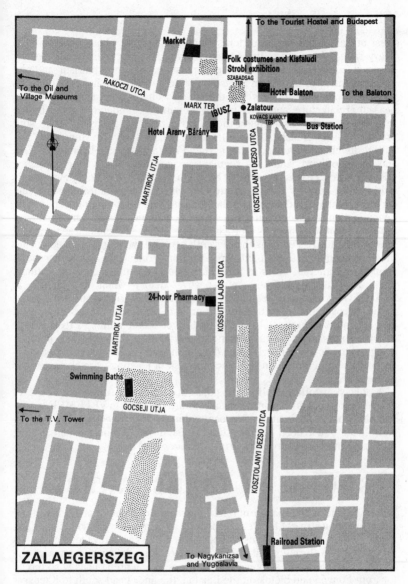

To the Tourist Hostel and Budapest

Market

Folk costumes and Kisfaludi
Strobl exhibition

SZABADSAG
-TER

RAKOCZI UTCA

To the Oil and
Village Museums

Hotel Balaton

To the Balaton

MARX TER

IBUSZ ● Zalatour

KOVACS KAROLY
TER

Bus Station

Hotel Arany Bárány

KOSZTOLANYI DEZSO UTCA

MARTIROK UTJA

KOSSUTH LAJOS UTCA

24-hour Pharmacy

MARTIROK UTJA

Swimming Baths

GOCSEJI UTJA

To the T.V. Tower

KOSZTOLANYI DEZSO UTCA

Railroad Station

To Nagykanizsa
and Yugoslavia

ZALAEGERSZEG

can't get moderately priced beds at the *Göcsej* hostel and pension at Kaszahászi u.2 (take bus #3, #3Y or #5), *Zalatour* on Kovács tér should be able to find private **rooms**—but it's tempting to move on as quickly as possible. While **trains** run to Budapest and Pécs, Keszthely (see *Lake Balaton and the Bakony*) and neighboring areas are better served by **buses** from Kovács tér.

Villages in the Őrség

West of Zala lies a region of forests and rolling hills whose poor soil and heavy rainfall have made **the Őrség** a byword for decline, as indicated by deserted cottages and a shrinking population. Whether tourism and the encouragement of traditional crafts like pottery will revive it—as is hoped—remains to be seen; meanwhile, the Őrség's charm lies in its landscapes, peasant architecture, and early medieval churches, rendered somber by the rain. You'll need to ask around to find good **pottery** (as distinct from stuff produced for the Budapest market); *fazekas* means "potter" in Hungarian.

With its cheap *Fogadó* and campground at Városszer 57, buses from Zala and Szentgotthárd, and less regular services to various Őrség villages, **ŐRISZENTPÉTER** is the obvious base. On the western edge of town stands a **thirteenth-century Romanesque church** with traces of frescoes and fine carvings around the doorway on the opposite side from an ugly lean-to. The denomination of Őrség churches can be a contentious issue, since many of the Protestant ones built by German settlers (whose religious freedoms had been guaranteed as early as the eleventh century) were appropriated during the seventeenth-century Counter-Reformation. Protestants, whose ancestors smuggled Lutheran bibles in wine barrels or were massacred by Catholic mobs at Csepzeg, claimed retrospective victory when the church at **SZALAFŐ** was recently deemed to be of *Református* origin—the proof being newly discovered sixteenth-century murals depicting the duties of women! Just beyond Szalafő (hostel at Felsőzer 14) you'll find a hilltop **Pityerszer** of heavy-timbered houses surrounding a courtyard, with connecting porches designed to allow neighborly chats despite the rain. Such groups of houses—sited apart on high ground to reduce the risk of flooding—are characteristic of the Őrség.

A folksy **wooden belltower** pops up at **PANKASZ**, 7km east of Őriszentpéter, but art historians usually award the prize to **VELEMÉR** for the beautiful fourteenth-century frescoes within its **Romanesque church**. To view these you'll need the key from a (signposted) house 400m before; there's nothing to fear from the armed border guard nearby.

SOUTHERN TRANSDANUBIA

Following one of the roads from Zalaegerszeg, the Balaton, or Budapest, I'd advise heading straight for **Pécs**, especially if the monthly market is due. The upper part of southern Transdanubia—**the Völgység**, or valley region—is pretty to drive through, but there's little accommodation and none of the towns are really worth stopping for. Journeys by rail aren't usually so direct: for from Fonyód and Siófok on the Balaton, the lines head south to Kaposvár (switch trains to reach Dombóvár, and then onto the main Budapest–Pécs service); while trains from Balatonszentgyörgy go to NAGYKANIZSA, and from there the track approaches Pécs via Barcs and Szigetvár (see below). For **crossings into Yugoslavia**, see "Travel Details."

Pécs and its Surroundings

If there was ever a uranium mining town worth visiting, **PÉCS**—pronounced "Paych"—is it. Tiled rooftops climb the vine-laden slopes of the Mecsek range, pinpricked by church spires, and the mines and mining community of *Újmecsekalja* nicknamed Uranium City—haven't contaminated Pécs's reputation for cultural and architectural excellence. One of Transdanubia's largest towns, and the region's leading center of education, its population of 150,000 includes a high proportion of students, creating a youthful profile. Besides some fine museums and a great monthly market, Pécs contains Hungary's best examples of Islamic architecture—a legacy of the long Turkish occupation, like the high cheekbones and Mongol eyes possessed by many of the townsfolk.

Around the Belváros

Heading up Bajcsy-Zsilinszky from the bus terminal, or by bus #30 from the station towards the center, you should pass Kossuth tér, whose main landmarks are the *Konzum Áruház* and Pécs's **Synagogue** (May 1–Oct 31; 9am–1pm, 1:30–5pm; closed Sat). The nineteenth-century interior is beautiful, but haunting, with Romantic frescoes swirling around space emptied by the murder of over 4000 Jews now listed in a Book of Rememberance; ten times the number that live in Pécs today. During the Turkish occupation (1543–1686) a similar fate befell the Christian population, whose principal church was torn down and rebuilt as the **Mosque of Gazi Kasim Pasha**—an act typical of the Ottomans, who came as destroyers but stayed on as builders and scholars. Though once again a Catholic church, the building's ornate window-grills and scalloped niches, with the finest calligraphy on the *mihrab* facing Mecca, are pure Islamic; sightseeing hours are noon–5pm.

With its ice cream parlor and **tourist offices**, modern **Széchenyi tér** is centuries removed from its Turkish predecessor, a dusty square crowded with "caravans of camels laden with merchandise from India and the Yemen." Nowadays there's more activity on **Kossuth utca**, Pécs's *korzó* a place to snack or window-shop, and meet people. For those who prefer indoor sightseeing, it's possible to visit a dozen museums and galleries en route between Széchenyi tér and Pécs Cathedral. Details of these appear below, following a round-up of the remaining monuments.

Though its architects have incorporated a crypt and side chapels from eleventh- to fourteenth-century churches, Pécs **Cathedral** is predominantly nineteenth-century neo-Romanesque, with four spires, three naves, and a lavish decor of blue and gold and floral motifs. The site has been used for religious and funerary purposes since Roman times, and **remnants of an early Christian basilica** are sunk into the park-like square below Dóm tér. At this point you can head east for the Csontváry Museum, nearby, or undertake a longer excursion starting from the Bishop's Palace.

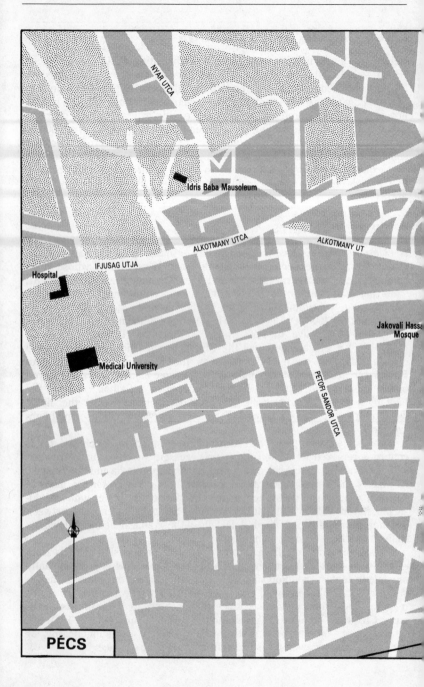

NYAR UTCA

Idris Baba Mausoleum

ALKOTMANY UTCA

ALKOTMANY UT

IFJUSAG UTJA

Hospital

Jakovali Hassa
Mosque

Medical University

PETOFI SANDOR UTCA

N

PÉCS

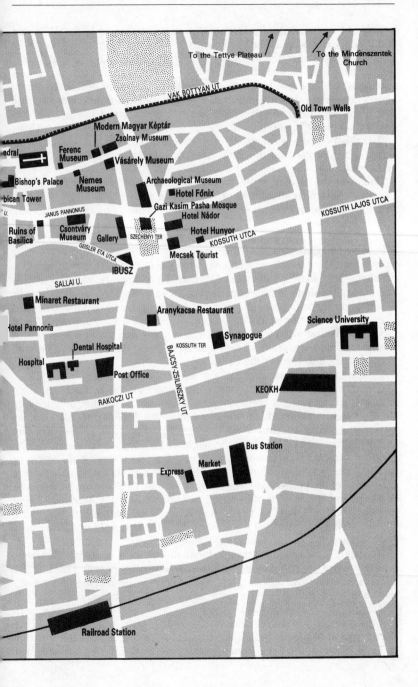

Behind this, a circular Barbican tower punctuates a gap in the **old town walls**—once a massive crenellated rampart 5500 paces long, buttressed by 87 bastions erected after the Mongol invasion—which stretch decrepitly along the northern flank of the Belváros. South of the Barbican, Landler utca slopes down past a *söröző* and *borozó* to meet Rákóczi út, where grubby buildings almost conceal the **Jakovali Hassan Mosque**. Unlike the structures at Eger and Szigetvár, this sixteenth-century mosque is still intact (though unfortunately its minaret is closed), with friezes, a superbly-carved *minbar* (pulpit), and Turkish carpets adorning its cool white interior. Around the corner on Sallai utca, you can see the ruins of a Turkish bath outside the *Minaret* restaurant.

Unless you're fascinated by Turkish death rites, it's not worth tracking down the *türbe* or **mausoleum of Idris Baba** at Nyár u.8, which is almost lost amid the redevelopment work around the children's hospital, and is way out of town as well.

Museums and Galleries

Pécs is loaded with both, so a little selectivity is in order. The trail begins on Széchenyi tér, where a gallery exhibits contemporary **work by local artists** and an **Archaeological Museum** displays lapidary and bronzes testifying to a Roman presence between the first and fifth century, when *Sophianae* rose from the rank of garrison town to become the capital of *Pannonia Inferior*. Since the **Mining Museum** (Déryné u.9) is pretty dull for all the sparkle of its crystals, most visitors head for Káptalan or Janus Pannonius utca instead, both of which lead towards the Cathedral.

Káptalan utca alone mounts half a dozen exhibits, starting with the Sixties Op-Art that hangs in the birthplace of the painter **Viktor Vasarely** (b.1908). Across the road you can see equally lurid **Zsolnay porcelain**, produced by the Pécs factory that made the tiles for Budapest's Applied Arts Museum, or be sobered by the **sculptures of Amerigo Tot**, whose *Erdély family* with its clamped grave-posts symbolizes the plight of the Magyars in Romania. The **Modern Magyar Képtár**, next door, presents a *tour d'horizon* of Hungarian art since the School of Szentendre, with an annex containing Constructivist evocations of the proletarian struggle by **Béla Uitz** (1887–1972), an associate of the journal *MA* and one of the activists who took over the Academy during the Republic of Councils. Other **temporary exhibits** of anything from Picasso etchings to medieval scrolls are held at the Ferenc Martyn and Endre Nemes museums, farther west along the street.

But Janus Pannonius utca trumps them all with the **Csontváry Museum**, devoted to the brilliant paintings of *Tivadar Csontváry Kosztka* (1853–1919). Born in the same year as Van Gogh, and likewise prone to schizophrenia and obsessed with following "the path of the sun," Csontváry was largely self-taught and unappreciated during his lifetime. His fascination with Hebrew lore and the Holy Land was expressed in huge canvasses—*Baalbek*, *Mary's Well at Nazarath*, and *Pilgrimage* and his hallucinatory vision of nature in *Tatra*, *Storm on the Great Hortobágy*, and *Solitary Cedar*. Don't miss them.

Backstreets, the Fair, and the University

For a fresh perspective on Pécs, catch bus #33 from Kossuth tér up to the **Tettye plateau**, where a ruined palace—once used as a Dervish monastery—stands in a park. Mező utca offers a succession of fine views as it winds around the hillside, down which slink picturesque **back streets**, some passing close to the Mindenszentek Church whose pastor supplements his income by selling poultry. Livestock of all kinds, plus crafts and fresh produce, are sold at the **Pécs Fair**—a chance for locals to engage in hard bargaining and drinking rather than a tourist event. However, you'll need to ask *Mecsek Tourist* for directions since the site changes from month to month; the event always occurs on the morning of the first Sunday.

Europe's fifth seat of learning when it was founded in 1367, Pécs **University** had a sickly childhood before it married the Humanities of Pozsony in the nineteenth century, eventually spawning thriving Science (*Tudományi*) and Medical (*Orvostudományi*) faculties, nowadays linked by buses #M14 and #30. The *Mecsek* and cellars along Landler utca are central **student hangouts**; *Ifjúság* and *Sophianai*, or the *büfe* behind Alkotmány utca's ABC, are closer to the science and medical faculties. The *Ifjúsági-ház* **club** halfway down Bajcsy-Zsilinszky caters to teenagers, so there's usually no alcohol at **discos** (Thurs & Sat 9–11pm).

Restaurants, Rooms, and the Mecsek Hills

The *Rózsakert* opposite the Csontváry Museum (9am–11pm; **disco** on Thurs) and the *Minaret* on Sallai u. are both nice, reasonably priced garden **restaurants**, while on Wednesday the *Aranykacsa* has **blues nights** (6–10pm). Although Kossuth utca abounds with pizzerias and cafés, **bars** are more numerous in the western part of the Belváros, where Landler utca's *Barbikán Pince* is open until 2 or 3am every night.

Downtown **hotels** tend to be on the expensive side, with doubles costing roughly 1300Ft at the *Pannonia*, slightly more at the small, modernistic *Fönix*, and approximately 2000Ft at the *Hunyor* and *Nádor*, two refurbished nineteenth-century establishments. Suburban hotels like *Dömörkapu* (Gyükés dülő 1) or the *Fenyves* at Szőlő u.64 (bus #33 to Kalinyin út, then walk) are moderately priced, but cheaper, centrally located **private rooms** available from *IBUSZ* or *Mecsek Tourist* are a better deal. In July and August, another budget option you could consider is **beds** in college dorms; see *Express* at Bajcsy-Zsilinszky út 6. Although bus #44 runs past *Mandulás* **campground** (with a hotel and cottages) in the woodlands below the TV tower, you can easily miss the turn off at Demokrácia út, and get lost in the hills after dark.

Anyone planning to stay in the towns mentioned below is advised to make **reservations** through *Mecsek Tourist* before going. If required, **visa extensions** are available from *KEOKH*, off Rózsa Ferenc utca. Travelers **heading for Yugoslavia** might avail themselves of trains to *Osijek*, which leave Pécs around 5am and 8:40pm.

The Mecsek Hills

For a break from the city, catch a bus from the terminal to Őrfü or Abaliget, an hour's journey away on an unexpected plateau set amid the softlycontoured Mecsek Hills. **ŐRFÜ** has a museum-piece mill, a modestly priced pension (Mecsekrákosi u.29) and hostel (Petőfi u.6), and a three-star campground near its small lake. **ABALIGET** down the road is larger, boasting **stalactite caves** inhabited by blind crabs beside one of its **lakes**. Accommodation is grouped around the campground (the *Fogadó* and hostel are cheaper than a cottage), which has a **disco** on Friday and Saturday (9pm–1am).

A tourist map is a wise investment if you're tempted to go **hiking** in the **Mecsek Hills**; whereas Őrfü and the *Kelet-Mecsek* hills to the northeast are open to all, access to the Pécs-facing slopes is partially restricted on account of the **uranium mines**. While Pécs takes its *bánya* for granted, plans to bury **nuclear waste** from the reactor at Paks have outraged communities elsewhere in the Mecsek. Protesting residents of ÓFALU and other villages south of Bonyhád have been supported by local government since a survey disclosed seven springs and an earthquake fault within a mile of the prospective site. The nuclear industry requires a new dump to replace Puspökszilágy outside Budapest, and handle the increase in solid waste forecast for the 1990s, so it's not inclined to budge, but the protesters still hope to prevail.

Szigetvár

Though a civic center designed by Hungary's avant garde *Makona* bureau is underway, **SZIGETVÁR**'s sole attraction at the moment is its sunbaked, quadrilateral **Castle** at the end of Vár utca. In 1566, when Szigetvár (Island Castle) was ringed by water and marshes, 2400 soldiers withstood the onslaught of 100,000 Turks here for more than a month, launching a final, suicidal sally when they could no longer hold the fortress. Enraged by this fierce resistance—which took 20,000 Ottoman lives and halted his seventh attempt to march on Vienna—the Turkish Sultan Süleyman burst a blood vessel and died. Szigetvár's defenders and their commander *Miklós Zrínyi* were hailed as saviors by Christendom, while the Turks honored Süleyman with a lovely *dzjami* in the fortress grounds. Today its minaret has disappeared but the interior—with ornamental grilles and Koranic inscriptions—survives. In an adjoining building, richly **colored miniatures** of Turkish life are counterpointed by praise for Magyar heroism, including copies of the epic *Szózat* ("Appeal") penned by Zrínyi's grandson, himself a general. A cry for liberty and a call for endurance, this seventeenth-century poem was adapted as a chorale by Kodály in 1956, and its single performance at the Budapest Academy was an emotional occasion. Crowds chanted its refrain, *Ne Bántsd a Magyarat!* ("Let the Magyars alone!") as a symbolic protest against the Rákosi regime, causing the government members present to walk out.

The castle's basements contain a tourist hostel (often full of army conscripts—Szigetvár is still a garrison town), while *Mecsek Tourist* in the lobby of the *Hotel Oroszlán*—on Zrínyi tér, opposite a Baroque church with Turkish-style windows betraying its origins as a mosque—can arrange private **rooms**, or beds in the *Zeneiskola* on Ságvári utca, nearby. If you're leaving by bus, there's a barely distinguishable ruin of a Koran school on Bástya utca, just around the corner from the terminal.

BARCS, 31km southwest by route 6 or railroad, is a **road crossing into Yugoslavia** (Terezino Polje). If you have to spend the night, the *Határ* campground and hotel at Nagyhíd u.28 are cheaper than the *Hotel Boróka* on Bajcsy-Zsilinszky út (tourist office at no. 78).

Harkány and Siklós

An open air **thermal pool** and the chance to wallow in **hot mud** (therapeutically rich in sulfur and fluoride) brings the punters to **HARKÁNY**, one hour's bus journey south from Pécs. There's certainly a lure to stopping for the mud and a cheap underwater massage, but aside from the baths (8am–4pm, 5–11pm; Sept–May 9am–5pm) there's not much to the place: a few snack stands, three pricy hotels and a campground with cottages and a hostel. The only bit of life, really, is the **market** near the **bus station**; a visit to *Bolgar Hadsereg* **museum** honoring the Bulgarian army's contribution to Hungarian liberation will worsen, not alleviate, terminal boredom.

Thankfully, most buses plow on for six more kilometers across the dusty plain to **SILKÓS**, another small town grown up around a castle. The birthplace of the late **George Mikes** (known for his humorous writings in the West), Siklós is sleepier but more appealing than Szigetvár—in short, a nice one-horse town. The **fortress**, visible from the bus station, has been continuously inhabited since its construction in the fifteenth century, and its rondellas and bastions form an impressive girdle around the eighteenth-century mansion at its heart. The main wing contains a hotel and *Mecsek Tourist*, who'll grudgingly unlock cheaper **rooms** in the hostel across the courtyard if you're persistent or, better, brandish a reservation from Pécs. Fragmented fifteenth-century frescoes and a rose-vaulted ceiling ennoble the **chapel**, located (with no sense of incongruity according to medieval values) within whipping distance of a dungeon filled with instruments of torture and rank air.

Locals and tourists make merry in the castle's wine cellar-cum-restaurant most evenings, while by day, action shifts to the *Sport Vendéglő* and dives around Kossuth tér, the site of a cheap *Fogadó*, and a derelict *Dzjami* undergoing slow restoration. From the terminal nearby, **buses** depart every hour for Harkány and Pécs, and less frequently **for Villány** (to which a few trains also run), where there are services **to Mohács**. Though there's a spasmodic service to DRÁVASZABOLCS, buses don't actually cross **the border** (which is open 24 hours) to Donji Miholjac in Yugoslavia.

Villány and Mohács

Acres of vineyards lap the slopes of Mt. Szársomlyo, and the appellation VILLÁNY appears on bottles of red **wine** sold in *ABC*s across the land. The local wine-making tradition goes back almost 2000 years but Villány's other noteworthy feature—its **sculpture park**—is of recent vintage. Bronze totems, concrete erections, and wooden structures mounted on the hillside testify to the activities of the annual **artists' summer camp**. As there's no tourist accommodation, you're best off returning to Pécs by train, or going on to Mohács by train or bus. Traveling directly from Pécs to Mohács, you'll pass a range of low hills to the northeast, where several villages have two names. SZÉKELYSZABAR (*Samar*) and HIMESHÁZA (*Nimmersch*) were originally settled by Germans in the Middle Ages, most of whom went back after World War II. Their places were taken by Székely folk from Bucovina, who no longer decorate their homes with ornate gateways, as their Székely kinsfolk still do in Transylvania.

Hot and dusty beside the pounding Danube, the small town of **MOHÁCS** is a synonym for defeat, for as a consequence of a single **battle** here in 1526, Hungary was divided and war-torn for 150 years, and the national independence lost then has yet to be recovered. The state was unsteady before Mohács, however: an empty treasury, bickering advisers, and an indecisive boy on the throne. Only after the Turks, under Süleyman "the Magnificent," had taken Belgrade and were nearing the Drava did Louis II muster an army, which headed south without waiting for reinforcements from Transylvania. The armies clashed a few miles south of Mohács on August 29. Attacking first, the Magyars broke ranks to loot the fallen and suffered a crushing counter-attack by élite Turkish Janissaries and cavalry, which caused a rout. Among the 25,000 who perished were Louis—killed in the ditches during flight—and most of Hungary's commanders and high clerics, which left the country unable to organize resistance while the Turks advanced on Buda. **Monuments** to the event rise over the battlefield, Sátorhelyi út, and on Széchenyi tér where a rather ugly Votive Church was erected to mark the 400th anniversary; a commemorative **museum** can be found on the corner of Szerb utca.

Aside from these, the River Danube rolling through town disconcertingly near street level is the only "sight" for 364 days of the year. The exception manifests itself on March 1, when the streets of Mohács come alive with the annual **Busójárás Carnival**. With its procession of grotesquely masked figures waving flaming torches, the carnival assumes a macabre appearance at night, although people are out purely to enjoy themselves. Hungarians generally pooh-pooh the carnival as a "tourist event"—which it is, to some extent—but lots of Yugoslavs from across the border appreciate it as a local version of an old Serbian festival. Originally, it was probably a spring ritual intended to propitiate the gods, but over time participants also began to practise ritualistic abomination of the Turks—hence the hideous masks—to magically draw the sting of reality.

It's the only time of the year when there might be an **accommodation** shortage, so if you're planning to attend the carnival, reserve beds through *Mecsek Tourist*—either in people's homes, or at hotels (the *Korona* on Jókai tér is cheapest). The local office (Tolbuhin u.2) can doubtless supply details of the **nudist campground** that's opened since my last visit. Because trains are infrequent, travelers generally rely upon **buses** to reach BAJA (see *The Great Plain*) on the Plain, or BÁTASZÉK, the junction for **trains** to Pécs, Szekszárd, Pörböly, or Baja. There's also a useful *Volán* bus service from Mohács **across the border** to *Osijek, Novi Sad,* and *Slavonski Brod* in Yugoslavia (one departure per destination most days, usually before 9am). The 24-hour checkpoint of UDVAR is 11km to the south of town.

Szekszárd and the Forest of Gemenc

The chance to sample red **wine** from vineyards dating from Roman times and buy inexpensive black **pottery** makes **SZEKSZÁRD** the prime stopover between Pécs and Budapest. With its somnabulant air and undistinguished architecture, the town itself is more restful than interesting; but the chance to visit the beautiful Gemenc Forest, or try your hand at flying, are incentives for a longer stay. Though it's rather shabby, Szekszárd's tourist hostel (Kálvária u.1) has fine views of the vineyard-laden Sió Hills.

Everything of interest in town lies along, or just off, Hunyadi út, the main drag. Starting from the bus terminal, you'll soon come to the **Béri Balogh Museum**'s rich collection of peasants' and nobles' artifacts, one block behind which stands the costly *Gemenc Hotel*. Shortly afterwards there's a junction at Garay tér, around which you'll find **Tolna Tourist** (Széchenyi u.38) and several **wine bars**. Continue uphill to Béla tér, where porticoed buildings tilt perceptibly around a statue marking the plague of 1730, and follow Munkácsy utca up past a supermarket to the hostel, or Babits M. u. towards the **house of Mihály Babits** (Tues–Sun 9am–6pm). Snug and homely, this exhibits photos and manuscripts related to *Nyugat* (West), the avant-garde journal that Babits edited, which published the Village Explorers' exposés of rural life in interwar Hungary, and launched the literary careers of Endre Ady and Gyula Illyés.

For 200Ft you can join one of *Tolna Tourist*'s **excursions to the Forest of Gemenc**, a remnant of the great wilderness of woods, reeds, and mudland (*Sárköz*) that once covered the Danube's shifting, flood-prone banks. Nowadays it's a nature reserve of sorts (the deer are fair game for hard-currency-paying hunters), with a miniature railroad and boat trips permitting glimpses of ospreys, black storks, and other **wildlife**. The package includes lunch and a visit to a folksy *Tájház* in the village of DECS, where old Sárköz **wedding customs and dances** are sometimes performed for visitors. Such tours are much easier than **getting there** independently, which entails an early start. From Szekszárd, you must catch bus #7 from Hunyadi út to KESELYÜS in time for the 7:10am train to *Gemenci delta* (weekdays only); coming from Baja, take the 6:53 to PÖRBÖLY and then the 7:30 train through the forest to Keselyüs. From there you'll have to rely upon taxis or walking.

For adventurous types, Tolna Tourist can also arrange **sightseeing flights** over Szekszárd (380Ft) or Gemenc (950Ft), and instruction in motorized **hang gliding** (220Ft) at the Őcsényi airfield outside town.

Moving on towards Budapest, the railroad runs through nowhere in particular while route 6 occasionally nudges close to the Danube, offering a **river crossing** at DUNAFÖLDVÁR (campground), and a succession of views which could be improved by removing the towns en route. Buses are fairly regular; hitching is poor.

The Danube's West Bank between Szekszárd and Budapest

Once full of mud and reeds where boats might run aground, the land west of the Danube has been subjected to technological fixes—the results of which can be seen although the consequences are still uncertain. The town of **PAKS** boasts Hungary's first **nuclear power plant**, a Soviet-designed VVER 440 type reactor, which supplies about sixteen percent of the country's electricity. Since the Chernobyl disaster, state planners have ordered two more reactors (of the 1000 megawatt, pressurized water VVER 100 type), despite opinion polls indicating public unease, and Szeged University's call for a referendum on the issue. Expansion entails a huge increase in nuclear waste, which the industry wants to dump in the hills south of BONYHÁD (see "The Mecsek Hills" above). In the unlikely event that you want a room, Paks' *IBUSZ* is at Táncsics u.2.

DUNAÚJVÁROS (Danube New Town), upriver, is a monument to Stalinist economics, created around a vast new steelmill which the Party saw as the lynchpin of its industrialization strategy for the 1950s. The construction of *Sztálinváros* (as it was originally called) was trumpeted as a feat by stakhanovites, though in fact much of the heavy work was performed by peasant women and "reformed" prostitutes (see "Beyond the Great Boulevard" in *Budapest*), living under appalling conditions. Guides who lead the **tours of the steelmill** (arranged at Korányi u.1 if twenty people are interested) are reticent about this, and future prospects; ironically, the government now deems the steelmill an economic liability, like so much of Hungary's heavy industry. Moderately priced **accommodation** is available at the *Szélkakas* pension (Lokomotiv u.1), a hostel (Római krt.38), or on Youth Island, where the campground has a *Fogadó* and cottages.

Leaving Hungary from Transdanubia

Transdanubia's geographical position and communications make this an easy place to leave the country. Motorists have a choice of road crossings into neighboring countries, open 24 hours; but traveling by public transit requires a little forethought. Tickets and seat reservations should be bought the day before, and anyone heading for Czechoslovakia must already have a visa.

Weekends are busiest for road crossings **into Austria**, with Mercedes-driving shoppers flowing across outside SOPRON and KŐSZEG, and at HEGYESHALOM, BÚCSÚ (near Szombathely), and RÁBAFÜZES (27km from Körmend). Getting a lift seems easy, and the Austrian *Grenzepolizei* are okay about hitchers. Traveling **by rail**, start from Szombathely, Sopron, or Győr, whose connections with GRAZ, WIENER NEUSTADT, and VIENNA are detailed under those towns. On timetables, remember that Vienna can appear as *Wien* or *Bécs.*. **By bus**, there are more destinations, with Sopron alone running services to eight towns and cities (see "Other things" above). Two other *Volán* terminals are less conveniently situated: BÜKFÜRDŐ (26km northeast of Szombathely), with buses to Vienna, Oslip, Schwarzenbach, Forchtenstein, Krumbach, and Wiener Neustadt; and ZALAKAROS (off rd.7 northeast of Nagykanizsa), with a service to Hartberg in Austria.

To the south are road crossings **into Yugoslavia** at BAJÁNSENYE (west of Zala); RÉDICS (just beyond Lenti); LETENYE (outside Nagykanizsa); BARCS; DRÁVASZABOLCS (south of Siklós); and UDVAR (south of Mohács). Hitch-hikers aren't welcome at any of them, an attitude widespread throughout Yugoslavia—so take a bus or train however tight your budget. **Buses** from Mohács run to NOVI SAD, SLAVONSKI BROD, and OSIJEK (the latter is also accessible by bus from Komló, north of Pécs), but they're not the most enticing destinations. LENTI, southwest of Zala, has two pensions (Zrínyi u.2 & Kossuth u.111) and a curious belfry raised on stilts to divert travelers waiting for the bus to LJUBLJANA, which runs most weekdays. Or you can sample the products of NAGYKANIZSA's brewery while preparing to board **trains** to ZAGREB—the *Dráva* (at around 9am) and the *Maestral* (4pm), which has connections to SPLIT and Rome until the end of September, are preferable to the *Adriactica*, which calls at Dombóvár in the small hours.

Armed with a visa, you can consider crossing **into Czechoslovakia**, where travelers without accommodation vouchers must change roughly $18 a day into Czech *kč* on arrival. Heading for BRATISLAVA or PRAGUE, you'll probably leave Hungary at RAJKA, like two international **trains** boardable at Győr (see "Diversions and practicalities"). Express trains from Budapest cross farther to the east, at KOMÁROM, where you're not allowed to board them. But local buses regularly truck across into Czech Komárno the two towns were a single municipality before World War I. Long-distance **buses** run from LETENYE on the Yugoslav border to Prague; from Tata and Sopron to Bratislava; and from Győr to Galanta and Trnava.

festivals

Spring
Grotesquely masked processions and much merriment at the MOHÁCS *Busójarás* on **March 1**.

Summer
Classical, folk, and opera music during SZOMBATHELY's **Savaria Festival** in **June**, hard on the heels of which comes SOPRON's

Festival Weeks (roughly June 22—**July** 14), with symphonic orchestras, folklore ensembles, and rock theater in the city, and smaller concerts in the FERTŐRÁKOS Quarry and the Eszterházy Palace at FERTŐD. At some time over the summer, organ recitals at PANNONHALMA and an Artists' Camp at VILLÁNY.

travel details

Trains

From Budapest to Győr (6–7 daily; 2–2hr 30min); Komárom (5–6; 1hr 30min–2hr); Pécs (3; 3hr 15min); Sopron (5; 2hr 15min); Tata (7; 1hr 15min).

From Dombóvár to Pécs (14; 1hr–1hr 30min).

From Győr to Sopron (5; 1hr 15min); Veszprém (4; 2hr 30min).

From Nagycenk to Fertőboz (hourly).

From Nagykanizsa to Balatonszentgyörgy (10; 45min); Pécs (3; 1hr 30min–3hr).

From Pécs to Mohács (5; 2hr).

From Sopron to Szombathely (7; 1hr 30min).

From Szekszárd to Budapest (4; 2hr 30min).

From Szombathely to Körmend (7; 1hr 30min); Kőszeg (11; 30min); Nagykanizsa (5; 1hr 30min–2hr 30min); Pécs (2; 4hr); Székesfehérvár (7; 2hr 15min–2hr 45min); Szentgotthárd (7; 2hr 15min).

Buses

From Győr to Pannonhalma (5–6 daily).

From Pécs to Orfű & Abaliget; Harkány; Siklós; Szigetvár (every 1–1hr 30min).

From Siklós to Harkány; Pécs (hourly).

From Sopron to Fertőd; Fertőrákos; Kőszeg (every 1–1hr 30min).

From Szekszárd to Budapest (4–5 daily); Baja (6–7).

From Szombathely to Ják (5–6); Körmend (hourly).

From Zalaegerszeg to Keszthely (hourly).

International trains

From Dombóvár to Zagreb & Rijeka (1 daily).

From Győr to Berlin (1 daily); Bratislava (2); Dresden (1); Gdansk (1); Prague (1); Vienna (2); Warsaw (1).

From Pécs to Osijek (2 daily).

From Nagykanizsa to Zagreb (2 daily); Split (1).

From Sopron to Wiener Neustadt & Vienna (4 daily).

From Szombathely to Graz (1 daily).

From Tatabánya to Bratislava, Warsaw & Gdansk (1 daily).

International buses

These leave once or twice a week (a few run daily), usually before 9am.

From Barcs to Zagreb.

From Bükfürdő to Forchtenstein; Krumbach; Oslip; Schwarzenbach; Vienna; Wiener Neustadt.

From Győr to Galanta; Trnava.

From Harkány to Sombor.

From Komló to Osijek.

From Lenti to Ljubljana.

From Letenye to Prague.

From Mohács to Osijek; Novi Sad; Slavonski Brod.

From Sopron to Bratislava; Eisenstadt; Forchtenstein; Neunkirchen; Oberpullendorf; Purbach; Semmering; Krumbach; Vienna; Weiner Neustadt.

From Szombathely to Bratislava.

From Tata to Bratislava.

From Zalaegerszeg to Murska Sobota.

From Zalakaros to Hartberg.

TELEPHONE CODES

BALF ☎99	KAPOSVÁR ☎82	SOPRON ☎99
DUNAÚJVÁROS ☎25	NAGYCENK ☎99	SZÉKSZARD ☎74
FERTŐD ☎99	ORFÜ ☎72	SZOMBATHELY ☎94
FERTŐRÁKOS ☎99	PÉCS ☎72	TATA ☎34
GYŐR ☎96	RAJKA ☎98	ZALAEGERSZEG ☎92

CHAPTER FIVE

THE NORTHERN UPLANDS

T
he **Northern Uplands** of Hungary are generally hilly, mountainous, and forested, but otherwise defy easy characterization. They take in the famous **wine**-producing towns of **Eger** and **Tokaj**, whose appeal goes beyond the local beverage, and a succession of **castles**, either well-preserved as at Sárospatak, or squatting in picturesque decrepitude on crags above the villages of Hollókő, Somoskő, Boldogkőváralja, and Füzer. This part of Hungary was the first region to be industrialized, and the idyllic woodlands of the **Bükk and Mátra mountains** lie cheek to cheek with drably-utilitarian **Miskolc**, the coal mines of the Borsod Basin, and the despoiled Sajó Valley, themselves less than 50km from the amazing **Aggtelek stalactite caves**. The environment and peoples' lifestyles run the gamut between two extremes—at one end, punks sniffing glue outside Miskolc's supermarkets; at the other, horse-drawn carts clopping around tiny **Zempléni villages**, where the siesta reigns supreme.

Approaching the Uplands

The westerly Cserhát range is adjacent to the Börzsöny Mountains (see Chapter Two), and thus accessible from Vác and Balassagyarmat, but the commonest **approaches** to the uplands are **from Budapest** or the Great Plain. Several times daily, express and slow trains leave the capital's Keleti station, passing through Hatvan and Füzesabony en route to Miskolc and Szerencs—all places to change onto **branch lines** heading farther north. Hatvan is the link with the Mátra; trains from Füzesabony run to Eger; Miskolc is the starting point for journeys into the Bükk; while from Szerencs you can reach Tokaj, Sárospatak, and many Zempléni villages. Balassagyarmat is accessible by train from Aszód, or bus from Hatvan (where buses also depart for Hollókő).

Again, trains are the easiest way of approaching **from the Plain**. From Nyíregyháza, frequent services run through Tokaj to Szerencs, before branching off towards Miskolc or Sátoraljaújhely; while Karcag, Tiszafüred and Szolnok are linked by rail to Hatvan and Füzesabony.

The Cserhát Region

The Cserhát range, like its more impressive neighbors, the Mátra and the Börzsöny, was once continuous forest. Farming and railroads in the Nógrád and Zagyva valleys have made inroads, however, and today there's little magic about the northern slopes or the monotonous flatlands around the Ipoly River, which marks the border with Czechoslovakia. What distinction and color that there is, is provided by the indigenous **Palóc ethnic group**,

who sport fantastic costumes which have long since become museum pieces elsewhere, evidence of a backward agricultural economy or an eye for the tourist trade rather than any "separatist" feelings.

Balassagyarmat

Since losing its medieval fortress and most of its population to the Turks, **BALASSAGYARMAT** (pronounced "Bolosho-dyurmot") has declined to a quiet market town. Nógrád Tourist are endeavoring to spruce up its few

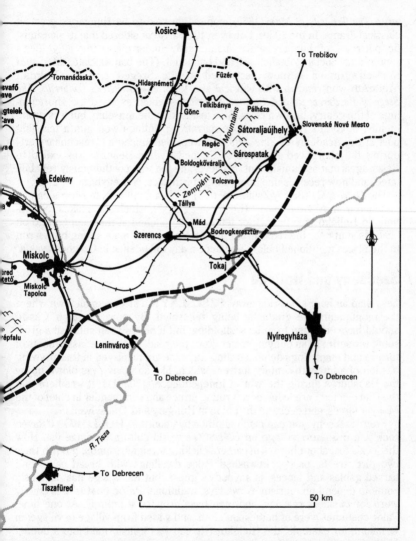

Baroque monuments and promote it as the "Palóc cultural capital," though few visitors will be impressed by the seedy main street or its Breughelesque folk.

The **Palóc Ethnographical Museum** (on Palócliget, off Bajcsy-Zsilinszky út) does little to dispel such impressions. The guide propels you at high speed past enticing displays of elaborate **costumes**—Palóc women's lacy headdresses are very distinctive—and a small collection of modern paintings. For the committed, two rooms are devoted to local writers: **Imre Madách** (1823–64) and Kálmán Mikszáth (1847–1910). Madách began his career as a clerk in the County Hall which still stands on Köztársaság tér, and went on to write *The Tragedy of Man* (1860), commonly held to be Hungary's greatest classical drama. In the 1950s, however, the Party considered that its pessimistic portrayal of human nature dangerously undermined the lofty ideals required of "Socialist Realist" art, and banned it. (The ban was later lifted, and Madách's drama is now performed at the Szeged festival). **Kálmán Mikszáth** won renown with satirical short stories—*St Peter's Umbrella*, *The Siege of Besztercze*, and *A Strange Marriage*—which exposed the shortcomings of the gentry, his own class. Also featured in the museum, but less prominently, is **Gyula Benczúr**, whose narrative paintings won him a teaching post at the Academy of Fine Arts, but were denounced as "reactionary art" during the short-lived Republic of Councils, when Benczúr was exiled to Balassagyarmat as punishment. However, he too was posthumously rehabilitated, and now receives due honor in his birthplace, Nyíregyháza.

The *Hotel Ipoly* (Bajcsy-Zsilinszky út 3) is cheap, but private **rooms** can be obtained from *Nógrád Tourist* (Köztársaság tér 7), which also makes reservations in Hollókő (see below); or tents can be pitched at the campground on Szabadság út near the river. From the terminal on the main street, **buses** run to the places mentioned below, and once a day to Lučenec in Czechoslovakia.

Szécsény and Hollókő

Less than an hour's bus-ride away, **SZÉCSÉNY** is a sleepy small town where the monuments are gradually being renovated. By now, **Forgách Castle** should have emerged from its scaffolding; but if not you can still visit a gruesome **museum** in an outlying tower down the road. Grotesque instruments of torture and engravings demonstrating their use are displayed in the surviving bastion of a fifteenth-century fortress which, like so many, was blown up by the Habsburgs during the War of Independence (1703–11). It was here that the Diet elected Ferenc Rákóczi II ruling prince and commander in chief of the Magyar forces, and declared the union of Hungary and Transylvania.

From Szécsény you can catch another bus south to **HOLLÓKŐ** ("Raven rock"), a **museum village** on *UNESCO*'s world cultural heritage list. How the locals feel about hordes of camera-clicking foreigners ambling down their two dirt streets, past whitewashed Palóc dwellings with broad eaves and carved gables and fences, is anybody's guess, but the village has obviously come to depend on tourism. Nowadays, traditional **Palóc costume** is chiefly worn for business reasons, and men have dropped it entirely. At one time, Palóc costumes were of homespun cloth, and varied from village to village; in Örhalom, for example, the Hollókő-style cap was transformed into a bonnet by the insertion of a stiff cardboard lining.

Nógrád Tourist in Salgótarján or Balassagyarmat can arrange weaving, woodcarving, or folk-dancing **courses**, and **rooms** (sometimes furnished with Palóc wardrobes and embroidered bolsters) here. Mass at the restored church—outwardly austere, but decorated inside with vibrant colors and flowers—provides the liveliest entertainment, while the locals' bar is decidedly cheaper and less tacky than the tourist restaurant. There are usually three **buses** a day to Pásztó and Szécsény, the jumping-off points for the Mátra or Salgótarján, respectively.

Salgótarján and the Castles of Somoskő and Salgó

After Szécsény and Hollókő, **SALGÓTARJÁN** whacks you with its modernity. This mining town—scarred since the nineteenth century by industrial squalor and poverty—was extensively rebuilt during the 1960s, a tardy response to workers' demonstrations in 1956, when the *ÁVH* shot dead 85 coalminers. Slums have been replaced by modern blocks and the downtown is a mass of supermarkets, which the government rightly deemed were sufficient, to "shut peoples' mouths with sausage." However, the old mines are now considered uneconomic, and the planned switch to open-cast mining and the closure of fourteen pits bodes ill for the workers of Salgótarján and Tatabánya. Access to unemployment benefits has been made easier, but so far little has been done to retrain workers or promote new industries.

The town's principal tourist attraction is the **Mining Museum** (*Banyámúzeum*) buried in the inclined shafts of the now-defunct "József" pit, with an entrance on Ady út, a block behind the market. Cramped and muddy, filled with props, tools, and cables, the tunnels lack the dust, danger, and noise of a working mine, but the explanatory leaflet still bids visitors "good luck," the traditional miners' greeting.

From Salgótarján's terminal, buses run 11km northwards to **SOMOSKŐ** on the Czech border, where a five-towered **ruined fourteenth-century castle** squats on vast blocks of stone, opposite **basalt formations** (*bazaltömlés*) resembling giant organ pipes. Since these lie over the border, tourists can only visit in groups accompanied by a guide from Nógrád Tourist, between April 15 and October 15. No such restrictions apply to the **ruined castle of SALGÓ**, about 3km southwest of Somoskő, which was constructed atop a 625m high basalt cone following the Mongol invasion. Before it was ruined during the Turkish occupation, Salgó was once owned by Count István Werbőczy, author of the *Tripartium* law which bound the peasants to "perpetual serfdom" after the nobles crushed the 1514 revolt.

Accommodation ranges from the pricy *Karancs Hotel* on Tanácsköztársaság tér, or a private room from *Nógrád Tourist* (Palócz Imre tér 3), to the campground at the end of the #6 bus route, and Salgó's two tourist hostels. The bus and train stations (separated by the railroad tracks) lie just south of the town center, close to the market and Mining Museum. If you're dependent on public transportation, **moving on** from Salgótarján amounts to heading northeast **towards Ózd** or south towards the Mátra region, assuming that you don't take the early morning bus **across to Lučenec in Czechoslovakia**.

Since the remote Aggtelek caves are the only reason for passing through Ózd, and bus connections are unreliable, **south** seems the obvious direction to take. Along the way to Hatvan (by bus or train), ore-buckets and slag hills disappear, vineyards and fields begin to flourish, and you can change buses at **PÁSZTÓ** and head **into the Mátra** by a scenic route. However, services might run more frequently from **HATVAN**, an old market town. From here, buses fan out towards Budapest and the Plain, Gyöngyös, the Mátra settlements, and as far afield as Eger.

Gyöngyös and the Mátra Mountains

Hungarians make the most of their highlands, and **the Mátra**—where Mount Kékestető just tops 1000m—is heavily geared to domestic tourism. Mt. Kékestető is a popular place for winter sports despite the relatively lackluster resort facilities at Mátraháza and Mátraszentimre, while during summer, families ramble the paths between picnic sites and beer gardens, ignoring the wild boar and deer that live deeper in the thickets of oak and beech. Few of the Mátra settlements have much of interest beyond their amenities, but the mountains and forests are in any case the main attraction.

Gyöngyös

Most visitors approach the Mátra via **GYÖNGYÖS** (pronounced "Dyurn-dyursh"), the center of the Gyöngyös-Visonta **wine** region, whence comes white *Muskotály* comes from. It's a pleasant enough town but nothing to write home about, unless you happen to catch one of local **Gypsy horse fairs** (usually in Aug). The bus station on Aprilis 4. körút is roughly mid way between the two centers of interest, the main square—called just that, Fő tér—and Dimitrov park, with its nearby museum.

Turn left down Kossuth utca—which soon becomes Lenin út—and nine-teenth-century buildings appear in garish blues and reds together with *IBUSZ* (no. 6), presaging the quaint old dwellings around **Fő ter**. Lively yet shadily tranquil, it's the place to join the Magyars around the wine stalls opposite the *Hotel Mátra*, before dutifully inspecting the picturesquely decrepit Gothic Church of Saint Bartholomew on the corner. Heading in the opposite direction from the terminal, Kossuth utca leads past benevolent-looking stone lions fronting Dimitrov park and the museum—both opposite a *Gimnázium*—to the station of the **narrow gauge railroad** (*Mátravasút*) to Mátrafüred in the mountains. Trains depart roughly every hour. If you've time to kill, the **Mátra Museum** at no. 40 has a reconstructed mammoth's skeleton and a collection of dazzling butterflies (among other dead Mátra wildlife).

The Mátra Settlements

The Mátravasút is the fun way to ride to **MÁTRAFÜRED**—and it takes no longer than buses. It deposits visitors at the lower end of this sloping, touristy settlement, where the costly *Hotel Avar* ("mit tennis platz") and *Mátra Tourist* (at Vörösmarty u.4) monopolize **accommodation**. Cheaper—and in many ways nicer—is the campground at **Sás-tó** (Sedge Lake), 3km uphill from Mátrafüred, where buses from Gyöngyös stop off on their way to Mátraháza, the next settlement. It's a friendly place, full of Hungarians boat-ing and fishing amid the usual *lángos* stands, a few hours by footpath from Mátraháza, with **wild boars** reputedly lurking in the forests to the west. At 8pm the restaurant closes and action shifts down to the disco and bars in Mátrafüred.

MÁTRAHÁZA consists mainly of Trade Union hostels, set on an incline with trees, a few bars, and lots of walks to take. Accommodation for foreigners is 2km along the road to Parádfürdő but you can easily do without and make a quick round-trip bus journey to see **Mount Kékestető**. Two **ski-runs** (*sípálya*) descend from the summit, 1015m high, crowned by a nine-story telecommunications **tower** (Tues–Sun 9:30am–3pm; 4pm in summer) offering an impressive view.

To the northeast, a group of similarly named villages gathers around **PARÁD**. Besides its hostel (Kossuth u.13) and campground with cottages, the commune's other feature of note is the *Palóc ház*, exhibiting costumes and artifacts of an ethnic past. From Parád, a promenade flanked by Metro-workers' vacation homes leads to **PARÁDFÜRDŐ**, a popular **thermal spa**, where people also drink the sulfurous, fizzy water for stomach and digestive complaints. The **Cart Museum** (*Kocsimúzeum*) here is more interesting than it sounds, as carved and brilliantly painted yokes and carts, on display here, were a Palóc specialty. For the record, the coach—which superseded the cumbersome wagon throughout Europe—was actually invented in a Hungarian village called, one might have guessed it, *Kocs*. In the crystal glass shop across the road you will find beautiful vases and glasses for sale. On Peres u. there's a private accommodation bureau (no. 39) and a cheap *Fogadó* (no. 8).

Mention **RECSK**, a village 2km east of Parádfürdő, and many older Hungarians will share recollections of terror. During the late 1940s and early Fifties, thousands of the tens of thousands of citizens arrested by the *ÁVO* were sentenced to labor in the **quarries** a mile to the southwest of here. Half-starved and frequently beaten by their jailers, prisoners died of exhaustion or in rockfalls, but more usually at night, while sleeping in muddy pits open to the sky. Recsk concentration camp was finally closed in 1953, during the brief premiership of Imre Nagy, and unlike notorious prisons such as Vác or Budapest's Gyütőfogház, it was never refilled when the hardliners regained control. Today, lacking any sign of its past, Recsk is merely a stopover for buses heading towards Eger and a halt on the branch line down from Mátramindszent to **Kál-Kápolna** (the station before Füzesabony on the Budapest–Miskolc line).

SIROK, one stop southeast on the same branch line, is worth visiting if you're wild about romantic views. Above the village one and a half kilometers northeast of the train halt, a **ruined thirteenth-century castle** broods on a mountain top, from which you can admire the mingled peaks of the Mátra, the Bükk, and Slovakia. A considerable detour—recommended only to antiquity buffs who have their own transport or are willing to hitch patiently—takes you to **FELDEBRŐ**, a village with one of the oldest church crypts still extant in Hungary, decorated with **twelfth-century frescoes** influenced by Byzantine art. The local **linden leaf wine** (*Debrői hárslevelű*) is good for refreshing weary travelers. Anyone intending to visit Sirok or Feldebrő, or go walking in the mountains, should buy a large scale **tourist map** (*A Mátra turistatérképe*) beforehand. But be warned that there's no tourist accommodation at either village.

Eger and Around

Situated in its own sunny valley between the Mátra and the Bükk, **Eger** is
famed for its wine, its minaret, and the heroic legend attached to its castle.
From town, buses and local trains lead to various villages bordering the Bükk
national park, notably Szilvásvárad near the beautiful Szalajka Valley to the
north, and Cserépváralja to the south, just below the "rocking" stones in the
Felső-szoros ravine. Thus you can enter the Bükk mountains from the west,
or cut straight through on a bus to Miskolc, and re-enter them by train from
Lillafüred (see "Exploring the Bükk" below) after you've finished with Eger.

Eger

With its colorful architecture suffused by sunshine, **EGER** seems a fitting
place of origin for *Egri Bikavér*, the potent, throat-rasping red wine, marketed
as *Bull's Blood* abroad, which brings hordes of visitors to the town. Despite
occasional problems with accommodation, it's a fine place to hang out and
wander around, not to mention all the opportunities for drinking. Travelers
arriving at the bus terminal can easily stroll into the center; coming from the
railroad station, walk up the road to Lenin út, catch a #10 or #12 bus and get
off when the cathedral comes into view.

   József Hild's rehearsal for the still larger Basilica at Esztergom, the neo-
Classical **Cathedral** is approached by a flight of steps, beneath which lies a
bizarrely furnished restaurant. Behind the cathedral's huge doors, the City of
God rises triumphantly inside the cupola as painted evildoers flee the sword,
and a clutter of supplications and testimonials around Saint Rita's shrine
evinces that faith in her miraculous powers hasn't disappeared. To the northwest, behind wrought iron gates, stands the former Archbishop's Palace.
Heading towards **the center** you pass several tourist offices and restaurants
before reaching **Dobó István tér**. With its wine bars and action-packed statues facing a stately Minorite Church, the main square is a pleasant spot, and
the starting point for further sightseeing. Cross the bridge, cut through the
open-air market and round a corner to find Eger's most photographed structure, a **minaret** standing 40m high. Slender and fourteen-sided, this looks
pathetic without its mosque, which was demolished during a nineteenth-
century building boom.

   Alternatively, head uphill from the square past the *Várkapitány* (Castle
Captain) restaurant, one of several ventures whose names or wares capitalize
on the memory of two **sieges** during the Turkish invasion. The first siege of
1552, described in Géza Gárdonyi's panegyric novel *Egri csillagok* ("Stars of
Eger"), was an unexpected victory for the Magyars. Ensconced in the castle
under the command of **István Dobó**, 2000 soldiers and Eger's **women** (who
hurled rocks, hot soup, and fat) repulsed a Turkish force six times their
number—shattering the impetus of the Ottoman advance until 1596. But in
their second attempt the Turks triumphed: Eger's garrison of foreign mercenaries surrendered after a week, and the Ottoman troops sacked the town,
leaving only "blackened walls and buildings razed to the ground" and "the
naked bodies of Christians baking in the sun, in some places four yards high."

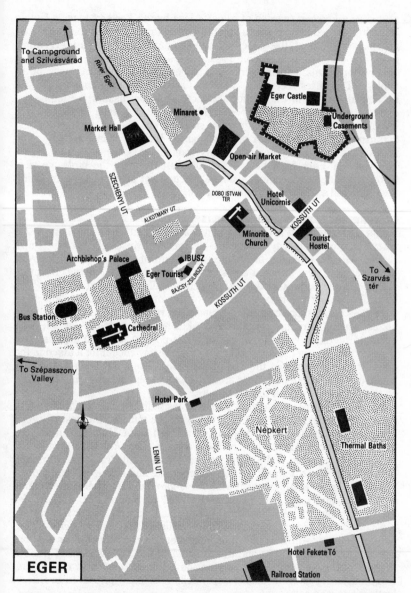

EGER

The **Castle** (9am–5pm daily) still commands the best view in town, though primed cannon no longer threaten Eger from its casements and ramparts. Gárdonyi's grave (inscribed "Only his body lies here") is enshrined atop the bastion overlooking the main gate, where a path leads up to the fifteenth-century Bishop's Palace and the jumble of medieval foundations aptly signposted as a *Romkert* (garden of ruins). Close by the *Romkert* (once a Gothic cathedral, turned into an arsenal by the Turks "to spite the Christians"), tour groups assemble at the concrete tunnel entrance to the **underground galleries**; a labyrinth of sloping passageways, gun emplacements, deep cut observation shafts, and mysterious chambers, which you can sneak off to explore. Tapestries, ceramics, Turkish handicrafts, and weaponry fill the **museum** upstairs in the Bishop's Palace, while downstairs are temporary exhibits and a **"Hall of Heroes"** (*Hősök terme*), where a lifesize marble István Dobó lies amid a bodyguard of siege heroes, the latter carved in best Stakhanovite style. In the **art gallery** near the Bishop's Palace are some fine Munkácsys and three romantic Transylvanian landscapes by Antal Ligeti. The **view of Eger** from here is actually surpassed by the birds-eye view through a nineteenth-century camera obscura, set atop the Lyceum facing the Cathedral steps, which visitors can see.

Drinking, and more Mundane Matters

Sights aside, drinking is obviously a major part of anyone's stay here. Local vineyards produce four types of **wine**—*Muskotály* (Muscatel), *Bikavér* (Bull's Blood), *leányka* (medium dry white with a hint of herbs), and *Medoc Noir* (rich, dark red, and sweet, it coats your tongue black)—all of which can be sampled in the **cellars of the Szépasszony Valley**, just west of town (50Ft by taxi). Finding the right cellar is a matter of luck and taste; some have musicians playing, or serve inferior booze, or reek of damp; I'd recommend no. 38, which is dry and spacious and takes its wine seriously—if you don't object to the aged vintner's spread of nudie posters. You can enjoy a meal beneath the vines of the *Kulacs Csárda*, and possibly encounter a **disco** in the open-air movie theater at the end of the valley. The *Park Szélló* is a likelier venue in town, where bars close around 10pm, except in hotels, but the place on the corner of Dobó tér does take-outs.

Its flamboyant way of serving wine and tasty dishes like *Szultána* at very reasonable prices makes the *Mecset*, opposite the minaret, the best of Eger's **restaurants**. Culinary standards are just as high at the *Vadászkert* next door to *IBUSZ* (specializing in game recipes) and the *Vörös Rák* (Alkotmány u.1), but neither are cheap, while the place beneath the cathedral steps is a rip-off. However, its decor is worth seeing—all concrete and split levels and gloom, like a set from *2001* crossed with the *Führerbunker*. There are various hamburger and juice outlets along the road to Szarvas tér, a *Tejivó* for breakfast near the Archbishop's Palace, and several *eszpresszó*-bars on Kossuth út. Other things available include the **horseback riding school**—*lovarda*—in the suburb of Felnémet (Sánu u., bus #10 or #11, but ask at a tourist office first) and the **thermal baths** and **swimming pool** to the east of the Népkert. A shop on the south side of Dobó István u. (linking Dobó István tér and the Castle steps) sells reasonably-priced **embroidery**, leatherware, and pottery.

Eger's best value lodgings are the **hostels** in the "Buttler house" (which was featured in Mikszáth's novel *A Strange Marriage*) at Kossuth út 26 and Szarvás tér 1 (just uphill from the square), both offering beds for around 90Ft. Dormitory beds arranged through *Express* (Széchenyi út 28) are likely to be at some college, way out along Lenin út, so the next best option is a room from the private sector (Agyagos u.16a & Legányi u.6) or one of the tourist offices—*Eger Tourist* (Bajcsy-Zsilinszky u.9; Mon–Sat 8am–6pm), *Cooptourist* (on the main square), or *IBUSZ*. Eger Tourist can also book slightly more expensive **rooms** in pensions at Kapási u:35a, Lenin út 11, Mekchey u.2, and on the campground (see below). These are several hundred forints cheaper than the *Unicornis*, while other **hotels** cost around 2000Ft for a double. To reach the **campground** at Rákóczi út 79, catch bus #10 or #11 from the railroad station or the stop near the cathedral.

Although hourly **trains** to Füzesabony constitute Eger's link with the Budapest–Miskolc line, there are direct services to Putnok (see "Stalactite Caves" below), and **buses** from the terminal on Felszabadulás tér cover a range of destinations. These include Budapest (2–5 buses daily), Mátraháza (2), Kecskemét (2), the Aggtelek Caves (departs at 8:30am daily), and hourly buses to Szilvásvárad, which call at Bélapátfalva along the way. On weekends there are two buses **through the Bükk mountains to Miskolc**, leaving at 7am and 11:25am; the latter goes via Felsőtarkány, one of several villages accessible by bus where you can than head into the mountains **on foot** (see opposite).

Up to Szilvásvárad and the Szalajka Valley

The road and railroad skirt the western foothills of the Bükk as they wiggle northwards towards Putnok, and 12km out from Eger the scenery is promisingly lush around SZARVASKŐ ("Stag rock"), a pretty village with a nearby *Fogadó* and very ruined fourteenth-century castle. However, quarries and an ugly cement factory ruin the view at BÉLAPÁTFALVA, where the sole reason to stop is a well-preserved Romanesque **abbey church** founded by French Cistercian monks in 1232, which hides between the main street and hills (open Tues–Sun 9am–4pm).

Eight kilometers farther, SZILVÁSVÁRAD occupies a dell beside wooded mountains rising to the east, once the private estate of the pro-fascist Pallavinici family, and then a workers' resort after 1945. While the narrow gauge railroad and snack stands date from the Fifties, Szilvásvárad's spruce streets and equestrian stadium were built for the World Coach-Driving Championships of 1984, and now serve for the annual **Bükk Trophy.** Usually held on the last weekend in August, this draws a big crowd (coach-driving is Hungary's second most popular sport, after soccer), so get there early. Puszta horsemen perform tricks while the contestants race around the SZALAJKA VALLEY, which really begins at *szikla-forrás*, a gushing rock cleft beyond the stalls and captive stags guarding its approaches. The **Erdei museum** in the vicinity exhibits weathered huts and tools (including an ingenious water-powered forge) once used by the charcoal-burners and foresters of the Bükk. Higher up, the valley is boxed in by mountains, and paths snake through trees to the triangular Istállóskői cave (*barlang*) and the barefaced Mount Istállóskő—which at 959m is the highest in the Bükk range. (The second highest, Bákvány, can be reached by footpath from Istállóskő or from NAGYVISNYÓ, the next settlement after Szilvásvárad.)

Szilvásvárad's **riding museum**, hotel, pensions (Szilvásváradi út 118 & Egri u.2), and campground are all easy to find (shower early morning or evening for hot water).

The Bükk Mountains

Beech trees—*bükk*—cover the mountains between Eger and Miskolc, giving the region its name. Unlike most of the northern mountains, **the Bükk** were formed from sedimentary limestone, clay slate, and dolomite, and are riddled with sinkholes and caves which were home for the earliest tribes of *Homo sapiens*, hunters of mammoths and reindeer. As civilization developed elsewhere the Bükk declined in importance—except as a source of timber—until the start of the nineteenth century, when Henrik Fazola built a blast furnace in the Garadna Valley, exploiting the iron ore which today feeds the Lenin metallurgical works in Miskolc. While industry continues to shape the grim towns of Miskolc, Ózd, and Kazincbarcika, almost 400 square kilometers of the Bükk have been declared a **national park and wildlife refuge**, which can be explored superficially by train and bus, or thoroughly if you're prepared to leg it.

Exploring the Bükk

Whether you start at Eger or Miskolc is likely to determine your route through the Bükk. **From Eger**, the most direct way is to take a bus, getting off somewhere along the route to Miskolc, or a suburban train to FELSŐTÁRKÁNY (hotel)—and start walking from there. Paths also lead into the Bükk from Bélapátfalva, Szilvásvárad, and Nagyvisnyó (see above), and from villages to the south, accessible by bus from Eger. Arrowheads and other remains were found in the Subalyuk cave, a Palaeolithic dwelling 2km from BÜKKZSÉRC and CSERÉPFALU at the start of one footpath, while farther east, "rocking stones" and hollowed-out pillars—used by medieval beekeepers and known as "hive rocks"—line the rocky **Felső-szoros ravine** north of CSERÉPVÁRALJA. At NOSZVAJ there's accommodation in the form of the *Pepsi Panzió* (József A. u.10; reservations from Gárdonyi u.43 in Eger).

From Miskolc (see next page), trains and buses go to LILLAFÜRED, where vacationing Trade Unionists throng the elegant old *Palace Hotel* overlooking Lake Hámori: not a tranquil place, but one with fine views, trains bursting forth from tunnels, and **caves** (*barlang*) in the vicinity. The **Anna-barlang** by the road wending up to the hotel has a long entrance passage and six chambers linked by stairs, formed from limestone, while the **István-barlang**, 1km along the road to Eger, is longer and less convoluted, with a "cupola hall" of stalactites, various pools, and chambers. Two hundred yards beyond the István cave is the wooden **house of Ottó Herman** (1835–1944), where the naturalist and ethnographer spent many years trapping and mounting local wildlife. Stuffed boars, birds, and rodents plus an extraordinary collection of giant beetles are the main attraction, but you can also see Ottó's top hat, butterfly nets, and a letter from Kossuth. The **Szeleta-barlang—**

where prehistoric spearheads were discovered—is tucked away above the road back to Miskolc, and all three caves may only be visited with a guide. Tours start roughly every hour at the entrances (9am–5pm; Oct 16–April 15, 9am–4pm).

Filled with shrieking children, **open trains** run from Lillafüred past **Lake Hámori** (opportunities for boating) up to ÚJMASSA in the Garadna Valley, which divides the Bükk plateau. Here **Henrik Fazola**, a Bavarian-born locksmith of Eger, established a blast furnace, while his son Frigyes built a foundry. Today it's a peaceful industrial ruin, surrounded by ferns, giant wild rhubarb, and the camps of **charcoal burners**, who live for part of the year in the forests.

From ÓMASSA, farther along the valley, it's a few hours walk up a well-marked path to **Mount Bálvány**, south of which lies the "Great Meadow" (*Nagymező*) where horses graze. A ski chalet *Síház* and two **more peaks**, Nagy-Csipkés (822m) and Zsérci-Nagy-Dél (875m), can be reached to the east, but more impressive crags lie to the south—Tárkő (950m) and Istállóskő. South of Tárkő the land drops rapidly, and water from the plateau descends through sinkholes, bursting forth in a spring at Vörös-kő ("red rock"). Among the Bükk's **flora** are violet blue monk's hood which blooms at the end of summer, yellow lady's slipper—an endangered species in Europe—and the Turk's cap lily. The undergrowth is home to badgers, beech martens, ermines, and other **animals**, and you might encounter rock thrushes and other **birds** in abandoned quarries, or see an Imperial eagle (*Aquila heliaca*) cruising overhead. The seldom-glimpsed "smooth" snake isn't poisonous. During winter when the plateau is covered with snow, a rising stream marks the entrances to **sinkholes** which carry the water deep underground to springs (*forrás*) in the foothills.

Practical Details

If you're planning more than just a ride up the Garadna Valley, a *Bükk hegység* **map** is essential. Since paths are well marked and settlements are rarely more than 15km apart, it's hard to go far astray **walking**, but a few **preparations** are advisable. Food and supplies should be purchased beforehand, together with insect repellent/bite cream and a canteen. Drinking water (*ivóvíz*) isn't always available, though many of the springs are pure and delicious.

The cheapest **accommodation** is at *Túristaszálló* and *Túristaház*, and you should make reservations in advance from *IBUSZ* and other agencies in Eger or Miskolc. The most useful are at Sikfőkúti (near Noszvaj, northeast of Eger); Bánkúti, 1km southeast of Mount Bálvány; and Bükkszentkéreszt, west of Miskolc. HOLLÓS-TETŐ, along the bus route between Miskolc and Eger, has a hotel and a campground, both prone to overcrowding. In addition, there are pensions at Noszvaj and Felsőtarkány, a private accommodation bureau at Locsoni u.21 in Lillafüred, and a campground—officially reserved for Young Pioneers—between Újmassa and Ómassa. Though it's illegal, some young Hungarians also camp out in the rain shelters (*esőház*) dotted throughout the mountains. Hollós-tető and Bükkszentkereszt can both be reached by walking from BÜKKSZENTLÁSZLÓ, which is accessible by bus #68 from Marx tér in Miskolc.

MISKOLC, TOWNS ALONG THE SAJÓ, AND THE STALACTITE CAVES AT AGGTELEK

Flanking Bükk National Park to the north and east, the polluted Sajó Valley and a clot of mountains ravaged for their ores form a common geographical link between Miskolc, Ózd, and Kazincbarcika, the upland's three industrialized giants. **Miskolc**—pronounced "MISH-koltz'—is a real city. It's difficult to avoid, since it straddles the road and railroad network, and perhaps it's worth visiting on account of its monolithic crudeness, the "Queen's Castle" in the Diósgyőr district, and the "thrashing" cave-baths in its resort suburb of **Miskolc-Tapolca**. **Ózd** and **Kazincbarcika** are both unadorned, industrialized towns. Ózd is a nineteenth-century settlement, while Kazincbarcika is the archetypal Soviet-trained city planner's design, one of the megadevelopments of the 1950s. As such they're hardly the stuff of tourism, unlike the wonderful **stalactite caves at Aggtelek**, situated on the Czech border, which can be reached by bus from Budapest, Eger, Miskolc, Ózd, or Putnok.

Miskolc and Miskolc-Tapolca

MISKOLC in the rain induces instant depression, and even on sunny days one feels oppressed by the windswept arterial roads and endless *lakótelep* of Hungary's second largest city (pop. 200,000). The hometown of ex-party boss Károly Grósz, Miskolc embodies the challenge facing Hungary's leaders: how to overhaul or dispense with unprofitable heavy industries without the workers striking en masse—or worse. In Miskolc, with its alienated youths and grim environment, mass lay-offs carry the risk of provoking social unrest. Although the city's tourist attractions are limited, the chance to see Hungarian life in the raw, and the strange melange of architecture, makes Miskolc worth a visit en route to somewhere more inviting.

Around the City

Your likeliest point of **arrival** will be the main *Tiszai pu.* station, or the bus terminal north of Búza tér. If you'd rather head straight for Diósgyőr Castle or Lillafüred (see below and "Exploring the Bükk" above), take a bus #1 or #101 from the station; otherwise, board a tram #1 or #2 and get off somewhere along the main street, Széchenyi út. Starting from the *Volán* terminal, you can reach Miskolc-Tapolca by bus (#2 or #102), or the downtown area on foot.

Heading west **along Széchenyi út**, boutiques and restaurants are interspersed with Baroque façades painted pea green, violet, and sky blue, or in the last stages of decrepitude, giving the impression of a boom and slump happening simultaneously. Here you'll find *IBUSZ* (no. 3; Mon–Fri 8:30am–4pm; Sat 8am–1pm), *Borsod Tourist* (no. 35; 7:30am–6pm; 8–noon at week-

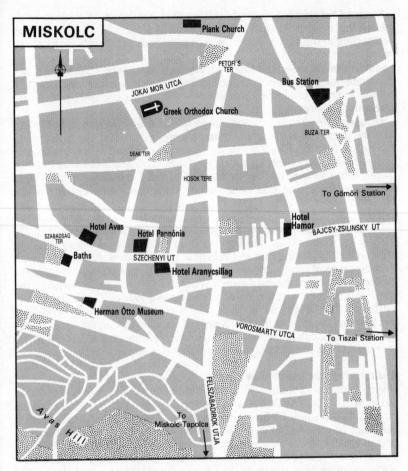

MISKOLC

Plank Church

PETOFI S. TER

JOKAI MOR UTCA

Greek Orthodox Church

Bus Station

BUZA TER

DEAK TER

HOSOK TERE

To Gömöri Station

Hotel Avas

Hotel Pannónia

Hotel Hamor

BAJCSY-ZSILINSKY UT

SZABADSAG TER

Baths

SZECHENYI UT

Hotel Aranycsillag

Herman Ôtto Museum

VOROSMARTY UTCA

To Tiszai Station

Avas Hill

To Miskolc-Tapolca

FELSZABADIROK UTJA

ends) and *Express* (no. 56), plus places to eat and drink in proximity to four hotels. These include a good self-service restaurant on the ground floor of the *Hámor*, *Aranycsillag*'s disco-bar, and *Pannónia*'s flash *Spatzen pince*, and the *Rác Kávéház* beyond the *Hotel Avas*.

In the back streets to the north and south, blocks of nineteenth-century artisan's dwellings with gardens are juxtaposed with concrete high-rises. Near Hősök tere, in the garden of no. 7, Deák tér, trees screen a **Greek Orthodox Church** whose iconostasis resembles a 16m-high advent calendar, inset with the "Black Mary of Kazan" presented by Catherine the Great of Russia and a cross from Mount Athos brought here by Greek refugees from the Turks, which play a major part in the impressive Sunday morning **services**. By contrast, the spooky wooden **Plank Church** (*Deszkatemplom*) rots away in a graveyard north of Petőfi tér like an unwanted import from Transylvania.

South of Széchenyi út a fin de siècle public bathhouse on Szabadság tér frames the view of **Avas Hill**, where a picturesque church and **wooden belfry** cling to the slopes, and a maze of paths snakes upwards to the observation tower on the summit. The right hand paths are more hazardous—leading through an extraordinary shantytown of tunnels, cellars, miniature villas, and hovels, guarded by ferocious dogs. Before risking your arm, check out the splendid exhibition of nineteenth-century folk costumes in the **Ottó Herman Museum**.

Diósgyőr vár—known as the **Queens' Castle**—hides in the western suburbs (bus #1 or #101); a sturdy four towered pile built in the thirteenth to fourteenth century, blown up in the Rákóczi wars, and nowadays crudely restored with cinder blocks and poured concrete. From the intact towers there's a fine view of the city hemmed in by hills, and of the nearby Bükk mountains. **Rock and jazz concerts** are sometimes held here during the *Miskolc Summer*, an annual festival (in June or July) that brings some cheer to the city.

Locals tend to go to Miskolc-Tapolca (see below) for fun, and happenings in the city are sparse. Most mornings the Búza tér **market** provides a splash of color with its glistening fruit and vegetables, weather-beaten peasant women wearing layers of aprons, and squawking poultry. Discos at the *Aranycsillag* or Cultural Centers are the main source of **nightlife**, for few locals can afford the Bar Varíte floorshow at the *Tokaj* penthouse overlooking Győri út (bus #1/ #101/tram #1). Disaffected Miskolc youths go in for drugs, petty vandalism, and fighting; the latter at the *DVTK* **soccer** stadium, or with the Gypsies resident in villages outside town, who've formed vigilante groups (one of which recently ambushed a German biker by mistake) in response to the threat.

Miskolc-Tapolca and the Cave Baths

Given the drabness of the city it's hardly surprising that so many people head out to **MISKOLC-TAPOLCA**, a suburb reached by bus #2 or #102 from the terminal. It's crammed with vacation homes, Young Pioneer groups, snack bars, and fat cats staying at the *Hotel Juno*, mostly drawn here by the prospect of walking in the woods or using the swimming pools and famous **cave baths**. Heavy petting by couples is almost the norm in this series of dimly lit warm water grottoes, which culminates in a "thrashing shower." Unaware of westerners' mistrust of most things nuclear, the tourist board guilelessly boasts of its "mildly radioactive" waters.

Transportation, Rooms, and Moving On

Despite Miskolc's size, it's easy to get around, with #1 **buses** running from the main Tiszai station, past Búza tér bus terminal, and westwards across town to Diósgyőr and Majális Park. From there you can catch a #5 or #105 to Lillafüred, or a #5 or #115 deeper into Bükk, to Ómassa (#5/#115)—see "Exploring the Bükk", above, for more details. **Narrow gauge trains** from the *Killian Észak* terminal in the western part of Miskolc chug up through Lillafüred and the Garadna Valley, or follow the more northerly Csanyik Valley.

As far as main street **hotels** go, you'll be charged over 1300Ft for a double at the *Pannónia* or *Hamor*, and somewhere in the region of 550Ft at the *Avas* or *Aranycsillag* (the cheapest of the four). Private **rooms** will almost certainly be amid the unnumbered *lakótelep*, and roughly twice as expensive as beds in **hostels** (around 120Ft). These are likely to be found in the *Egyetemváros* University Town (bus #12 from Hősök tere), or in college dorms elsewhere **in Miskolc**, for which you'll need directions and a good map of the city. You can get those, and reservations too, from *IBUSZ* or *Express*; while *Borsod Tourist*, which also arranges private rooms, can reserve beds at *Boldogkőváralja* (see "The Zempléni Range" below). **In Miskolc-Tapolca** the deluxe *Junó* charges twice what the *Lidó* and *Park* **hotels** do, while three **pensions** (at Iglói út 15, Fenyő u.19, & Kiss u:40) undercut the latter by half. *Éden* campground near the Junó is a ghastly manicured parking lot, but 2km up along Iglói út there's a leafier place **to camp**, popular with motorists.

If you're not **moving on** to the Bükk (see above), there are regular trains from Tiszai station to the Zempléni, Szerencs, the Great Plain, or Budapest, and buses from the terminal to Eger (leaving at 6am, 1pm & 4pm), Szeged (5:20am), Debrecen (6:30 & 7:30am), or the stalactite caves of Aggtelek (9:30am from stand 8). This last bus is better than catching a train from

ENVIRONS OF MISKOLC

To Kazincbarcika

Ómassa

Újmassa

Lake Hámori

MISKOLC

Express Hotel

Gömöri Railroad Station

To Szerencs

Diósgyőr

Queen's Castle

Lillafüred

THE

Tiszari Railroad Station

Egyetemváros

BÜKK

Hollóstető

Campground

Campground

Campground

To Eger

Miskolc-Tapolca

To Budapest

Miskolc's Gömöri station, which stops at the misnamed *Jósvafő-Aggtelek vá* en route to Tornanádaska. Should you think of a reason for going there, lots of trains run up the Sajó Valley to Kazincbarcika and Ózd. Alternatively, travelers with the requisite visa(s) can head north **into Czechoslovakia or Poland**. Besides *Volán* buses to the Slovakian towns of Rožňava (leaving at 9:30am, Mon–Fri) and Košice (6:30am Wed; 10:25am Thurs; 6pm Wed, Fri & Sat) there are express trains from Tiszai station to Kraków (the *Cracovia*, departing around 9:20pm), Warsaw (*Karpaty*; 4pm), and Poprad-Tatry (*Rákoczi*; 8:30am), all calling at Košice along the way.

Kazincbarcika and Ózd

A planner's dream and a resident's nightmare, **KAZINCBARCIKA** was created in the Fifties for the purpose of manufacturing chemicals and energy from the coal deposits of the north, laid out in a grid with endless rows of numbingly identical *lakótelep*, ineffectually separated from the smoggy industrial zone by half a kilometer of withered grass. Of the three villages that originally stood here, only the **fifteenth-century churches** of Barcika and Sajókazinc and the **wooden belfry** of Berente remain; it's hardly worth staying the night for, though the *Hotel Polimer* (Ifjúsági krt.1, just off Bolyai tér) and private accommodation bureaus (Tavasz u.7 & Lenin út 46) live in hope.

ÓZD, which likewise pollutes the River Sajó, is fractionally more appealing: its southeastern suburb of lace-curtained brick houses with pocket-sized gardens built around a wooded depression is reminiscent of small towns in the Ohio valley. Artisans' dwellings are gradually being replaced by high rises in the center, but the foundry and oxygen plant belch smoke unchecked near the railroad tracks, and few will wish to spend up to 700Ft to stay at the *Hotel Kohász* (Ív út 9), or get a cheaper room from *IBUSZ* (Vörös Hadsereg u.1).

In fact the only reason to come here is to catch one of the three daily buses from Ózd's terminal to Aggtelek, departing at around 8am, noon, and 3pm.

Stalactite Caves in the Aggteleki

Like the Bükk, the Aggteleki range bordering Czechoslovakia displays typical limestone features, where a mixture of water and carbon dioxide has dissolved gullies, sinkholes, and caves in the limestone. The **Baradla caves** between the villages of **Aggtelek and Jósvafő**, and the **Béke caves** to the southeast, constitute an amazing subterranean world with stygian lakes and rivers, waterfalls, countless stalactites, and 262 species of wildlife. Set in remote countryside that's ideal for walking and cycling, the caves are little visited except by factory outings on national holidays.

Getting there by bus entails catching an earlybird service from Budapest, Miskolc, or Eger; or traveling later in the day, starting from Ózd (see above) or from Putnok, where there are **buses** to Aggtelek and Jósvafő every hour and a half. **PUTNOK** (linked to Ózd, Eger, Miskolc, and Kazincbarcika by rail) is the last outpost of *IBUSZ* and banks. Although **trains** from Miskolc call at *Jósvafő-Aggtelek vá* en route to Tornanádaska, this halt is actually 10km east of Jósvafő, and with no certainty of catching a rural bus or ride to the cave entrance, it's a poor alternative.

The Caves at Aggtelek and Jósvafő

The main **Baradla cave passage** twists underground for 22km, and can be partially visited on **short tours** (lasting about 1hr 30min) that begin whenever enough people have assembled at the *bejárat* entrances at either end. The **Aggtelek end** of the passage is more convoluted and rewarding for a "short tour," and from here you can also sign up for longer **trips to the Domica caves** in Czechoslovakia (no passport is needed).

Trying to describe the variety and profusion of **stalactites and stalagmites** is impossible, and nicknames like *Tortoise, Slaughter House*, and *Diamond Mountain* can only hint at the fantastic rock formations. Glittering with calcite crystals, stained ocher by iron oxides, or blackened by smoke, the rocks resemble faces, bodies, fungal growths, and grotesque menageries. In the "Concert Hall" (inquire at the Aggtelek *bejárat* for performance details), boats sway on the River Styx, and the guide activates a light show and tape of Bach's *Toccata in D minor* to create a *Phantom of the Opera* ambience.

Long tours of the Baradla passage begin at the *Vörös-tó* entrance situated in a valley between the two villages, and require some stamina; five and a half hours is a long time to clamber around dank, muddy caves, however beautiful they may be. The same goes for guided tours around the **Béke caves**, which contain a sanatorium, the underground air being judged beneficial to asthmatics; most of these, however, are untamed, even unexplored, and as late as 1973 a new passage was discovered when cavers penetrated a 30m high waterfall. Visitors require boots and warm, waterproof **clothing**, and are issued helmets.

Underground wildlife—bats, rodents, and bugs, mostly—keeps out of sight, and is easiest to view in the **Cave Museum** by the Aggtelek entrance, which also has photos and mementos to gladden a speleologist's heart. Aside from the fortified church with its picturesque cemetery in Jósvafő, and the algae-green lake outside Aggtelek, both villages are unremarkable. Shops are few and social life centers around the church and *Italbolt* "drink shop" (active from 4pm). Aggtelek has a **campground**, *Túristaszálló*, and the **hotel** *Cseppkő*, which serves good meals; in Jósvafő the *Hotel Tengerszem* monopolizes food and accommodation.

Excursions in the Surrounding Countryside

Both hotels display **bus times** between Aggtelek and Jósvafő, but you can walk the 8km Cool Valley (*Hideg völgy*) to the Vörös-tó entrance. Other **walks** in the surrounding hills lead to **more caves** and various peaks marked on the *Aggtelek és Jósvafő környékének* tourist **maps**, which also warn of the **border zone**, where armed guards patrol; carry your passport and visa at all times. **RAGÁLY**, a pretty village, lies on the bus route back to Putnok, but without transportation it's difficult to reach **RUDABÁNYA**, where the 10,000,000-year-old jawbone of *Rudapithecus hungaricus*—an ancient primate—can be seen at the iron mine where it was excavated. At **EDELÉNY**, on the line to Miskolc, an eighteenth-century *kastély* is being converted into a five-star hotel.

THE ZEMPLÉNI RANGE

The **Zempléni range** is the best region in the north—largely unspoiled by industry and tourism, and richly textured by nature and history. **Tokaj**, the center of the *Tokaj-Hegyalja* wine-making district, absorbs most tourists, and surprisingly few make it up to **Sárospatak**, site of the superb Rákóczi castle, or beyond to the little **Zempléni villages**.

Most people **approaching by road or rail** usually go through SZERENCS, the junction between Nyíregyháza, Miskolc, Tokaj, and the northern Zempléni. A drab town, with a reeking chocolate factory and sugar refinery responsible for most of Hungary's output, its only claim to fame is the **fortified manor**—called a castle—which now serves as a hotel in the park at the far end of Rákóczi út.

Tokaj

TOKAJ is to Hungary what Champagne is to France, and this small town has become a minor Mecca for wine snobs. Perched beside the confluence of the rivers Bodrog and Tisza, Tokaj is a place of sloping cobbled streets and faded ocher dwellings with nesting storks and wine cellars—overlooked by lush vineyards climbing the hillside towards the "Bald Peak" and the inevitable TV transmission tower. From the **railroad station** it's ten minutes' walk under the arch and left along Münnich F. utca to the old **town center**, just past the bridge (which leads over to the campground). Here are the first of the wine-cellars (*bor pince*) which pop up along the main street to Kossuth tér, interspersed with fried fish (*sült hal*) shops, and the rainbow-striped *Hotel Tokaj*. Farther along are the few architectural "sights"—the old Town Hall and Rákóczi-Dessewffy mansion and a **ruined castle** by the river—but inevitably it's wine that attracts most people's attention.

The three main **Tokaj wines**—*Furmint* (dry), *Aszú* (sweet), and *Hárslevelü* (linden leaf)—all derive their character from the special soil, the prolonged sunlight, and the wine-making techniques developed here. Heat is trapped by the volcanic loess soil, allowing a delayed **harvest** in October, when many over-ripe grapes have a sugar content approaching sixty percent. Their juice and pulp is added by the *puttony* (butt) to 136-liter barrels of ordinary grapes, and the number of butts determines the taste and qualities of the wine: rich and sweet or slightly "hot," with an oily consistency, ranging in color from golden yellow to reddish brown.

Though some may find *Aszú* too sweet, Tokaj wine has collected some notable accolades since the late Middle Ages. Beethoven and Schubert dedicated songs to it; Louis XVI declared it "the wine of kings, the king of wines"; Goethe, Voltaire, Heine, and Browning all praised it; and Sherlock Holmes used it to toast the downfall of Von Bork, after troubling Watson to "open the window, for chloroform vapour does not help the palate." The **Tokaj Museum** (Bethlen G. u.7) complacently displays wine labels from Crimea, France, and the Rhineland, where attempts to reproduce Tokaj all failed; but the favorite place for pilgrimage is the **Rákóczi cellar** at Kossuth tér 15, where Mrs. Borika Vajtho presides over 24 cobwebbed, chandelier-lit passages containing 20,000 hectoliters of wine (8am–noon & 12:30–7pm). You can also drink in cellars belonging to private households, advertised around the backstreets above the main drag.

As for **eating**, the options boil down to cheap *halászlé* at the buffet by the campground; more expensive fish dishes at the *Halászcsárda*, accompanied by schmaltzy music; or whatever the *Vendéglő* on Kossuth tér has to offer. Other **activities** include rowing, water-skiing, and swimming in the Tisza, or fending off inebriated conscripts at the campground discos which, together with the mosquitos, might discourage you from **staying** there. The alternatives include a private room (from Ovar u.6, Münnich u.19, or the tourist office on the campground) for around 450Ft a night, or more expensive accommodation at the *Hotel Tokaj.*

Villages, Castles, and Walking in the Tokaj-Hegyalja

Behind Tokaj's Kossuth tér, a road winds up to the summit of "Bald Peak" through vineyards, each carefully labeled with its owner's name. From beside the TV tower (guarded to prevent photography), views scan the distant Plain and the lush green Tokaj-Hegyalja: the wine-growing region covering the western and southern slopes of the Zempléni. Some of the **Tokaj-Hegyalja villages** are beautifully situated, with the odd historic monument, while higher in the mountains, ruined castles brood on crags awaiting visitors. Most castles once belonged to the Rákóczi family (see below.) One such in **TOLCSVA**, a village better known for its **linden leaf wine**—*Tolcsvai Hárslevelű*—can be reached on the hourly Komlóska bus from Tokaj.

From Szerencs, seven trains a day strain up the Hernád Valley to Hidasnémeti, stopping at a string of settlements. Grape-growing **MÁD** is but a prelude to **TÁLLYA**, the second largest producer after Tokaj, where visitors can see a former Rákóczi mansion and the font in which Kossuth was baptized. **BOLDOGKŐVÁRALJA**, two and a half kilometers from its train halt, is the site of a massive, partially ruined **thirteenth-century castle** which now houses a *Túristaszálló*. (Reservations should be made at *Borsod Tourist*, Széchenyi út 33, in Miskolc.) Hikers might enjoy a hard day's **walking** between Regec and Gönc, on an ill-marked path skirting the 787m high Gergely-Hegy. **GÖNC** is set in splendid countryside and famed for the making of 136-liter **barrels** (called *Gönc*), traditionally used to store Tokaj wine. You can also get there on the Hidasnémeti train, which is just as well because **REGEC**—the starting point for the walk—lies 7km from its own train halt of *Korlát-Vizsoly.* Not including private rooms in TELKIBÁNYA (10km east of Gönc) and Boldogkőváralja's tourist hostel, there's officially **no accommodation** in this neck of the woods. Walkers should be prepared to camp out or rely on sympathetic locals, and bring food and a **map** of the *Zempléni hegység.*

Sárospatak

Half an hour's train journey from Szerencs, **SÁROSPATAK** ("muddy stream") basks on the banks of the Bodrog. Walking from the train or bus station through Iskola Park, you'll pass statues of famous alumni—testifying to Sárospatak's once-significant role in Hungarian intellectual life, which led Magyars given to hyperbole to describe the town as an "Athens on the Bodrog"—before reaching the Calvinist College on Rákóczi út. If resident scholars like the Czech Comenius brought Sárospatak prestige, it was the **Rákóczi family** who really put the town on the map. When Prince György I, the "first" Rákóczi, acquired **Sárospatak Castle** in 1616, the family power base was in Transylvania, but subsequently the impetuous György II aroused the wrath of the Turkish Sultan and the clan had to hot-foot it to Habsburg-controlled Hungary. Here the Counter-Reformation was in full swing, and Magyar landlords and peasants reacted against Habsburg confiscations by sporadically staging ferocious revolts of "dissenters." The original *kuruc* revolt led by Imre Thököly was bloodily crushed in 1685, but rekindled into a full-scale War of Independence in 1703. At its head was **Ferenc Rákóczi II** (1676–1735), who after initial hesitations led the Hungarians from victory to victory. But by 1711 the Magyars were exhausted and divided, abandoned by their half-hearted ally Louis XIV of France, and Rákóczi fled into exile as his armies collapsed under the weight of superior Habsburg power.

In the Renaissance wings grouped around a courtyard, the **museum** dotes on the Rákóczi dynasty, even down to a series of watercolors depicting the stages of Ferenc's exile (he died in Tekirdag, Turkey). Heavy inlaid furniture, jewelry, monstrous stoves, and a banqueting hall (complete with piped court music and portraits of tipplers) recreate domestic life *chez* Rákóczi. Among the paintings are life-size depictions of Rákóczi's fearsome irregular cavalry and the portrait of Ferenc by Ádám Mányoki that's reproduced on 50Ft banknotes. A romantic seventeenth-century loggia, like a prop from *Romeo and Juliet*, joins the residential wings to the fifteenth-century keep, known as the **"Red Tower."** Guided tours take in the dungeons and underground wells, the labyrinth of galleries used by gunners, and a series of impressive halls. The "Knights' Hall," somehow austere despite its throne and stained glass windows, saw sessions of Parliament during the Independence War, while in the adjoining circular balcony room, anti-Habsburg plots were hatched during the *Kuruc* wars. (Its ceiling is decorated with a stucco rose—hence the expression *sub rosa*, meaning conspiratorial.)

For a small town, Sárospatak has some remarkable architecture, starting with the gorgeously ornamental **Great Library** (*Nagykönyvtár*) where Kossuth, Gárdonyi, Zsigmond Móricz, and other notables once crammed for their exams. Farther south along Rákóczi út, the hand of the *Makona* design team is evident in a block of apartment buildings with humped roofs and eye-like windows, not far from Sárospatak's strikingly modern **Cultural Center**. Designed by Imre Mákovecz, Makona's founder, the building's glass and steel façade stares at you like a monstrous insect, almost opposite the elegant pink Baroque **Comenius College** on Eötvös utca.

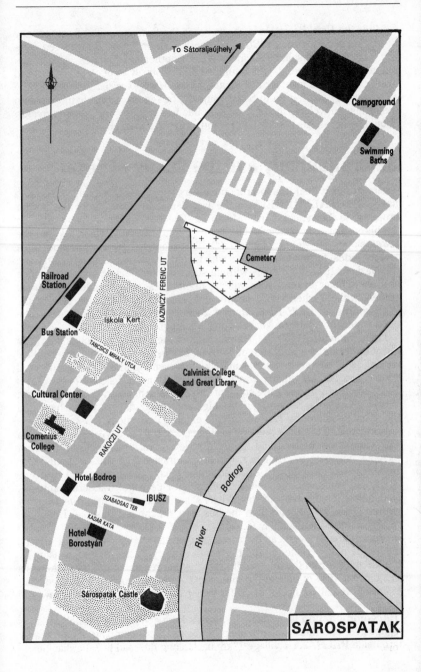

SÁROSPATAK

While the *Hotel Borostyán* is cheaper than the *Bodrog*, you'll still save money by getting **rooms** through *IBUSZ* (Kossuth u.50) or *Borsod Tourist*'s rep, actually a landlord himself, at Kazinczy út 28. Another five minutes' walk brings one to the campground, well equipped and relatively expensive. To eat and drink cheaply and meet local students, try the *Megyer kisvendéglő* opposite the *Hotel Bodrog*. Moving on to Sátoraljaújhely, **buses** are probably more useful than trains; travelers catching the 6am bus **to Trebišov in Czechoslovakia** should reserve seats the day before, and must have a Czech visa.

Sátoraljaújhely and the Castle of Füzer

Easier to reach than it is to pronounce—try saying "SHAR-tor-all-yah-oowee-hay'—**SÁTORALJAÚJHELY** is the last Zempléni town before the border crossing to Slovenskí Nové Mesto in Czechoslovakia (a daily **bus to Trebišov** leaves at 6:20am). The town is situated every which way on the lower slopes of Mount Magas (509m), surrounded by ravines and thick forests—ideal terrain for partisans who fought against the Czechs in 1919 and the Nazis in 1944 (both times without success, however). A massive wooden church, sinister beyond your wildest nightmares, rots outside the railroad station, while Várhegy utca, farther uphill, boasts the remains of a castle. With **rooms** at the *Hotel Zemlpén* (Széchenyi út 5) so cheap, there's little need to use the hostel on Várhegy utca's campground.

Lajos Kossuth (1802–94), leading light of the 1848 revolution and *de facto* dictator during the subsequent War of Independence, began his political career as a lawyer in Sátoraljaújhely, representing the interests of local gentry. His famous oratory was first displayed on the balcony of the Town Hall (Ady tér 5) during the Zempléni cholera epidemic and riots of 1830, but shortly afterwards, Kossuth quit the highlands for Budapest, where he edited the scandal-mongering *Pesti Hírlap* and entered Parliament.

Northwest of town the hills roll in ridges, working up to rocky spines laden with clumps of conifers, and highland valleys containing some of the most unspoilt villages in Hungary. From Sátoraljaújhely, buses bound for Hollóháza pass through **FÜZÉR**, an idyllic village of whitewashed cottages, vines, and sunflowers, inhabited by dignified elders and wandering animals. Depending on the time of day, Füzér's social center shifts from the tiny church to the *Italbolt* and then the bus stop, for the last buses to Hollóháza (8:50pm) and Sátoraljaújhely (6:50pm).

Almost directly overhead but screened by trees are the ruins of **the castle**, one of the many erected in the thirteenth century in case of a re-invasion by the Mongols. From the huge Gothic arches that remain of its chapel there's a magnificent view of blue-green mountains along the border, and the distant Plain, enlivened by flocks of swifts swooping and soaring on the powerful thermals.

Accommodation is available in Füzér's Bodnár Józsefné school, which is signposted, and there's plenty of space for unofficial camping, either nearby or outside **PÁLHÁZA**, a village 12km back along the road to Sátoraljaújhely.

Leaving Hungary from the North

Guardsmen patrolling with Alsatians just north of Nagybörzsöny and Aggtelek are an unpleasant sign of **the border with Czechoslovakia**, drawn by force in 1919 when the Czech Legion wrested highland Slovakia from Hungary, and subsequently affirmed by the Treaty of Trianon. Since Hungarian rule had until then extended over intermingled Slovak and Magyar communities, from Košice (known to the Magyars as *Kassa*) to Bratislava (*Pozsony*), the new frontier ruptured economic and social ties, and gave Magyar nationalists an interest in Czechoslovakia's dismemberment—an attitude that Hitler exploited. Awarded to Hungary as a by-product of the Munich sell-out, the disputed territory was returned to Czechoslovakia after World War II, complete with a 750,000-strong **Magyar minority**. Subsequently, the Magyars of Slovakia have been neglected rather than persecuted, which explains why Hungarian public opinion is more concerned with the fate of their kinfolk in Romania. Seemingly warm relations between the Hungarian and Czechoslovak Communist parties during the Kádár-Husak era probably owed something to the fact that both regimes were installed by Soviet tanks. Hungarian troops even participated in the invasion of Czechoslovakia in 1968, though without enthusiasm; an apocryphal story has a Soviet officer urging his Magyar colleague to "fight harder, and then we'll let you invade Romania."

Anyone hoping **to cross the border** will need a Czech visa, which can only be obtained from one of their consulates (in Budapest, allow seven working days). Drivers can cross **by road** at any of the following 24-hour checkpoints: PARASSAPUSZTA in the Börzsöny; BALASSAGYARMAT; SOMOSKÓÚJFALU, north of Salgótarján; TORNYOSNÉMETI; and a few miles beyond SÁTORALJAÚJHELY. Although **hitch-hiking** across is not recommended, car-less travelers can reach some of the Slovakian towns beyond **by Volán bus**. ROZNAVA, a medieval gold mining town near Krásna Hôrka castle and the Slovak Karst region, is most appealing; KOSICE (also accessible from Miskolc) boasts a fine Gothic cathedral, and the spectacular Herl'any Geyser thirty kilometers away; but there's nothing special about TREBISOV (buses from Sárospatak or Sátoraljaújhely) or LUCENEC (from Salgótarján or Balassagyarmat). The *Rákóczi*, calling at Poprad in the Czech Tatras, is one of three **trains** boardable at Miskolc's Tiszai station; the other two run to Kraków (*Cracovia*) and Warsaw (*Karpaty*), and likewise stop at Košice along the way. Another train **to Poland** (*Polonia*)—aiming for Katowice, Częstochowa, and Warsaw—halts briefly at Salgótarján during the small hours.

Finally, it's just conceivable that someone might take advantage of the service **from Ózd to Uzhgorod in the Soviet Carpathians**. However, you must already be in possession of a Soviet visa (apply two weeks before at the consulate in Budapest), which will only be valid for the date and place of entry specified on your visa application, so it's hardly a journey for the flexible traveler.

festivals

Summer

Jazz, rock, classical music, etc. during the MISKOLC Summer (**June** or **July**). Concerts in the stalactite caves at AGGTELEK as advertised.

Gypsy horse fairs may take place at GYÖNGYÖS in **August**. The last weekend normally sees the *Bükk Trophy* championship at SZILVÁSVÁRAD.

travel details

Trains

From Budapest to Miskolc, express (11 daily; 2–2hr 30min); Tokaj (1; 2hr 45min); Sártoraljaújhely (2; 4hr).

From Eger to Putnok (4; 3hr).

From Füzesabony to Eger (hourly; 20min).

From Gyöngyös to Mátrafüred (hourly; 1hr).

From Hatvan to Salgótarján (7 daily; 1hr 30min).

From Miskolc to Kazincbarcika (30min), Putnok (1hr) and Ózd (2hr), 7 daily; Tornanádaska (8 daily; 2hr); Nyíregyháza (8; 2hr); Sártoraljaújhely (3; 1hr 30min); Szerencs (hourly; 30min).

From Szerencs to Mád, Tállya, Boldogkőváralja, and Gönc (7 daily); frequent services to Tokaj, Miskolc, and Nyíregyháza.

Buses

From Balassagyarmat to Szécsény and Salgótarján (hourly; 30min–1hr).

From Eger to Aggtelek (1 daily; 4hr); Budapest (2–5; 3hr); Kecskemét (2; 5hr); Mátraháza (1–2; 1hr 30min); Miskolc via the Bükk (2; 2hr); Szilvásvárad (hourly; 1hr).

From Füzesabony to Tiszafüred (hourly; 45min).

From Gyöngyös to Eger (4–5 daily; 1hr); Mátrafüred (every 20min; 30min); Mátraháza (hourly; 30min).

From Hatvan to Gyöngyös (hourly; 30min); Hollókő (3 daily; 1hr 30min).

From Hollókő to Szécsény (3 daily; 45min); Hatvan (3; 1hr 30min).

From Miskolc to Aggtelek (1 daily; 3hr); Bükkszentlászlo (every 20min; 45min); Debrecen (3; 3hr 30min); Eger (2 daily; 2hr); Lillafüred (20min; 30min); Miskolc–Tapolca (10min; 15min); Ómassa (20min; 45min); Salgótarján (4; 2hr 30min); Szeged (1; 4hr); Tokaj (1; 2hr).

From Ózd to Aggtelek (3 daily; 1hr 30min).

From Putnok to Aggtelek (5–6 daily; 30min).

From Sárospatak to Sátoraljaújhely (hourly; 20min).

From Sártoraljaújhely to Füzér (hourly; 45min).

From Szécsény to Hollókő (3 daily; 45min).

International trains

From Miskolc to Košice (3 daily); Kraków (1); Propad–Tatry (1); Warsaw (1).

From Salgótarján to Warsaw (1 daily).

International buses

All services depart in the morning, weekdays only.

From Balassagyarmat to Lučenec in Czechoslovakia.

From Miskolc to Rožnava or Košice in Czechoslovakia.

From Ózd to Uzhgorod in the USSR.

From Salgótarján to Lučenec.

From Sárospatak to Trebišov in Czechoslovakia.

From Sátoraljaújhely to Trebišov.

TELEPHONE CODES

EGER ☎36	MÁTRAHÁZA ☎37
GYÖNGYÖS ☎37	MISKOK ☎46
LILLAFÜRED ☎46	SALGÓTARJÁN ☎32
MÁTRAFÜRED ☎37	SÁROSPATAK ☎11

CHAPTER SIX

THE GREAT PLAIN

C overing more than half of Hungary and awesome in its flatness, the **Great Plain** or **puszta** can shimmer like the mirages of Hortobágy, or be as drab as a farmworker's boots. Chance encounters and fleeting details are often more interesting than "sights" on the Plain, and if vast herds no longer roam freely as in the nineteenth century, many villages look virtually unchanged, their whitewashed *tanya* hung with strings of paprika, rustic artesian wells and clouds of geese about. One-street affairs with names prefixed *Nagy-* or *Kis-* (Big or Little), they're most archaic in Szabolcs-Szatmár county, where the majority of Hungarian Gypsies live.

Residents of **Debrecen** and **Szeged** disagree over which is the more sophisticated city; Szeged deserves the accolade if restaurants, architecture, and festivals are the main criteria, but both have lots of students and a high cultural profile. The **towns** of Kecskémet, Baja, Hajdúszoboszló, and Nyírbátor shine for one reason or another, and a few more have at least one redeeming feature, yet the main attractions are possibly the **national parks**, preserving the wildlife and landscape of the old *puszta*. **Bugac**, due south of Kecskemét, is rather overshadowed by the **Hortobágy**, a mirage-prone steppe where an equestrian Bridge Fair is held on August 19–20. This more or less coincides with **festivals** in Debrecen and Szeged: a Flower Carnival on Saint Stephen's Day, and the climax to the Szeged Weeks of music and drama. The Crafts Fair at Kecskemét in early September, and the *Téka Tabor* festival at Nagykálló, usually held in August, will delight anyone interested in Magyar folk arts.

A Little about the *Puszta*

The word *puszta* is practically synonymous with the Great Plain (*az Alföld*), but it's a name that describes the transformation of this huge lowland. During medieval times **the Plain** was thickly forested, with hundreds of villages living off agriculture and livestock rearing, and the mighty **River Tisza**, fed by its tributaries in Transylvania and Maramureş, determined all. Each year it flooded, its hundreds of loops merging into a "sea of water in which the trees were sunk to their crowns," enriching the soil with volcanic silt from the uplands, and isolating the villages for months on end. But the Turkish invasion of 1526 unleashed a scourge upon the land, 150 years of nearly unceasing warfare. The peasants that survived fled to the safer *khasse* (tribute paying) towns like Szeged and Debrecen, leaving their villages to fall into ruin, while vast tracts of forest were felled to build military stockades, or burned simply to deny cover to the *Hajdúk* (partisans). Denuded of vegetation, the land became swampy and pestilent with mosquitoes, and later the

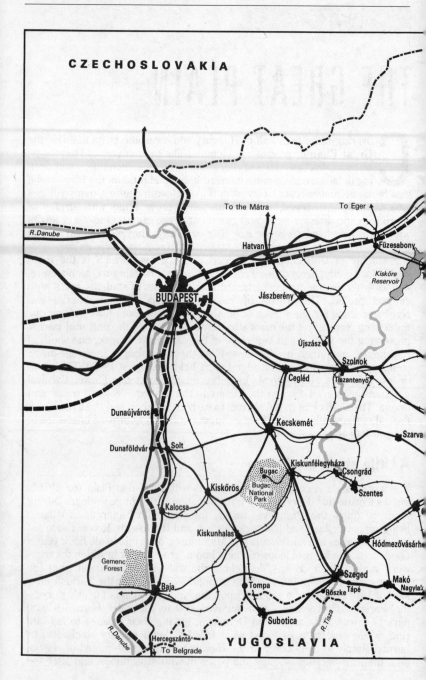

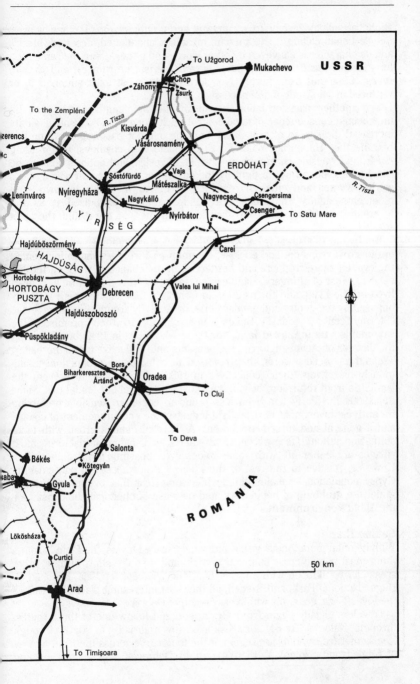

abode of solitary swineherds, runaway serfs, outlaws (*betyár*), and wolves. People began calling it **the puszta**, meaning "abandoned, deserted, bleak"; and its character is conveyed by other words and phrases with the same root, for example *pusztít* (to devastate), *pusztul* (perish, be ruined), and *pusztulj innen* (Clear out from here!). Not surprisingly, most folks shunned it, or ventured in solely out of dire necessity.

Yet another transformation began in the nineteenth century, as an unexpected consequence of flood-control work along the Tisza: soil alkalinity increased the spread of **grassland**. Suitable only for pasturage, in time this became the "Hungarian Wild West"; complete with cowboys, rough-riding *csikós*, and wayside *csárda* where lawmen, Gypsies, and outlaws shared the same tables, bound not to fight by the custom of the puszta. It was a man's world—women and children remained in the *tanyas* close to town—and nineteenth-century romantics like Sándor Petőfi rhapsodized it as the incarnation of Magyardom. "My world and home . . . the Alföld, the open sea."

But by the 1920s reality had crushed romance. Irrigation enabled landowners to grow crops on, and enclose, common pasture. Mechanization denied the evicted share-croppers and herders even the chance of work on the big estates. Most of Hungary's landless peasants, or **"three million beggars,"** lived on the Plain, and their efforts to form Agrarian leagues were violently opposed by the gentry and gendarmerie, particularly around *Viharsarok*—the "Stormy center," today's Békés County. True to their promises, the Communists **nationalized land** "for those who till it" in 1949, but, following the dictates of Stalinism, forced the peasants onto collective farms thereafter. Treated as socialist serfs, they reverted to subsistence production; unanimously dissolving "their" collectives in 1956, while vowing to prevent the landlords from returning, belying any nostalgic guff about feudal ties. Since the 1960s the Party has been less prone to coercion, sensibly preferring **incentives**: investment in rural light industry, the encouragement of co-ops, and a general nod to self-enrichment. As a result, shops groan with foodstuffs, and although farmworkers may still rise at 3am, in material terms most villages are better off, with some co-ops even boasting forint millionaires. However, relative to the rest of the Plain, the northeast—in particular its Gypsy population—remains poor; while some fear that over-production of grain, the grubbing of hedgerows, and over-use of chemicals hold risks for the Alföld's **environment**.

Getting There

With its often monotonous vistas and widely spaced towns, the Plain is something most people cross as much as visit, and if you're short of time, large areas can be skipped with a clear conscience. Except for Baja, Kecskemét, Bugac National Park, and Szeged, all the most interesting places are east of the River Tisza, generally within easy reach of Debrecen.

Travelers usually begin **from Budapest**, and follow one of three routes: through Kalocsa (rd.51) or Kiskőrös (by railroad) to Baja; through Kecskemét (rd.E5/rail) to Szeged; or the long curve across the Plain by way of Cegléd and Szolnok (E15/rd.4/rail) to Debrecen. The Friday evening "**black train**" to Debrecen is notorious for drunken passengers (home-brewed *pálinka* is sold in the toilets), gambling, thefts, and brawls, so women travelers in particular should avoid using it. Foreigners are likely to be accosted by Gypsies, whom the train's barmen accurately describe as "good company, but then they drink all their wages and want to fight." There are also trains from Budapest to Békéscsaba in the southeast.

Debrecen can also be reached **from the northern highlands** (by trains from Miskolc, Szerencs, and Tokaj), while people crossing the river at Dunaföldvár or Baja **from Transdanubia** are virtually forced towards Kecskemét and Szeged by road as there are no direct trains, but plenty of buses. **Hitching** along the E15 to and from Debrecen seems okay, and could well be feasible along other major roads. Between some towns and villages, slow **trains** (*személyvonat*) are the only form of public transit, but at all costs avoid them for the long hauls.

BETWEEN THE DANUBE AND THE TISZA

Approaching from the direction of Budapest, Transdanubia or Yugoslavia, your first experience of the Plain is of the region **between the Danube and the Tisza**. Here only a few towns are worth a visit, and the old puszta grass-lands have shrunk to a remnant, now protected as Bugac National Park. To reach Kalocsa or Baja by railroad from Budapest it's necessary to switch onto branch lines at Kiskőrös or Kiskunhalas. Both names are clues to the region's **archaeology**: the so-called *Kőrös people* raised sheep and tumuli here during the Neolithic era, while between the ninth and thirteenth centuries the land was settled by the Magyars' allies, the *Kun*, or Cuman, tribes. Farther north, the names of towns and villages are prefixed "Jász," after the Iranian-speaking Jazyges who preceded them; as Leigh Fermor writes, "this entire nation seems to have vanished like will o' the wisps and only these place-names mark the points of their evaporation."

South to Kalocsa and Baja

Road 51 isn't scenically exciting, and the main reason for taking it is BAJA, a nice town on the lower Danube and a river crossing. **KALOCSA**, along the way, is heavily promoted for its "**Painting Women**"—once decorators, now entertainers—and the equally flowery **Kalocsa embroidery**. Nowadays made in factories and sold across Hungary, the embroidery is too cute for many peoples' taste, but the older textiles, and those murals that still remain, seem wonderfully assured. One place to see them is the **Viski Károly Museum**, at 25, István Király út (ten minutes' walk from the bus station, past *Pusztatourist* and the *Hotel Piros Arany*). Nineteenth-century folk costumes from the Magyar, Swabian (*Sváb*), and Slovak (*Tót*) communities form a dazzling display upstairs, together with the overstuffed bolsters and quilts that were mandatory for a bride's dowry, but I couldn't help thinking of the woman in a Panaït Istrati novel, who rages "Why should I spend months sewing them, for some fat pig to muddy with his boots?"

Farther down the road stands Kalocsa's small cathedral, whose scruffy façade belies its delicate pink and gold interior. Follow Kossuth utca, to the right, as far as the hospital, where signs direct visitors towards the **Folk Art House** (*Népmüveszeti Szövetkezet*) on Tompa utca. Several rooms are decorated with exuberant floral murals, traditionally found in the *tiszta szoba* or "clean room" of peasant households, where guests were welcomed, the work of groups of "Painting Women." Finally, for something completely different, check out the 22m-high **Chronos 8 light tower** that beams over Kalocsa, where its designer, Parisian conceptual sculptor Nicolas Schöffer, was born.

BAJA, 76km farther south, has an almost mediterranean feel, with respectable citizens promenading up and down Eötvös utca, and young bloods revving their motorcycles around Béke tér. The shady banks of the Sugovica-Danube and **Petőfi Island** (with fishing, swimming, and boating) are the main attractions, for this is basically a town to rest in. Icon buffs might care to visit the Orthodox Church (catering to ethnic Serbs) on Táncsics utca, but it's not worth going out of your way to see the Turr István Museum (Roosevelt tér, off the main square), or the ugly Synagogue on Munkácsy u.

On Baroque Béke tér, overlooking the river, you'll find two **tourist offices** and the reasonably priced *Duna* hotel, which usually hosts **discos** (7–11pm) on Wednesday and Sunday. Live music sometimes features at *Belvárosi cukrászda*, and on Saturday there's another disco in the more expensive *Hotel Sugovica* on Petőfi Island. The cheapest place **to stay** is the campground with cottages, nearby, overrun by pheasants around dawn. From the long-distance terminal on Marx tér, **buses** cross the river into southern Transdanubia, cover various points as far east as Szeged, and once or twice a week strike off for Subotica in Yugoslavia. At time of writing, the 6:53am train to PÖRBÖLY enables you to catch the 7:30am train from there up to the FOREST OF GEMENC, a lovely nature reserve on the west bank of the Danube (see *Transdanubia*).

Farther East: Kecskemét and Bugac National Park

Seventy kilometers southeast of Budapest, en route to Kecskemét or Debrecen, **CEGLÉD** is a sleepy town where the peasants have been roused to arms twice. Both occasions are commemorated in the museum on Rákóczi út (between the railroad station and the center), where a large oil painting in the foyer depicts the gory end of György Dózsa, leader of the 1514 Peasants' Revolt; and proclamations and assorted bric-à-brac recall Lajos Kossuth, who abolished serfdom and fought against the Habsburgs, before fleeing into exile in 1849.

Szabadság tér is glorified by two churches, *IBUSZ*, and the bus terminal, and there's a fairly lively **market** off Kossuth tér, but there's no reason to stay longer than an hour or so. If you have to spend the night, the one hotel is at Rákóczi út 1. Most trains head east towards Debrecen, but some, and numerous buses, go south, passing through NAGYKÖRÖS, which has nothing to recommend it except for an ornamental garden (*Cifrakert*), to Kecskemét.

Kecskemét

Hungarians associate **KECSKEMÉT** with *barackpálinka* (the local apricot brandy) and the composer Zoltán Kodály, who was born in what is now the railroad station, but its cultural significance doesn't end there. Providing you don't stop for a drink at a bar on Rákóczi út, it's less than ten minutes' walk from either terminal into the center, a fine blend of diverse **architecture** and foliage. At one end stand both the Art Nouveau **Cifra Palace**, with mushrooms sprouting from psychedelic tiles above gingerbread façades, and the white, onion-domed **Technika-háza**, a former synagogue built in the Moorish style that was popular in the nineteenth century. If the **Library**, inspired by Transylvanian Gothic, seems designed to intimidate borrowers, the **Town Hall** seeks to charm with Gothic and Turkic motifs, which the architect, Ödön Lechner, used to create a self-consciously "Hungarian Style." This coincided with the nationalism of the 1890s, whose spirit permeates the rich murals (by Bertalan Székely) inside the building.

Kecskemét's annual **Crafts Fair** (Sept 8–10) has demonstrations of everything from pottery to how to felt and pitch a *yurt*, the Khirgiz equivalent of a mobile home, plus lots of things to buy. It's held under the auspices of the **Toy Museum** (*Szórakaténusz Játékmúzeum*), occupying an airy wooden building, which features regular crafts events for kids and a varied collection of instruments and playthings. The museum (Tues–Sun 10am–6pm) lies beyond the *Erdei Ferenc* Cultural Center, where **discos** are held on Tuesday (7–11pm) and Friday (8pm–1am) from late July onwards.

Together with Bartók, **Zoltán Kodály** (1882–1967) recorded Hungarian music's folk roots and found inspiration for his own compositions, largely rejecting the Baroque and Western strains that his colleague termed "New Style." Kodály's belief that only active participation allows one to understand music ("passive listening is not enough") is the guiding principle of Kecskemét's *Zenepedagógiai Intézet*, or **Institute of Music Teaching**. Students on the **one-year course** are exhorted to approach music through the human voice, "the most easily accessible instrument for all," and build upon their national folk traditions when teaching children, a task that Kodály considered supremely important. "No one is too great to write for the little ones," he said, "in fact one has to strive to be great enough."

The town can also boast of **József Katona** (1791–1830), the "father" of Hungarian classical drama, born and killed in Kecskemét, who left his name to the **theater** and the square on which it stands. Its company, directed by the film maker **Miklós Jancsó**, has a reputation for acts like staging *Dr. Faustus* with Mephistopheles in a Stalin T-shirt. Other things on the cultural front are more prosaic, ranging from antique furniture in the **Bozsó Collection** (Klapka u.34) to temporary exhibitions at the Cifra Palace or Technika Háza, with the Protestant and History museums farther back in the running.

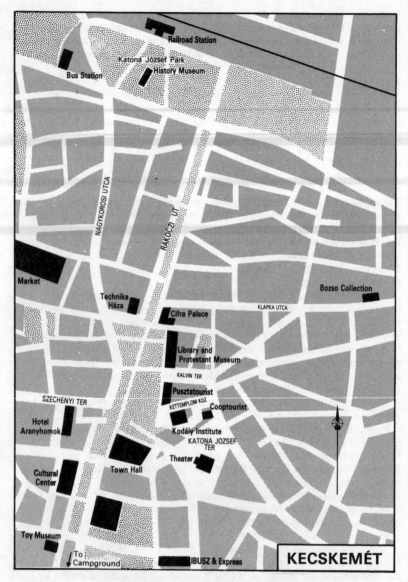

There are several decent **restaurants** along Rákóczi út, Kéttemplom köz, and the fringes of the main square; a fine *Delicatesse* patisserie (7am–10pm) in an arcade to the west; and a **market** for snacks and fresh produce. *Pusztatourist* (Mon–Thurs 8am–5pm; Fri 8am–4:30pm; closed Sat & Sun) and

Cooptourist are the most accessible **tourist offices**. Express and *IBUSZ* are on the first floor of block 11, Dobó körút, beyond two sprawling *Áruház* department stores. Private **rooms** from *Pusztatourist* or *IBUSZ* are much cheaper the *Aranyhomok* and *Tó* **hotels**, and cost several hundred forints less than the *Andi Fogadó* (Bácskai u.13). Outside of July and August, when Express can probably rustle up dormitory beds, the sole alternative is cottages at the **campground**. To reach this, ride a bus from the terminal (#1) or Május 1 tér (#1, #11) past the Soviet base and Uszoda **pool** on Izsáki út; then walk along Sport utca, off to the right.

Kiskunfélegyháza and Bugac National Park

About 6km south of Kecskemét a picturesque **windmill** stands by the road, taken from the courtyard of the Kiskun (Little Cumanian) Museum at Vörös Hadsereg út 9, thus robbing **KISKUNFÉLEGYHÁZA** of one of its two sights. The other is the Town Hall, an ornate Art Nouveau pile which brightens up this otherwise rather drab town, more primitive than Kecskemét and seemingly resentful of the fact. There's a cheap hotel on Petőfi tér, and a tourist-trap *csárda* opposite the Town Hall, but Kiskunfélegyháza's most useful feature is the bus service to Bugac (about every 1hr 30min).

BUGAC NATIONAL PARK (Tues–Sun, 10am–5pm, May 1–Oct 31) begins 3km beyond Bugac village, and buses pass by the entrance before continuing on to Jakabszállás along a new road (unmarked on most maps). From the entrance it's a walk of about 4km along a sandy track to the park's center; past flower-speckled meadows (rare blue globe-thistles appear in August) and lounging *juhász* shepherds, beneath an immense sky. *Csikós* in traditional white pantaloons stride across this remnant of the *puszta*, cracking whips and stampeding the horses for the benefit of geriatric Germans, who are then ferried away in buggies for lunch at the local *csárda*. In the small **Pásztormúzeum** are shepherds' felted cloaks and hand-carved pipes, and a grotesque tobacco pouch formed from a ram's scrotum.

The Park can also be reached **directly from Kecskemét** by narrow gauge railroad (trains depart at 7:55am and 2:30pm) or you can take one of the **bus tours** organized by *Express*. Kecskemét's Pusztatourist can reserve **beds** in the village, or you can make your own deals at no. 37 on Bugac's main street. **Farmstead accommodation** is available from the Lenin Cooperative by prior arrangement at 1, Blazha Lujza tér in Kiskunfélegyháza (☎169).

Paprika and the Legend of Attila

The countryside around Kalocsa and Szeged produces more **paprika** than anywhere else in Hungary, a country where this plant of the Capiscum genus is esteemed above all others. No one knows when paprika was introduced (during the Age of Migrations, via the Balkans, is one theory; from America, by Columbus, is another), but demand for it was assured by the continental blockades of the Napoleonic Wars, which compelled Europeans to find a substitute for pepper. The nineteenth-century preference for milder paprika spurred cross-fertilization and research, which led to the discovery of Capasacin, produced by the plant in response to drought and sunlight, and responsible for its piquancy. Inventions like the Pálffy roller frame eased the laborious task of chopping and grinding, while the plant's nutritional qualities (shepherds were said to remain healthy on a diet of paprika and bacon) were investigated by Dr. Szent-Györgyi of Szeged University, who was awarded a Nobel Prize for synthesizing vitamin C in 1933 (paprika is also rich in vitamin A). Around harvest season (which traditionally begins on Sept 8), the countryside is an Impressionist dream of verdant shrubs and tapering scarlet pods, with carpets and garlands of paprika in every hue of red on the roadsides and houses for weeks afterwards.

Somewhere around the lower reaches of the Tisza, Attila the Hun died of a nasal hemorrhage following a night of passion with a new bride, Kriemhild, in 453. According to **the legend of Attila**, the Scourge of God's body was buried within a triple-layer coffin of gold, silver, and lead, and submerged in the Tisza at an unknown spot—unknown beacause the pallbearers were slain before the Huns departed. Archaeological digs have yet to find it, but the legend gains credence from the "treasure of Attila" (actually thought to have belonged to a Hun general) discovered at Nagyszentmiklós (in what is now Romania), currently held by Vienna's Kunsthistoriches Museum.

Szeged

SZEGED straddles the Tisza like a provincial Budapest, "Great" and "Small" boulevards encircling its Belváros, as cosmopolitan a place as you'll find on the Plain. Much of its friendly atmosphere is due to students, while the old city's eclectic good looks have been saved by placing the ugly modern housing and industry over the river, in Újszeged. Though the goddess-worshiping Kőrös folk settled here 4000–5000 years ago, and the town flourished after 1225 because of its royal salt monopoly over the mines of Transylvania, Szeged's layout derives from the **great flood** of March 1879, which washed away all but 300 homes and compelled the population to start again from scratch. With aid from foreign capitals (after whom sections of the outer boulevard are named) the city bounced back, trumpeting its revival with huge buildings and squares where every type of architectural style got some playing time.

The result generally pleases the eye but makes initial **orientation** slightly harder. Basically, tram #1 (from the railroad station) or bus #70 (from the *Volán* terminal) will get you to one side or another of Széchenyi tér, a few minutes' walk from the Belváros center, Klauzál tér. Of the two **tourist offices** here, *Szeged Tourist* (9am–7pm) usually stocks town plans. *Omnibusz* and horse-drawn coach **tours** start from Somogyi utca, a couple of blocks south, but downtown Szeged is a pleasure to explore on foot, and the twin-spired Votive Church is an unmistakable landmark.

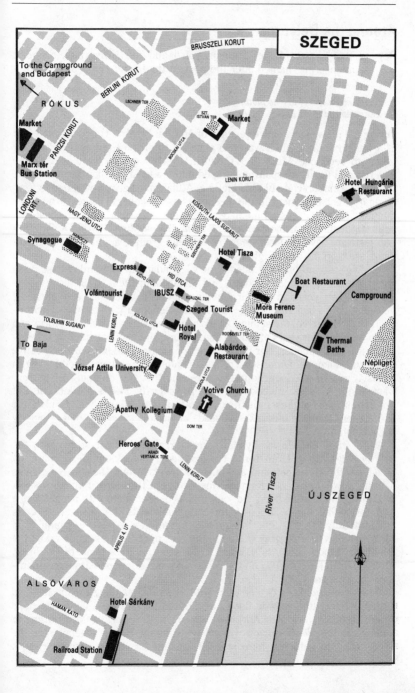

Around the Belváros

Beyond the "Water Music" fountain you'll find the **University**, Szeged's cultural mainspring, named after the poet **Attila József** (1905–37), whom it sternly expelled for writing:

I have no father, I have no mother,
I have no god and I have no country

during the ultra-conservative regency of Admiral Horthy. The illegitimate son of a washerwoman, Attila was also expelled from the Communist Party for trying to reconcile Marx and Freudian pyschology; he lived in extreme poverty, and finally, despairing, jumped under a train at Lake Balaton, at the age of 32. Unappreciated in his lifetime, Attila's popularity now extends from Hungary's establishment to the teenage "sewer dwellers" (*csöves*) who enjoy quoting "Culture drops off me, like the clothes off a happy lover." Local sub-cults still haunt the University's *JATE Klub* **discos** (8pm–4am Fri & Sat), but pop festivals have replaced gigs by amateur groups, a feature of Szeged's youth scene in the early Eighties.

The biggest and baddest was the now-legendary **CPG band**, whose rants about Brezhnev, alienated youth, and SS-20s won them a big local following—plus two years in jail for "inciting public disaffection" and allegedly decapitating a chicken on stage. CPG retain enough fans to make a comeback (like **Beatrice**, *the* seminal punk band, recently allowed to reform and begin touring after years of official harassment) but fashions have changed— in music and in politics. For the minority of Szeged students currently active (the entire campus demonstrated in 1956, ahead of Budapest), ethnocide in Transylvania or **environmental issues** such as the dumping of nuclear waste in the Mecsek Hills now take priority over the **Peace Movement**. But the hottest issue at present is the **corruption scandal** involving Gyula Papp and other council officials, accused of insider dealing and property speculation.

Aside from the University and ever-larger department stores like the nearby *Nagyáruház*, **Dóm tér** is the main object of civic pride. Flanked by arcades with twisted columns and busts of the illustrious, the square contains a vast brown brick, neo-Romanesque **Votive Church** that the townsfolk pledged to build after the flood, only finished—complete with a 10,180 pipe organ—in 1930. Banked opposite the church are seats for the **Szeged Weeks** (roughly July 20–Aug 20), when the program can include anything from Madách's play *The Tragedy of Man* to the rock opera that I saw, based on the life of the "Blood Countess" Báthori, which rejoiced in the name of *The Beast*. **Tickets**, from the *jegyiroda* on the corner of Klauzál tér and Kiss utca (10am– 8pm), are cheap.

When performances (which start with everyone standing for the national anthem) finish, the crowds flood out towards the **Heroes' Gate** that links Aradi Vértanúk tere with Aprilis 4. útja. Though its origins are no longer publicized, the *Hősök Kapuja* was raised to honor Horthy's henchmen, the "Whites," who gathered here in 1919, waiting for the Romanian army to defeat the Republic of Councils before they fanned out across Hungary to murder 5000–6000 Jews and "Reds" in the "White Terror." Fascistic stone guardsmen still flank the archway, but Horthy's murals have been erased by dirt and time.

Temporary **exhibits** are held in the library on Dóm tér and the chocolate and white Romantic-style annex at Somogyi u.13, but Szeged's past is mainly preserved in the **Móra Ferenc Museum**. Its standard mix of *objets d'arts* and artifacts of local significance hide behind an aging neo-Classical façade of columns, lions, and crumbling philosophers. The ruins in the park to the north once housed convicts, who labored on the river tow-paths during the eighteenth century, a period notable for its mass witch trials. Victims confessed to "stealing the rain and selling it to the Turks" after torture, organized by the church elders, and it took a scandal raised by foreign journalists to shame Maria Theresa into banning further trials.

Szeged's Suburbs

Beyond its inner boulevard, Lenin körút, Szeged is shabbier and more utilitarian. The northwestern **Rókus quarter** has several cheap eateries along the streets leading from the center to Marx tér (bus #70), the site of a **market** and the **bus station** (for services, see below). Around the outer boulevard (bus #11, #21), to the south, you'll find the **railroad station** in the **Alsóváros** or "lower town." Seedy and raucous by turns, the *Hotel Sárkány* and the railroadmen's *Tóth Vendéglő* make this a dubious area after dark. Farther along Háman Kató u. the lower town could almost be a village, with ocher-painted cottages, vegetable plots, and rutted streets once inhabited by the paprika growers whose lives inspired the nineteenth-century writer István Tömörkény.

Things are different across the River Tisza in **Újszeged**. On hot weekends people flock to the **swimming pool** (right of the bridgehead) or the grassy *strand* beside the river; they go in winter, too, for a wallow in the outdoor **thermal baths**. Don't swim in the river. The fenced-off riverbank expanse is also the setting for the *Tisza Gyöngye* **disco** (from 8pm daily) and a **campground**. For fresh air freaks, there's the **botanical garden** (*Füvészkert*) at the Újszeged end of the #70 bus line, and **excursions** as well. The two most accessible sites are the fishing village of **TÁPÉ** (bus #73/#73Y from Marx tér), and the **FEHÉR-TÓ NATURE RESERVE**, with organized peeping at its 250 kinds of migratory **birds**. Visits to the latter are arranged by *Szeged Tourist*, which should also be able to locate the **nudist site** that's recently taken root beside a lake somewhere near the city.

Restaurants, Rooms, and Transportation

Eating out is no problem in a city that's famous for its sausages, *halászlé* soup, *halpaprikás*, and other fish dishes. For grills, stews, and salads, the *Debrecen* (11am–11pm daily) and *Szeged* (violin music after 9pm) on the western side of Széchenyi tér are both good value; so too, for lunch, is the *Hági* around the corner from the *Hotel Royal*, which serves Brno beer and Slovak food. More expensive but still affordable are the *Alabárdos* (Oskola u.13), the *Tisza halászcsárda* at Roosevelt tér 12, and the *Szőke Tisza* boat-restaurant (both fish-oriented), hotel restaurants like the *Hungária*, and the quasi-Chinese *Pagoda* (Eötvös u.5). Like the late-night workers' *Búbos étterem* on Merey utca, near Marx tér, most of these places double as **bars**; but for a quiet drink I'd recommend the *Borkostoló* wine cellar (Somogyi u.19). As for **cakes and ices**, *Virág*, with chic salons on both sides of Klauzál tér, has to be the place. Sadly, decrepitude has ensured the closure of a once splendid Art Deco milk bar (Lenin krt.56).

Szeged Tourist or *IBUSZ* can arrange **private rooms** for a quarter of the cost of a double (1200Ft) in the *Royal* or *Tisza* hotels (the *Hungária* is even more expensive); and yet cheaper **dormitory beds** in the splendidly named *Ápathy kollegium* are usually available from *Express* (Kigyó u.3) during July and August. Szeged has two **campgrounds**; one near the thermal baths in Újszeged, the other (with a **motel**) on Dorozsmai út at the start of the Budapest highway (bus #78/#75/#75V from Marx tér, or tram #1 from Szeehevy tér and cross the bridge).

Moving on: Kecskemét, Cegléd, and Budapest are equally accessible by train or bus (5–7 of each, daily); Békéscsaba is best reached by rail, and Pécs by bus; while traveling to Debrecen entails catching the 5:50am or 4:05pm bus, or changing trains at Cegléd, neither of which will get you there in under five hours. (The daily Miskolc bus, leaving around 1:40pm, takes even longer.) Travelers **heading for Yugoslavia** can reach Dubrovnik by bus (departs 7:30pm on Fri between June 24–Sept 9), and Subotica by train (7am daily) or bus (6am & 8am Mon–Sat until Oct 1). International buses leave from stand 4 of the terminal; reserve seats the day before, at least. You can reach Arad in **Romania** by taking an early train from Újszeged to NAGYLAK, walking 1km to the border and hitching 4km to NADLAC, and then catching another train—it's easier than it sounds.

Crossing the Tisza at Szolnok or Csongrád

Heading eastwards across the Plain, the **River Tisza** is no longer the great barrier of old, "three parts water and two parts fish." One hundred and twenty river bends, some four hundred miles in length, were removed during the nineteenth century, and the river has been tamed, one of the many projects initiated by Széchenyi. The two main crossing points by road and rail are Csongrád and Szolnok, and it's tempting to dismiss both towns as no more than that.

SZOLNOK's origins are military—an eleventh-century castle which acquired a township in later life—and its strategic role as a bridgehead was reaffirmed in 1956, when the Russians seized it prior to crushing the Uprising. Much of the town is bleakly modern, but some old **gabled houses** crouch in the Tabán district alongside the Zagyva River, and there's a nice Franciscan church on Költői utca, a block back from the Tisza. In 1988, Szolnok's theater staged Eastern Europe's first ever production of *Dr.*

Zhivago. The *Áév* (Mártírok útja 8) aside, hotel prices are steep; but you can get cheap private **rooms** (from Kossuth u.18 or Ságvári krt.22) or avail your-self of cottages at the campground near the **thermal baths** on the other side of the Tisza. A nice campground at LAKITELEK is accessible by local train (20Ft).

Csongrád county has the highest suicide rate in Hungary—the world's most suicide-prone nation, with 45 **suicides** per 100,000 people—and the commune of ÁSOTTHALOM (which has a nice pool) has the worst rate of all. Nobody is sure why; some cite racial melancholy, hence the old saying that "the Magyar takes his pleasures sadly"; others blame the puszta, or believe that local funeral rites (the corpse is publicly displayed) encourage attention-seeking suicides. On a less morbid note, the county town of **CSONGRÁD** has thatched **peasant houses**, a museum, thermal baths, and **hotel** (on Felszabadulás út); though with rooms at 700Ft you'll save money by renting a cottage or pitching tent at *Köröstoroki* **campground**. Awash with purple sea lavender in early September, the surrounding countryside is wonderful for **cyclists**.

BEYOND THE TISZA: DEBRECEN AND THE HORTOBÁGY PUSZTA

East of the Tisza, the main routes from Budapest and the Northern Uplands converge on **Debrecen**, the Plain's "capital." Although **Hajdúszoboszló** spa lies along the way from Szolnok, and travelers approaching from Füzesabony or Tiszafüred pass by the **Hortobágy puszta**—Hungary's biggest national park—Debrecen is usually the starting point for visits to Hortobágy or the Hajdúság. Karcag and Püspökladány along the Szolnok–Debrecen route are both covered under "The Southern Plain" below.

Debrecen

Once upon a time **DEBRECEN** was the site of Hungary's greatest livestock fair, and foreigners tended to be snooty about "this vast town of unsightly buildings" with its thatched cottages and a main street that became "one liquid mass of mud" when it rained, "so that officers quartered on one side were obliged to mount their horses and ride across to have dinner on the other." Nevertheless, everyone recognized the significance of Debrecen (pronounced "DEB-retzen") economically, and as the chief center of Hungarian Calvinism. From the sixteenth century onwards, there wasn't a generation of lawyers, doctors, or theologians that didn't include graduates from Debrecen's famous Calvinist College (the city is still renowned for its university and teacher-training colleges); while in the crucial years of 1848–49 and 1944–1945, it was here that Hungary's future was debated. At present, Debrecen's churches and employers are helping to resettle hundreds of Magyar refugees from Romania.

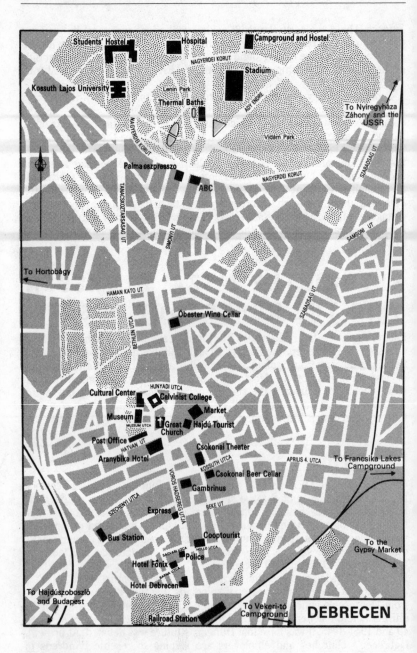

Students' Hostel
Hospital
Campground and Hostel
NAGYERDEI KORUT
Stadium
Kossuth Lajos University
Lenin Park
Thermal Baths
Vidám Park
To Nyíregyháza
Záhony and the
USSR
Palma eszpresszo
ABC
NAGYERDEI KORUT
TANACSKOZTARSASAG UT
SZABADSAG UT
SIMONYI UT
SAMSONI UT
To Hortobágy
HAMAN KATO UT
BETHLEN UTCA
SZABADSAG UT
Óbester Wine Cellar
HUNYADI UTCA
Cultural Center
Calvinist College
Museum
Market
MUZEUM UTCA
Great
Church
Hajdú Tourist
Post Office
Csokonai Theater
HATVAN UT
Aranybika Hotel
KOSSUTH UTCA
APRILIS 4. UTCA
To Francsika Lakes
Campground
Csokonai Beer Cellar
VOROS HADSEREG UTJA
Gambrinus
SZECHENYI UTCA
BEKE UT
Express
Bus Station
Cooptourist
HOLD UTCA
To the
Gypsy Market
SAGVARI UTCA
Polica
Hotel Fönix
BARNA UTCA
Hotel Debrecen
To Hajdúszoboszló
and Budapest
To Vekeri-tó
Campground
Railroad Station

DEBRECEN

Around the City

Modern Debrecen, Hungary's third largest city, still follows the old main street, now called Vörös Hadsereg útja in honor of the Red Army. From the railroad station, tram #1 follows it northwards through the city center, continuing on to the University (this last stretch might be covered by *Villamospótló* bus instead) before returning, which makes sightseeing easy. Along the útja the old County Hall crawls with Art Nouveau statuary, no. 54 puts up a brave show of domes and turrets, the *Hotel Aranybika* tries to live up to its faded regency decor, and on nearby Kossuth tér Hungary's largest bell, the *Rákóczi-harang*, summons people to worship at the old citadel of Calvinist power.

The **Great Church** is an appropriately huge monument to the *Református* faith that swept Hungary during the sixteenth century, and with space for 5000, the building was able to accommodate the Diet of 1849, which declared the country's secession from the Habsburg empire. **Calvinism** took root more strongly in Debrecen than anywhere else, partly because the local Calvinists struck a deal with the Turks, thus ensuring their security, but also because Catholics were forbidden to settle here after 1552. Debrecen's austere Calvinists also waged war on the pagan beliefs held by the peasantry of the Plain, who regarded *táltos* or village wise men with benevolence, while fearing *boszorkány*, their female counterparts.

Until the eighteenth century, women accused of **witchcraft** were able to plead that they were beneficient *táltos* (for example Frau Bártha, who claimed to have learned *táltos* skills from her brother), but as the Calvinists' grip tightened this defense became untenable. Midwives were particularly vulnerable as it was popularly believed that the murder of a relative or newborn child was a pre-requisite for acquiring their "magical" skills, but women in general suffered from the Calvinists' witch-hunting zeal, which also found scapegoats in herbalists, beggars, and vagabonds. **Witch trials** were finally banned by Maria Theresa in 1768 after the scandalous events in Szeged; and by the nineteenth century the bloody deeds of Debrecen's forefathers were buried beneath platitudes eulogizing the "Calvinist Rome."

On Kálvin tér, behind the Church, you'll find the **Calvinist College** or *Református Kollegium*. Though venerable in appearance, it's not the original edifice founded in 1538, but the enlarged college built during the nineteenth century, where the Provisional National Assembly of left-wing and center parties met under Soviet auspices late in 1944. To the west, on Déri tér, an excellent **museum** depicts women's life and household interiors in the nineteenth century, and mounts a dazzling display of shepherds' cloaks (*szűr*), worth a little digression. Traditionally, a herdsman would "forget" to remove his finest *szűr* from the porch when he left the house of the woman he was courting, and if she welcomed the idea it was taken inside within an hour, indicating that a formal proposal could be made. Otherwise the cloak was hung prominently on the veranda—giving rise to the expression *kitették a szűrét* ("his cloak was put out"), meaning to get rid of somebody. Aside from the cloaks, Mihály Munkácsy's dark oil paintings get star treatment together with the work of peasant artist László Holló, but my preference was for displays such as "Mihály Tort's kitchen: birthplace of the Workers' movement."

Visitors can see more artwork, and occasional folk or theatrical performances, in the Kölcsey Ferenc **cultural center** around the corner on Hunyadi utca, but only the ultra-dedicated should bother going in search of the old houses on Széchenyi utca, or Attila tér's neglected Greek Orthodox church.

North of Kálvin tér it's greener, with stylish residences lining the roads to **Lenin Park**, which provides the setting for a **pool** and **boating lake**, a **thermal bath** of sulfurous "brown water" (*bárna-víz*), and several hangouts. Sweaty **discos** take place at the *Pálma eszpresszó* (until 11-ish) and *Új Vigadó* (closing in the small hours) most nights, while the outdoor *Levelescsárda* is favored by students from **Kossuth Lajos University**. You'll find this beyond the lake and wooden footbridge, its columned bulk fronted by fountains where newlyweds pose for photos. The university is good for **making contacts** at any time, but particularly during the *Nyári-Egyetem* **Hungarian language summer course** (usually in late July), when students hail from nations as diverse as Sweden and Vietnam. Beyond the campus lies a **Botanical Garden**.

Debrecen's Markets and Festivals

Though the great bi-monthly Fairs "held here since time immemorial" no longer take place, Debrecen's **fruit and vegetable market** is a pungent, compulsive affair. Next door to the supermarket on Csapó utca, the *Vásárcsarnok* hall (Mon–Sat 4am–3pm; Sun 4–11am) is awash with kerchiefed grannies hawking pickles, meat, soft cheese, and strange herbs; the air filled with smells and Magyar interrogatives ("*Hogy a . . . ?*" is slang for "how much is the . . . ?").

Come in the morning, when there's more life in the **Polish market** behind the hall. Among the flea markets and stalls of tacky clothes, it's possible to find Poles or Romanians (recognizable by their Dacia cars marked *RO*) who are willing to **exchange forints for lei**. Romanian lei thus purchased is vastly cheaper than the lei one gets inside Romania itself, exchanging hard currency at the ludicrous official rate. However, both the transaction and the importation of lei into Romania are forbidden, so travelers heading that way should think twice before taking advantage of this ruse.

Haggling is also part of the experience at the so-called **Gypsy market** (*Cigány piac*), held on Saturday and Wednesday mornings in an industrial quarter of town. Take a #30 bus from the railroad station and get off with the crowd just past the cigarette factory (*Dohánygyár*). The market is across the road and through a portal, its 800-odd stalls selling clothes, tools, dubious watches, and other junk.

The date and duration of Debrecen's **Jazz Festival** (*Jazzfeszt*) varies each summer, but *Hajdú Tourist* can supply details and tickets if you're interested. A more predictable event occurs on August 20, when the **Flower Carnival** trundles north along Tanácsköztársaság útja: thirty floats laden with flowers, bands, and operatically dressed soldiers. People hang from windows en route, cheer wildly when the Young Pioneers' band plays tunes from *István a király* ("Stephen the King," a patriotic rock-opera), and surge behind the last float towards the stadium, where the show continues into the late afternoon. In the evening there's a **fireworks** display outside the Great Church.

Restaurants, Rooms, and Other Things

Places around Lenin Park (see above) suffice for lunchtime drinking and the odd meal, but proper **restaurants and bars** are indoors, closer to the center. For hearty roasts and violinists at above-average prices, there's the *Hunyadi* (50m up from the Great Church) or the *Gambrinus*, or the innermost sanctum of the Hotel Arany Bika. The hotel terrace is a pleasant hangout, with a cheap patisserie serving delicious cakes inside, and a stand-up salad/juice bar next door to *IBUSZ*. Across the road, various doors give access to the *Csokonai* cellar restaurant, with a stand-up workers' canteen selling grub from the Nádudvar Co-op on the ground floor. Nearby, you'll find a pizzeria (noon–6pm) in the glassy shopping mall beyond *Hajdútourist*. The *Óbester* cellar on Péterfia utca, where the wine is served from glass spigots, has a nice ambience (open until 10pm).

The *Főnix* (Barna u.17), charging 600Ft for a double, is Debrecen's cheapest **hotel**, but you can economize by booking **private rooms** through *IBUSZ*, or *Hajdútourist* in the shopping mall. Cheaper still are **dormitory beds** in the annex behind the university, which is usually less crowded than the **tourist hostel and campground** beyond the hospital. A student card isn't usually necessary to get beds at the university (from July to mid-Aug) or at other colleges (exact dates and locations vary each year, but the *kollégium* at Béke út 2 and Varga u. 2 seem good possibilities); see *Express* at Vörös Hadsereg útja 77 for details and reservations. Anyone needing to register or extend their visa should visit the **police** station on the corner of Ságvári utca. Two other **campgrounds** are **out of town**—at Vekeri-tó to the south (bus #26 from the terminal/rd.47), and by the **Fancika Lakes** to the east (Aprilis 4. utca/rd.48), which have facilities for horseback riding, boating, and fishing.

Hajdútourist, or the Hotel Aranybika (where international calls are more expensive but easier to make than from the stall in the university basement), will change your money quicker than *IBUSZ*; and the hospital reportedly gives preferential treatment to foreigners (pharmacy on Csapó utca). On Vörös Hadsereg útja, opposite the small church and at no. 47, you'll find two bookshops selling tourist **maps**, books in foreign languages, and records.

Moving On

Roughly half the places covered over the following pages can be reached **by train**, either directly or by changing. To avoid the latter and the chore of deciphering the revolving timetables in Debrecen's station, it's worth catching a bus #1 to the *Volán* terminal, and looking for **buses**. They're probably the quickest way to get to the northeast (though not everywhere is covered) and some run directly to towns on the southern Plain, which are otherwise awkward to reach. And during the summer, there may be special services to Hortobágy, or Eger in the Northern Uplands. To compare services, take bus #1 from terminal to terminal.

Aside from the much-visited **Hortobágy** puszta and the spa town of **Hajdúszoboszló** (both covered below), the Plain's attractions are split between north and south. To the north lies **Szabolcs-Szatmár county**, where drab Nyíregyháza is atypical of the surrounding *Nyírség*. Nyírbátor, an hour's ride from Debrecen, boasts a run of concerts and two remarkable churches, while Nagykálló (easier to reach from Nyíregyháza) hosts a folk arts festival. Farther to the northeast, around the Tisza's headwaters, ancient villages with vaguely pagan graveyards and churches form a distinct entity called the *Erdőhát*. The **southern Plain** is less distinctive, and with most trains limiting themselves to stops at Püspökladány and Karcag, en route to Budapest, it's hardly worth the effort of getting to Békéscsaba and Gyula unless you're planning to drive across into Romania.

Trains that run from Debrecen **to Romania** (and crossing the border in general) are covered under "Leaving Hungary from the Great Plain" below; the following is a summary of trains that run to other foreign cities. Passengers traveling on the *Budapest, Puskin,* or *Tisza* express (leaving town around 2am, 6:30am & 11pm, respectively), must already have a Soviet visa in order to reach **Moscow**; and a Polish visa is likewise necessary for the *Varna* to **Warsaw** (4:30pm). Traveling in the opposite direction, the *Puskin* (9:45pm) and *Varna* (midnight) run to **Belgrade** and **Varna**; the Yugoslavs grant visas at the border, but the Bulgars require travelers to obtain them in advance.

Hortobágy National Park

Petőfi compared **the Hortobágy puszta** of the central Plain to "the sea, boundless and green," and in his day this "glorious steppe" was astir with countless horses and cattle, tramping their way from well to waterhole urged on by mounted *csikós*, and Racka sheep grazing under the eyes of Puli dogs. Centuries before, Cuman tribes raised burial mounds (*kunhalom*) which were later taken for hills, one of which served as the site of a duel between Frau Bártha of Debrecen and two rival *táltos*. Nowadays, the grasslands have receded and mirages are the closest that Hortobágy gets to witchcraft, but the puszta can still pass for Big Sky country, its low horizons casting every copse and hillock into high relief. But come prepared for a relatively costly touristic experience—the puszta comes packaged at Hortobágy.

The 630-square kilometer **National Park** is a living heritage museum, with state-employed cowboys demonstrating their skills, and beasts strategically placed along the way to the nine-arched stone bridge (depicted in a famous painting by Csontváry) that lies just west of Hortobágy village. A succession of small tourist inns gives advance notice to drivers approaching via the Debrecen–Füzesabony road, but **getting there** by rail offers a subtler transition from farmland to puszta. Services from Debrecen (towards Tiszafüred and Füzesabony, or vice versa) are better than trains from Nyíregyháza, which leave you stranded at Óhat-Pusztakócsi, several miles west of Hortobágy village; and during summertime there might even be a steam train leaving Debrecen around 10:45am. Buses—calling at Hortobágy en route between Eger and Hajdúszoboszló (or direct from the latter during high season)—are another option.

Immediately to the south of Hortobágy railroad halt, the much-restored **Great Inn** (*Nagycsárda*) faces the **Shepherd's Museum**, whose embroidered *szűr*, carved powder horns, and other objects were often fashioned by the plainsmen to while away solitary hours. Status counted within their world—horseherds outranked shepherds and cowherds, who felt superior to the *kondás* or swineherd—although all slept equally beneath the stars, only building crude huts (*kunyhó*) or sharing a reed *szárnyék* with their animals if necessary. Across the bridge and to the north lies the Máta stock-breeding center, which hosts an international **Horse Show** (on the first Sun of July and the Fri and Sat before) and regular displays of controlled stampedes and bareback riding during the high season, culminating in the **Bridge Fair** (Aug 19–20)—a Magyar rodeo occasioning the sale of leatherwork, knives, and roast beef.

Wildlife on the Hortobágy

Silvery-gray cattle and corkscrew-horned Racka sheep can be seen just behind Máta, but most of Hortobágy's **wildlife** is dispersed over 100,000 hectares. The Hortobágyi-halastó lakes (6km west of the village) are the haunt of storks, buzzards, mallards, cranes, terns, and curlews; dry sheep-runs are preferred by the little ringed plover, the stone curlew, and the pratincole; while millions of migratory birds pass through during spring and fall. Red-footed falcons here behave unusually for their species, forming loose groups in the low foliage. Mammals frequent marshy thickets near Kecskéses (boars), Árkus (otters), and Kónya (ground squirrels) or, in the case of roe deer, a shifting habitat of reeds, meadows, and copses, between Óhat and Tiszaszőlős. Medieval tales of cities in the clouds and nineteenth-century accounts of phantom woods, or the "extensive lake half enveloped in gray mist" which fooled John Paget, testify to the occurrence of **mirages** during the hot, dry Hortobágy summers. Caused by the diffusion of light when layers of humid air at differing temperatures meet, these *délibáb* sporadically appear at certain locations—north of Máta, south of Kónya, and along the road between Cserepes and the *Kis Hortobágyi* inn.

Practicalities and Tiszafüred

All of these sites appear on the Hortobágy tourist **map**, and some are within walking distance of train halts (*vá.*) along the Debrecen–Tiszafüred, Tiszafüred–Karcag, and Nyíregyháza–Óhat–Pusztakócsi lines. However, if you can rent a bike from the campground or a local person, cycling is the best way of **getting around**. Unless you're equipped to camp, **accommodation** can be tricky, with the *Nagycsárda* and *Fogadó* and local private rooms all full up (though badgering the tourist office might still produce something).

One alternative is to stay at **TISZAFÜRED**, a junction linking the Plain and the Northern Uplands, currently expanding along the east bank of the

Kisköre reservoir. The railroad station is at the western end of the main street, Somogyi B. út; the bus terminal, *IBUSZ* (no. 15) and the main square lie to the east. Gáspár Nyuzó's poky **pottery** (Malom u.12, key from across the road) and the **Kis Pál Museum** (Kun u.6) are the only sights in town, but good **Gypsy music** throbs in the dim *Vendéglő* at Somogyi út 8. With private **rooms** and the *Hotel Vadász* (Lenin u.4) so inexpensive, there's little call to use the motel or pension on the **campground**, unpleasantly situated near a dead—and pestilent—tributary of the Tisza. But the flood-plain and ox-bow lakes are a paradise for **birdwatchers**, with Black and White storks, bitterns, Red-backed shrikes, and magnificent Golden Orioles.

The Hajdúság

The **Hajdúság** region north and west of Debrecen takes its name from *Hajdúk* communities that occupied eight derelict villages during the early seventeenth century. Originally cattle drovers and part-time bandits, their ranks were swollen by runaway serfs and homeless peasants, and they provided a fearsome army for István Bocskai's struggle against the Habsburgs. Bocskai achieved his ambition to be Voivode of Transylvania, while the Hajdúk were pensioned off with land to avert further disturbance. The result was a string of settlements with names prefixed Hajdú-, where the Hajdúk farmed, enjoyed the status of "nobles" (*natio*) and, if necessary, mustered to fight. The military aspect is still apparent in the layout of **HAJDÚBÖSZÖRMÉNY**, where old houses stand in concentric rings around a walled core—once a fortress—but nowadays the Hajdúság towns hardly differ from others on the Plain, and most have acquired a new role as spas.

Hajdúszoboszló and Nádudvar

Driven away from Lake Balaton by rising prices, many Hungarians take their vacations in **HAJDÚSZOBOSZLÓ**, where a spa has been operating since 1927. In the vicinity of the **thermal baths** practically everyone is dressed for the pool, and the consumption of beer and *lángos* is staggering. Modern housing and supermarkets along Vörös Hadsereg útja/Debreceni út (the main street) nourish the illusion of a hedonistic urban environment, but in the backstreets the agricultural past lingers on. Outside the **railroad station**, chunky whitewashed cottages—their vegetable gardens fringed with sunflowers—shimmer in the heat. Errant cows, old women, and wagon-loads of pigs move slowly in the dazzling sunlight, and a bus runs 2km into the town center, terminating 100m from the baths.

Hajdúszoboszló gets about one and a half million visitors each year, and the pools can be packed. Surveying the wallowing, guzzling crowds in the steaming brown waters (good for arthritis and other muscular ills), you might try the old Hajdúk war cry, *Huj, huj, hajrá!*, to clear some space before jumping in yourself. Away from the baths things are more relaxed, with **tennis courts** for rent in the park, and cafés and quaint old buildings around

Bocskai and Hősők squares. Sixty feet of **fortress wall**—part of the fifteenth-century defenses—lurk behind the inevitable Calvinist church, while a comically fierce statue of the Prince guards Bocskai tér and its two hotels.

Around the corner at Bocskai u.12 you'll find a **museum** exhibiting photos of nineteenth-century Hajdúk villagers, and assorted military relics—among them Bocskai's embroidered silk banner, given first place alongside the town's charter. Bocskai comes across as a benevolent man, although he didn't balk at betraying a different group of peasants who fought for him: the Székely of Transylvania, butchered during the so-called "Bloody Carnival" when they outlived their utility. The room across the hall commemorates Hajdúszoboszló's spa, cultural achievements, and natural gas extraction plant.

Rooms at the *Gambrinus* are far less costly than the *Hotel Délibáb*'s, but fractionally more expensive than private lodgings, available from *Hajdútourist* (József u.2), *Cooptourist* (Vörös Hadsereg útja 44), or *IBUSZ*. Otherwise, there's a middle-priced hotel and the possibility of hostel beds or cottages at the campground, beyond the natural gas tank. You'll spot this from the bus terminal, where **buses** depart regularly for Debrecen, Eger, or Nádudvar, and for Hortobágy during the summer.

Aficianados of **pottery** might wish to visit **NÁDUDVAR**, 18km away, where *Lajos Fazekas* carries on a family tradition by producing black, un-fired ceramics at his house and studio on Vörös Hadsereg útja (as always, the mainstreet). Otherwise this sleepy place has two petite churches, a spanking new cultural center, and **Nádudvar Co-operative farm** sprawled around its outskirts, where foreigners attending Debrecen's summer university are sometimes taken for a glimpse of rural prosperity. In the past, some visits have culminated in a riotous *pálinka* binge, with students and workers riding pigs across moonlit fields!

Szabolcs-Szatmár County

North of Debrecen, the Plain ripples with low ridges of windblown sand anchored by birches, apple groves, and tobacco fields. The soft landscape of the *Nyírség* ("birch region") makes a pleasant introduction to **Szabolcs-Szatmár**, an area scorned by many Magyars as the "black country." More densely settled than other parts of the Plain, Szabolcs would be wholly agricultural if not for industrialized Nyíregyháza, straddling the main routes to the Northern Uplands, the Erdóhát villages, and the USSR. Historically isolated by swamps, and then severed from Transylvania in 1920, the region has remained poor and backward in comparison to the rest of Hungary. If your interest in rural life is limited, the odd riding school or ruined castle shouldn't tempt you out beyond Nyíregyháza or Nyírbátor, whose Village Museum and striking churches convey something of the region's character. But for anyone seeking the challenge of remote areas, encounters with Gypsies on their own turf, or the folk customs and architecture of old Hungary, Szabolcs has much to offer.

Nyíregyháza

A sleepy provincial town of 19,000 just ten years ago, **NYÍREGYHÁZA** has grown into the Big Apple of Szabolcs as the food processing industry developed here; a cocoon of gray high-rise *lakótelep* enclosing the original core of three squares. Arriving at the chaotic **station** on the southwestern edge of the circular, you can obtain a street-map from *Express* (2, Arany utca) outside the terminal before catching bus #8 or #8A into the town center, or riding to the bathing resort of **Sóstófürdő** at the end of the line in the northern suburbs. The hostels and campground (April 15–Oct 15), and beds in the *KISZ Iskola* on Sóstoi út there, are all cheap alternatives to private **rooms** from *Nyírtourist* or the *Hotel Szabolcs* on Dózsa Gy. utca in the center.

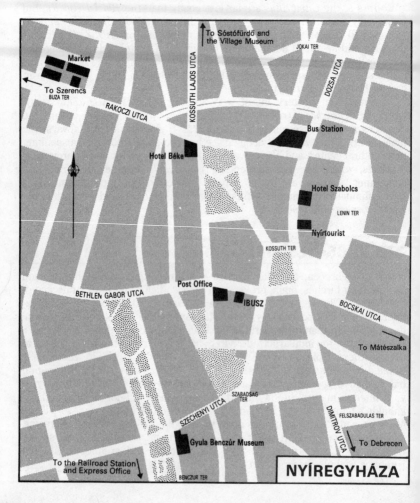

The town's only real attraction is the strangely eerie **Village Museum** (*Szabadtéri Néprajzi Múzeum*), located on Berenat utca in the vicinity of Sóstófürdő. With clothes on the clothes-line, tables laid, and boots by the hearth, the farmsteads seem to have been abandoned by their occupants only yesterday, leaving mute testimony to their lives in a nineteenth-century black country village. The size of the barns (*csűr*) and stables (*istálló*) denotes a family's wealth, as does the presence of a Beam Gate onto the street: "A gate on a hinge, the dog is big, the farmer is great" as the old proverb has it. Other clues to social standing are knick knacks adorning the homes of petty gentry (or "sandled nobles"); the placing of a bench between two windows, the sign of an Orthodox householder; and the single communal bowl in the poorest dwellings.

Downtown centers on Kossuth tér, where the Catholic church stands tall. From there a shopping precinct runs southwards to pastel-hued Freedom Square with the hotel and tourist office on Dózsa utca, nearby. Benczúr tér, to the west, has a beer garden and the local **museum** that displays ancient junk, Party relics, and the dark formal paintings of **Gyula Benczúr**— denounced as a "reactionary" artist during the Republic of Councils, but now reinstated as a worthy son of Nyíregyháza. Kossuth tér's *Kis Étterem* offers seedy grandeur, but the cheapest place to eat is the *Kolumbia* on Egyház utca. Other places worth noting include *IBUSZ* and the post office on Bethlen utca; the **market** on Búza tér; and Jókai tér's **bus terminal**.

Moving On

Assuming that you don't take the train north to Tokaj, the main **routes** into the Szabolcs hinterland lead up to Kisvárda (rail or the T1 highway) or east-wards: through Nyírbátor and Mátészalka, or Vaja and Vásárosnamény, towards the headwaters of the Tisza. Visitors without a car are more or less compelled to travel **by train** in an area with few private vehicles or buses; there are five trains every day from Nyíregyháza to Nagykálló, Nyírbátor and Mátészalka, and less frequent services along the branch lines; all of them are slow but punctual. Hardest, perhaps, is trying to leave town, for Nyíregyháza's station has no platforms, and the indicator boards give cryptic directions. To give you an idea, "*Debrecen—7 balra*" means that the Debrecen train leaves from the left hand side of the seventh track from the main building.

Nagykálló and Nyírbátor

"Go to **NAGYKÁLLÓ**!" used to be a popular insult east of the Tisza, referring to the large mental asylum in this small town of converging houses painted a flaky ocher. From a visitor's standpoint, its sole attraction is an annual work-shop-cum-**festival** of Hungarian folk arts, the *Téka Tábor*, normally held during the first or second week of August inside a weird "barn" shaped like a Viking's helmet, on the outskirts of town; hence another name for the festival, the *Csűr at Nagykálló*. Debrecen's tourist office should be able to supply more details. At other times, happenings are whatever takes place in the local *ital-bolt* (bars), from which youths are excluded. The pall of their small-town life is exacerbated by the visions of Budapest sophistication beamed in via their TVs.

Aware of this, the government endeavors to disseminate metropolitan culture, dispatching troupes from leading theaters and ensembles from the State Philharmonic on tours. At **NYÍRBÁTOR** there's a well-established "season" of **concerts**—mainly choral and chamber music, performed in the Gothic vault of the Calvinist church (from mid-July to Sept; see tourist offices for details)—preceded by a dramatic recitation of verses by Ady or Petőfi ("It's about the sea," my companion muttered). The *protokol* of such events is amusing, with unwilling school kids firmly seated at the back, town belles wearing dresses with the most daring necklines their parents will allow, seeking admiring eyes from gallants, in the middle rows, and along the front local worthies and the Party boss.

The **Calvinist church**, where concerts are held, stands upon a hillside overlooking town, an austere structure with a web-vaulted nave built between 1484 and 1511 on the orders of **István Báthori**. His tomb at the back is conventional, with a sleeping figure indicating that he died in bed but revealing nothing about the character of this Transylvanian Voivode. A power-mad schemer whom the Transylvanian Saxons (among others) hated, he periodically endowed churches in pious atonement for his well-known bouts of orgiastic cruelty. Most likely these had a hereditary origin, for similar hysterical rages and sadism were also characteristic of "Crazy" Gábor Báthori, a short-lived Transylvanian ruler, and István's cousin Erzsébet, known to history as the "Blood Countess." As Counter-Reformation ordinances required, the church's belfry is separate—and in this case, is a splendid seventeenth-century example of the type of **wooden bell tower** once common in rural Szabolcs, Maramures, and Transylvania. Wide-skirted at its base, the belfry rises 20 meters, with a spire like a wizard's hat sprouting four little towers known as *fiatorony* ("sons of the tower"), which symbolized a civic authority's right to execute criminals. Inside the belltower, which is surfaced with hand-cut shingling, you can climb a crooked stairway among ancient joists and beams, to the balcony and the huge bells.

On Károlyi utca, on the far side of the main street, is more of Báthori's legacy to Nyírbátor. The **Minorite Church**, paid for by the spoils of war against the Turks (who, perhaps appropriately, gutted it in 1587) has fantastic wood carvings. The altars (carved by Krucsay's workshop in Eperjes) swarm with figures wearing disquieting expressions. To gain admission, ring at the side door marked *plebánia csengője*, which leads to an exhibition of photos of ancient Szabolcs churches. Next door you'll find a **museum** where various relics with unintelligible captions trace the history of the Báthoris, whose holdings stretched well into Transylvania, but were especially concentrated around **Szatmár**. Though predominantly inhabited by Hungarians, this area was bisected by the diplomats at Versailles, who allotted the provincial capital (nowadays called Satu Mare) and its surroundings to Romania. International relations have been awkward, if not hostile, ever since; which partly explains the small number of border crossings in these parts.

Private rooms can be arranged at Nyírtourist on Szabadság tér, where the *Kakukk* restaurant offers good cheap **meals** and the occasional video-disco. For fruit and vegetables, try the **market** at the junction of Váci and Fürst utcas. Men might enjoy the "old time" barber at 10, Báthori utca.

Gypsy Communities in the Northeast

In the Magyar towns and cities, the **Gypsies** you see are cleaners, flower-sellers, construction workers, hustlers, or drudges; housed in *Munkásszálló* hostels, and universally referred to by the vaguely pejorative term *Cigány*. However, Magyar society has always made an exception for Gypsy entertainers, showering esteem and wealth on a few favorites, and the "Gypsy Music" (*Cigányzene*) associated with Hungary reflects this. To satisfy their audiences, the Gypsy violinists spun together "Old Style" Magyar folk airs and foreign dances and marching tunes of the seventeenth and eighteenth centuries; a mixture that Hungarian purists later deplored, which is equally at variance with the Gypsies' cultural origins. Away from the *gadjé*, among their own people, they are *Rom*: the descendants of tribes who left India to escape their low caste and wandered across the continent, entering Europe around the twelfth century (other Rom headed south to Egypt and Arabia). Foreign countries reacted suspiciously to this peaceful invasion, and at different times Rom have been enslaved, banished, or forced to assimilate.

Their permanent **settlements** are generally on the outskirts of towns (Gyöngyös, Miskolc, Szolnok, etc), or in the the Szabolcs hinterland, and together with urban Gypsies and transient workers, there are somewhere in the region of 250,000–500,000 Rom in Hungary, although nobody knows for sure. Ethno-musicologists occasionally enter these *cigánytelep* to record the communal singing and stick-dancing, but wild horses wouldn't drag the average Magyar into the Gypsy settlements and foreigners are sternly advised against going near them. Health care and education have improved slightly since conditions were exposed in Pál Schiffer's shaming documentary film, *Gyuri*, but Gypsies are still light-years from integrating into Hungarian society. The Catholic Church has taken an interest in the matter, providing religious services and primary education in Romany for Gypsies living just outside HODÁSZ, a commune between Nyírbátor and Mátészalka.

Mátészalka and Vaja

A shabby fusion of flaking estates and low yellow houses, **MÁTÉSZALKA**'s sole claim to fame is that it's the birthplace of Tony Curtis's parents, whose original family name was Kertes (Gardener). In the town center—where each Sunday the population gravitates in homage to the Catholic and Orthodox churches and a thermal bath—you'll find the *Hotel Szatmár* (Szabadság tér 8) and *Nyírtourist* (Bajcsy-Zsilinszky u:30), which can arrange private **rooms** or direct you to the campground. However, more interesting places are accessible using Mátészalka's **trains and buses**, which depart from the western end of the mainstreet, Bajcsy-Zsilinszky utca. Five trains a day head north to Vásárosnamény and Záhony (see below), while three or four pursue branch lines to Fehérgyarmat or Csenger in the Erdőhát region (see below); and there's a single train—currently departing at around 7:20am—to Carei in Romania (see "Leaving Hungary from the Great Plain" below).

En route to the Hungarian frontier post of Ágerdőmajor, some trains call at **NAGYECSED**, the birthplace of the "Blood Countess" Erzsébet Báthori.

Raised at the family château (where she witnessed a Gypsy sewn into a horse's stomach and left to die—a formative experience), she died a prisoner in her own Castle Čachtice, and was buried nearby, to the outrage of her victims' parents, who eventually ensured that Erzsébet's body was transferred to the Báthori vault at Nagyecsed.

Less morbidly, by traveling 14km northwest by bus from Mátészalka, you'll come upon the commune of **VAJA**. The lure is a **castle** (more a fortified manor, really) once owned by Ádám Vaj, one of the earliest adherents to Ferenc Rákóczi's campaign against the Habsburgs. Within the thick stone walls, visitors in felt slippers shuffle across the parquet from room to room, gaping at painted furniture and the grand meeting hall, the *Rákóczi-terem*. But with no accommodation here, visitors must return to Mátészalka or Nyíregyháza, or continue on to Vásárosnamény, for lodgings.

The Erdőhát

The **Erdőhát** is Hungary's most isolated region, a state imposed by nature and confirmed by history. Meandering and flooding over centuries, the headwaters of the Tisza and its tributaries carved out scores of enclaves beneath the flanks of the Subcarpathians, where dense oak forests provided acorns for pig-rearing and ample timber for building. Though invaders were generally deterred by Escedi Swamp and similar obstacles, scattered communities maintained contact with one another through their intricate knowledge of local tracks and waterways, which paid no regard to sovereign borders. Today, the chief sign of this link is the similarity in traditional wooden architecture throughout the Erdőhát and parts of neighboring Maramureş, for the **borders** have come down like shutters during the twentieth century. Although, as a local rightly put it, "From here, twenty kilometers—Russia, twenty kilometers—Romania!," there's nowhere to cross into the adjacent Subcarpathian Oblast of the USSR (traditionally known as Ruthenia), and only two, shaky crossings into Romania.

Exploring the Villages

Roads are poor and motor vehicles are rare in these parts, but if you're interested in rural lifestyles, customs, and architecture practically extinct elsewhere in Hungary, some **villages** are worth the effort. The first clutch are more or less accessible by bus from **VÁSÁROSNAMÉNY**, a small town that was once a trading post on the "salt road" from Transylvania (hotel at Beregszászi u.4; campground). Across the river in **TÁKOS** stands a wattle-and-daub Protestant **church** with bold floral paintings on its gallery and coffered ceiling; outwardly less striking than the thirteenth-century wooden-spired **church** in neighboring **CSARODA**. Such Gothic-inspired architecture predated "folk Baroque" and subsequently enjoyed an eighteenth-century revival, giving rise to the *biserici de lemn* of Maramureş, and formidable-looking structures like the **wooden belfry** in **VÁMOSATYA**, 8km away.

The restorers have been at work in **TARPA** (to the southeast, easier to reach from Fehérgyarmat), and among the wooden cottages stands a large horizontal "dry" **mill** (*száraz-malom*), beneath an intricate conical roof known

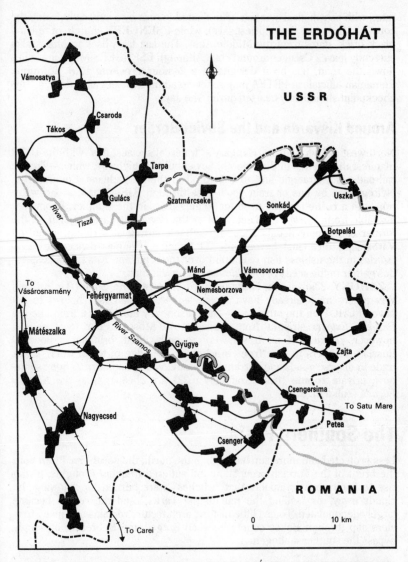

THE ERDŐHÁT

as "the tent of the merry-go-round." MÁND, NEMESBORZOVA, VÁMOSOROSZI and a string of villages bordering the USSR have surrendered their choicest wooden buildings to Szentendre's Village Museum, but **SZATMÁRCSEKE** has retained the "boat-shaped" oaken **grave markers** that vaguely resemble the heads on Easter Island. There's a pension and hostel at Honvéd u.6. To the south of Fehérgyarmat are two more villages with picturesque **churches**: the tiny one at **GYÜGYE** has its panelling decorated with astrological symbols (illuminated in turn by a sunbeam during the course of the year, so the priest says); while **CSENGER**'s church, of red and black brick, dates from the Middle Ages. The last train back to Mátészalka currently leaves Csenger around 8pm. Although CSENGERSIMA, a few miles down the road, has been designated a 24-hour **crossing into Romania**, Romanian officials at PETEA may refuse to admit travelers after dark, so this checkpoint should only be used during the day.

Around Kisvárda and the Soviet Border

Northwest of Nyíregyháza, Hungary's "fraternal socialist ties" with the USSR manifest themselves in the smooth, Soviet-built T1 highway, which—like the railroad—is a strategic link to Uzhgorod in the Carpathians. Coming from Nyíregyháza by bus or train you'll pass through **KISVÁRDA**, a backwater **spa** with a **ruined castle** used for staging plays in the summer. Rooms are available from *Nyírtourist* (Lenin u.2) or the *Fogadó* at Városmajor u.37; the former can supply details about **horseback riding** at a riding school on Városmajor utca, just beyond the T1 junction. Couples dance the *disco-csárdas* in the fishless fish restaurant over the road, and Kisvárda's desperados gather in the seedy *Sport Falatózo* bar on Vár utca.

    ZÁHONY, 23km north, is the only crossing **into the Soviet Union**, and Westerners must already have a **visa** and travel plan (see below) to get beyond CHOP on the other side—the reason why most take a train like the *Pushkin Express* straight from Budapest to Moscow. For local people, however, restrictions on travel were recently lifted, bringing a flood of Russian shoppers to the **"free" market** on the edge of town, where Poles trade in diverse goods and currencies. Should you get stuck in Záhony somehow, private **rooms** (from Szamuely u.22) are cheaper than the *Kemény Fogadó* (Zalka M. u.1).

The Southern Plain

Less protected and more sun-baked than the north, the **southern Plain** bore the brunt of the Turkish occupation and suffered frequent droughts, giving rise to such popular anxiety that "witches" were burned for "blowing the clouds away" or "selling the rain to the Turks," and the region became largely depopulated. Today, little historic architecture remains and many travelers slip through Békés county between Szeged and Debrecen, or simply bypass the southeast altogether.

Püspökladány and Karcag

Along the Budapest–Szolnok–Debrecen route, Karcag and Püspökladány are the junctions for the railroad branch lines south. Aside from its station (with trains for Romania), the most notable feature of **PÜSPÖKLADÁNY** is the large number of aging, former *Munkásrendőrség*. Founded in 1956, this Workers' Militia was employed to break strikes in the aftermath of the

Uprising, and remained the Communist Party's private army until it was dissolved in 1989 as a prelude to Hungary's first free national election. For anyone compelled to stay, there's a campground and hostel at Peto"fi u.62.

KARCAG is likewise slightly Orwellian—"Better work is achieved through Socialism" proclaim the billboards in front of grubby high-rises—and boasts of the largest rice-hulling mill in Europe (rice is grown around Hortobá.) During my visit, the town's **Folk Art Museum** and Orthodox church (both on Horváth utca) were closed, but the *Kunsági* restaurant at 1, Dózsa út, was keen to serve **Cumanian food**. Although of dubious authenticity (the Cuman tribes disappeared centuries ago), the recipes are very tasty, particularly *kunsági pandurleves*—a soup of chicken or pigeon, seasoned with ginger, garlic, nutmeg, and paprika. Cheap rooms can be had at the *Otthon* hotel (no. 33) or *Tiszatour* (no. 10) on Vörös Hadsereg útja, if required; buses run to the campground and thermal baths at BEREKFÜRDŐ, 12km along the Kunmadaras road.

Békéscsaba and Gyula

Traveling between Szeged and Debrecen, **BÉKÉSCSABA** is practically unavoidable. Its central shopping precinct, Tanácsköztarsaság útja, is where to find *Békéstourist* (no. 10), *Express* (no. 29), and an excellent *Halász étterem* with music in the evenings; while the **museum** at Széchenyi út 9, near the canal, exhibits paintings by Mihály Munkácsy and oddments concerning the eighteenth-century Slovak settlers, who revived Békéscsaba after a ruinous succession of earthquakes, invasions, plagues, and fires. There's more about their lifestyle in the ornate **Slovák Tájház** on Garay utca. Over the canal bridge from the museum is another, albeit unofficial, sight, the *István Malom*. This nineteenth-century flour mill, automated at the turn of the century, is crammed with wardrobe-sized shakers, rotating sieves, and wooden chutes, objects of pride to the workers who showed me around.

From the Hunyadi tér station, buses head off northeast to BÉKÉS—a boring place with a thermal bath and a half-obliterated castle—or southwest to **GYULA**, the last town before the Romanian border. Named after a tribal chieftain from the time of Magyar conquest, it became a twin town after the Turkish withdrawal, with Hungarians living in *Magyargyula* and the Romanian and German newcomers in *Németgyula*. In a park on the eastern side of town, a fourteenth-century brick **fortress** now lends its thick walls to the **Castle Plays** held here in July and August, the old chapel occupied by a museum and the Powder Tower by a wine bar. Glittering icons fill one wall of the **Greek Orthodox Church** on Groza tér nearby but secular pleasures are pursued in the steamy *Várfürdő* to the south, a complex of twelve **thermal pools** constructed by the townspeople. In the park along Béke sugárút, visitors to the **György Kohán Museum** are greeted by some of the 3000 works that he bequeathed to his hometown—most notably boldly painted horses, women, and houses, lit by flickering hexagonal track lights. The **Erkel Museum** on Dürer utca makes much of Ferenc Erkel, founder of Hungarian opera, who was born here, and the painter Albrecht Dürer, whose ancestors lived here, but does little to inspire.

Curiously, there's loads of **accommodation**, ranging from the three-star *Aranykereszt* (Eszperantó tér 2) to pensions with rooms for around 300Ft, namely the *Benedeki* (Szt. Benedek u.83), *Komló* (Béke sugárút 6), and *Park* (Park u.15); plus three campgrounds. The *Márk* site (Vár u.5) with a few rooms is nicer than the larger *Termál* and *Camping* grounds, southeast of the fortress, both of which have cottages to compensate. Private rooms are available from Békéstourist (Kossuth u.16) or Gyulatourist (in the Hotel Aranykereszt), and there's a **24-hour currency exchange** at Hétvezér u.5. For cheap food, try the *Gulyáscsárda* near the junction of Városház and Kossuth utca, or the excellent *cukrászda* (Szt. István u.2) in the vicinity of the bus station. The railroad station lies northwest of the town center.

Leaving Hungary from the Great Plain

Bordering Yugoslavia, Romania, and the USSR, the Great Plain also has direct links with places farther afield thanks to international express trains routed via Budapest, which make stopovers at Szolnok or KISKUNHALAS. If you're planning to board there, it's important to buy tickets the day before; seat reservations are compulsory, even for Eurailers. Remember, too, that visas for some countries can *only* be obtained from a consulate, in advance; and that it's cheaper to buy a round-trip ticket in Hungary than to pay the fare back from Bulgaria or Romania.

Unfortunately, a combination of factors virtually rules out entering the **Soviet Union**—not least **visas**, which can take up to 14 days at the Soviet consulate in Budapest, and require you to specify the time and place of entry to the USSR in advance. Few travelers are willing to commit themselves to leaving Debrecen on a particular day, despite the bus service to MUKACHEVO or the three trains to MOSCOW (originating from Budapest), which leave Hungary at ZÁHONY. Motorists with the appropriate visa can cross there **by road**, but their itinerary and accommodation from CHOP onwards must have already been approved by *Intourist*—a regulation which severely hampers independent travel in the USSR (see "Onwards from Hungary" in *Contexts*).

Happily, there are no such restrictions on visiting **Yugoslavia**, where political unrest has yet to affect tourism or border formalities. EC citizens can get **visas** at any of the 24-hour checkpoints; US, Canadian, New Zealand or Australian passport-holders are supposed to obtain them beforehand from a Yugoslav consulate, though only if crossing by rail. You can drive across at HERCEGSZÁNTÓ, south of Baja; TOMPA, on the road down from Kiskunhalas; or RÖSZKE, in the vicinity of Szeged; or even travel **by bus**. Services normally depart on weekday and Saturday mornings before 9am, so you'll need to buy a ticket the day before. *Volán* buses run from Baja, Gyula, Kecskemét, and Szeged to SUBOTICA, and from Szeged to DUBROVNIK. It's easier than trying to board the *Puskin* (2:50am), *Polonia* (7:40am), or *Meridian* (5:25pm) **trains** during their one-minute stopover at Kiskunhalas before leaving Hungary at KELEBIA, bound for SUBOTICA and BEOGRAD (Belgrade).

The pros and cons of visiting **Romania** (see "Onwards from Hungary" in *Contexts*) are finely balanced, and there's no doubt that many travelers are deterred by the idea of exchanging $10 per day and paying $30 for a **visa** at the border, where tourists in transit are charged for the latter, plus three days stay! Assuming you're still interested, stock up on non-perishable food (and gas if you're driving) before leaving Hungary. Motorists crossing **by road** at NAGYLAK, ÁRTÁND, GYULA (open 24-hours) or CSENGERSIMA (daytime only) should be prepared for delays as Romanian border guards shake down Hungarian vehicles—the reason why no buses cross over. International **trains** are likewise delayed, but the following services should arrive during daylight hours—an important consideration in blacked-out Romania. Although estimated departure times refer to Szolnok, most trains also stop at Békéscsaba or Püspökladány en route to the LÖKÖSHÁZA or BIHARKERESZTES frontier posts. CLUJ is best reached by the *Trakia* (6:50am), *Nord–Süd* (9:30am), or *Mamaia* (11:20am); BRAȘOV by the *Vitosha* (4:40am), *Pannonia* (7:20am), or *Orient* (10:15am); and SIGHIȘOARA or BUCHAREST by the *Balt–Orient* (7:15pm). As the express train from Debrecen (4:50pm) arrives in SATU MARE at night, making it hard to push on into Maramureș, you might consider "**local**" **services** from Debrecen (7:30am) or Mátészalka (7:20am), which should reach VALEA LUI MIHAI or CAREI in time for connections to Baia Mare, the hideous portal to Romania's most enchanting region. But customs inspections are rigorous, so there's nothing to be gained from using "local" trains from Békéscsaba to CURTICI or SALONTA.

Travelers to **Bulgaria** must already have a **visa**, and settle for the *Meridian* to SOFIA (boardable at Kiskunhalas around 5:25pm) unless they're willing to bear the expense of passing through Romania. The second option allows a choice of destinations and **trains**: Szolnok is the boarding-point for the Sofia-bound *Vitosha* (4:40am), *Pannonia* (7:20am), and *Karpaty* (4:30pm); the *Transdanubium* (9:15am), *Nord–Süd* (9:30am), and *Nesebar* (1:30pm) to BURGAS; and the *Trakia* (6.50am) to VARNA; while the latter is also accessible by the *Varna* from Debrecen (11:50am). Varna-bound services excepted, all trains stop at RUSE along the way.

Though **Greece** doesn't require visas, you'll have to pay to travel through Yugoslavia on the *Meridian* to THESSALONÍKI and ATHENS. Apply to the consulate for a visa to **Czechoslovakia** a week or so before reserving seats on the PRAGUE-bound *Mamaia* (leaving Szolnok around noon), or get a Czech transit-visa plus a visa for **Poland** prior to catching the *Varna* to WARSAW (from Debrecen at 4:25pm).

festivals

Summer

In **July**, an international **Horse Show** at HORTOBÁGY (on the first Sun and the two days before), **Castle Plays** at GYULA, and the SZEGED **Weeks of music and drama**. The latter starts around July 20 and runs through into

August, a month which also sees the *Téka Tábor* folklore camp at NAGYKÁLLÓ (exact dates vary) and the **Bridge Fair** at HORTOBÁGY on the 19–20, which overlaps with DEBRECEN's **Flower Carnival** on Constitution Day. KECSKEMÉT has as interesting annual **Crafts Fair** in **September** (8–10).

travel details

Trains

From Budapest to Debrecen (13 daily; 2hr 30min–3hr 30min); Kiskőrös (7; 1hr 30min); Kiskunhalas (7; 1hr 45min–2hr 45min); Szeged (2; 2hr 15min).

From Cegléd to Szeged (2; 1hr 45min).

From Debrecen to Hortobágy (6; 1hr); Mátészalka (10; 1hr 30min); Nyírbátor (8; 1hr); Nyíregyháza (20; 30–45 min).

From Füzesabony to Debrecen (6; 2hr); Hortobágy (5; 1hr).

From Kecskemét to Bugac (2; 1hr); Szeged (9; 1hr 15min–2hr).

From Kiskőrös to Kalocsa (7; 1hr).

From Kiskunhalas to Baja (7; 1hr–1hr 30min).

From Mátészalka to Csenger (4; 1hr); Vásárosnamény (5; 30min); Záhony (5; 2hr 30min).

From Nyíregyháza to Mátészalka (5; 1hr); Nagykálló (6; 15min); Nyírbátor (5; 45min); Záhony (5; 30min).

From Szeged to Békéscsaba (7; 1hr 30min–2hr 15min); Keceskemét (7; 1hr 15min).

Buses

From Baja to Szeged (4–5 daily); Szekszárd (6–7).

From Békéscsaba to Békés; Gyula (hourly).

From Debrecen to Hajdúszoboszló (hourly); Nyírbátor (4–5 daily).

From Hajdúszoboszló to Debrecen; Nádudvar (hourly); Hortobágy (during the high season).

From Mátészalka to Vaja (5–6 daily).

From Kalocsa to Baja (hourly).

From Kecskemét to Kiskunfélegyháza (hourly).

From Kiskunfélegyháza to Bugac (every 1hr 30min).

International trains

From Békéscsaba to Arad (3 daily); Bucharest (3); Burgas (2); Curtici (2); Salonta (2); Sofia (3).

From Debrecen to Belgrade (1 daily); Moscow (3); Satu Mare (1); Valea lui Mihai (2); Varna (1); Warsaw (1).

From Kiskunhalas to Athens (1 daily); Belgrade (2); Kiev and Moscow (1); Sofia (1).

From Kötegyán to Salonta (2 daily).

From Mátészalka to Carei (1 daily).

From Püspökladány to Bucharest (3 daily); Constanţa (1); Varna (1).

From Szolnok to Arad (3 daily); Bratislava (1); Bucharest (7); Burgas (3); Cluj (5); Constanta (1); Moscow (3); Oradea (4); Prague (1); Sofia (3); Varna (1).

International buses

From Baja to Subotica.

From Debrecen to Mukachevo.

From Gyula to Subotica.

From Kecskemét to Subotica.

From Szeged to Dubrovnik; Subotica.

TELEPHONE CODES

BAJA ☎79	NYÍREGYHÁZA ☎42
CEGLÉD ☎20	SZEGED ☎62
DEBRECEN ☎52	SZOLNOK ☎56
KECSKEMÉT ☎76	

PART THREE

THE

CONTEXTS

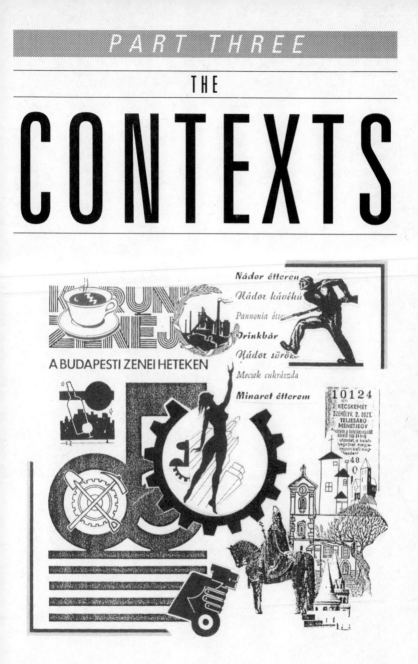

A BUDAPESTI ZENEI HETEKEN

Nádor étterem

Nádor kávéhá

Pannonia étt...

Drinkbár

Nádor söröz...

Mecsek cukrászda

Minaret étterem

10124
KECSKEMÉT
SZEMÉLYV. 2. OSZT.
TELJESÁRÓ
MENETJEGY

HISTORICAL FRAMEWORK

The region of the Carpathian basin known as Hungary (*Magyarország*) changed hands many times before the Magyars arrived here at the end of the ninth century, and its history is marked by migrations, invasions, and drastic changes, as Asia and Europe have clashed and blended. Over the centuries borders have shifted considerably, so geographical limits as well as historical epochs are somewhat arbitrary. Transylvania, an integral part of Hungary for hundreds of years, was lost to Romania in 1920; the plight of its Magyar minority is currently a major issue (see "Ethnocide in Transylvania" below).

PREHISTORY AND THE ROMANS

Although recorded history of the area now covered by Hungary begins with the arrival of the Romans, archaeological evidence of **Stone Age** (3,000,000–8000 BC) humans has been found in the *Istállóskő* and *Pilisszántó* caves in northern Hungary, suggesting that the earliest inhabitants lived by gathering fruit and hunting reindeer and mammoths. The end of the Ice Age created favorable conditions for the development of agriculture and the domestication of animals, which spread up through the Balkans in the Neolithic era, and was characteristic of the **Körös culture** (5500–3400 BC); clans herding sheep and goats and worshipping fertility goddesses, living alongside the River Tisza. As humans became more settled and spread into Transdanubia, evidence survives of mounds (*tell*) full of artifacts, seemingly leading towards the rise of the **Lengyel culture** around Lake Balaton.

During the **Bronze Age** (2000–800 BC), warlike tribes arrived from the Balkans and steppes, introducing cattle and horses. Subsequent migrants brought new technology—the Cimmerians iron, and the Asiatic Scythians (500–250 BC) the potter's wheel and manufactures from Greek traders on the Black Sea coast—while the Celts, who superseded them in the early third century BC, introduced glassblowing and left mournful sculptures and superb jewelry (most notably the gold treasures of *Szárazd-Regöly*), before being subdued by the Romans.

The **Roman conquest** was initiated by Augustus at the beginning of the Christian era, primarily to create a buffer zone in *Pannonia* between the empire and the barbarians to the east. By the middle of the first century AD Roman rule extended throughout Transdanubia, from the Sava to the Danube, which was fortified with *castrum* and formed the *limes* or military frontier. Trade, administration, and culture grew up around the garrison towns and spread along the roads constructed to link the imperial heartland with the far-flung colonies in Dacia (Romania) and Dalmatia (Yugoslavia). Archaeological finds at Pécs, Sopron, Szombathely, and Buda show that these were originally Roman towns; aqueducts and baths at *Római-fürdő* and *Aquincum*, *Gorsium* near Tác, and Szombathely's *Temple of Isis* are the best-preserved Roman remains.

During the fourth century the Romans began to withdraw from Pannonia, handing over its defense to the Vandals and Jazygians who lived beyond the Danube. In 430 they fell under the invading **Huns**, whose empire reached its zenith and then fragmented with the death of Attila (453). Other warring tribes—Ostrogoths, Gepidae, and Langobards—occupied the region for the next 150 years, before being swept aside by the **Avars**, whose empire survived until the beginning of the eighth century, when the region once again came up for grabs for any determined invader.

THE MAGYARS

The **Magyars'** origins lie in the *Finno-Ugrian* peoples that dwelt in the snowy forests between the Baltic and the middle Urals. Around the first century AD, some of these tribes migrated south across the Bashkiran steppes and fell under the influence of Turkic and Iranian culture, gradually becoming tent-dwelling nomadic herders who lived on a diet of mare's milk, horse flesh, fish, and berries. Some archaeologists believe that they mingled with the ancient Bulgars north of the Caspian Sea (in a land known as "Magna Bulgaria"), before the majority fled from marauding Petchenegs (c. 750) and moved westwards to settle on the far bank of the River Don in the so-called *Etelköz* region, around the year 830. Ties with the Huns and Avars have been postulated—including a common language—but there's stronger evidence to link the seven original Magyar tribes with three Kavar tribes, known collectively as the *Onogur*, or "Ten Arrows."

Overpopulation and Petcheneg attacks forced the Onogur to move westwards in 889, and tradition has it that the seven Magyar chieftains elected **Árpád** as their leader, pledging fealty to his heirs with a blood oath. Accompanied by smaller Kun (or Cuman) tribes, the Onogur entered the Carpathian basin and began its **conquest** in 896. Six Magyar tribes settled west of the Danube and in the upper Tisza region, the seventh took the approaches to Transylvania, while the lower Tisza and the northern fringes of the Plain went to the Kuns and Kavars. For the next 70 years the Magyars remained raiders, striking terror as far afield as Constantinople and Orleans (where people thought them to be Huns), until a series of defeats persuaded them to settle for assimilating their gains.

Civilization developed gradually, after Árpád's great-grandson Prince **Géza** established links with Bavaria and invited Catholic missionaries to Hungary. His son **István** (Stephen) took the decisive step of applying to Pope Sylvester for recognition, and on Christmas Day 1000 István was crowned as a "Christian King," and began converting his pagan subjects with the help of Bishop Gellért. Royal authority was extended over the non-tribal lands by means of the **Megye** (county) system, and defended by fortified *vár*, artisans and priests were imported to spread skills and the new religion; and tribal rebellions were crushed. For trying to unify the tribes and establish order, István was subsequently credited with the **foundation of Hungary** and canonized after his death in 1038. His mummified hand and the "Crown of Saint Stephen" have since been revered as both holy and national relics.

THE MIDDLE AGES

Succession struggles raged for decades following István's death, and of the sixteen kings who preceded Andrew II (1205–35), only the humane László I (also canonized), Kálmán "the Booklover," and Béla III (1172–96) contributed anything to Hungary's development. Fortunately, invasions were few during the eleventh and twelfth centuries, and **German and Slovak immigrants** helped double the population to about 2,000,000 by 1200. Parts of **Transylvania** were settled by the Magyars and Székely, perhaps before the second half of the eleventh century, when the "lands of Saint Stephen" were extended to include **Slavonia** (between the Sava and Drava rivers) and the unwillingly "associated" state of **Croatia**. The growth in royal power caused tribal leaders to rebel in 1222, when Andrew II was forced to recognize the "noble" status and rights of **the Natio**—landed freemen exempt from taxation—in the *Golden Bull*, a kind of Hungarian Magna Carta.

Andrew's son **Béla IV** was trying to restore royal authority when disaster struck from the east—the **Mongol invasion** of 1241, which devastated Hungary. Hundreds of towns and villages were sacked; refugees fled to the swamps and forests; crops were burned or left unharvested; and famine and plague followed. Population losses ranged from 60–100 percent on the Plain to 20 percent in Transdanubia, and after the Mongol withdrawal a year later (prompted by the timely death of the Khan), Hungary faced a mammoth task of **reconstruction**—the chief achievement of Béla's reign, to which foreign settlers made a large contribution. Renewed domestic feuding (complicated by foreign intervention and the arrival of more Cuman tribes) dogged Andrew III's reign; and worsened when he died heirless in 1301, marking the **end of the Árpád dynasty**.

Foreign powers advanced their own claimants, and for a while there were three competing kings, all duly crowned. **Charles Robert** of the French Angevin (or Anjou) dynasty eventually triumphed in 1310, when his rivals went home in disgust; and despite colonial skirmishes with Venice, Serbia, and Wallachia, Hungary itself enjoyed a period of peace, for the Mongols and other great powers were occupied elsewhere. Gold mines in Transylvania and northern Hungary—the richest in Europe—stabilized state finances and the currency. Charles's son Lajos, **Louis the Great**, reigned (1342–82) during a period of expansion, when the population rose to 3,000,000, and by war and dynastic aggrandizement, crown territory grew to include Dalmatia, the Banat, Gallicia, and (in theory) Poland. But Louis had only daughters, so after his demise, another foreigner ascended the throne in 1395—**Sigismund of Luxembourg**, Prince of Bohemia, whom the nobles despised as the "Czech swine." His extravagant follies and campaigns abroad were notorious, and while Sigismund recognized the growing threat of the Turks, he failed to prevent their advance up through the Balkans.

During the fourteenth century, the realm contained 49 boroughs, about 500 market towns, and 26,000 villages. Everyone benefitted from peace and expanded trade, but the rewards weren't shared evenly, for the Angevins favored towns and guilds, and most of all the top stratum of the Natio, on whom they depended for troops (*banderia*) when war posed a threat. The burden fell upon the **peasantry**, who lacked "free" status and were compelled to pay *porta* (gate tax) to the state, tithes to the church, and one ninth of their produce to the landlords—plus extra taxes and obligations during times of war, or to finance new royal palaces.

Sigismund died in 1447 leaving one daughter, Elizabeth, just as **the Turks** were poised to invade and succession struggles seemed inevitable. The Turks might have taken Hungary then, but for a series of stunning defeats inflicted upon them by **János Hunyadi**, a Transylvanian warlord of Vlach (Romanian) origin. The lifting of the siege of Nándorfehérervár (Belgrade) in 1456 checked the Turkish advance and caused rejoicing throughout Christendom—the ringing of church bells at noon was decreed by the pope to mark this victory—while Hunyadi rose to be *Voivode* or Prince of Transylvania, and later regent for the boy king László. Following Hunyadi's death, László's early demise, and much skullduggery, Mihály Szilágyi staged a coup and put his nephew Mátyás (Matthias), Hunyadi's son, on the throne in 1458.

RENAISSANCE AND DECLINE

Mátyás Corvinus is remembered as the "**Renaissance King**" for his statecraft and multiple talents (including astrology), while his second wife **Beatrice** of Naples lured humanists and artists from Italy to add luster to their palaces at Buda and Visegrád (of which some remains survive). Mátyás was an enlightened despot renowned for his fairness: "King Mátyás is dead, justice is departed," people mourned. By taxing the nobles (against all precedent) he raised a standing force of 30,000 mercenaries, called the Black Army, which secured the realm and made Hungary one of Central Europe's leading powers. But when he died in 1490, leaving no legitimate heir, the nobles looked for a king "whose plaits they could hold in their fists."

Such a man was Ulászló II (whose habit of assenting to any proposal earned him the nickname "King Okay"), under whom the Black Army and its tax base were whittled away by the Diet (which met to approve royal decrees and taxes), while the nobility filched common land and otherwise increased their exploitation of the peasantry. Impelled by poverty, many joined the crusade of 1514, which under the leadership of **György Dózsa** turned into an **uprising against the landlords**. Its savage repression (over 70,000 peasants were killed and Dózsa was roasted alive) was followed by the **Werbőczy Code** of 1517, binding the peasants to "perpetual **serfdom**" on their masters' land and 52 days of *robot* (unpaid labor) in the year.

Hungary's decline accelerated as corruption and incompetence bankrupted the treasury, forts along the border crumbled, and the revived *banderia* system of mobilization was makeshift. Ulászló's son Louis II was only nine when crowned, and by 1520 the Turks, under Sultan Süleyman "the Magnificent," had resumed their advance northwards, capturing the run-down forts in Serbia. In August 1526 the Turks crossed the Drava and Louis hastened south to confront them at the **battle of Mohács**—a catastrophic defeat for the Magyars, whose army was wiped out together with its monarch and commanders.

THE TURKISH CONQUEST

After sacking Buda and the south, the Turks withdrew in 1526 to muster forces for their real objective, Vienna, the "Red Apple." To forestall this, Ferdinand of Habsburg proclaimed himself king and occupied western Hungary, while in Buda the nobility put **János Zápolyai** on the throne. Following Zápolyai's death in 1541 Ferdinand claimed full sovereignty, but the Sultan occupied Buda and central Hungary, and made Zápolyai's young son ruler of Transylvania. Thereafter Transylvania became a semi-autonomous principality, nominally loyal to the Sultan and jealously coveted by the Habsburgs. The tripartite **division of Hungary** was formally recognized in 1568. Despite various official or localized truces, warfare became a feature of everyday life for the next 150 years, and the national independence lost then was not to be recovered for centuries afterwards.

Royal Hungary—basically western Transdanubia and the north—served as a "human moat" against the Turkish forces that threatened to storm Austria and Western Europe, kept at bay by Hungarian sacrifices at Szigetvár, Temesvár, Kőszeg, and other fortresses. Notwithstanding constitutional arrangements to safeguard the Natio's privileges, real power passed to the Habsburg chancellory and war council, where the liberation of Hungary took second place to Austria's defense and aggrandizement, and the subjugation of Transylvania.

Turkish-occupied Hungary—*Eyalet-i Budin*—was ruled by a Pasha in Buda, with much of the land either deeded to the Sultan's soldiers and officials, or run directly as a state fief (*khasse*). The peasants were brutally exploited, for many had to pay rent both to their absentee Magyar landlords and to the occupying Turks. Their plight is evident from a letter to a Hungarian lord by the villagers of Batthyán: "Verily, it is better to be Your Lordship's slaves, bag and baggage, than those of an alien people." Peasants fled their villages on the Alföld to the safer fields around the expanding "agro-towns" of Debrecen and Szeged, the nexus of the cattle trade which gradually supplanted agriculture, while neglect and wanton tree-felling transformed the Plain into a swampy wasteland—the *puszta*.

The Voivodes of **Transylvania** endeavored to provoke war between the Habsburgs and Turks, increase their independence from both, and satisfy the feudal **Nationes**. The latter, representing the élite of the region's Magyars, Saxons, and Székely, combined to deny the indigenous Vlachs political power, while competing amongst themselves and extending the borders of Transylvania (then much bigger than today). István Bocskai's *Hajdúk* forces secured the Szatmár region; Gábor Bethlen promoted economic and social development; but Prince György Rákóczi II aimed too high and brought the wrath of the Sultan down on Transylvania.

Religion was an additional complicating factor. The Protestant Reformation gained many adherents in Hungary during the sixteenth century, and while religious toleration was decreed in Transylvania in 1572, in Royal Hungary the counter-reformation gathered force under Habsburg rule. The Turks, ironically, were indifferent to the issue and treated all their Christian subjects (*Rayah*) with equal disdain. After the expulsion of the Turks, Protestant landowners were dispossessed in favor of foreign servants of the crown—a major cause of subsequent anti-Habsburg revolts.

THE HABSBURGS

A multinational army evicted the Ottomans after heavy fighting between 1683 and 1699, and the Turks relinquished all claims by signing the *Peace of Karlowitz*. Yet for many years peace remained a mirage, for the Hungarians now bitterly resented Habsburg policy and their plundering armies. The **Kuruc revolt** (1677–85) led by **Imre Thököly** was but a prelude to the full-scale **War of Independence** of 1703–11, when peasants and nobles banded together under **Ferenc Rákóczi II**, György's grandson, and initially routed the enemy. Ultimately, however, they were defeated by superior Habsburg power and the desertion of their ally, Louis XIV of France, and peace born of utter exhaustion came at last to Hungary.

Habsburg rule combined force with paternalism, especially during the reign of Empress

Maria Theresa (1740–80), who believed the Hungarians "fundamentally a good people, with whom one can do anything if one takes them the right way." The policy of *impopulatio* settled thousands of Swabians, Slovaks, Serbs, and Romanians in the deserted regions of Hungary, so that in areas such as the "Military Border" along the Sava, **Magyars became a minority**, and by the end of the eighteenth century they formed only 35 percent of the population of the huge kingdom. For the aristocrats it was a *belle époque*: the Esterházy, Grassalkovich, and Batthyány families and their lesser imitators commissioned over 200 palaces, and Baroque town centers and orchestras flourished. Yet the masses were virtually serfs, using medieval methods that impoverished the soil, mired in isolated villages. Cattle, grain, and wine—Hungary's main exports—went cheap to Austria, which tried to monopolize industry.

The **Germanization** of culture, education, and administration was another feature of Habsburg policy. Whilst the richest nobles and most of the urban bourgeoisie chose the Habsburg style, the petty gentry and peasantry clung stubbornly to their Magyar identity. The ideals of the Enlightenment found growing support among intellectuals, and the revival of the **Magyar language** became inseparable from nationalist politics. **Ferenc Kazinczy**, who refashioned Hungarian as a literary language and translated foreign classics, was associated with the seven Jacobin conspirators executed for plotting treason against the Habsburgs in 1795.

THE NINETEENTH CENTURY

Magyar nationalism, espoused by sections of the Natio, became increasingly vocal during the early nineteenth century. Hungary's backwardness was a matter for patriotic shame and self-interested concern, especially after peasant riots in the impoverished, cholera-ridden Zempléni, and the publication of *Hitel* ("Credit"), which crushingly indicted the country's semifeudal economy. However, most nobles were determined to preserve their privileges. One wrote that "God himself has differentiated between us, assigning to the peasant labor and need, to the lord, abundance and a merry life." Moreover, national liberation was seen in exclusively Magyar terms—the idea

that non-Magyars within the multinational state might wish to assert their own identity was regarded as subversive.

The **Reform Era** (roughly 1825–48) saw many changes. Business, the arts, and technology were in ferment, with Jews playing a major role in creating wealth and ideas (although they remained second-class citizens). The **Diet** became increasingly defiant in its dealings with Vienna over finances and laws, and parliamentarians like Ferenc Deák, Count Batthyány, and Baron Eötvös acted in the shadow of the "giants" of the time, Széchenyi and Kossuth, who expounded rival programs for change. Count **István Széchenyi**, the landowning, Anglophile author of *Hitel*, was a tireless practical innovator, introducing silkworms, steamboats, and the Academy, as well as an unprecedented tax on the Natio to pay for the construction of his life's monument, the Chain Bridge linking Buda and Pest. His arch rival was **Lajos Kossuth**, smalltown lawyer turned Member of Parliament and editor of the radical *Pesti Hirlap*, which scandalized and delighted citizens. Kossuth detested the Habsburgs, revered "universal liberty," and demanded an end to serfdom and censorship, but Magyar chauvinism was his blindspot. The law of 1840, his greatest prerevolutionary achievement, inflamed dormant nationalist feelings among Croats, Slovaks, and Romanians by making Magyar the sole official language—an act for which his ambitions would later suffer.

The fall of the French monarchy in February precipitated a crisis within the Habsburg empire, which Kossuth exploited to bring about the **1848 revolution** in Hungary. The emperor yielded to demands for a constitutional monarchy, universal taxation, widened voting rights, and the union of Transylvania with Hungary; while in Budapest the nobles took fright and abolished serfdom when the poet **Sándor Petőfi** threatened them with thousands of peasants camped out in the suburbs. But the slighted nationalities rallied against the Magyars in Croatia and Transylvania, and the reassertion of Habsburg control over Italy and Czechoslovakia closed the noose. The new emperor Franz Joseph declared that Hungary would be partitioned after its defeat, in reaction to which the Debrecen Diet declared **Hungarian independence**—a state crushed by August 1849, when Tsar Nicholas of Russia sent armies to support the Habsburgs, who instituted a reign of terror.

Gradually, brute force was replaced by a **policy of compromise**, by which Hungary was economically integrated with Austria and given a major shareholding in the Habsburg empire, now known as the "Dual Monarchy." The compromise (*Ausgleich*) of 1867 engineered by **Ferenc Deák** brought Hungary prosperity and status, but tied the country inextricably to the empire's fortunes. Simmering nationalist passions would henceforth be focussed against Hungary as much as Austria, and diplomatic treaties between Austria and Germany would bind Hungary to the "Central Powers" in the event of war. In 1896, however, such dangers seemed remote, and people celebrated **Hungary's millenary anniversary** with enthusiasm.

1918–1945

Dragged into **World War I** by its allegiance to the Central Powers, Hungary faced defeat by the fall of 1918. The Western or "Entente" powers decided to dismantle the Habsburg empire in favor of the "**Successor States**"— Romania, Czechoslovakia, and Yugoslavia— which would acquire much of their territory at Hungary's expense. In Budapest, the October 30 *"Michaelmas Daisy Revolution"* put the Social Democratic government of Mihály Károlyi in power. But the government avoided the issue of land reform, attempted unsuccessfully to negotiate peace with the Entente, and finally resigned when France backed further demands by the Successor States.

On March 21 the Social Democrats agreed on cooperation with the **Communists**, who proclaimed a **Republic of Councils** (*Tanácsköztársaság*) led by **Béla Kun**, which ruled through local Soviets. Hoping for radical change and believing that "Russia will save us," many people initially supported it until the enforced nationalization of land and capital, and attacks on religion, alienated the majority. Beset by the Czech Legion in Slovakia and internal unrest, the regime collapsed in August before the advancing Romanian army, which occupied Budapest.

Then came the **White Terror**, as right-wing gangs spread out from Szeged, killing "Reds" and Jews, who were made scapegoats for the earlier Communist "Red Terror." **Admiral**

Miklós Horthy appointed himself regent and ordered a return to "traditional values" with a vengeance. Meanwhile, at the Paris Conference, Hungary was obliged to sign the **Treaty of Trianon** (July 4, 1920) surrendering two thirds of its historic territory, and three fifths of its total population (3,000,000 Magyars) to the Successor States. The bitterest loss was **Transylvania**, whose 103,093 square kilometers and 1,700,000 Magyars went to Romania—a devastating blow to national feelings, reflected in the popular slogan of the times, *Nem, Nem, soha!* (No, No, never!).

During **the Twenties and Thirties**, campaigning for the overturn of the Trianon *diktat* was the "acceptable" outlet for politics; while workers' unions were tightly controlled and peasants struggled to form associations against the landlords and the gendarmerie, who rigged ballots and gerrymandered as in the old days. Politics were dominated by the *Kormánypárt* (Government Party) led by Count Bethlen, representing the Catholic Church and the landed gentry, which resisted any changes that would threaten their power. Social hardships increased, particularly in the countryside where the **landless peasantry** constituted "three million beggars" whose misery concerned the "**Village Explorers**" (*Falukutató*): a movement of the literary intelligentsia ranging across the political spectrum. With the Social Democrats co-opted by conservatism and the Communist Party illegal, many workers and disgruntled petit bourgeois turned to the "**radical right**" to voice their grievances, and were easily turned against Jews and the "Trianon Powers."

Resentment against France, Britain, and Romania predisposed many Hungarians to admire **Nazi Germany**'s defiance of the Versailles Treaty; a sentiment nurtured by the Reich's grant of credits for **industrialization**, and Nazi sympathizers within *Volksdeutsche* communities, commerce, the civil service, and the officer corps. Rampant nationalism and **anti-semitism** raised to power politicians like Gyula Gömbös, and Hungary's belated industrial growth was partly due to the acquisition of territory from Czechoslovakia, following Germany's dismemberment of the latter. The annexation of Austria made the Reich militarily supreme in Central Europe, and Hungary's submission to German hegemony almost inevitable.

With the outbreak of **World War II**, the government's pro-Nazi policy initially paid dividends. Romania was compelled to return **northern Transylvania** in July 1940, and Hungary gained additional territory from the invasion of Yugoslavia a year later. Hoping for more, Premier Bárdossy committed Hungary to the Nazi invasion of the USSR in June 1941—an act condemned by the former Prime Minister, Teleki (who had engineered the recovery of Transylvania), as the "policy of vultures." The Hungarian Second Army perished covering the retreat from Stalingrad, while at home, Germany demanded ever more foodstuffs and forced labor. As Axis fortunes waned Horthy prepared to declare neutrality, but Hitler forestalled him with *Operation Margarethe*—the outright **Nazi occupation of Hungary** in March 1944.

Under Sztójay's puppet-government, Hungarian **Jews** were forced into ghettos to await their deportation to Auschwitz and Belsen, a fate hindered only by the heroism of the underground, a handful of people organized by the Swedish diplomat Raoul Wallenberg, and by the maneuvering of some Horthyite politicians. Mindful of Romania's successful escape from the Axis in August, Horthy declared a surprise armistice on October 15, just as the Red Army crossed Hungary's eastern border. In response, Germany installed the native **Arrow Cross fascists**, or *Nyilas*, led by the deranged Ferenc Szálasi, whose gangs roamed Budapest extorting valuables and murdering people on the frozen Danube, while the Nazis systematically plundered Hungary. They blew up the Danube bridges and compelled the Russians to take Budapest by storm—a siege that reduced much of Buda to ruins. Meanwhile in Debrecen, an assembly of anti-fascist parties met under Soviet auspices to nominate a **provisional government**, which took power after the Germans fled Hungary in April 1945.

THE RÁKOSI ERA

In the November 1945 **elections** the Smallholders' Party won an outright majority, but the Soviet military insisted that the Communists and Social Democrats (with seventeen percent of the vote) remain in government. **Land reform** and limited **nationalization** were enacted; while the Communists tightened their grip over the Ministry of the Interior (which controlled the police) and elections became increasingly fraudulent. **Mátyás Rákosi**, Stalin's man in Hungary, gradually undermined and fragmented the "bourgeois" parties with what he called "salami tactics," and by 1948—officially called the "**Year of Change**"—the Communists were strong enough to coerce the Social Democrats to join them in a single **Workers' Party**, and neutralize the Smallholders. Church schools were seized, Cardinal Mindszenty was jailed for "espionage" and the peasants were forced into collective farms. More than 500,000 Hungarians were imprisoned, tortured, or shot in native concentration camps like Recsk, or as deportees in the Soviet Union, victims of the *ÁVO* secret police (renamed the *ÁVH* in 1949), which spread terror throughout society.

Soviet culture and the personality cults of Rákosi (known as "Baldhead" or "Asshole" to his subjects) and Stalin were stiflingly imposed. Hungarian classics like the *Tragedy of Man* were banned for failing to meet the standards of "Socialist Realism." Under the 1949 **Five Year Plan**, heavy industry took absolute priority over agriculture and consumer production. To fill the new factories, peasants streamed into towns and women were dragooned into the labor force. Living standards plummeted, and the whole of society was subject to the laws and dictates of the Party. "Class conscious" workers and peasants were raised up to high positions and "class enemies" were discriminated against, while Party *funkcionáriusok* enjoyed luxuries unavailable to the public, who suffered hunger and squalor.

Although the Smallholders retained nominal positions in government, real power lay with Rákosi's clique, known as the "Jewish Quartet." Like elsewhere in Eastern Europe at this time, Hungary saw bitter **feuds within the Communist Party**. In October 1949, the "Muscovites" purged the more independently-minded "national" Communists on the pretext of "Titoism." The former Interior Minister **László Rajk** was executed; and his friend and successor (and, some say, betrayer), **János Kádár**, was jailed and tortured with others during a second wave of purges. Two years later, following Stalin's death in March 1953, Kremlin power struggles resulted in a more moderate Soviet leadership and the abrupt replacement of Rákosi by **Imre Nagy**. His **"New Course,"** announced in July, promised a more balanced industrial strategy and eased pressure on the peasants to collectivize, besides curbing the *ÁVH* terror. But Nagy had few allies within the Kremlin, and in 1955 Rákosi was able to strike back—expelling Nagy from the Party for "deviationism" and declaring a **return to Stalinist policies**. However, this brief interlude had encouraged murmurings of resistance.

THE 1956 UPRISING

The first act of opposition came from the official Writers' Union: the *November Memorandum*, objecting to the rule of force. The Party clamped down, but also began to "rehabilitate" the Rajk purge victims. During June **1956** the intellectuals' **Petőfi circle** held increasingly outspoken public debates, and **Júlia Rajk** denounced "the men who have ruined this country, corrupted the Party, liquidated thousands and driven millions to despair." Moscow responded to the unrest by replacing Rákosi with **Ernő Gerő**—another hardliner—in July, a move which merely stoked public resentment. The mood came to a head in October, when 200,000 people attended Rajk's reburial; Nagy was readmitted to the Party; and **students** in Szeged and Budapest organized to demand greater national independence and freedom.

In Poland, Gomulka's "reform communists" had just won concessions from the Kremlin, and Budapest students decided to march on October 23 to the General Bem statue, a symbol of Polish-Hungarian solidarity. About 50,000 assembled, patriotic feelings rose, and the procession swelled as it approached Parliament. A hesitant speech there by Nagy failed to satisfy them, and students besieged the Radio Building on Bródy utca, demanding to voice their grievances on the airwaves. The *ÁVH* guards opened fire, killing many. Almost immediately, this triggered a city-wide **uprising** against the *ÁVH*, which the regular police did little to control; and when Soviet tanks intervened, units of the Hungarian army began to side with the insurgents.

Over the next five days fighting spread throughout Hungary, despite Nagy's reinstatement as premier and pleas for order.

Revolutionary councils sprang up in towns and factories and free newspapers appeared, demanding "*Ruszkik haza*" (Russians go home), free elections, civil liberties, industrial democracy, and foreign neutrality. Intellectuals who had led the first protests now found themselves left behind by uncontrollable dynamism on the streets. The Party leadership temporized, reshuffled the cabinet, and struggled to stay in control, as the "bourgeois" parties reappeared and the newly liberated Cardinal Mindszenty provided a focus for the resurgent Right.

The negotiated **Soviet withdrawal**, beginning on the 29th, was a delaying tactic. The Russians regrouped in the countryside and brought in fresh troops from Romania and the USSR. On November 1, Nagy announced Hungary's withdrawal from the Warsaw Pact and asked the UN to support **Hungarian neutrality**; that night, Kádár and Ferenc Münnich slipped away from Parliament to join the Russians, who were preparing to crush the "counter-revolution." America downplayed Hungary in the United Nations while the Suez crisis preoccupied world attention, but the CIA-sponsored **Radio Free Europe** encouraged the Magyars to expect Western aid. Having surrounded Budapest and other centers with tanks under cover of a snowstorm, the **Soviet attack** began before dawn on November 4.

Armed resistance was crushed within days, but the workers occupied their factories and proclaimed a **general strike**, maintained for months despite **mass arrests**. Deprived of physical power, the people continued to make symbolic protests like the "Mothers' March" in December. Inexorably, however, the Party and *ÁVH* apparatus reasserted its control. Over 200,000 **refugees** fled to the West, while at home, thousands were jailed or executed, including Nagy and other leading "revisionists," shot in 1958 after a secret trial.

KÁDÁR'S HUNGARY

In the aftermath of the Uprising, the new Party leader **János Kádár** ruthlessly suppressed the last vestiges of opposition. After the mid-1960s, however, his name came to be associated with the **gradual reform** of Hungary's social and economic system from a totalitarian regime to one based, at least in part, on **compromise**. Kádár's famous phrase, "Whoever is not against us is with us" (a reversal of the Stalinist slogan) invited a tacit compact between Party and people. Both had been shaken by the events of 1956, and realized that bold changes—as happened in Czechoslovakia in 1967 and 1968—only invited Soviet intervention, justified by the Brezhnev doctrine of "limited sovereignty."

Having stimulated the economy by cautious reforms in the structure of pricing and management, and overcome opposition within the Politburo, Kádár and Reszö Nyers announced the **New Economic Mechanism** (NEM) in 1968. Though its impact on centralized planning was slight, the NEM was accompanied by measures to promote "socialist legality" and make merit, rather than class background and Party standing, the criteria for promotion and higher education.

While generally welcomed by the populace, these reforms angered "New Left" supporters of either Duboek's "Socialism with a human face" in Czechoslovakia or of the Chinese Cultural Revolution, and also, more seriously, conservatives within the Party. With backing from Moscow, they watered down the NEM and ousted Nyers, its leading advocate, from the Politburo in 1973; expelling Hegedüs and other "revisionist sociologists" from the Party later.

Following a power struggle, Kádár was able to reverse the reactionary tide, and reduce constraints on the so-called "second economy." While structural reforms were extremely limited, consumerism, a private sector, and even "forint millionaires" emerged during **the Seventies**, when Hungary became a by-word for **affluence** within the Socialist bloc—the "happiest barracks in the camp," as the joke had it. Mechanics and other artisans with marketable skills were able to moonlight profitably, as demonstrated by the boom in private home-building; and workers and unions acquired some say in the management of their enterprises. This **"market socialism"** attracted the favors of Western politicians and bankers, and before *perestroika* the "Hungarian model" seemed to offer the best hope for reform within Eastern Europe.

In **the Eighties**, however, economic and social problems became increasingly obvious—ranging from thirty percent **inflation**, whose effect was felt hardest by the **"new poor"** living on low, fixed incomes, to Hungary's $14.7 billion foreign debt (per capita, the largest in

Eastern Europe). Despite reformist rhetoric, vested interests successfully resisted the logic of the market, whose rigorous application would entail drastic lay offs and, almost certainly, **unemployment** in towns dominated by the unprofitable mining and steel industries. Although frank analyses of Hungary's economic plight started appearing in the media during the mid-Eighties, **other issues** ran up against the limits of state tolerance. These included fears for **the environment** in the wake of Chernobyl and the decision to build a dam at Nagymaros (see "Nagymaros and the Dam" in *The Danube Bend*); an unofficial **peace movement** that was quickly driven back underground; and any discussion of the Party's "leading role" or Hungary's alliance with the Soviet Union. Discussion of such topics could only be found in **samizdat** (underground) magazines like Beszéld, whose publishers were harassed as **dissidents**. Although in 1983 the Party announced that "independents" could contest elections, it proved unwilling to let them enter Parliament, as demonstrated by the official gerrymandering used against László Rajk in 1986.

Yet the need for change was becoming evident even within the Party, where the caution of the "old guard"—Kádár, Horváth, and Gáspár—caused increasing frustration among **reformists**, who believed that Hungarians would only accept sales tax, income tax, and economic austerity if greater liberalization seemed a realistic prospect. Happily, this coincided with the advent of **Gorbachev**, whose interest in the Hungarian model of socialism and desire to bring a new generation into power was an open secret.

RECENT DEVELOPMENTS

The rapidity of change over the last year or so has surprised even reformists, and there's no way that any survey of the scene will remain up to date. At time of writing Hungary is awaiting its first free national election since 1945, which seems set to be followed by even greater changes. Consequently I've merely summarized some developments and central issues: but any Hungarian should be able to fill you in on the latest details.

Some of the most publicized developments have involved the **Communist Party** which reconstituted itself as a **Socialist Party** in the fall of 1989, simultaneously jettisoning forty years of Marxist-Leninst ideology. This represented the culmination of a **struggle between reformers and conservatives**, which had raged at the highest levels ever since the 1988 Party Congress, when Kádár and seven colleagues were ousted from power. Kádár's successor **Karóly Grósz** vacillated, disgusting both sides; but it was the reformists (meeting earlier at Kecskemét and Szeged) who shunted him aside in July 1989, forcing conservatives and hardliners onto the defensive. As the ascendancy of **Imre Pozsgay**, **Rezsö Nyers**, **Miklós Nemeth** and other committed reformers became apparent there was a "traffic jam on the road to Damascus" as lesser figures hastened to pledge support for reforms. Fears that hardliners might use the local Party machinery to block change, or even employ the 60,000-strong **Workers' Militia** to stage a coup subsequently proved groundless. Instead, thanks to the pressure of public opinion, the government agreed to wind up Party cells in work places and institutions across Hungary, and abolish the despised *Munkásrendőrség*.

By pledging **free elections** in 1990, the Party has accepted the possibility of sharing power with the democratic opposition, or even being voted from office; Pozsgay supposedly believes that a reformed Socialist Party could be popular with the electorate, but others aren't so optimistic. The **Democratic Forum**, which trounced the old MSzMP in two by-elections in August 1989, is currently the front-runner among the **new political parties**; the **Smallholders'** and **Christian Democrats** are actually resurrected parties of the 1930s. Although Hungary's **increasing media freedom** has worked to their advantage, all of them are short on funds and administrative experience. Nevertheless, a loose alliance called the Opposition Round Table conducted negotiations with the party and the government over Hungary's **transition to multi-party democracy**. The opposition objects that Imre Pozsgay was appointed Prime Minister under the old system yet retains this office in the new **Hungarian Republic** proclaimed on October 23, 1989.

Whatever the eventual outcome, certain problems must be confronted—above all, **the economy**. Inflation has topped eighteen percent, real wages and living standards have sunk, and poverty and unemployment have risen; yet Hungary still owes Western creditors $14.7 billion and has hardly started the long-promised radical overhaul of industry and administration. In other ways, however, progress is tangible, if only on **symbolic issues**. Thirty-three years after the event, the Party submitted to the verdict of ordinary Hungarians by proclaiming **the 1956 Uprising** a popular revolution whose participants were heroes and heroines, rather than branding it an "imperialist-backed conspiracy" carried out by "bandits" and "counter-revolutionaries". In a similar vein, Imre Nagy and others executed after the Uprising received **honorable reburials** (June 16, 1989) and posthumous acquittals by the Supreme Court three weeks later. Many Hungarians saw the **death of János Kádár** (July 6) as the end of an era; the media revelations of his guilt over Nagy's murder were a form of catharsis.

So too were the removal of barbed wire and mines along **the border** with Austria, and orders that guards could no longer shoot escapers. This prompted thousands of East Germans to use Hungary as a staging-post on their escape to West Germany, causing an awkward diplomatic situation. By eventually deciding to let the **refugees** leave *en masse*, the Hungarian government clearly made its relations with the West a higher priority than appeasing the DDR.

Relations with the Czechoslovak government had already worsened after Hungary suspended work on the Nagymaros Dam (May 1989; the project was abandoned altogether in November), broadcast an interview with Alexander Dubček and stated its regret for participating in the Warsaw Pact invasion of 1968. Hungary's running feud with the Ceauşescu regime (see below) shows no signs of abating, and a more assertive response can't be ruled out if the Democratic Forum gains power. But everyone knows that **international relations** are delicately poised. Within the Warsaw Pact, only Poland is a likely ally, whereas Romania, Czechoslovakia, and the DDR are hostile. Despite hints that the Kremlin might accept Hungary leaving the Warsaw Pact no-one's too keen to put the matter to the test . . . at least not yet. Requests for economic help from the West have so far elicited more advice than cash, although this may change.

MONUMENTAL CHRONOLOGY

8000BC	Palaeolithic cave-dwellers in the Bükk Mountains.	Remains found at Subalyuk, Szeleta and other caves.
400BC	Celts enter Transdanubia.	Pottery, glassware; gold treasure of Szárazd-Regöly.
1st–4th c.	**Romans** occupy Pannonia, founding numerous towns.	Ruins at **Aquincum**, **Gorsium**, **Szombathely**, Pécs etc.
896	Magyar conquest. The state and Christianity are established in Hungary by István I during the eleventh century.	Ruins of the Székesfehérvár Basilica; eleventh-century crypts at Pécs and **Tihany** Abbey are virtually all that remain.
13th c.	Mongol invasion. Castles and new towns are founded during the reign of Béla IV.	**Romanesque churches** at **Ják**, **Lébény**, **Zsámbék**, **Oskü**, and **Velemér** stand comparison with **Pannonhalma Monastery**. Ruined *vár* at **Esztergom**, **Füzér**, **Boldogkőváralja** sited on precipitous crags.
14th–15th c.	Zenith of Hungarian power in Europe under the Angevin monarchs and then Mátyás Corvinus.	Remains of **Buda** and **Visegrád** where **Gothic and Renaissance architecture** attained great heights; **Diósgyőr** castle in Miskolc.
1526–1680s	After defeat at **Mohács**, Hungary is occupied for next 150 years by **Turks** and Habsburgs, and ravaged by warfare.	**Kőszeg**, **Sárospatak**, **Siklós**, and other **castles** have remained largely intact; as have a few **Turkish** *türbe*, ex-*djami* and **minarets** at **Pécs** and **Eger**; but most medieval towns were destroyed, although on the Plain, Szeged and Debrecen expanded vastly.
1703–11	Rákóczi War of Independence.	
17th–18th c.	Under **Habsburg rule**, many towns are wholly rebuilt around new centers; while Buda Palace and other monumental buildings are begun.	The **wooden belfrys**, pew-carvings and colorful coffered ceilings found at **Nyírbator**, **Zsurk**, **Csaroda**, and other remote churches in eastern Hungary are part-Gothic, and partly the "folk" equivalent of the **Baroque style**. This characterized much of seventeenth- and eighteenth-century architecture, eg. in the *Belváros* districts of **Győr**, **Veszprém**, **Székesfehérvár** etc, and at the **Esterhazy Palace** in **Fertőd**.
1830–1880s	After the Reform Era and the struggle for independence (1848–49), Hungary accepts the "Compromise" of 1868. Development of new centers of industry—Miskolc, Salgótarján, Csepel etc.	The **Chain Bridge** presages a spate of construction in Budapest, where large houses are built alongside the new **boulevards**. Szeged rebuilt after 1879 flood. The rise of **Neo-Classicism**—with Ybl and Hild's huge Basilicas in Eger, Pest and Esztergom—but also **Neo-Gothic**—the **Fishermen's Bastion** and **Vajdahunyad Castle** (in 1896, like the Metro)—plus Lechner's attempts to develop a uniquely "**Hungarian Style**" for the **Applied Arts Museum** and the public buildings in **Kecskemét**.
1896	1000th anniversary of the Magyar conquest.	

1918–1919	Habsburg empire collapses; Hungary briefly becomes a "Republic of Councils."	
1920s &1930s	Hungary loses two thirds of its territory to neighboring states. Regency of Admiral Horthy.	Deliberate evocation of past national glories—the erection of "Heroes' Gates" in **Szeged**, **Kőszeg** etc.
1944–45	Nazis occupy Hungary; heavy fighting with Soviet army.	Budapest and many towns incur massive damage. This is swiftly repaired.
1948–56	"**Rákosi era**" characterized by Five Year Plans, police terror, and a propaganda blitz.	**Dunaújváros** and other new towns; crash urbanization and industrialization; the **Liberation Monument** and other Soviet-style projects exemplify this phase.
1956	**Hungarian Uprising**.	Widespread urban damage—Budapest is worst affected.
1960s & 1970s	Emergence of "**Kádárism**"—economic reforms to encourage greater public affluence. During this period, Hungary becomes a byword for "**consumer socialism**" in Eastern Europe.	The **Metro** is completed. **Modernistic** cultural centers at Győr and Sárospatak are notable examples of Sixties and Seventies **architecture**; while supermarkets, hotels and resorts around Balaton are more typical of the period.
1980s	Economic problems, made worse by energy shortfall after the Chernobyl disaster.	Go ahead for construction of **Nagymaros dam** and more nuclear reactors at **Paks**. Closure of mines and other loss-making industries is proposed by the state.
1988	**Grósz** replaces Kadar as Party leader.	
1989	Grósz replaced by **Nemeth** and **Pozsgay**.	Nagymaros dam project abandoned.
1990	Proposed democratic elections.	

"ETHNOCIDE" IN TRANSYLVANIA

Imagine that the language and songs of your childhood, and the names of your own children, are regarded as subversive; that visits to or from relatives in a neighboring country are severely restricted; and that your house and village are liable to be demolished, leaving you to survive a below-freezing winter—well, that's life for the Hungarian minority in Romania.

It's also the cause of public outrage in Hungary, which has hardly been assuaged by the Hungarian government's feeble response. In 1988, a hastily-arranged summit resulted in further humiliation for the Magyars: Grósz returned home and announced "progress" only to be mousetrapped by the Romanian media's attack against "Hungarian chauvinism" and "Horthyite fascism."

At issue are the lives of one to two million Magyars living in Romania, mostly on the plain of the Banat and in the valleys of Transylvania, with smaller enclaves in the Moldavian Subcarpathians. Included in this total are two kindred minorities, the Magyar-speaking **Székely** and **Csángó** folk of the eastern Carpathians, but more precise demographic figures are unavailable. Romanian statistics are patently false, while those from Budapest are liable to reflect wishful thinking—besides which, thousands are fleeing Romania every year. This also applies to **other ethnic minorities**, notably the German-speaking Saxons and Swabians, whose emigration from the Transylvanian and Banat towns is permitted in return for millions of Deutschmarks from the West German government.

All are hoping to escape from **Ceaușescu's Romania**—a country richly endowed by nature, but reduced to penury and near-starvation by the policies of a megalomaniac dictator. In what used to be the breadbasket of Eastern Europe, housewives start lining up for food at 5am; lights and heating are sacrificed in winter so that heavy industries may be empowered to produce unsaleable goods; and acres of the capital have been razed to build homes for Party bureaucrats and Romania's

rubber-stamp National Assembly (rumored to be the intended site of Ceaușescu's mausoleum). *Securitate* informers are almost as ubiquitous as posters hailing the Leader, yet popular discontent can still catch the regime by surprise—as happened in November 1987, when 10,000 workers rioted in the Transylvanian city of Brașov.

Rather than moderate his policies, Ceaușescu launched **sistematizare** the following year. This "systemization" envisages **the destruction of half the villages in Romania** by the year 2000, and the herding of the peasantry into 500 Agro-Industrial Complexes: high-rise apartment buildings with communal bathrooms and kitchens on separate floors. According to the government, 6000–8000 villages occupy "too much" land, and their private plots and livestock are "less efficient" than collectivized agriculture. That most highland villages already make optimal use of the available land, that private plots are all that stand between the populace and starvation, and that Romania lacks the means to transport millions of workers to far-flung fields, or complete these Agro-Industrial units—all this is discounted; as are objections on humanitarian or cultural grounds. Villages everywhere are threatened, but it's the ethnic minorities—whose communities are already beleaguered—who are most vulnerable.

Reactions in Hungary and Romania are inextricably bound up with the history of **Transylvania** (*Erdély* in Hungarian). This mountainous land "beyond the forest" has long been the subject of **rival claims**, backed by abstruse, contradictory evidence and arguments. Greatly simplified, **the Hungarian version of history** asserts that the Magyars and Székely found *Erdély* largely unpopulated when they began colonizing it in the tenth century; and that Romanians (or "Vlachs," as medieval chroniclers called them) only arrived as wandering pastoralists 200 or 300 years later—and thus lack any historic right of ownership. Conversely, the Romanians claim descent from Transylvania's original inhabitants, the Dacians, who interbred with their Roman conquerors and remained there throughout the Age of Migrations—the **Daco-Romanian Continuity Theory**—only to be subjugated by the Magyars, who annexed Transylvania to the Kingdom of Hungary.

Magyar rule over the region was marked by discrimination along feudal and ethnic lines (between the fifteenth and nineteenth century), and pogroms in northern Transylvania (1940–1944). Since it passed under Romanian rule (in 1918, and again in 1944), Transylvania has witnessed a reversal of fates, with the Magyars bearing the brunt of official hostility. The Romanian Communist Party has attempted to conceal this behind a facade of minority rights, and dismisses complaints from Budapest as "Hungarian revanchism" in disguise. So far, Ceaușescu has shown no sign of heeding Hungarian, Soviet, or Western displeasure, let alone protests by his own subjects, even by senior figures within the Romanian Communist Party. Soviet pressure could well force Ceaușescu to compromise on *sistematezare*, but if it doesn't, **the future** looks grim.

BOOKS

TRAVEL BOOKS AND GENERAL ACCOUNTS

Gyula Antalffy, *A Thousand Years of Travel in Old Hungary* (Corvina, UK). Slightly stodgy in places, but with enough anecdotes and odd details to keep your attention as it surveys a millennium of Hungary through the eyes of foreign and native travelers.

Stephen Brook, *The Double Eagle: Vienna, Budapest and Prague* (Hamilton, UK, £14.95). Taking their Habsburg traditions as a starting point, Brook's readable, personal exploration of three cities concludes that war and Stalinism have dissolved the bonds of common experience, giving rise to "three ways of living." Though more chapters are devoted to Vienna, it's the sections on Budapest, and above all Prague, that really shine.

Gyula Illyés, *People of the Puszta* (Corvina, UK, available in libraries). An unsentimental, sometimes horrifying immersion in the life of the landless peasantry of prewar Hungary, mainly set in Transdanubia rather than on the Plain. Illyés—one of Hungary's greatest twentieth-century writers—was born into such a

background, and the book breathes authenticity. Highly recommended.

Patrick Leigh Fermor, *A Time of Gifts* (Penguin, $6.95), *Between the Woods and the Water* (Penguin $6.95). In 1934 the young Leigh Fermor started walking from Holland to Turkey, and reached Hungary in the closing chapter of *A Time of Gifts*. The Gypsies and rusticated aristocrats of the Great Plain and Transylvania are superbly evoked in *Between the Woods and the Water* (a third volume, covering Moldavia and Bulgaria, is underway), and this elegiac account reads all the more poignantly today, as Ceauşescu's bulldozers destroy the centuries-old villages of Transylvania. Wonderfully lyrical and erudite.

Claudio Magris, *Danube* (Collins, UK, £15). Recently published and highly praised account of the Danubian countries, interweaving history and contemporary reportage. Read in conjunction with Brook and Leigh Fermor, it helps place Hungary in context.

John Paget, *Hungary and Transylvania* (Ayer Co. Publishers, $59.50). Paget's massive book attempted to explain nineteenth-century Hungary to the English middle class, and within its aristocratic limitations, succeeded brilliantly. Occasionally can be found in secondhand bookshops.

Walter Starkie, *Raggle-Taggle* (UK edition only, available in libraries). The wanderings of a Dublin professor with a fiddle, who bummed around Budapest and the Plain in search of Gypsy music in the 1920s. First published in 1933 and last issued by Murray in 1964—a secondhand bookshop perennial.

Ivan Volgyes, *Hungary, a Country of Contradictions* (Westview, out of print). A thorough if pretty tedious introduction to Hungarian history, politics and society. Rather negative picture by a bitter expatriate.

Although restrictions on bringing "politically sensitive" books into Hungary were lifted in 1989, and Hungarian publishers are now translating, importing, or commissioning dozens of previously forbidden works, ranging from *Animal Farm* to favorable accounts of the 1956 Uprising, anyone visiting other, less liberal Eastern Bloc countries should be cautious regarding certain titles below. The best all round **bookshops** (*könyvesbolt*) in Hungary are on Váci utca, and in the Párizsi udvar, in the V district of Budapest.

HISTORY, POLITICS, AND SOCIOLOGY

Tamás Aczél, *Revolt of the Mind* (Greenwood Press, $35). Describes how and why sections of the intelligentsia revolted against Party control. Khrushchev, the Soviet leader, is alleged to have said that the 1956 revolution would never have occurred had a few intellectuals been shot earlier—one of the propositions discussed in *Ten Years After* (Macgibbon & Kee, UK): a series of eye-witness accounts and essays, published to commemorate the tenth anniversary of the Uprising.

Noel Barber, *Seven Days of Freedom* (Stein and Day, out of print). Vivid but oversimplified account of the Uprising, focused mainly on events in Budapest, by the top reporter of England's *Daily Telegraph* newspaper.

John Bierman, *Righteous Gentile* (Viking, $12.95). The best biography yet of Raoul Wallenberg, the Swedish diplomat whose daring efforts partly frustrated Eichmann's attempt to exterminate the Jews of Hungary during 1944 and 1945.

Miklós Haraszti, *A Worker in a Workers' State* (Universe, $5.15). Factual, gritty investigation of "Piecework" (the book's Hungarian title) in Budapest's Red Star factory, which earned Haraszti a prison term for "defaming socialism." He's now active in the *samizdat* (underground publishing) movement. *The Velvet Prison: Artists Under State Socialism* (Basic, $14.95), Haraszti's other important dissident work, is fiercely critical, although less specific to Hungary than *Worker*...

András Hegedüs, *Socialism and Bureaucracy* (St Martin, out of print) and *The Humanization of Socialism* (Allison & Busby, UK). Two heavyweight critiques of Eastern European socialism from a Marxist perspective. The latter book of essays, by other members of the "Budapest School," includes two excellent pieces on women in socialist countries by **Maria Márkus** and **Ágnes Heller** (now in exile). *Structure of Socialist Society* (St Martin, $19.95), gives you some interesting facts but otherwise dry, dull academic writing and pretty Stalinist too.

Pál (Paul) Ignotus, *Hungary* (Praeger, out of print). An excellent short history, more colorful than McCartney's, by a former Social Democratic politician who was jailed and tortured in Vác during the Rákosi era—an experience described in *Political Prisoner* (RKP).

David Irving, *Uprising* (Noontide, $16.95). Massively detailed on every aspect of 1956, including events in Győr and the countryside, but marred by crude commie-bashing and the taint of Irving's notorious anti-semitism.

János Kenedi, *Do It Yourself* (Pluto Press, UK). Building your own home is a herculean task in Hungary today, and Kenedi gives a full account of the necessary wheeling and dealing, laced with tongue-in-cheek Marxist terminology, showing how fine the lines are between private enterprise, "socialist construction," and outright cheating.

György (George) Konrád, *Antipolitics* (H. Holt & Co., $9.95). Inspiring, witty, and humane, described by E.P. Thompson as a "book of exceptional importance," it examines the possibility of transforming Hungarian society and East–West relations "from below." Still essential reading for peace activists and cold warriors alike, although it predates Gorbachev, *perestroika*, and Grósz; it's written in an easy style.

Ferenc Kőszegi & E.P. Thompson, *The New Hungarian Peace Movement* (Longwood Pub. Group, $1.59). A pamphlet that seems sad in retrospect, despite its optimistic tone; the unofficial "Peace Group for Dialogue" has been forced to disband since their meeting with Thompson in Konrád's flat, and the publication of this in 1983. **END**, the European Disarmament Movement, is the publisher, and their journal prints the latest news of the peace struggle inside Hungary (and worldwide).

Bill Lomax, *Hungary 1956* (Allison & Busby, UK). Probably the best—and shortest—book on the Uprising, by an acknowledged expert on modern Hungary. Lomax also edited *Eyewitness in Hungary* (Spokesman 1980), an anthology of accounts by foreign communists (most of whom were sympathetic to the Uprising) that vividly depicts the elation, confusion, and tragedy of the events of October 1956.

C.A. McCartney, *Hungary: A Short History* (Edinburgh University Press, UK). A basic outline of events from the Magyar conquest to the Rákosi era, in readable if unexciting prose.

The bulkier and dryer *October Fifteenth . . .* is restricted to the period 1918–45, which Nagy-Talavera (see below) handles with more flair.

George Mikes, *A Study in Infamy* (Deutch, UK). Better known in the West for his humorous writings, Mikes exposes the activities of the secret police during the Rákosi period, using captured *ÁVO/ÁVH* documents which explain their methods for surveillance of the population and using terror as a political weapon.

N.M. Nagy-Talavera, *Greenshirts and Others* (Stanford University Press, out of print). A well-written and researched study of the social dislocations, racism, and paranoid nationalism which afflicted Hungary and Romania between the wars, giving rise to native fascist movements and bitter anti-semitism, culminating in the massacre of Hungarian and Romanian Jews.

W.F. Robinson, *The Pattern of Reform in Hungary* (Praeger, UK). A thorough, academic report on the "Kádár model" of socialism in Hungary. All solid stuff, but certainly not bedtime reading.

William Shawcross, *Crime and Compromise* (Dutton, out of print). Former Party leader János Kádár is an intriguing figure for a biographer, having been reviled as the "Butcher of Budapest" after 1956, only to become "good old Jancsi" during the Seventies (when this book was written). Surveying Kádár's life and deeds, Shawcross poses the question "Unprincipled opportunist or principled pragmatist?," but fails to decide either way.

I. & N. Völgyes, *The Liberated Female* (Westview, out of print). Despite minor faults, a revealing (if ultimately depressing) survey of women's place in modern Hungary, as contrasted with their status—or rather, lack of it—during feudal and "liberal" times. Essential reading for anyone interested in understanding Hungarian society—although it doesn't go beyond the 1970s—and a small contribution to the feminist/socialist debate.

Iván Völgyes, ed., *Hungary in Revolution, 1918–1919: Nine Essays* (University of Nebraska Press, $19.95). A rather academic treatment of a crucial period in Hungary's history usually ignored by Western Europe. *Hungary, a Country of Contradictions*

(Westview, out of print). A thorough if pretty tedious analysis of Hungarian politics and society.

ART, FOLK TRADITIONS, CINEMA, AND COOKING

Corvina (UK) publishes a number of books covering Hungary's folk traditions and artistic treasures, mostly translated into English or German. Some editions are available on import, and some of its British titles are available through US publishers of fiction and poetry, below. You can also browse through the range of them in Váci u. bookshops in Budapest.

Val Biro, *Hungarian Folk Tales* (Oxford University Press, $14.95). Merry tales of dragons and the like in a crisp, colloquial rendering close to original recountings. Intended for children but more readable than Hegedus, at least.

Susan Derecskey, *The Hungarian Cookbook* (Harper and Row, $9.95). A good, easy-to-follow selection of traditional and modern recipes.

Tekla Dömötör, *Hungarian Folk Beliefs* (Indiana University Press, $20). A superb trove of social history, folk beliefs, and customs, recently made available in an English translation.

Tamás Hofer et al, *Hungarian Peasant Art* (Oxford University Press, out of print). An excellently produced examination of Hungarian folk art, with lots of good photos.

George Lang, *The Cuisine of Hungary* (Atheneum, $11.95). A well-written and beautifully illustrated work of coffee-table dimensions, telling you everything you need to know about Hungarian cooking, its history, and how to do it yourself.

Fred Macniol, *Hungarian Cooking* (Penguin, UK). A much cheaper if less glossy alternative to Lang's book, but unfortunately out of print.

Graham Petrie, *Hungarian Cinema Today: History Must Answer to Man* (NY Zoetrope, $8.95). Though you wouldn't guess so from the title, this is an unpretentious and very readable account of Hungarian film, surveying its history from the beginnings to the work of directors like Bacsó, Szábó, Jancsó, Makk, Kézdi-Kovács. Could do with an update, though.

FICTION AND POETRY

Most **Hungarian classics in translation** are published by Corvina in the UK. Inside Hungary, you might find the swashbuckling romances of **Géza Gárdonyi**, or the *Dark Diamonds* by **Mór Jókai**—a rather padded novel by the Magyar equivalent of Dickens—in English; and short stories by **Frigyes Karinthy** in German. Despite his stature, the romantic poems of **Sándor Petőfi** only appear in English thanks to the Hungarian Cultural Foundation in Buffalo, New York (1969; editor A. Nyerges).

The same publisher and editor are responsible for the collected poems of **Attila József** and **Endre Ady** (1973). Corvina publishes *Explosive Country*, a selection of essays by Ady, and poems by **Miklós Radnóti**, an antifascist killed by the Nazis in 1944, but that's currently the extent of its coverage of the **modern poets**.

Of the two **modern authors** whose work has appeared in translation abroad, one is little known inside Hungary, the other highly-esteemed by his compatriots, who speak of four or five writers as standard-bearers of Magyar literature. **Illyés** is well-represented by *People of the Puszta* (see "Travel Books" above), while twenty-five authors have been selected for *Nothing's Lost* (Corvina 1988), an anthology of short stories; **Endre Vészi**, **Ferenc Karinthy**, and **Erzsébet Galgóczi** turn in real stunners, but the contributions by **Péter Esterházy** and the late **József Lengyel** are disappointing.

ANTHOLOGIES

Loránt Czigány, *The Oxford History of Hungarian Literature from the Earliest Times to the Present* (Oxford University Press, $75). An excellent collection, probably the most comprehensive in print to date. Chronological structure; good coverage of political and social background.

Albert Tezlsa, *Ocean at the Window: Hungarian Prose and Poetry since 1945* (University of Minnesota Press, $25). A good selection.

Miklós Vajda, *Modern Hungarian Poetry* (Columbia University Press, $16). A reasonable selection of postwar poetry.

Paul Varnai, ed., *Hungarian Short Stories* (Toronto: Exile Editions, out of print). An excellent collection of modern work ranging from the "magical realist" to astringent social commentary.

POETRY

Endre Ady, *Poems of Endre Ady* (Hungarian Cultural Foundation, $24).

George Faludy, *Selected Poems, 1933–80* (University of Georgia Press, $8.95). Firey, lyrical poetry by a victim of both Nazi and Russian repression. Themes of political defiance and the nobility of the human spirit, the struggle to preserve human values in the face of oppression.

Ágnes Nemes Nagy, *Selected Poems* (University of Iowa Press, out of print). A major postwar poet, often speculating intellectually on knowledge and the role of poetry in trying to impose order on the world, despite the jarring and bitter realization that it can't.

Jónas Pilzinsky, *Selected Poems* (Dufour, out of print). A major poet, with themes of humanity's suffering and sacrifice.

Miklós Radnóti, *Under Gemini: The Selected Poems of Miklós Radnóti with a Prose Memoir* (Ohio University Press, $9.95). The best collection of Radnóti's sparse, anguished poetry. *The Complete Poetry* (Ann Arbor, out of print). A more complete although poorly translated collection. From exotic and erotic celebrations of nature to the agonies of repression and injustice. *Subway Stops: Fifty Poems* (Ann Arbor, out of print). Over-scholarly introduction not so great; otherwise a reflective collection contrasting love with the brutal surroundings of Radnóti's last years in a Nazi labor camp. *Clouded Sky* (Harper & Row, out of print). Radnóti's last poems before his murder in a mass grave by the Hungarian fascist army in 1944 at a labor camp. Love poems to his wife poignantly mixed with poems on the brutality of life in the camp.

Sándor Weöres and Fernec Juhász, *Selected Poems* (Peter Smith, $12.00). Two successful modern poets. Weöres is more preoccupied with primitive myth and mystical themes; Juhasz, often quirkily, with folklore and rural culture and the folk oral poetic tradition.

FICTION

Géza Csáth, *The Magician's Garden and Other Stories* (Columbia University Press, $24); *Opium and Other Stories* (Penguin, $6.95). Both of these volumes of stories are in a "magical realist" genre, questioning "reality," Csáth himself tormented by insanity and opium addiction; he committed suicide in 1918.

Tibor Dery, *The Portuguese Princess* (Northwestern University Press, $9.95). Short stories by a once-committed Communist, who was jailed for three years after the Uprising, and died in 1977.

Mór Jókai, *Tales from Jókai* (Ayer Co. Publishers, $5.37). *Dr. Dumany's Wife: A Romance* (Doubleday, out of print). A nineteenth-century author.

György (George) Konrád, *The Case Worker* (Penguin, $6.95); *The City Builder* (Penguin, $6.95); *The Loser* (Harcourt Brace Jovanovich, $7.95). In contrast with his optimistic *Antipolitics* (see above), Konrád's novels are overwhelmingly bleak—dealing with misery, alienation, escapism, hypocrisy, and madness. Despite the subject matter, his powers of insight and rich use of language are seductive and compelling.

József Lengyel, *Acta Sanctorum* (Peter Owen, £9.95); *Prenn Drifting* (Beekman Publishers, $14.95); *From Beginning to End/The Spell* (Englewood Cliffs, out of print); *The Judge's Chair* (Beekman Publishers, $16.95), and *Confrontation* (Lyle Stuart, $6.95). A dedicated Communist since his youth, Lengyel apparently kept his faith though he was in the Gulag for some years, but later began to display doubts. His colorful semi-autobiographical novels concern morality under stress, ambition, and the question of ends versus means. *The Bridgebuilders* (Corvina, UK) is the least gripping, although Lengyel reportedly considered it one of his best.

László Nemeth, *Guilt* (Dufour, $17.95). A Thirties novel of tragedy and its effect on a young couple.

A Tezla, *Hungarian Authors: A Bibliographical Handbook* (Harvard University Press).

ÉMIGRÉ WRITERS AND FOREIGN WRITERS ON HUNGARY

Heinrich Böll, "And Where Were You, Adam" in *Adam and the Train* (McGraw Hill, $7.95). A superb short novel by one of the major German novelists since World War II, consisting of loosely connected and semi-autobiographical short stories modelled on Boll's experiences as a soldier on the Eastern Front. It describes the panic-stricken retreat of Hitler's forces from the puszta, in eastern Hungary, before the Red Army in 1944. Told through both Hungarian and German eyes, these stories are a haunting evocation of the chaos, cruelty and horror of the retreat, but also of a rural ethnic culture that seems to resist everything thrown at it.

Hans Habe, *Black Earth* (NEL 1968, UK, available in libraries). The story of a peasant's commitment to the Communist underground, and his disillusionment with the Party in power; a good read, and by no means as crude as the artwork and blurb suggest.

Cecilia Holland, *Rakossy, The Death of Attila* (Knopf, out of print). *Rakossy* is a bodice-ripping tale of a shy Austrian princess wed to an uncouth Magyar baron, braving the Turkish hordes on the Hungarian marches; while the *Death of Attila* evokes the Huns, Romans, and Goths of the Dark Ages, pillaging around the Danube. Two well-crafted historical romances.

Stephen Vizinczey, *In Praise of Older Women* (Atlantic Monthly, $6.95 but out of print). The memoirs of a randy egocentric lad growing up in refugee camps and in Budapest during the Rákosi years. Soft porn mixed with social comment and supposedly profound insights into the nature of women, which made a splash when first published in the West in 1967.

MUSIC AND RECORDS

Hungarian music enshrines the trinity of Liszt, Bartók, and Kodály: Liszt was the founding father, Bartók one of the greatest composers of the twentieth century, and Kodály (himself no slouch at composition) created a widely imitated system of musical education. When you also take into account talented Hungarian soloists like Perényi, it's clear that this small nation has made an outstanding contribution to the world of music.

HUNGARIAN COMPOSERS

Ferenc Liszt (1811–1886), who described himself as a "mixture of Gypsy and Franciscan," cut a flamboyant figure in the salons of Europe as a virtuoso pianist and womanizer. The Hungarian Rhapsodies and similar pieces reflected the "Gypsy" side to his character and the rising nationalism of Liszt's era; while later work like the Transcendental Etudes (whose originality has only recently been recognized) invoked a visionary, "Franciscan" mood. But despite his patriotic stance, Liszt's first language was German (he never fully mastered Hungarian), and his expressed wish to roam the villages of Hungary with a knapsack on his back was a Romantic fantasy.

That was left to **Béla Bartók** (1881–1945) and **Zoltán Kodály** (1882–1967), who began exploring the remoter districts of Hungary and Transylvania in 1906, collecting peasant music. Despite many hardships and local suspicion of their "monster" (a cutting stylus and phonograph cylinders), they managed to record and catalog thousands of melodies, laying down high standards of musical ethnography still maintained in Hungary today, while discovering a rich source of inspiration for their own compositions. Bartók believed that a genuine peasant melody was "quite as much a masterpiece in miniature as a Bach fugue or a Mozart sonata . . . a classic example of the expression of a musical thought in its most conceivably concise form, with the avoidance of all that is superfluous."

Bartók created a personal but universal musical language by reworking the raw essence of Magyar and Finno-Ugric folk music in a modern context—his six String Quartets in particular, although Hungarian public opinion was originally hostile. Feeling misunderstood and out of step with his country's increasingly pro-Nazi policies, Bartók left Hungary in 1940, dying poor and embittered in the United States. Since then, however, Bartók's reputation has soared, and the return of his body in 1988 occasioned national celebrations, shrewdly sponsored by the state.

Kodály's music is more consciously national: Bartók called it "a real profession of faith in the Hungarian soul." His Peacock Variations are based on a typical Old Style pentatonic tune, and the Dances of Galanta on the popular music played by Gypsy bands. Old Style tunes also form the core of Kodály's work in musical education; the "Kodály method" employs group singing to develop musical skill at an early age. His ideas have made Hungarian music teaching among the best in the world, and Kodály himself a paternal figure to generations of children.

For others Kodály was a voice of conscience during the Rákosi era, writing the Hymn of Zriényi to a seventeenth-century text whose call to arms against the Turkish invasion—"I perceive a ghastly dragon, full of venom and fury, snatching the crown of Hungary . . ."—was tumultuously acclaimed as an anti-Stalinist allegory (see "Szigetvár" in *Transdanubia*). Closely followed by the Uprising, the Hymn was not performed again for many years, and no recordings were made available until 1982.

HUNGARIAN FOLK MUSIC

Until Bartók and Kodály's research, **Hungarian folk music** (*Magyar népzene*) was identified with Gypsy bands in cafés, whose popular songs were influenced by the stirring *verbunk* (recruiting tunes) of the Rákóczi wars, and Austrian music—the sort of thing that Brahms and Liszt made into Hungarian Dances, and is still heard in Budapest restaurants. Bartók and Kodály were more excited by what the former called "Old Style" music: simple pentatonic (5-note) tunes stretching back to the days when Magyar tribes roamed the banks of the Don and Volga, where similar music has been handed down and recorded by ethno-musicologists.

In Hungary today, folk music has little connection with rural communities, whose taste in music (as in other things) has been transformed by urban influences, TV, and the radio. Folk music and village life are still closely linked **in Transylvania**, which was seen as a repository of Magyar traditions even in Bartók's day, but now faces obliteration by the Ceauşescu dictatorship. Recordings of haunting Csángó airs and wild Mezőség dance music could well be the only trace of the Transylvanian Heath and Gyimes regions' centuries-old cultures once the bulldozers are finished. In Hungary, by contrast, Magyar folk music has enjoyed a revival in towns and cities thanks to the **Táncház**. These dance houses are very popular with young people interested in traditional music and dances—mostly from Hungary and Transylvania, but also from the "South Slavs," Yugoslavia and Bulgaria. Foreigners are welcome to attend Táncház meetings (see under Budapest entertainments or ask the tourist office in other towns for details) or join other devotees of Magyar folk music at Nagykálló's *Téka Tábor* **festival** (see "Nagykálló and Nyírbátor" in *The Great Plain*).

RECORDS

Good quality **records and tapes** produced by *Hungaroton* retail for half or a third of what you'd pay abroad, which makes it well worth rooting through *zeneművesbolt* shops. After Western and Hungarian **pop**, the bulk of their stock consists of **classical music**. A full discography of the works of Liszt, Bartók, and Kodály, directors like Dohnányi and Doráti, and fine contemporary Hungarian soloists and sing-

ers would fill a catalog; and the following recordings (on tape or vinyl, sometimes in boxed sets with an English commentary) are merely an introduction to the equally wide field of Hungarian **folk music**.

VII. Magyarországi Táncház Találkozó A great mixture of dances, ballads, and instrumental pieces from all over, recorded at the Seventh Dance House Festival in 1988. One of a series (MK 18152).

Magyar népzene 3 (Hungarian folk music). A 4-disk set of field recordings covering the whole range of folk music—Old and New style songs, instrumental music, and music for occasions that's probably the best overall introduction. In the west, the disks are marketed as "Folk Music of Hungary Vol.1."

Magyar hangszeres népzene (Hungarian Instrumental Folk Music). A very good 3-disk set of field recordings of village and Gypsy bands, including lots of solos. (Hungaroton LPX 18045-47.)

Muzsikás Beautiful arrangements of traditional ballads by the Muzsikás group and Márta Sebestyén, Hungary's leading Táncház singer. Highly recommended (Hannibal HNBL 1330).

The Prisoner's Song More haunting songs by Márta and Muzsikás, released in the US on the Hannibal label, distributed by Carthage.

Bonchidától Bonchidáig The Kalamajka Ensemble, another Táncház group, plays Transylvanian and Csángó ballads and dances (Hungaroton MK 18135).

Este a Gyimesbe' Jártam Music from the Csángó region performed by János Zerkula and Regina Fikó; sparser, sadder, and more discordant than other Transylvanian music (Hungaroton MK 18130).

Táncházi muzsika (Music from the Táncház). A double album of the Sebö Ensemble playing Táncház music from various regions of Hungary. Wild and exciting rhythms (Hungaroton SPLX 18031-32).

Jánosi Együttes (Jánosi Ensemble). Another young group, performing "authentic" versions of some of the folk tunes that Bartók borrowed in his compositions. A record that makes a bridge between classical and folk music. (Hungaroton SPLX 18103.)

Serbian Music from South Hungary played by the Vujicsics Ensemble. More complex tunes than most Magyar folk music, with a distinct Balkan influence. (Hannibal HNBL 1310.)

ONWARDS FROM HUNGARY

Hungary is linked to dozens of European cities by rail, with direct flights to dozens of nations, as summarized in the *Budapest* "Travel Details". Below, you'll find a brief rundown on the most obvious possibilities, complementing the practically-oriented "Leaving Hungary . . ." sections which precede the "Travel Details" of chapters Four, Five, and Six. Would-be hitchers might benefit from contacting *Ötödik Sebesség* (see "Getting There" in *Basics*).

AUSTRIA

Austria, a few hours' journey from Budapest or western Transdanubia, is an expensive place to stay, but it's worth considering a stopover in imperially elegant **Vienna** (see "Getting There" in *Basics* for some accommodation hints). If you're Eurailing westwards, brief visits to **Graz** or lovely (but ultra costly) **Salzburg** are also feasible.

WEST GERMANY

There are more options for budget travelers in **West Germany**, which you can reach by bus or train, or even by hitching, from Budapest. Though details of everything from **Munich** nightlife to the **Bavarian Alps** appear in the new *Real Guide to Germany* ($13.95), it's worth mentioning that the cheapest way to reach **Berlin** from Budapest is by rail via Czechoslovakia and the DDR—even taking into account the cost of transit visas. You don't need a visa for Austria or West Germany.

YUGOSLAVIA

Yugoslavia is a medley of regions and peoples, whose political discords have yet to put a damper on tourism. **Zagreb**, the medieval capital of Croatia, is accessible from southern Transdanubia, where buses also occasionally run to **Ljubljana**, the center of Slovenia

(whose cultural life includes the group Laibach). There's a direct train to **Split**, and weekly buses from Budapest and Szeged to **Dubrovnik** on the Adriatic. Other trains from Budapest and the Plain aim for **Belgrade**, from where it's tempting to hurry on to choicer destinations (covered in the *Real Guide to Yugoslavia*). Holders of US, Australian, New Zealand, or Canadian passports are supposed to obtain visas beforehand (easily done at the consulate in Budapest) though EC citizens can get them at the border.

ROMANIA

Adventurous travelers often find **Romania** fascinating, despite hard conditions there (see "Ethnocide in Transylvania" above). But with visas (best obtained at the border) costing $30, it's not a place to visit lightly. You need to bring food from Hungary, and must change $10 per day into *lei* at a rate which makes hotels very expensive, so a tent for camping in the rough is another essential. Numerous trains from Budapest and Szolnok to **Bucharest** call at picturesque towns in **Transylvania** along the way. Start with Gothic **Sighişoara** or **Braşov** rather than **Cluj** or the Saxon stronghold of **Sibiu** (only accessible by the *Karpaty*), where you arrive in the small hours; the most useful trains are listed under "Leaving Hungary from the Great Plain" in *The Great Plain* chapter, together with "local" services from eastern Hungary. These travel towards **Maramureş**, where grim Baia Mare is the starting point for exploring amazing wooden churches and medieval-looking villages. Afterwards, follow the Iza Valley into **Moldavia** to see the **Painted Monasteries** or one of Romania's great folklore **festivals**—all detailed in the forthcoming *Real Guide to Eastern Europe*, which also covers Hungary (more briefly than this book) and Bulgaria.

BULGARIA

To visit **Bulgaria**, you must get a visa before hand, and either pass through Yugoslavia (the cheaper option) or Romania. From **Sofia**, best reached by the *Meridian*, head south to **Rila Monastery** and **Melnik**, or eastwards towards the historic cities of **Plovdiv** and **Veliko Târnovo**. Bulgaria's **Black Sea coast** improves the farther south one goes, but

Varna, accessible by the *Nord–Süd* or *Transdanubium*, is a nice place to begin, with lots happening during summer.

CZECHOSLOVAKIA

Czechoslovakia also requires visitors to obtain visas beforehand, and change a set amount (currently about $18 per day) into Czech koruna. There are direct services from Budapest and western Hungary to Prague, Europe's loveliest city, and Bratislava, and from northern Hungary to Rožnéava, near Krásna Hôrka Castle and the dramatic Slovak Karst region. Tatranská Lomnica in the High Tatra and the handsome town of Banská Bystrica can both be reached by bus from Budapest, where the Rákóczi express runs to Propad-Tatry, the gateway to the medieval Spiš towns, whose romance is only exceeded by the castles of Bohemia. Simon Hayman's *A Guide to Czechoslovakia* (Brandt) is good on monuments and history, but short on practicalities.

POLAND

Travelers to **Poland** as well have to get visas first, and change about $16 per day. The country is directly accessible from Budapest (where you should also obtain a Czech transit visa): several trains to **Warsaw** carry on to **Gdansk**, the birthplace of Solidarity; the *Polonia* calls at Poland's holiest shrine, **Czętochowa**, along the way; and a weekly bus runs to **Kraków**, the former capital, famed for its architecture and subversive cabaret. Tim Sharman's *Travelscapes: Poland* (UK only; Harrap Columbus £9.95) or Philip Ward's *Polish Cities* (focused on Kraków, Warsaw, and Gdansk; Pelican $13.95) will fill you in on sights and the history, if nothing else.

EAST GERMANY

East Germany is also directly accessible by rail, and with a transit visa (readily available in Budapest) you can see something of east **Berlin** en route to the western sector. A longer stay necessitates reserving (usually costly) accommodation; more reasonably priced student deals are sometimes available from the *Reisebüro der DDR* (V, Dimitrov tér 2). A *Real Guide* to Czechoslovakia, Poland, and the DDR is planned for 1990.

THE SOVIET UNION

The cost of accommodation ($60–90 a night), which must be reserved, makes independent travel prohibitively expensive in the **Soviet Union**; travelers need to confirm their itinerary with the state tourist organization, *Intourist*, before getting a visa specifying the time and place of entry to the USSR. It's cheaper to take some kind of package deal—for example, the "youth tours" that are sometimes available from *Intourist* in Budapest (V, Felszabadulás tér)—which also saves you from standing in line for meals, tickets, and other things in the bureaucracy-ridden Soviet Union.

CHINA

Despite recent tragic events, **China** remains an intriguing destination for many budget travelers, some of whom get there by train from Budapest. It's not quite as easy as it was, but the great railroad journey from **Budapest to Beijing** is still the cheapest way to China. Tickets tend to be in short supply from May to October, but if you're prepared to spend time in Budapest doing the legwork there's still a vast saving to be had compared to the price of tickets purchased in the west.

The first thing to do is visit *IBUSZ* (VII, Tanács krt.3c/☎226-638) or the MÁV office (VI, Népköztársaság útja 35/☎228-049), who allocate seats on the **Trans-Mongolian Express**. Your seat reservation will be telexed to Moscow, and you don't actually buy **tickets** until a reply is received (1–2 weeks). Get an open-ended round-trip ticket for the *Trans-Manchurian Express*—one-way tickets back to Budapest cost twice as much in Beijing, where some travelers sell theirs for a profit and travel first class: after all, the journey takes nine days. This is by no means expensive—a first class round-trip ticket costs roughly $150 ($70 one-way)—and still less with an **IUS card** ($130; $62 o/w), which even non-students can usually obtain at the hectic *Express* office in Nyugati Station (photo needed). Second class fares are in the region of $101 for a round trip ($50 o/w) or $86 ($43 o/w) at the student rate.

Next you must acquire three **visas**, starting at the Chinese Embassy (VI, Benczúr u.17/☎224-872), where the process costs $10 and takes one day. Then, with railroad ticket and Chinese visa, go to the Soviet Embassy

(Népköztársaság útja 104/☎318-985) and apply for one of their visas ($10), which takes eight to ten days. Since they don't retain your passport, you can simultaneously obtain a Mongolian visa from XII, Istenhegyi út 59–65 (☎151-412), which costs the same or $15 for immediate issue. For all this you'll need six to eight photos—see "Listings" in *Budapest* for the locations of photomats.

Before leaving Budapest, buy plenty of food and drink for **the journey** to Moscow (2 days), where there's time to wander around before boarding the *Trans-Mongolian Express*. Soviet trains are "dry" and catering is worse than on Amtrak, with the honorable exception of the *provodnitsa* who serve Russian tea from a samovar at any hour. Winning the favor of these formidable ladies may require some effort and a smattering of Russian, but a sympathetic *provodnitsa* will make your journey much smoother. Although the scenery goes on forever in a boring, steppe-ish way, other passengers—hailing from every continent and all over the USSR—can be endlessly diverting. If they're not, take refuge in *The Big Red Train Ride*, Eric Newby's classic account of travel on the *Trans-Siberian Express*. It's possible to trade T-shirts for food, wine, or vodka on all these Trans-Union routes, but Soviet customs won't take kindly to the import of a dozen T-shirts wrapped in plastic, nor obviously saleable quantities of anything else. To prepare yourself for arrival in Beijing, and travels thereafter, bring along the British *Rough Guide to China*, a revised edition of which will be published as the *Real Guide to China* early in 1991.

LANGUAGE

Hungarian is a unique, complex, and subtle tongue, classified as belonging to the Finno-Ugric linguistic group, which means that it's totally unlike any other language that you're likely to know. Its closest (though still distant) relatives are Finnish and the Siberian Chuvash language, although odd grammatical structures and words from Turkish have crept in, together with some German, English, and (a few) Russian neologisms.

Consequently, foreigners aren't really expected to speak Hungarian, and natives are used to (but don't honestly appreciate) being addressed in **German**, the *lingua franca* of East European tourism. It's understood by older people—particularly in Transdanubia—and by many students and professional types, besides virtually everyone around the Balaton or in tourist offices. For a brief visit it's probably easier to brush up on some German for your means of communication, but a few basic Magyar phrases can make all the difference. Even halting efforts elicit praise, and a cheery *Jó napot kiévánok!* can usually sweeten the surliest shop assistant. People are likeliest to understand **French** or **English** if you mix in educated circles; though I knew a teenager who'd gleaned his entire English vocabulary from Judas Priest records! Despite obligatory basic instruction in schools, people rarely know **Russian** and use it most unwillingly if they do.

In addition to the following, you'll find a detailed food glossary and a selection of phrases pertaining to transportation in *Basics*. If you're prepared to seriously study the language however, *Colloquial Hungarian* (Routledge $15.95) is the best available book. As a supplement, invest in the handy little *Angol–Magyar/Magyar–Angol Kisszótár* dictionaries; available from bookshops in Hungary for 60Ft.

VERY BASIC GRAMMAR AND PRONUNCIATION

Although its rules are fiendishly complicated, it's worth describing a few features of **Hungarian grammar**, albeit imperfectly. Hungarian is an agglutinating language—in other words, its vocabulary is built upon **root-words**, which are modified in various ways to express different ideas and nuances. Instead of prepositions—"to," "from," "in" etc.— Hungarian uses **suffixes**, or tags added to the ends of genderless **nouns**. The change in suffix is largely determined by the noun's context eg. (the) book = *könyv*; (give me the) book = *könyveket*; (in the) book = *könyvben*; (to the) book = *könyvnek*. But it is also affected by complicated rules of vowel harmony (which you're bound to get wrong, so don't worry about them!). Most of the nouns in the vocabulary section below are in the subject form—that is, without suffixes. In Hungarian, "**the**" is *a* (before a word beginning with a consonant) or *az* (preceding a vowel); the word for "**a/an**" is *egy* (which also means "one"). **Adjectives** precede the noun (*a piros ház* = the red house), adopting suffixes to form the comparative (*jó* = good; *jobb* = better), plus the prefix *leg* to signify the superlative (*legjobb* = the best). **Negatives** are usually formed by placing the word *nem* before the verb. *Ez* (this), *ezek* (these), *az* (that), and *azok* (those) are the **demonstratives**.

PRONUNCIATION

Achieving passably good **pronunciation**, rather than grammar, is the first priority (see the box on p.262 for general guidelines). **Stress** almost invariably falls on the first syllable of a word and all letters are spoken, although in sentences, the tendency is to slur words together. Vowel sounds are greatly affected by the bristling **accents** (that actually distinguish separate letters) which, together with the "double letters" *cs, gy, ly, ny, sz, ty,* and *zs*, give the Hungarian **alphabet** its formidable appearance.

BASICS

Do you speak . . .	*beszél . . .*	good day	*jó napot*
English	*angolul*	good evening	*jó estét*
German	*németül*	good night	*jó éjszakat*
French	*franciaul*	how are you?	*hogy vagy?*
yes—OK	*igen—jó*	how are you? (more formal)	*hogy van?*
no/not	*nem*	could you speak more	*elmondaná*
I (don't) understand	*(nem) értem*	slowly?	*lassabban?*
please—excuse me	*kérem—bocsánat*	what do you call this?	*mi a neve ennek?*
two beers, please	*két sört kérek*	please write it down	*kérem, iérja ezt le*
thank you (very much)	*köszönöm (szépen)*	today—tomorrow	*ma—holnap*
you're welcome	*sziévesen*	the day after tomorrow	*holnapután*
hello/goodbye (informal)	*szia*	the day before	*az előző nap*
goodbye	*viszontlátásra*	yesterday	*tegnap*
see you later	*viszlát*	in the morning—in the	*reggel—este*
I wish you . . . (formally)	*. . . kiévánok*	evening	
good morning	*jó reggelt*	at noon—at midnight	*délben—éjfélkor*

QUESTIONS AND REQUESTS

Legyen sziéves ("Would you be so kind") is the polite formula for attracting someone's attention. Hungarian has numerous interrogative modes whose subtleties elude foreigners, so it's best to use the simple *van?* ("is there?"/"is it?"), to which the reply might be *nincs* or *azok nincsenek* ("it isn't"/"there aren't any"). Waiters and shop assistants often rely upon the laconic *tessék?*, meaning "What do you want?," "go ahead" or "next." *Kaphatok . . . ?* ("Can I have . . . ?") is politer, but less widely used than *Szeretnék . . .* ("I'd like . . ."); in restaurants you can also order with *Kérem, hozzon . . .* ("Please bring me . . ."); *Kérem, adjon azt* ("Please give me that"); *Egy ilyet kérek* ("I'll have one of those"); or simply *. . . kérek* (". . . please").

I'd like/we'd like	*Szeretnék/szeretnénk*	It's too expensive	*Ez nagyon drága*
Where is/are . . . ?	*Hol van / vannak . . ?*	anything cheaper?	*van valami olcsóbb?*
Take me to . . .	*Vigyen kérem a . . .*	a student discount?	*van diák kedvezmény?*
Hurry up!	*Siessen!*	Is everything	*Ebben minden*
How much is it?	*Mennyibe kerül?*	included?	*szerepel?*
per night	*egy éjszakára*	I asked for . . .	*Én . . . .-t rendeltem*
per week	*egy hé}tre*	The bill please	*Kérem a számlát*
a single room	*egyágyas szobát*	we're paying	*Külön-külön*
a double room	*kétágyas szobát*	separately	*kiévánunk fizetni*
hot (cold) water	*meleg (hideg) viéz*	what?—why?	*mi?—miert?*
a shower	*egy zuhany*	when?—who?	*mikor?—ki?*

SOME SIGNS

entrance—exit	*bejárat—kijárat*	room for rent	*szoba kiadó*
arrival	*érkezés*		(or *Zimmer frei*)
departure	*indulás*	hospital	*kórház*
open—closed	*nyitva—zárva*	pharmacy	*gyógyszertár*
free admission	*szabad belépés*	(local) police	*(kerületi) Rendőrség*
women's—men's	*női—férfi mosdó* (or *WC* -	caution/beware	*vigyázat!*
toilet	"Vait-say")	no smoking	*tilos a dohányzás*
shop—market	*bolt—piac*	no bathing	*tilos a fürdés*

DIRECTIONS

Where's the . . . ?	hol van a . . . ?	Do I have to change	át kell szállom
campground	kemping	for . . .?	. . .-be?
hotel	szálloda	towards	felé
railroad station	vasútállomás	on the right (left)	jobbra (balra)
bus station	buszállomás	straight ahead	egyenesen előre
(bus or train) stop	megálló	(over) there—here	ott—itt
Is it near (far)?	közel (távol) van?	Where are you going?	Hova megy?
Which bus goes to . . . ?	Melyikbuszmegy . . .-ra/re	Is that on the way to . . .?	Az a . . . úton?
a one-way ticket to . . .	egy jegyet kérek . . .	I want to get out at . . .	le akarok szállni . . .
please	ra/re egy útra	please stop here	it álljon meg
a round-trip ticket to . . .	egy retur jegyet . . .-ra/re	I'm lost	eltévedtem

DESCRIPTIONS AND REACTIONS

and	és	good	jó	quick	gyors	ugly	csúnya
or	vagy	bad	rossz	slow	lassú	Take your	nem fogdoss!
nothing	semmi	better	jobb	now	most	hands off me!	
perhaps	talán	big	nagy	later	később	Help!	Segiétség!
very	nagyon	small	kicsi	beautiful	szép	I'm ill	beteg vagyok

TIME

Luckily, the 24-hour clock is used for timetables, but on movie theater programs you may see notations like ¼4, ¾4 etc. These derive from the spoken expression of time which, as in German, makes reference to the hour approaching completion. For example 3:30 is expressed as *fél negy*—"half (on the way to) four"; 3:45—*háromnegyed negy* ("three quarters on the way to four"); 6:15—*negyed hét* ("one quarter towards seven") etc. However, ". . . o'clock" is . . . *óra*, rather than referring to the hour ahead. Duration is expressed by the suffixes *-től* ("from") and *ig* ("to"); minutes are *perc*; to ask the time, say " *Hány óra?*."

NUMBERS AND DAYS

1	egy	20	húsz	900	kilencszáz
2	kettő	21	huszonégy	1000	egyezer
3	három	30	harminc	half	fél
4	négy	40	negyven	a quarter	negyed
5	öt	50	ötven	a dozen	egy tucat
6	hat	60	hatvan	each	darab
7	hét	70	hetven	Sunday	vasárnap
8	nyolc	80	nyolcvan	Monday	hétfő
9	kilenc	90	kilencven	Tuesday	kedd
10	tiéz	100	száz	Wednesday	szerda
11	tizenegy	101	százegy	Thursday	csütörtök
12	tizenkettő	150	százötven	Friday	péntek
13	tizenhárom	200	kettőszáz	Saturday	szombat
14	tizennégy	300	háromszáz	on Monday	hetfőn
15	tizenöt	400	négyszáz	on Tuesday	kedden etc.
16	tizenhat	500	ötszáz	day	nap
17	tizenhét	600	hatszáz	week	hét
18	tizennyolc	700	hétszáz	month	hónap
19	tizenkilenc	800	nyolcszáz	year	év

PRONUNCIATION

A o as in hot

Á a as in father

B b as in best

C ts as in bats

CS ch as in church

D d as in dust

E e as in yet

É ay as in say

F f as in fed

G g as in go

GY di as in medium, or d as in due

H h as in hat

I ee as in feet

Í ee as in see, but longer

J y as in yes

K k as in sick

L l as in leap

LY y as in yes

M m as in mud

N n as in not

NY ni as in onion

O aw as in saw, but shorter

Ó aw as in awe, with the tongue kept high

Ő ur as in fur, but without any "r" sound

Ő ur as in fur, as above, but with the lips tightly rounded

P p as in sip

R r pronounced with the tip of the tongue

S sh as in shop

SZ s as in so

T t as in sit

TY tty as in prettier, said quickly

U u as in pull

Ú oo as in food

Ü u as in the German "unter"

Ű u as above, but longer and with the lips tightly rounded.

V v as in vat

W v as in "Valkman," "vhiskey" or "WC' (vait-say)

Z z as in zero

ZS s as in measure

HUNGARIAN TERMS: A GLOSSARY

ABC national chain of supermarkets.

ALFÖLD plain; it usually means the Great Plain (*Nagy Alföld*) rather than the Little Plain (*Kisalföld*) in northwestern Hungary.

ÁLLATKERT zoo.

ÁRUHÁZ department store.

ÁVO (*Államvédelmi Osztály*) the dreaded secret police of the Rákosi era; renamed the *ÁVH* in 1949, and nowadays considerably reduced in power.

BARLANG cave; the most impressive stalactite caves are in the Aggteleki karst region.

BELVÁROS inner town or city, typically characterized by Baroque or neo-Classical architecture.

CALVINISM the Reformed (*Református*) faith, which established itself in Hungary during the sixteenth century.

CASTRUM (Latin) a Roman fortification.

CIGÁNY Gypsy (in Hungarian); hence *Cigánytelep*, a Gypsy settlement; and *Cigányzene*, Gypsy music.

CSÁRDA inn; nowadays, a restaurant with rustic decor.

CSÁRDÁS traditional wild dance to violin music.

CSIKÓS *puszta* horse herdsman; a much romanticized figure of the nineteenth century.

DOMB hill; *Rózsadomb*, "Rose Hill" in Budapest.

DJAMI or **DZAMI** mosque.

DUNA the River Danube.

ERDÉLY Transylvania; for centuries a part of Hungary, its loss to Romania in 1920 still rankles.

ERDŐ forest, wood.

FALU village; **FALUKUTATÓ** "Village Explorers" who investigated rural life and pressed for reforms in the countryside during the 1930s.

FŐ UTCA main street.

FORRÁS natural spring.

FÜRDŐ public baths, often fed by thermal springs.

GYÓGYFUÓRDŐ mineral baths with therapeutic properties.

HAJDÚK cattle-drovers turned outlaws, who later settled near Debrecen in the **HAJDÚSÁG** region.

HAJÓÁLLOMÁS boat landing stage.

HÁZ house.

HEGY hill or low mountain (pl. **HEGYSÉG**).

HÍD bridge; *Lánchíd*, the "Chain Bridge" in Budapest.

HONVÉD Hungarian army.

ISKOLA school.

ITALBOLT "drink shop," or a village bar.

KÁPOLNA chapel.

KAPU gate.

KASTÉLY fortified manor or small castle.

KERT garden, park.

KÖRÚT boulevard. Some cities have semicircular "Great" and "Small" boulevards (**NAGYKÓRÚT** and **KISKÓRÚT**) surrounding their Belváros.

KÖZ alley, lane; also used to define geographical regions, eg. the "Mud land" (*Sárköz*) bordering the Danube.

KÚT well or fountain.

LAKÓTELEP high-rise apartment buildings.

LÉPCSŐ alley with steps ascending a hillside.

LIGET park, grove, or wood.

LIMES (Latin) fortifications along the Danube, marking the limit of Roman territory.

LOVARDA riding school.

MAGYAR Hungarian (pronounced "*Mod*-yor"). Also **MAGYARORSZÁG**, Hungary.

MEGÁLLÓ a railroad halt or bus stop.

MEGYE county; originally established by István I to extend his authority over the Magyar tribes.

MIHRAB prayer niche in a mosque, indicating the direction of Mecca.

MSzMP (*Magyar Szocialista Munkáspárt*) the Hungarian Communist Party.

MŰEMLÉK historic monument, protected building.

MŰVELŐDESI HÁZ community arts and social center; literally, a "Cultural House."

NYILAS or "Arrow Cross"; Hungarian fascist movement.

OTTOMANS founders of the Turkish empire, which included central Hungary during the sixteenth and seventeenth century.

PALOTA palace; *Püspök-palota*, a Bishop's residence.

PÁLYAUDVAR (*pu.*) railroad terminal.

PIAC outdoor market.

PINCE cellar; a **BOR-PINCE** contains and serves wine.

PUSZTA another name for the Great Plain, coined when the region was a wilderness.

RAKPART embankment or quay.

ROM ruined building; sometimes set in a garden with stonework finds, a **ROMKERT**.

STRAND beach, or any area for sunbathing or swimming.

SZIGET island.

TANÁCS council; also **TANÁCSKÓZTÁR-SASÁG**, the "Republic of Councils" or Soviets, which ruled Hungary in 1919.

TEMETŐ cemetery.

TEMPLOM church.

TÉR square; **TERE** in the possessive case, as in *Hősök tere*, "Square of the Heroes."

TEREM hall.

TÓ lake.

TORONY tower.

TÜRBE tomb or mausoleum of a Muslim dignitary.

UTCA (*u.*) road or street.

ÚT avenue; in the possessive case, **ÚTJA**— eg. *Vörös Hadsereg útja*, "Avenue of the Red Army."

VÁR castle.

VÁROS town; may be divided into an inner Belváros, a lower-lying *Alsóváros* and a modern *Újváros* section. Also **VÁROSKÓZPONT**, the town center.

VÁSÁRCSARNOK market hall.

VASÚTÁLLOMÁS railroad station.

VÖLGY valley; *Hűvösvölgy*, "Cool Valley."

ZSIDÓ Jew or Jewish.

ZSINAGÓGA synagogue.

INDEX